Working with Zia

**Pakistan's Power Politics
1977-1988**

Working with Zia

Pakistan's Power Politics
1977-1988

General Khalid Mahmud Arif, NI(M), S Bt

Karachi
Oxford University Press
Oxford   New York   Delhi
1995

Oxford University Press, Walton Street, Oxford OX2 6DP
Oxford   New York
Athens   Auckland   Bangkok   Bombay
Calcutta   Cape Town   Dar es Salaam   Delhi
Florence   Hong Kong   Istanbul   Karachi
Kuala Lumpur   Madras   Madrid   Melbourne
Mexico City   Nairobi   Paris   Singapore
Taipei   Tokyo   Toronto
and associated companies in
Berlin   Ibadan

Oxford is a trade mark of Oxford University Press

© Khalid Mahmud Arif 1995

All rights reserved. No part of this publication may be reproduced, stored in a retrieval system, or transmitted, in any form or by any means, without the prior permission in writing of Oxford University Press.

This book is sold subject to the condition that it shall not, by way of trade or otherwise, be lent, re-sold, hired out or otherwise circulated without the publisher's prior consent in any form of binding or cover other than that in which it is published and without a similar condition including this condition being imposed on the subsequent purchaser.

ISBN 0 19 577570 8

Printed in Pakistan at
The Army Press, Rawalpindi.
Published by
Oxford University Press
5-Bangalore Town, Sharae Faisal
P.O. Box 13033, Karachi-75350, Pakistan.

CONTENTS

	Foreword	ix
	Preface	xvii
1.	The Gathering Storm	1
2.	East Pakistan Amputated	19
3.	Prelude to Intervention	61
4.	The Military Option	93
5.	Voyage of Discovery	109
6.	The Political Juggernaut	148
7.	Verdict of Guilty	176
8.	The Tragic End	189
9.	From the Pinnacle	213
10.	Interceding Links	250
11.	Relations with Iran	276
12.	Turmoil in Afghanistan	298
13.	An Unequal Friendship	331
14.	The Nuclear Ballyhoo	349
15.	A Stormy Summer	385
	Epilogue	410
	Notes	415
	Index	426

ILLUSTRATIONS

Between pages 112 and 113

1. The author
2. General Ziaul Haq
3. Zulfikar Ali Bhutto
4. Zia receiving Bhutto
5. Bhutto reviewing parade
6. VCOAS Arif with COAS Zia
7. COS Arif with Zia and Ghulam Ishaq Khan

Between pages 208 and 209

8. Bhutto at Dir
9. Bhutto's coffin being unloaded
10. Bhutto addressing a public meeting
11. Bhutto's *namaz-i-janaza*
12. Prime Minister Junejo with top military brass
13. Investiture ceremony
14. Presidents Zia and Carter

FOREWORD

Scholars have long rejected Samuel Huntington's persuasive but wholly ahistorical view that the armed forces in the Third World are instruments of modernization, political stability, and economic development. Nevertheless, in Pakistan the armed forces, especially the army, are a central factor in the country's politics and the decision-making process. For much of Pakistan's history, the military has played an active role and has intervened three times to capture power. And even though it failed to institutionalize the role of the military in the formal political processes, it continues to enjoy considerable public esteem and is seen by many in Pakistan as the ultimate arbiter in the affairs of the country. In short, an understanding of the military as a factor in Pakistan's politics is essential to a comprehension of Pakistan's post-independence history.

While all Chiefs of Army Staff (COAS) in Pakistan have, in varying degrees, exercised political influence and have been seen as presidents-in-waiting, most people perceived General Muhammad Ziaul Haq as the least likely coup-maker. His public image was that of an apolitical soldier, and if he had any political ambitions these were carefully concealed. It was perhaps his lack of charisma, his religious piety, the ostensible bluntness of a soldier, and a carefully cultivated simplicity that seems to have so endeared him to Zulifikar Ali Bhutto that it led to his elevation as the army chief in preference to several other contenders for the job. The choice was understandable: Bhutto was ambitious and not content to be a popularly elected leader whose powers were limited by the Constitution. He wanted to monopolize power in his own hands and to reduce his political opponents to servile submission. He needed a loyal army chief who would render unquestioning loyalty to the prime minister. The choice fell on Zia because, as Bhutto confided to Princess Ashraf Pahlavi, 'he is in my pocket'. Bhutto, like most other politicians and analysts in Pakistan, greatly underestimated the shrewdness and the political acumen of Zia.

Unlike Field Marshal Muhammad Ayub Khan, Pakistan's first military ruler, Zia did not have a blueprint for capturing political power. In some ways it was thrust on him by Bhutto's misdemeanour and the encouragement from the leaders of the Pakistan National Alliance (PNA), who could not hope to oust Bhutto through the ballot and therefore viewed the military as the alternative route to power. But once in power Zia showed an uncanny ability to outmanoeuvre his opponents and became Pakistan's longest serving military ruler. Zia was a master survivor, a skilled tactician, and a deft handler of political crises. Several interrelated factors helped Zia to survive politically virtually unscathed until his death in a plane crash on 17 August 1988.

It is considered flippant and perhaps unscholarly to attribute the success of a person to luck. But luck did favour Zia. Each time the man was confronted with a problem, it seems that his stars bailed him out. The execution of Bhutto coincided with the overthrow of the Shahinshah of Iran and thereby not only removed one of Bhutto's staunchest supporters, but also greatly muted the international outcry which might otherwise have followed. In November 1979 Zia had become an international pariah, following the burning of the US embassy in Pakistan; but all his worries were wiped out when the Soviet Union invaded Afghanistan in the following month. Zia emerged as the leader of the pro-US front-line state fighting against communism. On two other occasions, external help came to his aid: Indira Gandhi bailed him out by declaring support for the popular uprising in Sindh which had seriously shaken the regime; and the hijacking of a PIA plane in March 1981 by the Al-Zulfiqar group put the emerging coalition of political parties on the defensive.

Zia was not just lucky; he also possessed an instinctive understanding of the political dynamics in the country. Like many other soldiers, he had contempt for politicians; however, his dislike of politicians was not a matter of military distaste for civilians but was rooted in a knowledge of the seamier aspects of their personal and public behaviour. It was the politicians who connived with him to postpone the elections because, despite their public stance, they were afraid of contesting the polls whilst Bhutto was alive. To them, politics was a means to 'profit and patronage' and they therefore required little persuasion to supplicate for the crumbs that fell from Zia's table. Zia was convinced that most politicians had a price; and experience confirmed his opinion that only a few were prepared to rise above their petty personal ambitions. Moreover, the hostility of the PNA leaders to Bhutto's Pakistan People's Party (PPP) far outweighed the inconvenience of military rule.

FOREWORD

There was another reason which made Zia both acceptable to the politicians and less objectionable to the public at large. In marked contrast to Bhutto, Zia's public image was one of a decent, honest, and humble public servant, inspired by religious zeal. It has been claimed that Bhutto 'took the decency out of politics'; humiliated and harassed his opponents; and very often even his own recalcitrant supporters became the victims of his vindictiveness. On the other hand, Zia's unfailing courtesy, the now famous 'double handshake and triple embrace', his broad smile and (perhaps a put on) self-effacing humility seldom failed to impress his visitors and won over many of his erstwhile opponents. Even those who despised Zia's political manipulation admired his *desi* attire and manners, compared to Bhutto's highly westernized behaviour and haughtiness.

Although Zia's temporary 'Operation Fair Play' became the longest stint of military rule and he was successful in warding off any serious threat to his own position, he failed to legitimize his rule through popular endorsement. The 'referendum', instead of bolstering his position, merely highlighted his political isolation. And even though the opposition failed to mount a credible popular movement against him until 1986, the Zia regime did not quite capture the full political initiative. His approach was ad hoc, piece-meal, and reactive; he did not attempt to disturb the *status quo*; and he ensured the continuance of his regime, not by building institutions or mobilizing popular support, but by taking advantage of the disunity among the politicians. In this respect, the Zia regime stands in marked contrast to that of Ayub, who had engineered the elaborate scheme of 'basic democracy' in an attempt to institutionalize his rule. And yet Zia was in many ways more successful in both blunting the thrust of the opposition and ensuring the continuance of his regime. He did not, unlike Ayub, seek to write his own made-to-measure Constitution but amended the Constitution of 1973 to transfer the balance of power from the parliament to the president; the politicians, and subsequently the political parties, were compelled to collaborate with him on his own terms; all the major institutions including the civil bureaucracy, the judiciary, the political parties, and the parliament were, compared to the armed forces, weakened; although in the formal structure there was no institutionalized role for the military, it nevertheless continued to play a decisive role in political decision-making.

Zia's policies were often contradictory; he was personally enigmatic and unpredictable. He had the dissident journalists publicly flogged but allowed considerable freedom to the Press (in many cases censorship was self-imposed by the editors and individuals); intellectual dissent was not altogether stamped out even though, as Mushahid Hussain points out, the 'hundred flowers never bloomed'; and belated recognitions were offered to staunch dissidents like the poet Faiz Ahmed Faiz and the 'Frontier Gandhi' Khan Abdul Ghaffar Khan. Zia was ruthless in hounding out some of the PPP leaders but, in marked contrast to Bhutto, his treatment of his political opponents was decent and humane; he was not averse to muzzling the judiciary but promoted some independent-minded judges who gave verdicts in defiance of the known preferences of the government; and, while he was staunchly pro-American, he defied his American benefactors by continuing Pakistan's nuclear programme. However, in one sphere there was no ambiguity or ambivalence. Zia's ability to hold power and to wield it to his advantage was consistent and quite ruthless. His concept of 'restoring' democracy was not meant to transfer power to the elected representatives but was designed to share power with the civilians. The unprovoked dismissal of the elected prime minister, Muhammad Khan Junejo, confirmed that clubs are trumps. In this respect, Zia showed a much more perceptive awareness of the reality of power in Pakistan. Even after being ostensibly 'elected' as the president, he did not relinquish his position as the army chief.

Military rulers are apt to get a bad Press. Perhaps quite rightly so. The record of military rule in Pakistan is far from unblemished. It has been argued that military rulers bequeath to their civilian successors more problems than they resolve. Zia was no different. Under him, the institutions of civil society were allowed to atrophy or were deliberately neglected. But he has left behind some lasting legacies for Pakistan. His Islamization of Pakistani society may have been politically motivated but today it is a reality in the country. Islam is no longer the preserve of official propaganda but has permeated society; and among its adherents are not only the traditional folk but also the Western-educated urban and professional groups. He failed to crush the PPP but helped to foster a distinct constituency in opposition to the PPP which espoused some of his cherished values. The considerable success of the Pakistan Muslim League under his protege, Mian Muhammad Nawaz Sharif, shows that the group has

FOREWORD

developed a mass following without continued official patronage. Zia did not succeed in institutionalizing the role of the military in decision-making but he imposed his political agenda sufficiently to set the parameters within which all political parties had to function, and they continue to do so after his death. The army also emerged as the dominant 'arbiter' in Pakistan's politics and it has become a fact of life which can no longer be ignored. His zealous espousal of the Afghan war, which divided the Pakistan polity and imported into the society many of the more baneful consequences of the war, not only inflicted a humiliating defeat on the Soviet Union but also greatly contributed to the demise of communism. Perhaps Zia, more than Ronald Reagan, was responsible for the eventual disintergration of the 'evil empire'.

General K. M. Arif's *Working with Zia* is easily the most interesting and the best informed account of the Zia years, and provides information which has hitherto not been available to scholars. Few persons in Pakistan could have been better qualified than General Arif to have undertaken this task. He was both an actor and a spectator and observed events from an unrivalled vantage point. He not only enjoyed the confidence of General Zia but was also the person (in his capacity as the chief of staff to the Chief Martial Administrator and later to the President) through whose hands passed all the vital policy documents, and who was personally present in most of the meetings which Zia had with politicians, foreign visitors, and his army colleagues. General Zia's esteem for the author and his key role in that regime have been succinctly summed up by a perceptive Pakistani analyst: 'It is Pakistan's only regime in which a number two man was clearly identifiable and allowed to function with considerable power without arousing any feelings of insecurity in the top man. General Arif's role since 1980 has been quite unique and probably without precedent in our previous power structures. ' Arif was the key witness to the unfolding history and drama in Pakistan for most of the Zia era.

General Arif writes with ease, elegance, and sensitivity. His detailed personal knowledge of the events is backed by scrupulous and painstaking research. The result is a highly readable, if often chilling account of the high politics in Pakistan. His meticulous reconstruction of Zia's coup plan, Zia-Bhutto personal relations and antagonisms, and the final hours of Bhutto prior to his execution are based on detailed and personal knowledge which no scholar can hope to surpass. He also provides a wealth of information on Zia's Afghan strategy, on the nuclear issue, on Indo-Pakistan relations which greatly add to the existing knowledge. His writing shows a deep insight into the working of civil-military relations; and some of his thumbnail sketches of the leading *dramatis personae* are at once both fascinating and revealing.

While reading the manuscript of this book, I asked myself two questions: Has this book been written by the General in self-justification for the policies of the regime with which he was so closely involved? And second, has the author distanced himself sufficiently from the events to provide an unbiased and truthful account of the period? Readers will form their own opinion but for myself I have no doubts on either score. General Arif's main concern has been to narrate things as they happened and as seen by those who were responsible for decision-making. There is hardly any attempt at justification or *post hoc* rationalization of the actions of the regime. He has indeed used the benefit of hindsight to gain a better perspective but not to explain away the mistakes and follies of Zia. His loyalty and admiration for Zia are beyond question but this has not made him uncritical of the leader. The author's concern for accuracy of the narrative is most scrupulous. He has not only relied on his own records and notes of the events but has crosschecked with others who were involved in the affairs of the period.

The answer to the question whether this is a dispassionate and objective study is more complex. Indeed, no study, not even the so-called academic works, are truly objective. Every author is very much the product of his or her own experiences. Our outlook and views are very much conditioned by our experience and the vantage point from which it is obtained; and therefore our analyses are invariably determined or coloured by our perceptions. General Arif's work is no exception. The strength of the book lies in the unique perspective which the author has to offer. It provides a penetrating insight into the minds of the soldiers, their hopes and aspirations for Pakistan, their world view, and the role they perceive for themselves in the order of things. The view may at times be subjective, but it offers an unrivalled understanding of Pakistan's politics as seen from the vantage point of General Headquarters and the cantonments. Not everyone will agree with some of General Arif's opinions, but no one can fail to take these seriously. The importance of this view will be self-evident to

FOREWORD

any one familiar with the politics of Pakistan. Of course, this is not a definitive study of the period, as indeed no book of this genre can be. But it is by far the most authoritative book on the subject and an invaluable source which no scholar or person interested in Pakistan's politics can ignore.

Nuffield College
Oxford
October 1993

Gowher Rizvi
Fellow in International Relations

PREFACE

When I retired from the army in March 1987, I had no plan to write a treatise on the political developments in Pakistan during the Zia era. I did not consider myself qualified for the unfamiliar task; besides, political expediency had spawned a number of myths based on half-truths, giving rise to all kinds of controversies. And telling the truth, the whole truth—which was for me the minimum requirement of writing—carried its own risks. But above all it was the highly complex personality of President General M. Ziaul Haq which defied a simple explanation. Having been one of his close associates, I could not claim complete objectivity and detachment.

For nearly seven years, I was the President's Chief of Staff and for another three years the Vice Chief of Army Staff. In the last appointment I was the *de facto* commander of the Pakistan Army, as all the powers of the Chief of Army Staff were delegated to me by the government. With this background, I could either put on record the full facts relating to an important period in our history, or recede into oblivion. The proverbial failing of an active participant made me think hard about whether I could do justice to the work. The other inhibiting factors were the Official Secrets Act and considerations of Pakistan's national security.

I was privy to a great deal of inside information on policy matters and took part in the formulation of national policy plans relating to the internal and external affairs of the country. General Zia trusted me on most issues. Many people envied my position. But my colleagues in the government knew that when I spoke, I seldom minced my words.

My well-wishers advised me to maintain silence and pointed out the pitfalls in opening Pandora's box. An absolute ruler, even if he is noble as an angel, is hard to defend. Why reopen political wounds that had barely started healing, and ignite controversies? Stay away from the hornet's nest and let history be written after Time has subdued public sentiments and taken care of the main actors. Some others suggested a variant—write a book, but defer its publication for two or three decades.

There was also the opposite view. I was reminded by many that I owed it to posterity to narrate events as I saw them, before my faculties were impaired by age. Ignore the inhibiting factors and reveal the truth. Those advocating this approach included Dr Waheeduz Zaman, an eminent historian, who volunteered to read the manuscript. I yielded to his persuasive logic. In so doing, I was compelled by an inner urge to share the facts with the people of my country in the hope that these facts may fill in some blanks when the national history of the period is written. I was convinced of the futility of taking my decade-long observations, experiences, and knowledge—whatever their worth—to my grave. I have endeavoured to narrate events as I saw them, resisting the temptation of justifying decisions and refraining from defending any person, including myself. Little did I know that Waheed was in a hurry to meet his Creator. I was denied the benefit of his professional expertise. His passing away strengthened my resolve to fulfil my commitment to him.

This work is neither an attempt to write the history of Pakistan nor an indepth analysis of the Zia years. It is a profile of the period 1977-88, in which momentous developments took place within and around Pakistan. The narration faithfully describes, so I feel, the political game played on Pakistan's canvas during that fateful decade, without attempting to eulogize or downgrade the key players involved. I am conscious of the possibility that my perception of facts, my assessment of different personalities, and the conclusions drawn by me might differ from the views held by some other people. A ten-year period is difficult to condense in a single capsule. The choice of what to include in the book or exclude from its text was not easy. Limitations of space forced me to omit certain issues. I concede the reader's right to differ with my selection. A conscious attempt has been made to lift the curtain of secrecy from some major, though highly contentious, events. If this work stimulates others to write about this period, the time and the effort spent by me will have been amply rewarded.

That the military became an important, and gradually a decisive factor in Pakistan's power politics soon after her birth, is not in dispute. How it happened has been discussed earlier but not at length. The dearth of biographies of some of the major actors, the pretext of misplaced secrecy, the play-safe tactics, and the reluctance of those possessing inside knowledge to share it with others are some of the reasons why our history has mostly remained obscured for so long. The periods of military rule under Generals Muhammad Ayub Khan, Yahya Khan, and Ziaul Haq deserve unemotional and objective analysis to determine the reasons for the repeated failure of Pakistan's fragile and corruption-prone political system and the inability of her feudal-dominated political parties to govern the country according to democratic norms.

Once out of power, Pakistan's political leaders vociferously preach the enforcement of unadulterated democracy; but, in power, they practise it selectively, not hesitating to disrupt the democratic process for self-perpetuation. As a result, personality-dominated institutions have remained weak and the politicians have failed to promote the smooth and uninterrupted growth of democracy in the country. This complex issue defies an easy solution or a simple interpretation. There may be disagreement with the conclusions drawn by me but I would be writing in the light of fresh evidence. In man-made history, the final word is seldom written.

I belong to a generation proud but guilty. Proud, because it participated in the freedom struggle that created Pakistan. And guilty, because it has the dubious distinction of losing East Pakistan through its incompetence. It is not a healthy reflection on our political maturity that, despite the trauma of 1971, the country blundered into another martial law barely six years later.

General Zia's military intervention may appear strange to a reader not familiar with the human carnage that preceded the dawn of freedom in Pakistan and the rapid erosion of the political system soon after her birth. The chaotic conditions prevailing during the 1947 Hindu-Muslim communal disturbances in undivided India resulted in the migration of eight million people between India and Pakistan in search of safety and honour. Our road to freedom, thus, passed through the valley of death, and the price paid for liberty, in blood and money, was heavy. Nevertheless, Pakistan's struggle for independence was conducted politically and the goal of freedom reached through a constitutional process. Our politics decayed rapidly in the post-Mohammad Ali Jinnah-Liaquat Ali Khan period. The loosening political grip created a vacuum which came to be dominated by the bureaucratic and military pillars of power. This background is briefly summarized in the first chapter.

To facilitate an understanding of the Zia era—the main theme of this work—it is necessary to recapitulate the rise of Mr Zulfikar Ali Bhutto to power and the amputation of East Pakistan in 1971. The fall of Dhaka demands a comprehensive analysis to determine what went wrong—in the political, military, diplomatic, and other fields—to avoid repeating such errors in the future. In the history of nations, not just the glorious but even the inglorious events are worth repeating. In Pakistan's context, the amputation of East Pakistan is one such tragedy. The political high drama played in the corridors of power, and the acts of omission and commission committed by those who mattered are discussed in chapter two.

The political turmoil that gripped the country just before the military axe fell on the cornered Bhutto regime in July 1977 is described in the third chapter. The fourth, fifth, and sixth chapters contain details of the military take-over and some insights into the working of the Bhutto administration.

Much has been said and written about Mr Bhutto's death. But a great deal more needs to be said. The seventh and the eighth chapters cover his trial, conviction, and execution.

Some glimpses of the major domestic, internal security, political, and administrative developments, and the internal policies adopted during the Zia era are contained in the ninth and the tenth chapters. The next four chapters deal with Pakistan-Iran relations, the Soviet aggression in Afghanistan, Pakistan-US relations, and Pakistan's nuclear programme. The concluding chapter narrates the dismissal of the Junejo government and the aircraft crash that killed General Ziaul Haq.

I thank all those who encouraged me to undertake this work and gave me the benefit of their views. Their contribution is gratefully acknowledged. While their advice was helpful, the views expressed in the book are exclusively mine and I take full responsibility for them. Space does not permit me to mention all the names; and to indicate some and omit others would be unfair. I am particularly thankful to Dr Gowher Rizvi for reading the manuscript and contributing the foreword. I am obliged to Mohammad Nawaz Sial for typing the manuscript and am indebted to my brother Mr Ahmad Mahmud Tabassum for putting the text on computer. Finally, a word of thanks to my wife, Khalida, without whose patience and encouragement my task might have been more arduous.

CHAPTER 1

The Gathering Storm

For the fourth time in her post-independence history of three decades, the sun of democracy set in Pakistan. On 5 July 1977, the government of Prime Minister Zulfikar Ali Bhutto was overthrown by the Chief of Army Staff, General M. Ziaul Haq, in a bloodless *coup d'etat*. The military operation, code-named Fair Play, claimed to save the country from a possible civil war. Paradoxically, the rot had started with the holding of national elections in March 1977, in which the ruling Pakistan People's Party (PPP) had won a landslide victory, capturing 155 out of the 192 contested National Assembly seats.

The result of the massively rigged elections was rejected by the combined opposition group called the Pakistan National Alliance (PNA, winning 36 seats) who claimed that a premeditated farce and a fraud had been perpetrated on the nation. Mr Bhutto denied the allegations, while conceding that some irregularities might have taken place. The PNA used street power to pressurize the administration to annul the ill-fated elections. The government employed force to suppress the popular demand. Newton's third law of motion coming into play polarized the country. Massive country-wide demonstrations against the government shook the foundations of the seemingly stable Bhutto administration. With death and destruction taking a heavy toll, the administration paralysed, and the government and the opposition unable to reach an agreement, the military intervened. By that act, General Zia joined the company of dictators — Field Marshal Muhammad Ayub Khan and General Muhammad Yahya Khan — who had earlier imposed martial law in Pakistan on 7 October 1958 and 25 March 1969 respectively. Zia was the fourth Chief Martial Law Administrator, Mr Bhutto having been the third from 20 December 1971 to August 1973.

Bewildered, the intelligent, articulate, and usually crafty Bhutto had used all the charm in his political armoury to regain the political and administrative control slipping from his once firm autocratic grip. He used the weapons of diplomacy, dialogue, concessions, coercion, threats, intimidation, arrests, alleged foreign interference, as well as religion to wiggle out of his self-created quagmire. The more he played his life-saving gimmicks, the more he failed to pull his sinking administration out of the turbulent waves of public hostility. Once a popular leader, Bhutto had earned the people's wrath during his five and a half year-long rough and harsh rule. The PNA agitation took the country by storm. With educational institutions closed, economic activities in limbo, the wheels of industry slowing down, exports shrinking, the streets filled with riotous crowds, and the government losing the moral right to rule, the writ of the Bhutto government collapsed. A cornered Bhutto groped for a solution to salvage his political future. He started parleys with the PNA to seek a face-saving way out of the impasse. As discussed later in greater depth, after protracted negotiations an agreement was all but reached. The talks failed to clinch an accord because mutual confidence remained starkly absent.

As the military axe fell on the seemingly democratic Bhutto rule, the squabbling politicians were arrested. Normalcy rapidly returned to the country but the surgical act inflicted a wound, invisible and deep, which has failed to heal.

Much has been said on Zia's years in power. Much more will follow when the curtain of officialdom is lifted from the events of that era. In the annals of history, there has been no ruler—democrat or autocrat, politician or general—who did not err while governing his country. General Zia was no exception. Like every mortal, he had his strong and weak points, likes and dislikes, virtues and vices. Notwithstanding the drawbacks of analysing a contemporary era, it is necessary to discover the real person hiding in Zia—the soldier turned absolute ruler, who, despite the predictions made by many political pundits, managed to stay entrenched in power for eleven years.

A complex and a controversial personality, a haze of mystery surrounds General Zia and his decision-making processes. Some vital questions concerning his personality, views, behaviour, style of governance, and decision-making remain unanswered. Was he ambitious or did he merely get sucked into a political quagmire? Was his *coup* justified? Was Bhutto's execution legally justified or did personal animus play a part in it? Was he a lover of Islam or a hypocrite who exploited religion for self-aggrandizement and for prolonging his rule? Did he really believe that he had a legitimate right to rule? Was he always master of his actions? If not, what were the chief influences on him? Did he believe in democracy and sharing power with others?

Were his domestic policies adequate or faulty? Did he mastermind the Afghanistan conflict for personal ends or did he merely seize the opportunity to take advantage of it? What was his grasp of international affairs and how were foreign policy options tackled in his administration? What was he like — as a person, as a leader, as an administrator, as an opponent, and as the President of Pakistan? These, and a host of similar issues need a deep probe to comprehend the enigma and the aberrations of the Zia years.

Before the Zia era, I, like my fellow citizens, had already experienced the two earlier periods of martial law. During the Ayub years, as a major, I saw martial law mostly from a distance. Only once (in early 1962) was I detailed for three months to perform the duties of a summary military court. This brief exposure proved sufficiently disturbing, as I learnt of the excesses committed against the accused persons held in police custody, the wilful distortions introduced in the first information reports, and the low calibre of prosecution witnesses, called police touts.

I also served on the staff of General Yahya Khan during his martial law, from March 1969 to July 1971, when I reverted to the field army. During this tenure I handled martial law matters and intelligence work. Though I was not personally involved in formulating policy matters, being only of the rank of lieutenant colonel, I was able to observe at close quarters the political storm brewing in East Pakistan, and the manner in which events were handled and mishandled on the political chessboard.

When Zia assumed power, I occupied a position on centre-stage as Chief of Staff to the President (1977-84) and as Vice Chief of Army Staff (March 1984 - March 1987). In the latter appointment, I was the *de facto* commander of the Pakistan army, as all the powers of the Chief of Army Staff were delegated to me by the government. In these assignments, I participated actively in the decision-making process at the national level in the midst of momentous events. I have discussed the course of events as I saw them from my unrivalled vantage point, where I had ready access to inside information.

General Zia's emergence as the central figure on the national stage was not an isolated event. The phenomenon of the rising influence of the military in Pakistan's internal affairs has a history behind it. It dates back to the creation of the country and the manner in which Pakistan has failed to evolve a vibrant political culture based on democratic norms.

Pakistan was created on the basis of the Two-Nation Theory according to which Muslims demanded, struggled for, and won a separate homeland forthemselves when British rule in the subcontinent ended in 1947. The partition of India was preceded by widespread communal riots in the closing stages of the British Raj,with incidents of death,destruction, abduction, and rape. Eight million people migrated between India and Pakistan in search of asylum, security, and self-respect. Such despicable ethnic madness deserves unqualified condemnation.

Pakistan was thus born in turmoil. The road from slavery to freedom passed through the valley of death in which human blood was shed in abundance, regretfully in the name of both religion and secularism. The joy of the dawn of independence was submerged in the pain of human suffering which came in its wake.

Pakistan inherited administrative structures in its constituent provinces but that for the centre had to be improvised from scratch. The country started without the traditional pillars of democracy — the supreme court, the parliament (a constituent assembly existed), a functioning federal government, and the necessary paraphernalia of a bureaucratic establishment. The visible symbols of the state—the flag, the federal bank, the currency notes, the revenue postage stamps, and the diplomatic missions in foreign countries—were conspicuously absent. The country was without a national anthem. Her armed forces consisted of truncated units equipped with obsolescent hardware.

The difficulty of the task of national consolidation was compounded by the inflow of millions of refugees. As their numbers swelled, so did the magnitude of the required effort to provide them succour, sustenance, and rehabilitation.

The pangs of its painful birth notwithstanding, Independence created euphoria. It had been achieved through a political struggle and there was a pervasive desire to see a strong and prosperous country emerge. The Quaid-i-Azam's dynamism generated immense public confidence; the people believed that the difficulties they were facing were transient and surmountable.

Mr Mohammad Ali Jinnah, reverently called the Quaid-i-Azam (great leader), was a man of total commitment, with a strong will—a tenacious personality with an overpowering charisma and an awe-inspiring aura. His friends and critics alike acknowledged his unassailable honesty and tremendous will-power. Westernized in his life-style, he led a regulated life, devoid of greed, cheapness, and scandal. Chiselled by age and experience, he was a perfect leader and a brilliant orator, whose cold logic disguised a warm heart. Firm but not arrogant, he spoke with ease, poise, and authority. His pronounced leadership qualities so endeared him to the masses that they ignored his minor inadequacies. A liberal democrat, he was an enlightened Muslim. Addressing the Karachi Bar Association on 25 January 1948, he said : 'Islam is not a set of rituals, traditions and spiritual dogmas. It is based on the highest principles of honour, integrity, fair play, and justice for all. '[1]

Despite her credentials of political plurality, Pakistan became a habitual deviator from the path of democracy. Her frequent supraconstitutional detours were partly the outcome of what she inherited at the time of Independence; thereafter the course of events compounded the situation. The military entered the political arena for reasons which, even with hindsight, seem hard to justify. The weaknesses of the political parties and the alleged indifferent performance of the governments did not bestow an imperial right on the military brass to march in and declare 'Enough is enough. We have taken over. Out you go'. But this is what happened — and more than once.

The Situation at Independence

The Muslim League, which was formed in 1906 and which led the freedom struggle, enjoyed the support of the Muslim elite, the feudal lords, the influential business community, and the titled gentry. Dominated by the upper middle class, it was not a party of the masses in the early decades of its existence. Mr Jinnah took charge of the Muslim League in the mid-thirties and initiated measures to transform its character. With the organization process underway, the party participated in the 1937 elections held in India and failed to acquit itself well.

The Pakistan resolution adopted by the Muslim League in 1940 caught the public imagination and gradually the slogan of Pakistan became synonymous with the people's salvation. Almost overnight, the Muslim League turned into a political movement taking India by storm. Riding a crest, it contested the 1945 elections on the issue of Pakistan. It won all the 30 Muslim seats for the Indian Central Legislative Assembly and secured 86.6 per cent of the votes in the Muslim constituencies in the provincial elections.[2] In the North-West Frontier Province (NWFP), it won only 17 of the 36 Muslim seats. The Muslim League became a mass organization, without the prolonged filtering process of electoral successes and failures which helps to groom leadership and provide vitality to a party. With the emergence of Pakistan, the Muslim League became the ruling party. Those religious parties which had opposed the creation of Pakistan receded into the background. The mood of the people in the NWFP, where Dr Khan Sahib had formed a Congress ministry in 1945, underwent a sea change. The accession of NWFP to Pakistan was decided in a referendum held in 1947 in which over 50 per cent of the total electorate participated.[3] Pakistan received 289,244 votes and India 2,974.

The Political Slide

During the freedom struggle, the Muslim League, a vibrant party, had a goal—Pakistan; a strategy—a constitutional approach; a determined leader—Jinnah; and the public support to accomplish its mission. In the immediate post-Independence era, the Muslim League failed either to evolve a plan to consolidate its success or to maintain its link with the people. Devoid of vigour, it started decaying.

On 11 September 1948, the Quaid-i-Azam, aged seventy-two, died at Karachi. His departure caused an enduring political vacuum. India seized the opportunity and invaded the State of Hyderabad Deccan.

Prime Minister Liaquat Ali Khan guided the country with courage and conviction during a difficult period. While he was respected by the provincial leaders, he lacked the authority and the stature of the Quaid-i-Azam. Factions developed and drift ensued. Chaudhry Khaliquzzaman, given the task of reorganizing the Muslim League, struck a nought. As centralized control loosened, the provincial leadership became increasingly assertive and powerful. The infighting eroded the League from within.

After Liaquat Ali Khan's assassination in 1951, the Muslim League leadership behaved like a bunch of minions, unable to meet the challenge of the time. Political bankruptcy was writ large in their behaviour. Devoid of enlightened leadership, the Muslim League went into limbo.

Pakistan's weak political base was not a case in isolation. Some other Third World countries, after gaining independence, have faced similar situations. Usually, the military became a dominant factor in those states in which the political system was weak and the leadership failed to handle the post-independence state responsibility to the satisfaction of their people. On the other hand, in countries with well-established political parties and tiers of groomed leadership, the transition to freedom followed a smooth and democratic path.

In a democratic polity, it is not the business of the military to rule the country on any pretext whatsoever. This responsibility rightfully belongs to the people who elect their leadership from amongst the candidates offered by the political parties. A strong political system with built-in checks and balances is a *sine qua non* for the growth of a democratic order. Such a base has generally been either elusive or weak in Pakistan. A brief look at the political developments in the provinces and at the centre illustrates the point.

The Provincial Scene

The Congress ministry of 1946 in the NWFP found itself at odds with Pakistan. Its ministers showed disrespect to the national flag by declining to attend the hoisting ceremony.[4] The ministry was dismissed on 22 August 1947, and a Muslim League government formed under Khan Abdul Qayyum Khan. In the words of Lord Birdwood, 'it [the ministry] presided over its own demise by refusing to take the oath of allegiance to the new state.'[5]

The Governor of Sindh, Ghulam Hussain Hidayatullah, accused Chief Minister Muhammad Ayub Khuhro of maladministration and corruption. A judicial tribunal found the Chief Minister guilty. He was dismissed in April 1948. Khuhro's successor, Pir Ilahi Bakhsh, got involved in cases of jobbery and nepotism. Governor's rule was imposed in the province of Sindh.

In the Punjab, an ambitious Minister, Mumtaz Muhammad Khan Daultana, vied for the job of his easy-going Chief Minister, the Khan of Mamdot. The power tussle led to the dismissal of the ministry in early 1949, the dissolution of the Punjab legislative assembly, and the imposition of Governor's rule.

Initially, East Bengal remained stable under the amiable and weak personalities of Chief Ministers Khwaja Nazimuddin and Nurul Amin. A feeling of deprivation gradually developed, leading to the accusation that the Central Government was unsympathetic towards provincial sensitivities and rights. Put on the defensive and unsure of an electoral success, the government felt shy of holding by-elections. Such tactics intensified public alienation.

The term of the East Pakistan Legislative Assembly ended in March 1953. Fearing an electoral defeat, the Muslim League government extended the term of the assembly by one year. The prevailing mood in the province ruling out the grant of further arbitrary extension, the elections were, perforce, held, in which the Muslim League won a mere 10 seats in a house of 309 members. Placed in a quandary, the central government dithered for two months, reluctantly allowed the United Front leader Mr A. K. Fazlul Haq to form the provincial government but dismissed his popularly elected government after two months on charges of maladministration. Mr Iskandar Mirza was posted as the Governor and Governor's rule was imposed. The people of East Pakistan were thus punished for expressing their will. This short-sighted policy planted the seeds of separation. East Pakistan threw up a party of its own. The Awami League initially started as a national party under Mr H. S. Suhrawardy but turned regional when Sheikh Mujibur Rahman became its president.

After the rout of the Muslim League in East Pakistan, the politicians in power could not muster up the courage to face the electorate. Democracy without elections led to dictatorship.

In September 1955, the East Pakistan Legislative Assembly declared its own Speaker insane. The Deputy Speaker was beaten to death inside the house. In West Pakistan, the Khan of Kalat demanded the restoration of his state, pulled down the Pakistan flag from the Miri Fort, and hoisted his own ancestral flag there. The government's political grip on events started loosening.

The Tussle at the Centre

A power tussle at the Centre between the ailing and authoritarian Governor-General, Ghulam Muhammad, and a mild Prime Minister, Muhammad Ali Bogra, took an ugly turn. In September 1954, Bogra had a bill passed in the Assembly making it obligatory for the Governor-General to act on the advice of the Prime Minister. In retaliation, on 24 October 1954, Ghulam Muhammad dismissed the Central Cabinet, dissolved the Constituent Assembly, and declared a state of emergency throughout Pakistan on the plea that 'the constitutional machinery had broken down and the Assembly had lost the confidence of the people'. A three-member bench of the Chief Court in Sindh, presided over by the Chief Justice, Sir George Constantine, held the dissolution of the assembly a nullity in law.[6] The issue was taken up in appeal before the Federal Court of Pakistan. The Chief Justice, M. Munir, in a judgment more political than legal, held that the Chief Court of Sindh had no jurisdiction in the matter but, significantly, gave no ruling on the vital issue whether the Governor-General could legally dissolve the Constituent Assembly.[7]

In October 1954, General Muhammad Ayub Khan joined the federal cabinet as Defence Minister. He accepted the cabinet post on condition that he continue as the Commander-in-Chief.[8] The Army Chief becoming a defence minister in a democratic dispensation was an unprecedented event and, as it turned out, a dangerous development. Ambitious Ayub tasted political power and became intoxicated by it. The army became a participant in the national power game.

During the next four years, the politicians changed their party affiliations with ease and without any qualms. The lust for power, through any means, was all-pervasive. Ethics and principles lost relevance. 'Power unto us' became the cry. Between the years 1953 through 1958, seven prime ministers were appointed and removed through palace intrigues. Every newly nominated incumbent promptly received a vote of confidence from the rubber-stamp assembly that had lost the mandate of the people.

The First Martial Law

With the democratic structure weakened by the quarrelling politicians, President Iskandar Mirza and General Ayub Khan connived to overthrow the government. On 7 September 1958, the President abrogated the 1956 Constitution, declared martial law in the country, dismissed the central and the provincial governments, dissolved the national the provincial assemblies, abolished all political parties, and appointed General Ayub Khan as the Chief Martial Law Administrator. Two weeks later in a palace coup Iskandar Mirza was eased out of power by General Ayub Khan.

A bureaucrat turned politician, President Iskandar Mirza had risen to the pinnacle of power through a combination of brilliance and intrigue. While playing his last official act, he failed to fathom the reality that the ambition of the person holding the gun—Ayub

Khan—was as high as his own. The error of judgement consigned him to the wilderness.

Mr Muhammad Ayub Khuhro, in the presence of the author, told General Zia in August 1977 that Iskandar Mirza had planned to remove Ayub Khan within three months and replace him with Mr Qizilbash as the Prime Minister of Pakistan. Ayub pre-empted his move. Ousted from power, Iskandar Mirza migrated to Britain, where many years later he died in poverty.

Miss Fatima Jinnah, while welcoming the exit of Iskandar Mirza, said, 'A new era has begun under General Ayub Khan and the armed forces have undertaken to root out the administrative malaise and the anti-social practices to create a sense of confidence and stability to bring the country back to a state of normalcy'.[9] This was an expression of anguish and disgust at the chaos that prevailed in the country just before the military take-over. Later, Miss Fatima Jinnah was to severely criticize Ayub's dictatorial policies; she contested the 1965 presidential election against Ayub Khan as a candidate of the Combined Opposition Parties.

The new supremo, General Muhammad Ayub Khan, felt that the parliamentary form of government did not suit the genius of the people. He introduced a presidential form of government in which 80,000 Basic Democrats, elected on the basis of adult franchise, formed the electoral college to elect the President of Pakistan. With the entire state administrative apparatus at his beck and call, it was easy for General Ayub Khan to win over a majority of a mere 80,000 votes. As the system was tailor-made to rubber-stamp his candidature, Ayub's 'babes' dutifully voted him to power. Following his election, Ayub introduced the presidential form of government in the country.

The Rise of Bhutto

Mr Zulfikar Ali Bhutto rose from political anonymity to become a minister in General Ayub's cabinet at the young age of 28. Working under the patronage of his benefactor, Bhutto gained prominence and stature, showed promise, and subsequently rose to become the foreign minister. On different occasions, he praised Ayub Khan lavishly, calling him a dauntless leader, an Ataturk, and a Salahuddin. Bhutto was the foreign minister during the Indo-Pakistan war of 1965, which ended in a stalemate. Under the brokerage of the Soviet Union, India and Pakistan disengaged their armed forces, after agreeing to a

United Nations sponsored cease-fire, and signed the Tashkent Declaration in January 1966. The people of Pakistan perceived the Tashkent Declaration to be biased in favour of India, and Ayub was accused of capitulation. Initially, Foreign Minister Bhutto vehemently defended the agreement. Subsequently, sensing the public mood, he distanced himself from it. Ayub eased him out of the federal cabinet in November 1966. A peeved Bhutto vowed to avenge the insult. Cashing in on public emotions and sensitivities, he bitterly accused Ayub of a sell-out, conveying the impression that he had opposed the agreement at the negotiating stage. A PPP leader, Salman Taseer, writes that, 'as a politician, Bhutto exploited Tashkent to its limit . . . He was mercilessly and unscrupulously to play upon public disillusionment of a secret clause to the Declaration . . . although the rabbit was never produced from the hat'.[10]

The Second Martial Law

Ayub Khan's coronary thrombosis in 1968 adversely affected his statecraft. His failing health compelled him to increasingly rely upon the filtered advice of a coterie of close advisers and sycophants. His slipping grip on the administration was capitalized on by his opponents, who started an agitation against him. His inability to handle the situation became evident as the public storm against him gained momentum. Unable to rule any longer, and unwilling to follow the constitutional route for transfer of authority, he asked General Yahya Khan, in March 1969, to take full control of the affairs of the country.[11] Yahya was not a guileless recipient of power. Ayub had done what Yahya wanted him to do.

On 25 March 1969, General Yahya Khan placed the country under its second martial law and himself became the Chief Martial Law Administrator. History repeated itself. It was Ayub's turn to be at the receiving end. Yahya desired him to vacate the President's House and leave the capital, Islamabad. While relinquishing power, Ayub breached the Constitution that he had promulgated in the country with much fanfare. As Ayub left and Yahya took charge, the change of guard was an unconstitutional act.

Yahya's rule was a horrendous failure. As discussed in chapter 2, in 1971 India imposed a war on Pakistan which resulted in the amputation of East Pakistan. Defeated in war, General Yahya quit. The ambition of Mr Z. A. Bhutto's life was fulfilled when he rose to the ultimate political height, to lead what remained of Pakistan.

The Third Martial Law

Mr Bhutto and General Yahya Khan had failed to grasp the intensity and the seriousness of the people's upsurge in East Pakistan, and to comprehend the machinations of Sheikh Mujibur Rahman. Pakistan was dismembered. The foundation of the Bhutto rule was laid on the debris of the Yahya regime and the ashes of East Pakistan. The crash of East Pakistan was not a sudden phenomenon. The catastrophe which physically divided the country in December 1971 was the culmination of a tragedy of errors committed since 1947.

The end of Yahya's rule and the beginning of the Bhutto era did not result in the lifting of martial law in the country. Mr Bhutto became the President and the Chief Martial Law Administrator, the first civilian in Pakistan to hold the latter post. Initially, he lifted the sagging morale of a nation defeated in war with commendable courage and gusto. The 1973 Constitution was passed by the parliament; martial law gave way to civilian rule. But the relief given to the people was partial. Throughout the five and half years of his harsh rule, the state of emergency was kept imposed in the country, denying fundamental rights to the people. Bhutto the democrat did not even hold elections within his own party. This shortsightedness turned the PPP into a cult organization.

The rise of Mr Bhutto, the style of his government, and his fall from the pinnacle of authority are inextricably linked with Pakistan's power politics of the times in general and the beginning of the Zia era in particular. Mr Bhutto's rule ended on a sad note. The end of his life was even more tragic. The elections held in March 1977 pushed the country into a political abyss, paving the way for military intervention for the fourth time in the short history of this unfortunate nation.

The Fourth Martial Law

Martial Law was clamped on the country for the fourth time on 5 July 1977 by General M. Ziaul Haq. He inherited the assets and liabilities of the Bhutto administration, and these profoundly influenced his views about the person he replaced, and his deeds and misdeeds.

Estrangement developed between them from the moment Mr Bhutto was rearrested on a murder charge. From then onwards, their paths diverged, never to meet again. The passage of time further strengthened their mutual distrust and dislike. They started hating and fearing each other. If Mr Bhutto turned into a devil for General Zia, the soldier was no less abhorrent for the politician.

Political Frailty

Pakistan has the political paraphernalia essential for running a democratic system. A political structure exists, but many of those who run the system and many more in the public do not have the patience or the heart for real democracy. The plethora of political parties, mostly tiny and regional, does not augur well for the growth of a democratic order. They hamper the functioning of even the larger parties. The national political parties, shallow in their outlook and led by the feudal aristocracy, mostly lack political depth.

Perhaps the seven year duration of the Pakistan movement was too short to give the Muslim League any firm roots in the masses. Once Pakistan was achieved and following the deaths of Mr Jinnah and Khan Liaquat Ali Khan, the party fell prey to divergent pressures, lost its links with the masses, and gradually disintegrated into quarrelling factions. A handful of landlord families have dominated Pakistan's politics since 1947.

Communist ideology and atheism have traditionally not appealed to the religion-loving people of Pakistan. The socialist ideologues have had no worthwhile public base in the country. They have never achieved any electoral success.

The religio-political parties, divided on fundamentals and small in size, exercise considerable influence on the people on religious issues, particularly in the rural areas. But their vote-catching ability in an electoral contest has traditionally been low. By and large, a vast majority of the electorate has invariably voted in favour of the parties belonging to the centre, with leanings towards left or right.

Weak and fragile, the democratic structure could not withstand internal intrigues for power. Lacking inherent vitality, civilian governments looked for crutches to sustain themselves in power and frequently used the coercive instruments of the state authority under their control to prolong their rules. The bureaucracy and the military waited in the wings to seize the chance for their own vested interests because they too had the same feudal background and upbringing.

The Bureaucracy

Saddled with the responsibility of forming a government in 1947, the shortage of talented politicians in the Muslim League became apparent. Some technocrats were inducted to hold key appointments: Sir Muhammad Zafarullah Khan became the Foreign Minister, Mr Ghulam Muhammad the Minister for Finance, and Chaudhri Muhammad Ali occupied the prominent position of the Secretary-General of the new state.

Chaudhri Muhammad Ali laments the fact that, 'The biggest administrative problem facing Pakistan (at the time of independence) was the shortage of competent and experienced personnel in the central and provincial governments'.[12] After tasting power, the inductees became addicted to it. The honorary rank of Major-General was bestowed on another civil servant, Lieutenant-Colonel Iskandar Mirza. These bureaucrats turned politicians achieved dizzy heights and dominated the political scene till 1958. Chaudhri Muhammad Ali became the Minister for Finance in 1951. Four years later, he rose to become the Prime Minister. During his tenure as prime minister, Pakistan adopted the 1956 Constitution—full nine years after achieving independence. Mr Ghulam Muhammad was elevated to the high office of the Governor-General of Pakistan and later Major-General Iskandar Mirza became the President of the country. In the Ayub administration, Mr Aziz Ahmad became the Secretary-General. Later, he held the posts of the Minister of State for defence and foreign affairs in the Bhutto administration. Mr Altaf Gauhar, Ayub's information secretary, wielded far more influence and authority than that suggested by his post.

Mr Agha Shahi became the minister for foreign affairs in the Zia era. Mr Ghulam Ishaq Khan, the powerful finance minister in the Zia administration, became the Chairman of the Senate and rose to be the President of Pakistan. Mr Roedad Khan and Mr Ijlal Haider Zaidi later became advisers to Prime Minister Nawaz Sharif, but then developed differences with him and joined the opposition camp. Mr Sartaj Aziz, the Minister for Finance in Nawaz Sharif's administration, was a former bureaucrat. So was Dr Mahbubul Haq who served as a minister in more than one government.

THE GATHERING STORM

In Pakistan's post-independence history, the bureaucracy has established itself as a permanent pillar of power. It has faced purges. Attempts to trim it, like those in a rose creeper, have helped the bureaucratic system to blossom with greater vigour and vitality. The bureaucrats have concentrated real power under their own control and have mastered the art of survival. They excel in weaving cobwebs of rules, regulations, and officialdom around new incoming ministers. A minister who follows the rules rigidly becomes a prey of the bureaucracy and loses his freedom of action. If he violates them, the system exposes him. After having spread the net, the bureaucrats relax and watch the fun.

The official dice in Pakistan has always been heavily loaded in favour of the administration. The power-wielding administrators, parading as men of high virtues, complain that they have to deal with people with lower moral values. The bureaucrats have created mini empires within the government, in which the supremacy of officialdom is overwhelming and over-powering.

Many bureaucrats at the policy-making levels—honourable and experienced persons—have not hesitated in taking risk-free decisions. They have excelled in passing the buck on to their seniors when faced with knotty problems. Many senior bureaucrats were happier working under a military government which interfered less with their decision-taking process. They complained that the elected ministers, under political pressure, demand undue favours from the civil servants. A wily bureaucrat had a readymade answer for most of his acts of omission and commission. He would plead that, as an innocent and dutiful civil servant, he was too weak and insecure to resist the pressure brought to bear on him by his military or political boss. A good bureaucrat could conjure up convincing logic and usually kept an escape route open to bail him out of a difficult situation.

The Military

From day one of his induction into the profession of soldiering, it is ingrained in every officer, soldier, sailor, and airman that he must respect his national flag and defend his country even at the supreme personal cost. Every day, the flags are ceremoniously hoisted at dawn and lowered at sunset with great respect, in order to inculcate a sense of belonging and attachment to the country.

Likewise, a military commander charged with the responsibility of defending the territorial integrity of the motherland is honour-bound to do everything professionally possible to accomplish his assigned responsibilities, irrespective of the risks and cost involved. An act of conspiracy, a threat of a civil war, and any fissiparous tendency endangering the territorial unity of the country are viewed with grave concern by him. Wishing to nip the evil in the bud, his reaction against such attempts is invariably harsh. Such a motivation, noble and well-intended, however, does not give him authority to intervene in the affairs of the state. In a democratic dispensation, every soldier is subordinate to a representative government and he cannot act unilaterally without lawful authority. The violation of this rule has harmed the country and the military no less.

In democratic societies the civil supremacy and control of the civil service over the military is achieved through a process of accountability, budgetary control, a fixed tenure of top appointment holders, and by a process of discussion and debate on non-classified defence issues in the legislatures and in the media. Such a system has generally been weak in Pakistan. Here, under the falsely exaggerated cover of national security, defence-related issues have usually escaped indepth political scrutiny and debate within the government and on public platforms. The concept of a loyal opposition has been foreign to Pakistan. Nor has the system of parliamentary committees been practised in the parliament. Such voids have retarded the growth of a political system.

Pakistan's weak and inefficient democratic structure coexisted with a strong and well-organized defence establishment dominated by the Pakistan army. The extended tenures of appointments of some of the army chiefs made them headstrong. General Ayub Khan, the first Pakistani Commander-in-Chief of the Pakistan army, held that powerful office for seven and a half years (17 January 1951 through 26 October 1958). He placed the country under martial law in 1958 and became the President of Pakistan. General Muhammad Musa, loyal to Ayub and incapable of posing a danger to his authoritarian rule, dutifully served as the Commander-in-Chief for eight years (27 October 1958 through 17 September 1966). He was replaced by General Yahya Khan who promulgated martial law in 1969. His presidency was an appalling interregnum, resulting in the surrender of Dhaka in December 1971. The next Commander-in-Chief, Lieutenant-General Gul Hassan Khan, fell foul of Prime Minister

Bhutto and was made to resign in an undignified manner within two and a half months of his taking over. His successor, General Tikka Khan, stayed in office for four years (3 March 1972 through 28 February 1976). A down-to-earth soldier and a Bhutto loyalist, he joined the ruling Pakistan People's Party after his retirement. General Zia became the Chief of Army Staff on 1 March 1976. He imposed martial law in 1977 and ruled the country till his death in 1988. His political instincts guided him to trust his subordinate army commanders to the extent necessary. To keep his grip on the army, which traditionally obeyed its commander, he did not take the risk of appointing anyone to succeed him in his coveted military post.

Low-quality democracy interspersed with four martial laws has been the fate of Pakistan. In addition, parts of the country also faced two mini-martial laws for short periods. Paradoxically, on both occasions, these extra-constitutional measures were ordered by elected civil governments.

Caught between a fragile, ineffective, and corrupt political system, and a well-organized and potent military institution, Pakistan has been searching for its identity and ideals. The administrative and political weaknesses of the country and the high ambitions of the army's top brass introduced the military factor into its national politics at an early stage of its life. The country was caught in a vicious circle in which political instability created opportunities for military interference. The egocentric commanders intervened to preserve the unity of the motherland. The motives of some of them were in doubt *ab initio*. Others found it hard to rid themselves of the intoxication of power. In a society in which individuals overshadowed institutions and a democratic political system was preached but not practised, the fibre of national unity remained weak and under stress. Pakistan has yet to develop as a nation-state.

Some day, historians will analyse the causes of the frequent military interruptions in the civil rule in Pakistan. They will pass judgement whether Ayub Khan, Yahya Khan, and Ziaul Haq were all power-hungry, ambitious, and opportunistic commanders, bursting with egoism and seeking self-glorification. Or were they sucked into a quagmire created by unscrupulous politicians? It is a historical reality that on three occasions the Pakistani people had welcomed the imposition of martial law; it saved them from the chaotic conditions which prevailed at the time of each military take-over. It may be premature to suggest that the frequent imposition of martial law became inevitable merely because of the unworthy conduct of the political masters. The malaise lay deeper, and the reasons were varied. Politicians, generals, judges, bureaucrats and administrators—individually and collectively—share the blame for the harm done to democracy and to the prestige of the country. None can escape that responsibility. They were all parties to the crime; they all contributed to the rot. On the face of it, all of them deserve to be condemned in varying degrees.

The narrative that follows starts from the worst catastrophe faced by the country—the amputation of East Pakistan. It ends with the death of General Zia under mysterious circumstances, the causes of which remain undetermined. In between lie glimpses of the Bhutto era and a more detailed account of the twelve summers of Zia's rule.

CHAPTER 2

East Pakistan Amputated

President Ayub Khan's lust for power prevented him from leaving his high office with grace after his heart attack in 1968. His directive to General Yahya Khan to take control of the country was illegal and unconstitutional. He should have allowed the constitutional process to prevail after his exit. If General Yahya Khan imposed the decision on him, then Ayub showed a moral weakness.

The Yahya administration held the first-ever national elections on adult franchise basis in Pakistan in 1970. The year-long election campaign, noisy and acrimonious, polarized the country. Emotions ran high. The simple and mostly uneducated voters were given unrealistic promises by the crafty politicians.

Mr Zulfikar Ali Bhutto's Pakistan People's Party (PPP) enjoyed overall public support in West Pakistan only. He had skilfully exploited the Tashkent Agreement and the prevailing feelings against military rule. The PPP slogan of *roti, kapra, aur makan* (food, clothing, and shelter) for all touched the hearts and the sensitivities of the underprivileged and portrayed Bhutto as the liberator of the poor.

Sheikh Mujibur Rahman's Awami League, confined to the province of East Pakistan, contested the election on the basis of a Six Point Programme, demanding dilution of the federal power structure and making the two wings semi-autonomous with enhanced powers.[1] The Awami League's six-point programme, announced at a party conference at Lahore in February 1966, was opposed by most political parties in West Pakistan. They considered it a subterfuge for the division of the country.

Sheikh Mujibur Rahman gained strength and stature during the campaign period. He played on the bruised sentiments of East Pakistanis and kept repeating the theme that their due rights had been denied to them. The only alternative left to the people of East Pakistan was, he argued, to vote for the six-point programme of the Awami League. His emotional and defiant slogan made him a local hero. The Awami League workers disturbed the pre-election public meetings of other political parties in East Pakistan. In private, Mujib kept assuring the government that he firmly believed in a united Pakistan, that the six-point programme was negotiable, that he had a flexible approach, and that, after the elections, his hands would be strengthened to deal firmly with those hard-liners within the Awami League who wanted to secede from Pakistan.

The government claimed to be neutral but covertly provided moral and material assistance to the right-wing Islamic parties in both the wings, the major share going to the Jamaat-i-Islami. It failed to turn the tide, as was reflected in the election results:

Awami League	– 160 seats
Pakistan People's Party	– 81
Pakistan Muslim League (Qayyum Group)	– 9
Pakistan Muslim League (Convention Group)	– 7
Pakistan Muslim League (Council Group)	– 2
Jamiat-i-Ulema-i-Islam	– 7
Jamiat-i-Ulema-i-Pakistan	– 7
National Awami Party	– 6
Jamaat-i-Islami	– 4
Independents	– 15

Sheikh Mujibur Rahman's attitude hardened after the elections. He argued that the people of East Pakistan had given their clear verdict on the six-point programme and he had no authority to deviate from it. His rigid and uncompromising attitude created a political deadlock and put the country on the road to disaster.

The situation in West Pakistan was no less complex. Mr Bhutto, regarded as the administration's unofficial political adviser, was on friendly terms with General Yahya Khan and his military coterie. Mr G. W. Choudhury, a cabinet member and close confidant of Yahya, maintains that there was a 'secret deal' between Bhutto and Lieutenant-General S. G. M. M. Peerzada, Yahya's Principal Staff Officer. This deal 'played an important part' in national developments at that time and 'he (Bhutto) was even reported to have prepared Yahya's various statements, including the decision to postpone the assembly.'[2]

Peerzada confirms that Bhutto had frequent *tete-a-tetes* with Yahya on political issues, but is unsure of how much of his advice was actually accepted by the President.[3] He denies having made a secret deal with Bhutto and claims ignorance of issues which the President sometimes discussed individually with the Foreign Office officials or others. An ill-informed Peerzada is, however, hard to imagine.

Mr Bhutto, in a press conference on 27 March 1971, declared that 'Sheikh Mujibur Rahman wanted to establish an independent, fascist and racist regime in East Pakistan. He did not really believe in the integrity of the country.'[4] Notwithstanding his own political stance, Mr Bhutto's assessment of Sheikh Mujib cannot be lightly dismissed as totally devoid of truth. However, the Bhutto rhetoric was no less laced with threat: 'Majority alone does not count in national politics ... No constitution could be framed, nor could any government at the centre be run without my party's co-operation.' He went on to add: 'People have voted for the Pakistan People's Party in great majority in West Pakistan, and for the Awami League in East Pakistan. Both these parties (are) the majority parties.'

Mr Bhutto announced on 14 February 1971 that the PPP would not attend the forthcoming session of the National Assembly at Dhaka. He threatened to break the legs of all those persons who dared to attend the session. In a defiant tone, he declared: *Idhar hum udhar tum,* meaning 'we represent [the country] here and you represent [it] there.' He argued that: 'Pakistan might have to recognize two majority parties and even two prime ministers in one country.'[5]

Pressure tactics notwithstanding, the elected leaders of the two major political parties adopted rigid and diametrically opposed views on national affairs, both claiming a public mandate in support of their arguments.

Placed in a quandary, the government honoured the verdict of the people. After some hesitation, the National Assembly was called to meet in Dhaka on 3 March 1971.

The adamant Bhutto kept lobbying with the government for a rapprochement between the two major parties—the PPP and the Awami League—before a session of the National Assembly was held. Otherwise, he warned, there would be a deadlock inside the National Assembly. General Yahya came to accept this view.

A high-level conference, presided over by General Yahya, was held at the President House, Rawalpindi, on the evening of 22 February 1971. It was attended by all the provincial governors, the four provincial Martial Law Administrators, the Chief of Staff of the Pakistan Army, General Abdul Hameed, the Director-General of Intelligence Bureau, a senior police officer Agha Muhammad Ali, and the Principal Staff Officer to the President, Lieutenant-General S. G. M. M.

Peerzada. Major-General Civil Affairs East Pakistan, Rao Farman Ali Khan, had arrived in Islamabad in advance on 19 February 1971. He had earlier met the President and the PSO separately. Sipping a drink, General Yahya expressed deep disappointment at the political impasse. The prevailing polarization, Yahya felt, was not conducive to holding a session of the National Assembly on 3 March as previously announced. That statement surprised some and shocked the East Pakistan Governor, Admiral S. M. Ahsan, and the East Pakistan Martial Law Administrator, Lieutenant-General Sahabzada Yaqub Khan. Both took pains to explain that Bengali nationalism ran deep and the cancellation of the National Assembly session would produce serious consequences which might erode national unity. General Yahya cut the discussion short and asked Ahsan and Yaqub to meet him separately.

In the exclusive meeting, the President told Hameed, Peerzada, Ahsan, and Yaqub that he had decided to strengthen martial law in East Pakistan. Yaqub stated that the eastern wing was slipping out of the federation.[6] The support of the civil administration and the local intelligence agencies was suspect and he feared that the soldiers of the East Bengal Regiment and the East Pakistan Rifles might manifest disaffection due to emotional stress. Any military measure, Yaqub felt, would result in bloodshed and be counter-productive. He apprehended India's clandestine support to the local uprisings. The crisis needed a political solution. Yaqub proposed that the political leaders in both the wings should be made to assume or share the responsibility for their actions, which could lead to the disintegration of the country. Admiral Ahsan agreed with Yaqub's assessment. Not sharing Yaqub's 'pessimism', General Yahya declared that: 'The Assembly will not meet on March 3 and I intend making martial law effective in East Pakistan.' He asked the Governor and the MLA to meet him again in his office at 10 a.m. the next day.

After this unhappy meeting, Sahabzada Yaqub Khan drafted a letter to the President summarizing his arguments. His purpose was 'to remove any ambiguity and to maintain a record of the historic event.' On 23 February Yaqub gave the letter to the PSO for submitting it to the 'old man.' He had earlier shown it to Ahsan. 'The President would not be happy to read this letter,' quipped Peerzada. Yaqub replied that it contained nothing that he had not said the previous night.

After reading Yaqub's letter, General Yahya Khan became tense but did not show his annoyance. Yaqub elucidated the contents further. Ahsan agreed with Yaqub's prognosis. They suggested that the National Assembly session should not be postponed and that the President should visit Dhaka for an on-the-spot personal assessment of the situation. The President said that he would think over the issue. There is a missing link. On their return to Dhaka, Ahsan and Yaqub told Farman that initially General Yahya Khan had told them that Mr Bhutto was adamant that the Assembly session be postponed. When Ahsan and Yaqub pressed their point, Yahya told them, 'Go and convince Bhutto.'[7] Both of them met Mr Bhutto at Karachi; he declined to budge from his position. Mr Bhutto told Ahsan and Yaqub that the Awami League was a bourgeois party and was incapable of starting a people's war in East Pakistan. Ahsan and Yaqub reported the failure of their talks with Mr Bhutto to General Yahya Khan before they left for East Pakistan.

Having returned to Dhaka empty-handed, Admiral Ahsan and Lieutenant-General Yaqub were directed to inform Sheikh Mujibur Rahman that the Assembly session due to be held on 3 March would not be held. They met him together on 2 March. Aghast, Mujib said that the cancellation would be an invitation to disaster, that he would be unable to control the situation, and suggested that the session might be postponed, provided a fresh date was announced by the government. The Governor forwarded that request to the President, who rejected it.

The government thus lost the initiative and the course of events was thenceforth determined by the prevailing mood in East Pakistan.

Admiral Ahsan relinquished his governorship on 4 March and Sahabzada Yaqub Khan became the head of the provincial government, in addition to his responsibilities as the Martial Law Administrator. On his urging, General Yahya agreed to visit Dhaka; he stopped en route in Karachi. Mr Bhutto met the President in Karachi and prevailed on him not to travel to Dhaka at that point time.[8] The President's visit was suddenly postponed and the PSO to the President informed Yaqub about the change in the President's plan. Dejected, Yaqub debated the choice of continuing to serve or quitting. Some might accuse him of shirking responsibility, buckling under pressure, and being unsoldierly. Others might call him a staff type, a theoretician who paddles a safe course. Yaqub felt that his decision affected not only his own future but also that of his country and the forces under his command. If he quit, posterity might label him a rat, abandoning a sinking ship. On the other hand, if he stayed in power, he would be honour-bound to implement the government policies and orders which, he felt, were against the national interest. He surprised Peerzada by saying: 'In that event I hereby tender my resignation. I will confirm it in writing tomorrow.'

On 5 March Lieutenant-General Sahabzada Yaqub Khan sent a flash message to Peerzada confirming his resignation. It read:

> Reference our telephone conversation of last night. General Farman has left for Rawalpindi fully briefed. Only solution present crisis is a purely political one. Only President can take this far-reaching decision by reaching Dacca by 6th which I have repeatedly recommended. Am convinced there is no military solution which can make sense in present situation. I am consequently unable to accept responsibility for implementing a mission namely military solution which would mean *civil war and large scale killing of unarmed civilians and would achieve no sane aim. It would have disastrous consequences.* I, therefore, confirm tendering my resignation which I communicated to you by telephone last night. Pending arrival relief DMLA General Raja is fully in picture. (Emphasis added.)

Did Yaqub chicken out in adversity or display moral courage by upholding his principles? General Yahya reportedly felt that the storm for him was 'too rough to ride out.'[9] If Yaqub was judged to be wrong by his superiors, his act justified a trial. The army took an easier way out by not holding one.

Yaqub reported to General Headquarters, met General Hameed and sought permission to call on the President. Hameed told him that General Yahya might or might not be able to meet him and advised him to proceed on leave. Yaqub took the hint. Weeks later, he was reverted to his substantive rank of a Major-General and retired from the army.

On 2 March Mujib called upon 'every Bengali including the government employees not to co-operate with the anti-people forces.' He started issuing a series of directives to implement a 'non-violence and non-cooperative movement,' which included non-payment of taxes to the government. The administration was paralysed by the rowdy street power.

On 3 March 1971, the President invited twelve elected members of the parliamentary groups in the National Assembly to meet in

Dhaka on 10 March as a prelude to the Assembly session to be held 'within a matter of weeks after the conference.' Sheikh Mujibur Rahman rejected the invitation.

On 6 March 1971, it was announced that the inaugural session of the National Assembly would be held on 25 March. Addressing a public meeting in Dhaka on 7 March, Sheikh Mujib put forward a four-point demand for acceptance by the central government before the Awami League could consider the question of attending the National Assembly session. The four points were:

1. Immediate withdrawal of martial law.
2. Immediate recall of all military personnel to their barracks.
3. An enquiry into the loss of life.
4. Immediate transfer of power to the elected representatives of the people.

The government ignored the demands. It was aptly commented: 'Sheikh Mujib appears to have declared the independence of East Pakistan, thinly disguised in demands.'[10]

Sheikh Mujibur Rahman's Six-Point Programme was a subterfuge. He revealed his real intentions when he proudly claimed that: 'My path was of a different kind where Bengalis had to break bondage with Pakistan.'[11] On 10 January 1972, Mujib said: 'I had been working for this independence for the last 25 years. Now my dream has come true.'[12]

On 7 March, Lieutenant-General Tikka Khan arrived in Dhaka to assume the roles of Governor and Commander Eastern Command. Quoting prevailing chaotic conditions as the reason, the Chief Justice of the East Pakistan High Court made himself unavailable to administer the oath of office to the new governor. Bengali nationalism had eroded the fibre of national unity. Tikka Khan was administered the oath after the military crackdown of 25 March by the same judge who had earlier expressed his inability to do so, due to fear.

By the time President Yahya Khan reached Dhaka on 15 March 1971, the secessionists controlled East Pakistan. Mujib suggested that Yahya convert Pakistan into a confederation.[13] Yahya did not immediately share this advice with the West Pakistan leaders, fearing that the scheduled talks might be aborted. On 22 March, Mujib submitted the confederation plan in a written form to the President. General Yahya spent the next ten days negotiating with the Awami League leaders—Mujib, Nazrul Islam, Tajuddin Ahmad, Dr Kamal Hossain, Khondkar Mushtaq Ahmed, and others. At the President's invitation, the West Pakistani leaders—Bhutto, Daultana, Shaukat Hayat, Mufti Mahmud, Wali Khan, Bizenjo, and Noorani—were on hand in Dhaka. By 25 March, the parleys had reached the dead end of the dark political tunnel.

The government claimed that the Awami League had planned to launch an armed rebellion in the early hours of 26 March 1971. The night of 25-26 March saw the perpetration of 'unmentionable brutalities' by the Awami League sympathizers on West Pakistani personnel and their families. In cantonments throughout East Pakistan, all officers and men of West Pakistan domicile serving in the East Pakistan Rifles and the East Pakistan Regiment, along with their family members, were killed in cold blood. In one incident, Lieutenant-Colonel Rashid Janjua, Commanding Officer 6 East Bengal Regiment, was killed in Chittagong, his body tied behind a jeep, and dragged through the town. It was reported that 'when the East Pakistan Rifles mutinied, their first reaction was to wipe out the non-Bengalis in their own ranks.'[14] Another report indicated that 'Thousands of West Pakistanis and Indian migrants [settled in East Pakistan since 1947] were put to death in Chittagong between 25 March and 11 April.'[15] Such acts were premeditated.

This massacre of innocent persons created anarchy and put the soldiers under tremendous emotional stress. When the army was subsequently deployed to restore normalcy, there were occasional reports of excessive force used against the miscreants.

In West Pakistan, the obdurate Bhutto had threatened to 'launch a movement from Khyber to Karachi' and warned that 'any member of his party attending the assembly session would be liquidated by the party workers.' He said that: 'In case it was the intention of someone to create different independent states in Pakistan, let it be said so clearly.'[16] On 14 March, he demanded the transfer of power to the Awami League in East Pakistan and to the PPP in West Pakistan, 'if power was to be transferred before reaching a constitutional settlement.'[17] His ambition got the better of him when he stated that 'Sheikh Mujib could become the Prime Minister of East Pakistan and he would be the Prime Minister of West Pakistan in a confederation.'[18]

The political scene was dominated by the three musketeers—Yahya, Mujib, and Bhutto—trying to outwit one another and vying for power. Sheikh Mujibur Rahman and Mr Bhutto had high ambitions. They disliked each other; their mutual distrust was surpassed only by their common hatred of President Yahya Khan. Each one in the trio tried to use the other two for his self-aggrandizement. Mujib wanted to become the founding father of Bangladesh rather than the Prime Minister of Pakistan; he said as much to the foreign ministers of Turkey and Iran when they met him in Dhaka.[19] The impetuous Bhutto could not control his impatience to wield power. And Yahya was all too eager to exploit the two warring politicians to carve a role for himself in the future political framework. Mujib promised him the President's post in the future government.[20] The only sufferer was Pakistan.

On 25 March 1971, the government, having lost patience, used force to suppress the popular uprising in the East Wing. Sheikh Mujibur Rahman and some other leaders were arrested. Many more went underground or escaped to India. Pakistan was close to collapse.

Returning to West Pakistan, General Yahya Khan addressed the nation from Karachi on 26 March 1971. The tone of his seventeen-minute speech was harsh. All political activities in the country were banned and the Awami League outlawed. The President charged Mujib with attacking the solidarity and integrity of the country and warned that his crime would not go unpunished. He said: 'Mujib's obstinacy, obduracy and absolute refusal to talk sense can lead to one conclusion—the man and his party are enemies of Pakistan and they want East Pakistan to break away completely from the country.'[21]

Mr Bhutto, returning to West Pakistan from Dhaka on 26 March 1971, issued a press statement supporting the military action in East Pakistan. He said: 'By the Grace of Almighty God, Pakistan has at last been saved.'[22] His judgement was faulty.

The military action caused casualties which further alienated the people. At considerable political cost, a modicum of order had been restored. But the people lost confidence in the government. Their wounds were bleeding. By the time Tikka Khan was eventually replaced, he had earned a dubious distinction of being named 'the butcher of Bengal'.

Dr A. M. Malik and Lieutenant-General A. A. K. Niazi were appointed the Governor and the Martial Law Administrator of East Pakistan respectively on 3 September 1971. This was a weak team, faced with an uphill task. Dr Malik was helped by the military adviser on civil affairs, Major-General Rao Farman Ali, who enjoyed the confidence of President Yahya Khan, had his ear, and was known to wield influence in excess of what his appointment indicated. The East Pakistan crisis exposed General Niazi's inadequacy. His operational plan was faulty, its implementation less than professional, and he rapidly succumbed under pressure. His reservoir of talent—juicy tales and unprintable anecdotes— did not help him in combat. A wise man has said: 'In war: resolution; in defeat: defiance; in victory: magnanimity; in peace : goodwill.' These traits were conspicuous by their absence. A weak strategy was further rendered untenable because of leadership failure.

India got an opportunity to convert her hitherto covert interference in East Pakistan into overt aggression. From March 1971 till the fall of Dhaka on 16 December 1971, Pakistan kept sliding down the slope. A crisis of confidence and a crisis in leadership gripped East Pakistan. The situation was akin to the vision of an Urdu poet who had once said:

> Don't give all these excuses;
> Tell me why the caravan has been looted.
> I have no concern with the robbers.
> It's the question of your leadership.
> Shall I tell you why the caravan was looted?
> Because you were in league with the robbers;
> I have no complaint against the looters;
> But I regret your leadership.

General Yahya Khan presided over the destruction of his own country. Fortune had favoured him earlier. General Muhammad Musa recalls his conversation with Field Marshal Muhammad Ayub Khan, when Musa took to him a list of the names of three general officers to replace him as the Commander-in-Chief of the Pakistan Army. Ayub added the fourth name—Yahya Khan's. Says Musa : 'I told him (Ayub) that, professionally, there was no remarkable difference between him and the other three officers, but whatever soldiering virtues Yahya possessed were by and large vitiated by his personal shortcomings ... The President concurred with my assessment of the four officers but felt my fears about Yahya were somewhat unfounded.'[23] Musa was overruled. Yahya was promoted. The country suffered.

General Yahya was a shrewd and intelligent person. He possessed a discerning mind which quickly grasped the essentials of a problem. A pleasant conversationalist, he spoke with ease and mixed freely. Known for taking quick decisions, he cleared his file work speedily and seldom had a backlog. During the first few months of martial law, he worked hard and took timely decisions which met with public approval. Thereafter, he became overconfident and complacent. Gradually, statecraft took a backseat. He started relying heavily on the coloured advice of a handful of his advisers who put a ring of isolation around him. As the pressure of work increased, so did his urge for hard drinks. Towards the latter part of his disastrous rule, he drank excessively and indulged in activities unworthy of his high office. Whether it was it to drown his sorrows and failures or to seek an easy escape from harsh realities, one can only guess. To draw a comparison, if Nero played the lyre while Rome burned, Yahya kept drinking while East Pakistan was sinking in an ocean of chaos.

Yahya enjoyed ephemeral pleasures. He shared his hours of leisure with General Abdul Hameed Khan, the Chief of Staff of the Pakistan Army. His close associates included Lieutenant-General Peerzada, Major-General Gul Hassan Khan, Major-General Ghulam Umer, and Mr Z. A. Bhutto. General Hameed had advised the military governors of the provinces not to implement the President's verbal orders, if given to them personally by him after 10 p.m., without reconfirming with the President the following morning.

A number of factors caused the debacle of 1971. These included the geographical separation of the two wings of the country and the inability of the political leadership to create a united and cohesive country. The people of East Pakistan resented the greater economic strides made in the western wing but ignored the reality that this part had inherited a better communications and industrial infrastructure at the time of independence. The inter-wing economic disparity, massively exploited by the Awami League for political gain, created hatred against West Pakistan and a feeling of bitterness developed against the federal government. Diplomatically, the country stood isolated in 1971. And finally, the operational plan made for the defence of East Pakistan was faulty and its implementation left much to be desired. Notwithstanding these difficulties, events in East Pakistan might have taken a different course if India had not played a Machiavellian role through covert and overt operations.

The fact of India's involvement in the fall of Dhaka has been well established by many neutral foreign political analysts. Even Indian writers acknowledge the Indian participation and express pride in having defeated Pakistan.

India and the Soviet Union had signed a Treaty of Peace and Co-operation on 9 August 1971. The treaty committed both the countries 'to consider attack on one as an attack on the other.' This treaty was invoked by India when she aggressed against East Pakistan.

With the arrest of Sheikh Mujibur Rahman, the provincial administration moved against the Awami League leaders, most of whom had gone underground. Many fugitive Awami League leaders and workers trekked across the border to the safety of a haven in India. They were joined by the miscreants who, after committing acts of violence in East Pakistan, went across the border. Some others left the country out of fear. India welcomed the immigrants, issued them weapons, and imparted guerrilla training to them. The trained saboteurs were then infiltrated back into East Pakistan to create destruction and panic. They had the full sympathy and support of the local population, who had been alienated by the misguided policies of the central government.

Adopting a double-faced policy, India claimed that the 'refugees', besides hurting her economy, also endangered her security. Significantly, she did not close her border with East Pakistan because her intention was to wage a war. The refugees were used as a 'pretext for war' and the Mukti guerrillas were merely a 'decorative facade.'[24] An Indian journalist reported that the Muktis were in fact Indian soldiers and if he had written about it 'when he was in India, he would undoubtedly have been arrested.'[25] In the words of the Prime Minister of India, 'the only solution of East Pakistan was independence of Bangladesh.'[26]

On 30 March 1971, both houses of the Indian Parliament passed a resolution moved by the Indian Prime Minister expressing 'profound sympathy and solidarity with the people of East Pakistan' and assuring them that 'their struggle will receive the wholehearted sympathies and support of the people of India.'[27]

On 31 March 1971, the Director of the Indian Institute for Defence Studies and Analysis, Mr K. Subramanyam, said: 'What India must realize is the fact that the break-up of Pakistan is in our interest and we have an opportunity the like of which will never come again.'[28]

On 4 April 1971, Mr K. K. Shukla, Secretary General of the West Bengal unit of the All India Congress Committee confessed that 'Sheikh Mujibur Rahman was fighting India's war.'[29]

The Indian Prime Minister declared on 15 June 1971 that 'India would not for a moment countenance a political settlement which meant the death of Bangladesh.'[30] Thakar Prasad of the Jan Sangh declared: 'We shall not rest content till Pakistan is destroyed and merged with Bharat.'[31]

On the diplomatic front, Mrs Indira Gandhi undertook a tour of the USSR, France, the UK, and the USA to gain their support for India's stand. While she spoke for peace, her generals planned for war.

In March 1971, Mrs Gandhi had directed the military to attack East Pakistan. Her calculating Chief of Army Staff, General Manekshaw, 'did not want his army to be get stuck in the quagmire of the monsoon.'[32] He asked for sufficient time to plan for the operation and train his troops for riverine warfare, indicating that success would be doubtful if the operation was launched earlier. By October, the monsoon season would be over, the ground offered space for manouevre, and the snow on the Himalayan range rendered the passes in the high ranges impassable. 'Manekshaw preferred to fight one enemy at a time, and the weaker one first. He preferred November, when the Chinese participation was considerably reduced because the Himalayan passes would then be closed.'[33] Accepting Manekshaw's professional advice, Mrs Gandhi approved the November 1971 date.

Early border skirmishes started in September 1971 when the districts of Khulna, Bogra, Jessore, Comilla, Sylhet, and Dinajpur were subjected to artillery shelling. Pakistan's diplomatic protests were rejected by India as 'false and fabricated'. The frequency of border violations increased in the month of October, with the districts of Noakhali and Kushtia as added targets. A protest note delivered to India on 4 November said: 'Pakistan takes a serious view of instances of continued and unprovoked shelling on Pakistan territory by the Indian Army in gross violation of the ground rules.' The note listed 22 incidents of unprovoked and wanton acts of aggression between 19 October and 24 October, in which 19 persons were killed and 45 injured. While Pakistan talked of peace, India's Defence Minister threatened that: 'Pakistan should voluntarily concede Bangladesh or India will impose it [the establishment of Bangladesh] on Pakistan.'

A British paper summed up the situation thus: 'India's attempt at subversion in Pakistan, of sponsoring a fifth column in East Pakistan, and her machinations to undo Pakistan itself... started from the very day in 1947 when Pakistan was created.'[34]

Without a formal declaration of war, India launched a multi-directional attack on East Pakistan in the first week of November 1971. Sydney H. Schanberg, wrote: 'Unimpeachable Indian sources said today, despite official denials, that Indian troops had crossed into East Pakistan.'[35]

The Indian invasion was not a surprise. On 6 September the Inter Services Intelligence Directorate (ISID) had placed copies of Manekshaw's operational instructions, issued in mid-August 1971, before the President of Pakistan, the services chiefs, and the Secretary Defence.[36] A month later, it had given prior information about the projected 'big' Indian attack on East Pakistan on 21-22 November 1971. On 3 December 1971, a copy of the latest Indian order of battle had been provided to the services headquarters. Notwithstanding the timely availability of strategic and technical level intelligence, there was something lacking in putting together of the Pakistani act.

The main Indian offensive in East Pakistan was launched on 21 November 1971, with eight divisions. Opposing them was one infantry division, having one reconnaissance regiment equipped with 40 light tanks. Pakistan had augmented this force with some infantry battalions, less their heavy equipment, moved from West Pakistan on an emergency basis. Out of this force, two *ad hoc* infantry divisions were created. These divisions were in skeleton form, having no integral tank, artillery, engineers, or logistic support components.

Manpower was airlifted through a circuitous route—Karachi-Colombo-Dhaka—as India had prohibited flights of all Pakistani civilian and military aircraft over her territory. Sri Lanka withstood the Indian pressure to stop Pakistan International Airlines from using refuelling facilities at its airports.

The operational details of war are not the burden of this narrative. In the real sense, it was more treachery than war which engulfed East Pakistan. The military deserters and the civilian dissidents, turned Mukti Bahini, familiar with the defensive layout, led the Indian Army on to the Pakistani posts by the safest possible routes. Much before the Pakistani soldiers were defeated in the battle, they had been stabbed in the back by the hostile locals. In the classic military sense, India did not win. Only Pakistan lost. So dominant was the role of betrayal that even the Indian attackers were amazed at the rapidity of their success. The other factors causing an early collapse were the exhaustion of the Pakistani troops due to the prolonged civil strife, lack of fire power and administrative support, and, above all, the faulty defence plans.

As an aggrieved party, it was natural for Pakistan to lodge an immediate protest with the United Nations Security Council and seek its early intervention to get the Indian aggression vacated. This did not happen. On 22 November 1971, Mr Agha Shahi, Pakistan's permanent representative at the UN, sent an urgent cable back home pointing out that, 'as the Indian armed forces had crossed the border of East Pakistan, they were committing aggression and the friends of Pakistan in the UN were wondering why Pakistan was not requesting the UN Security Council to become seized of the act of aggression.'[57] To his request for instructions, the Foreign Office categorically directed him not to take any initiative in the matter without specific instructions from the Foreign Office. Such an authorization was never given.

Mr Bhutto was then the Deputy Prime Minister and the Foreign Minister. With his vast experience in domestic and foreign relations, Pakistan's suicidal policy of diplomatic inactivity in the face of external aggression is intriguing. The Indian attack had tilted opinion in UN circles in favour of Pakistan and against India. An immediate approach to the Security Council might have given a chance to international diplomacy to call for an immediate cease-fire and halt the Indian aggressor from overrunning East Pakistan.

Internal disunity, diplomatic isolation, indecisive leadership, and the inability to activate the West Pakistan border in time caused the military debacle. The battle in East Pakistan was wrongly planned and inexpertly conducted. In West Pakistan, troops waited for orders but the decision-makers in Islamabad remained unmoved. On 11 or 12 December 1971, Brigadier Amir Gulistan Janjua, the Military Secretary to the Commander-in-Chief told me in a telephonic conversation that 'our friends from the north' would soon be intervening. Janjua held too sensitive an appointment to be so vocal on an issue of national security without good reasons. If Pakistan really had believed in such a possibility, it was a sad reflection on her policymakers.

Professor G. W. Choudhury writes: 'Kissinger was reported to have told the Indian ambassador in Washington after his visit to Beijing that China would intervene, if India attacked Pakistan, and the United States might not come to India's help as it had done in 1962 and 1965, when it had warned China against intervention.'[38] Choudhury claims that the information was given to him by General Yahya himself. This appears plausible. The Chief of General Staff, Lieutenant-General Gul Hassan Khan, verbally passed information about 'friends from the north' intervening, to the Commander Eastern Command, based on the instructions received by him from General Hameed. Earlier, on 5 December 1971, GHQ had clearly informed Eastern Command (signal no. 0233) of every hope of Chinese activities soon. Was it unwarranted complacency, wishful thinking, or intrigue?

The inevitable happened. East Pakistan was amputated on 16 December. A humiliated Pakistan earned the dubious distinction of creating a motherland and then destroying it within the life-span of just one generation. The Indian dream of dismembering Pakistan was fulfilled. 'The Indians have been rough and irresponsible,' wrote a newspaper, adding, 'they have encouraged and directly taken part in the dismemberment of a sovereign state . . .'[39] The Indian euphoria was summarized by the Indian Prime Minister, Mrs Indira Gandhi, thus: 'India has avenged the defeat of the last one thousand years.'

The news of the surrender was, ironically, heard by the Pakistani people through the Indian Prime Minister's broadcast, over All India Radio. The announcement of surrender was sugarcoated by Radio Pakistan in its 5 p.m. news bulletin in these words: 'Following an arrangement between the commanders of India and Pakistan, fighting has ceased in the Eastern theatre and the Indian troops have entered Dhaka.'

The President's radio broadcast at 7:15 p.m. on 16 December, confirming the surrender in East Pakistan was heard by the shocked nation in grim silence. The people felt humiliated, betrayed, misled, and cheated. Soon after the President's radio speech, Mrs Indira Gandhi once again spoke on All India Radio to declare a unilateral cease-fire all along the western border effective from 7:30 p.m. on 17 December 1971. India's immediate aim having been achieved, she was in a position to suspend hostilities. Or was there some other reason behind that decision? Nixon writes: 'India dismembered and threatened to extinguish Pakistan, a goal I may have helped to deny by "tilting" U. S. policy in the conflict towards Pakistan.'[40]

Pakistan's public relations' effort was niggardly. Once again, All India Radio was the first to announce, at 4:30 p.m. on 17 December 1971, Pakistan's acceptance of the cease-fire along the West Pakistan border. Radio Pakistan broadcast that news half an hour later. A pall of gloom engulfed Pakistan in the wake of shameful defeat.

From 8 December onwards, the Indian military commander had been sending surrender messages to Major-General Rao Farman Ali in Dhaka. On 9 December the Governor East Pakistan sent a distress signal to the President of Pakistan, painting a grim situation and requesting for a political solution of the crisis. The will to resist had collapsed. In reply, General Yahya delegated the responsibility of taking the final decision to the Governor by saying, 'I have and am continuing to take all measures internationally but in view of our complete isolation from each other decision about East Pakistan I leave entirely to your good sense and judgement. I will approve of any decision you take and I am instructing General Niazi simultaneously to accept your decision and arrange things accordingly.'[41] This was passing on the buck to a subordinate to place the onus of surrender on him. The Chief of Army Staff's signal to General Niazi read: 'President has left the decision to the Governor in close consultation with you as no signal can correctly convey the degree of seriousness of the situation. I can only leave it to you to take the correct decision on the spot. It is however apparent that it is now only a question of time before the enemy . . . will dominate East Pakistan completely . . .'[42] Yahya and Hameed had acted in unison. Based on the authority delegated to the Governor of East Pakistan, Major-General Rao Farman Ali addressed a note to the UN representative in Dhaka, Mr Paul Mark Henry, calling upon the United Nations to arrange for a peaceful transfer of power. It was strange tactics. Such a request should have originated from the government of Pakistan. Farman claims that he did so on the orders of the Governor.[43] Farman's note suggested an immediate cease-fire, and the repatriation of the Pakistani armed forces and civilians to West Pakistan in safety (the full text of the note is at Annexure 4). This was a request for an honourable surrender in which no mention was made of the Indian aggression. Those sending that note should have known that the surrender terms are imposed by the victors, not demanded by a defeated army. The text of the note was sent by the Governor to the President under signal number A7107 dated 10 December 1971 with the remark, 'General Niazi has been consulted and submits himself to your command.'

In New York, at 4:30 a.m. on 10 December, an official of the UN Secretariat read out over the telephone to Pakistan's representative, Agha Shahi, the full text of Farman's note along with the personal observations of Paul Mark Henry on the prevailing situation in Dhaka.[44] In the assessment of Paul Mark Henry, confusion prevailed in Dhaka where Hotel Intercontinental had been converted into a Red Cross protected zone for the official personnel from West Pakistan, and the policymakers—Governor Malik, and Generals Niazi and Farman—were in a state of nervous exhaustion. Shahi was informed that the Secretary General planned to circulate Farman's note to all members of the Security Council. Shahi pleaded against such a step, arguing that it would foreclose Pakistan's case in the Security Council. Nevertheless, the report was circulated to the five permanent members only. They must have leaked it out to the other members of the Council.

Later in the day, Shahi received Mr Bhutto, who arrived at New York airport from Frankfurt. In the car, he told Bhutto what he had been told about Farman's message that morning by the UN Secretariat official. Bhutto's reaction was; 'I have been betrayed.'[45] The Foreign Minister was either unaware of the developments back home, which would appear improbable, or his arrival in America had been carefully timed to enable him to be away from the scene of activity in Pakistan as well as the UN at the critical time, to escape the stigma of becoming party to the surrender of East Pakistan.

In the final analysis, Pakistan's internal mismanagement, the treachery of Sheikh Mujibur Rahman, the overambitiousness of Mr Bhutto, and the inept leadership of General Yahya Khan contributed to converting East Pakistan into Bangladesh, no less than the covert and overt aggression committed by India.

War is a business of timely decisions. A strategist who fails to grasp fleeting opportunities invariably surrenders the initiative to his adversary. Pakistan's defeat in the battlefield was symbolic. She was, in fact, beaten in the corridors of power in Islamabad much before the visible fall of Dhaka.

The defeat in East Pakistan was made worse by officially maintaining a cloak of unwise secrecy. The people were not psychologically prepared for the disaster and one saw drooping heads, gloomy and dejected faces, blank eyes staring into the wilderness, and chests choked with suppressed and bruised emotions. A telling description in *Time* magazine, that 'between dusk and dawn, Pakistan was ruled by pimps', seemed only too true.

On 19 December General Abdul Hameed Khan, the Chief of Staff of the Pakistan Army addressed the army officers in the National

Defence College auditorium at Rawalpindi. He faced a volley of hostile questions from the agitated junior officers and barely managed to extricate himself from an awkward situation. The time for explanations had passed. It was time for some heads to roll. The disaster had sealed General Yahya Khan's fate as President of Pakistan. His desire to hang on to power had blinded him beyond measure. While every person in the country knew that the game was over for him, he played a last-minute gimmick to prolong his rule. A Constitution, secretly prepared, was released to the Press in December 1971. It was withdrawn posthaste when the inevitability of his political end hit Yahya like a thunderbolt.

Left with no choice, General Yahya Khan had to call upon Mr Zulfikar Ali Bhutto, then aged 43, the leader of the Pakistan People's Party, which had won a majority of seats in West Pakistan, to succeed him. Mr Bhutto was sworn in as the President and the Chief Martial Law Administrator of the country on 20 December 1971. It was a rare phenomenon in history that an elected political leader became a martial law dictator. The act earned harsh comments: 'It is a measure of Pakistan's desperation that in its darkest hour it has to turn for leadership to the very man who helped bring disaster to the country.'[46]

After the loss of East Pakistan, Mr Bhutto emerged as a populist leader in what was left of Pakistan. Firm, resolute, and charismatic, he had undiluted authority at his command. He took Pakistan out of the debris of war with skill, courage, and determination, gave his countrymen a sense of awakening, and promised them prosperity and a better future. He handled his subordinates, colleagues and opponents firmly, even harshly when needed. He had the drive and the ability to get his decisions implemented.

In an emotion-packed address to the nation on radio and television on 20 December, Mr Bhutto said: 'We are facing the worst crisis in our country's life—a deadly crisis . . . We have to pick up the pieces, very small pieces, but we will make a new Pakistan. A Pakistan free of exploitation . . . Pakistan was at the edge of the precipice . . . East Pakistan was an inseparable and indissoluble part of Pakistan.' Speaking with confidence, he pledged to rebuild Pakistan anew. His spirited extempore address, aimed at injecting vigour and confidence in the sagging morale of the nation, was well received. While referring to the armed forces he said: 'My dear *jawans* [soldiers] and my dear officers and dear brothers, you have fought bravely. You have nothing to worry about, you have nothing to be ashamed of, you have been victims of a system. We will put this right.'

Bhutto announced the retirement of General Abdul Hameed Khan, Lieutenant-General S. G. M. M. Peerzada, and Major-Generals Ghulam Umer, Abubakar Osman Mitha, Khuda Dad, and Hamid Asghar Kiyani. Lieutenant-General Gul Hassan Khan was made the Acting Chief of the Pakistan Army. Three days later, some senior naval officers, including the Naval Commander-in-Chief, Vice Admiral Muzaffar Hasan, were retired. All the Generals retired were serving in West Pakistan.

The unusual mode of retiring the general officers—in a media talk—was to serve the cause of expediency. That uncharitable act was resented and cost Mr Bhutto the goodwill of many of his admirers in the defence services. Notwithstanding his public rhetoric, Mr Bhutto proceeded to cut the army to size. A film on the surrender ceremony at Dhaka was telecast. The public reaction was strong and adverse. Mr Abdul Hafeez Pirzada, a minister in the Bhutto cabinet, justified the Government's decision by stating that the 'truth must be told.'

After his arrest in March 1971, Sheikh Mujibur Rahman had been brought to West Pakistan. Lodged in the Faisalabad jail, he was tried in a Field General Court Martial, presided over by Brigadier Rahimuddin Khan, on charges including that of sedition. The members of the court were an officer from the Pakistan Navy, two officers from the Pakistan Army, and a civil sessions judge. The trial commenced in mid-1971 and was spread over a period of six months. At the trial, Sheikh Mujibur Rahman was defended by the well-known constitutional lawyer, Mr A. K. Brohi. The court submitted the trial proceedings to the government in December 1971. On completion of the trial, Sheikh Mujibur Rahman was shifted to Mianwali jail.

On becoming the head of state on 20 December 1971, Mr Bhutto decided to release Sheikh Mujibur Rahman. He was first transferred from the Mianwali jail to a rest-house in Chashma. Mr Bhutto had two lengthy meetings with him in Rawalpindi, the first on 27 December 1971, and the second on 7 January 1972. These were expertly stage-managed. The conversation was secretly taped with Mr Bhutto aware of the fact and Sheikh Mujibur Rahman ignorant of it. In those meetings, Mr Bhutto and Sheikh Mujibur Rahman bitterly criticized General Yahya Khan. Sheikh Mujibur Rahman indicated that America and India were implicated in the East Pakistan crisis. Mr Bhutto praised Sheikh Mujibur Rahman lavishly, calling him the greatest son ever born in the subcontinent. He proposed to him that an inter-state link, even a loose confederation, be maintained between Pakistan and Bangladesh. Sheikh Mujibur Rahman initially remained evasive. Subsequently, he agreed and remarked 'otherwise there was no hope for West Pakistan.' Sheikh Mujib asked Bhutto to appreciate his difficulty as he had to deal with a triple menace—armed guerrillas, the occupation army, and Maulana Bhashani. He stressed the urgency of his reaching Bangladesh to prevent India from gaining a firm foothold there.

Mr Bhutto took pains to convey the impression to Sheikh Mujibur Rahman that he (Bhutto) was personally responsible for saving him from the jaws of death. He repeatedly mentioned that General Yahya Khan had been determined to execute Sheikh Mujibur Rahman, even if he had to backdate his orders for that purpose. He told Sheikh Mujibur Rahman that he had been deeply worried about his personal safety. For that reason, said Bhutto, he had had him shifted from the Mianwali jail to Chashma rest-house, to take him out of the reach of General Yahya Khan. He repeatedly requested Sheikh Mujibur Rahman that on his arrival at Dhaka he should disclose publicly that Bhutto had saved his life.

Sheikh Mujib told Mr Bhutto that the game was to kill both of them and those earmarked for high appointments were Khan Abdul Qayyum Khan and Mr Nurul Amin. Mr Bhutto asked Mujib who he thought was a bigger villain, Yahya or Peerzada. Mujib responded: 'Both'.

Was there a plan to execute Sheikh Mujibur Rahman? The available evidence does not support this allegation. Those wielding authority at that time are no longer alive. Professor G. W. Choudhury, known to have enjoyed Yahya's confidence, recalls his first meeting with General Zia in March 1979 in these words: 'He (Zia) also asked me about Bhutto's advice to me in September 1971 to urge President Yahya to execute Mujib before Yahya would go to attend the two-thousand year anniversary of the Iranian monarchy—an occasion where many world leaders were expected to gather in Tehran at the invitation of the late Shah of Iran. Bhutto's contention to me was that Yahya, being a weak person, was likely to succumb to world pressure and may release Mujib or might even transfer power to Mujib. It was, therefore, needed, according to Bhutto, to execute Mujib before Yahya went to Tehran in late 1971. When I gave General Zia the documentary evidence of the late Bhutto's outrageous suggestion, Zia was simply shocked and surprised.'[47]

The Last Days of United Pakistan was published in 1974 when General Yahya was out of power, Sheikh Mujibur Rahman was the President of Bangladesh, and Mr Bhutto was the Prime Minister of Pakistan. It contains a detailed narration on the subject thus: 'In the meantime there began a "trial" of Mujib by a military tribunal, and Brohi was allowed to act as Mujib's defence counsel. In fact, the "trial" was never a serious one. Thanks to pressure from the White House, the safety of Mujib's life was guaranteed. In fact, even before Mujib surrendered to the Pakistan Army in March, there was a secret deal, again through the good offices of the American officials, ensuring that Mujib's life would be protected . . . Mujib and his family were treated in a strangely pleasant way by the army. The fabricated story of digging a "graveyard" for Mujib on the floor of his cell in the prison has been exposed by the journalist, Oriana Fallaci, in her [book] *Mujib in Power: A Portrait*. It is, however, true that some hawkish generals, in collaboration with Bhutto, would have preferred to execute Mujib if it had been feasible. Yahya had no such plan. He was rather relieved to receive Nixon's letters on this matter which strengthened his hands in restraining the hawks.'[48]

President Nixon claims that he had '. . . obtained assurances from the Government of Pakistan that Mujib would not be executed.'[49]

Sheikh Mujibur Rahman was released and quietly flown to London on 7 January 1972 in a special aircraft. A sum of $50,000 was placed at his disposal to cover incidental expenses. For his homeward journey, Sheikh Mujibur Rahman left London on board a British Air Force Comet on 10 January. He made a brief halt in New Delhi to thank the Indian leadership for the help provided, before reaching Bangladesh. In Dhaka, he declared that the link between East and West Pakistan 'has been snapped for all time to come.' The Bhutto plan misfired. On 15 August 1975, Mujib was assassinated in his house along with his wife and his sons and their families by some Bangladeshi army officers. His death was a loss to India.

Mrs Indira Gandhi and Mr Zulfikar Ali Bhutto met at the hill resort of Simla, India, in the summer of 1972 to negotiate a settlement for the return of Pakistan's POWs, the pulling back of military forces to the Indo-Pakistan borders, and other allied matters. Before Mr Bhutto went to India, he met a broad cross-section of public opinion-makers in Pakistan to formulate a negotiating strategy. He enquired from the services headquarters about their preference between: 1) the return of POWs, and 2) the exchange of captured territories. He was advised that the exchange of captured territories should be given preference over the return of the prisoners. The advice was based on the logic that the POWs could not be kept as permanent hostages by any victor.

The Simla talks resulted in the Simla Agreement.[50] As a consequence, the POWs returned to Pakistan and the diplomatic links between the two countries were restored. On the vital question of the return of the captured territories, Mrs Gandhi and Mr Bhutto correctly realized that any readjustment in the international boundary would add friction to their trouble-ridden relationship. Such territories, therefore, were vacated by India and Pakistan. However, the areas captured by the two countries in the State of Jammu and Kashmir during the hostilities were not returned. This decision went to the advantage of India which had made greater territorial gains in the war. The term 'cease-fire line' was replaced by the words 'line of control'. India extracted the price of victory from a defeated Pakistan.

Six years after the signing of the Simla agreement, the Indian External Affairs Minister, Mr Atal Behari Vajpayee, claimed that Mrs Indira Gandhi had reached 'a secret understanding' in her confidential conversation with Mr Bhutto at the Simla summit over the State of Jammu and Kashmir. A section of the Indian press carried a report that: 'Mrs Indira Gandhi and Mr Z. A. Bhutto reportedly agreed at Simla in 1972 that the only solution to the Kashmir issue would be to freeze the cease-fire line [in Jammu and Kashmir] with minor adjustments . . . Both, however, noted that in neither country was the atmosphere propitious for such a settlement to be put through.'[51]

Mrs Indira Gandhi denied the allegation. So did Pakistan's former Minister of State for Foreign Affairs, Mr Aziz Ahmad, and the ex-Minister for Foreign Affairs, Mr Agha Shahi. Mr Vajpayee beat a tame retreat in the Indian Lok Sabha (Lower House) when the opposition members challenged him to substantiate his charge by either tabling the documents or naming the persons on whom he had relied for his information.

The second summit of the Islamic Conference countries was held in the city of Lahore in February 1974. The visiting dignitaries included King Faisal of Saudi Arabia, President Moammar Qadaffi of Libya, Palestine Liberation Organization Chief, Yasser Arafat (to whom I acted as Military Secretary), and President Sheikh Mujibur Rahman of Bangladesh. Lahore wore a bridal look.

A public reception was hosted in honour of the dignitaries by the Mayor of Lahore at the Shalimar Gardens built by the Emperor Shah Jehan in 1642. The guests appeared on the balcony in small groups to the applause of the thousands of invitees. The clapping reached its climax when Mr Bhutto and Sheikh Mujibur Rahman made an appearance with their hands clasped together. Mr Bhutto had achieved the primary objective of hosting the summit conference: Pakistan accorded recognition to Bangladesh 'at the instance of the leaders of the Islamic World.' It had taken the government over two years of intense diplomatic effort and numerous solicitations to provide an opportunity to Pakistan to recognize Bangladesh 'with grace.'

* * *

General Gul Hassan Khan's tenure as the army chief was short. He and Air Marshal Rahim Khan, as friends and supporters of Mr Bhutto, had reportedly helped him to reach the pinnacle of power. They were now an embarrassment to the President. Bhutto was headstrong and ruthless. Gul Hassan was possessive of his command. A strike in the police force created a flashpoint. The government wanted the army to frustrate the strike. It bypassed General Headquarters and ordered an artillery unit at Nowshera to deploy guns against a police station at Peshawar. Bhutto's adviser (a retired general) met Gul Hassan Khan to complain when his orders were not implemented. In turn, Gul Hassan Khan blasted him for interfering in the army's chain of command. The bruised adviser conveyed the military language used by Gul Hassan Khan to Mr Bhutto.

On 3 March 1972, General Gul Hassan and Air Marshal Rahim were invited to the President's House for an impromptu meeting. They were asked to resign from service. Both obliged. Simultaneously, the Chief of General Staff, the Director of Military Operations, and the Director of Intelligence at General Headquarters were called for a fake meeting in a nearby building. They were kept waiting till the resignations were obtained. Police contingents were posted at the television and radio stations in Rawalpindi to prevent a 'possible' *coup d'etat* attempt. From the President's House, General Gul Hassan and Air Marshal Rahim were taken to Lahore by road by Mr Ghulam Mustafa Khar, the Governor of the Punjab. The five-hour journey was undertaken to gain time. Meanwhile, Dr Mubashir Hasan, a minister in Bhutto's cabinet, took a special plane to Sahiwal to fetch Lieutenant-General Tikka Khan to Rawalpindi. Tikka Khan was promoted to the rank of General and appointed as the Chief of Army Staff. The two ex-service chiefs were set free the following day and later given diplomatic assignments abroad. Air Marshal Zafar Choudhary was appointed as the new Air Chief. This undignified episode exposed Mr Bhutto's intriguing nature, feudal traits, and lack of moral scruples.

On 29 February 1976, General Tikka Khan retired from the army. He was replaced by Lieutenant-General M. Ziaul Haq.

General Zia superseded some general officers senior to him to become the Chief of Army Staff; he subsequently ousted Bhutto from power. This raised questions as to what motivated Mr Bhutto to appoint him to that coveted post.

In mid-1975, Mr Bhutto started sniffing around for a successor to General Tikka Khan, who was due to retire in March 1976. At one stage, Mr Bhutto had considered granting Tikka Khan a one-year extension, but the idea was dropped after he assessed that such a measure would not go down well in the army. At about this time, the COAS' address to the officers at one or two garrisons had also not gone off too well for the General. This was taken as a sign of 'rumbling' in the army, and the Prime Minister had become hypersensitive to such soundings after the episode of the 1973 abortive conspiracy in which some middle-rung army officers were tried in a court-martial for collectively criticizing the government policies which had led to the dismemberment of the country.

The seniority status of the then lieutenant-generals in descending order was: Muhammad Shariff, Muhammad Akbar Khan, Aftab Ahmad Khan, Azmat Buksh Awan, Agha Ali Ibrahim Akram, Malik Abdul Majid, Ghulam Jilani Khan, and Muhammad Ziaul Haq.

Mr Bhutto personally knew the eight lieutenant-generals in the run, but to satisfy himself fully, he had their antecedents, reputation, and other qualities verified through the network of intelligence agencies, special branches, and other sources employed to keep watch over the people and the armed forces. Over a period of time, he discussed the eight names with the head of his principle intelligence agency, Mr M. Akram Sheikh (Director, Intelligence Bureau), as also with Mr Saeed Ahmad Khan (Chief Security Officer to PM), Mr Masood Mahmud (Director, Federal Security Force), Lieutenant-General Ghulam Jilani Khan (Director General, Inter-Services Intelligence), and

Brigadier Muzaffar Khan Malik of the National Security Council.[52] He always met the latter two together in this regard. In addition, he consulted his kitchen cabinet, Maulana Kausar Niazi, Major-General Imtiaz Ali (his Military Secretary) and the 'Bhutto Boy' in the Intelligence Bureau—Lieutenant-Colonel Mukhtar Ahmad, who had been specially inducted in that organization to keep a watch on the army. Mukhtar had accompanied Mr Bhutto to the United Nations session in December 1971. The Prime Minister also elicited the views of his close political workers, advisers, and confidants before he finally took a conscious decision.[53] This is borne out by the fact that he had full information and knowledge about the professional competence and other qualities of the general officers.

When General Tikka Khan learnt about his impending retirement, he took it upon himself to write to Mr Bhutto, recommending Lieutenant-General Muhammad Akbar Khan, an ex-DGISI, to succeed him. Normally, one avoids naming one's own replacement in any appointment, unless asked. It was naive to imagine that General Headquarters' unsolicited recommendation on this issue would be accepted by the appointing authority. Mr Bhutto drove the point home by ignoring the uncalled-for intrusion on his discretion.

Having done his homework systematically, Mr Bhutto met General Jilani and Muzaffar together some time towards the end of October/November 1975.[54] In that meeting he made unsavoury remarks about practically every prospective candidate! These are omitted here. To him, Shariff was the Field-Marshal's (Ayub's) man, but, after some initial reluctance he hinted that he might be willing to consider appointing him as Chairman, Joint Chiefs of Staff Committee, if and when the appointment was sanctioned. He then talked about General Tikka Khan's replacement and asked for comments. Jilani advised him not to waste the talent pool drastically and to select the next Chief of Army Staff of his choice from amongst the top few general officers, who were all experienced and competent professionals. The rank structure of the army might be destabilized if too many senior officers were superseded and sought premature retirements, he pleaded. Unimpressed by that logic Bhutto enquired, 'What about Zia?'

'As compared to others, I do not really know him as a person, and, therefore, it would not be fair to comment on him,' replied Jilani, adding that 'the last time Zia and I had served together was when we were both captains in Kohat in 1950.' Mr Bhutto then asked Muzaffar for his comments on Zia. 'Before you even consider appointing him,' said Muzaffar, 'you should know that he has a strong religious bug, and once it enters his head, it does not get out easily.' Bhutto smiled but did not reveal his mind. Bhutto seems to have developed confidence in Zia when they came in contact with each other during the course of the 1973 Conspiracy trial, presided over by the general officer. Jilani feels Bhutto had felt personally obliged to Zia for convicting the officers who had wanted to topple his government. During the trial, Zia used to report to Bhutto almost daily, either directly or through the Military Secretary, Imtiaz. Soon after the trial, Zia, in his capacity as the senior-most serving armoured corps general, had invited Bhutto to be the honorary Colonel-in-Chief of the Armoured Corps. The initiative for Bhutto's selection had come from Major-General S. Wajahat Hussain, Commander 6 Armoured Division, at Kharian. Zia had agreed to that proposal. Zia maintained his rapport with Mr Bhutto and paid his respects to the latter whenever he visited Multan. During such visits, Mr Bhutto stayed at the 'White House,' the residence of Governor Sadiq Hussain Qureshi. Zia used to be a favourite topic at the 'White House'. Bhutto was indeed charmed by him during his visit to the Multan garrison. The Prime Minister was given a rousing ovation by a turn-out of the wives and children of officers at the station, who showered flower petals on the visiting dignitary. Bhutto selected Zia to succeed Tikka Khan as the Chief of Army Staff. Shariff became the Chairman of the Joint Chiefs of Staff Committee.

A little before his promotion was made public, General Zia was invited to meet Mr Bhutto. General Zia came to Rawalpindi and stayed with Brigadier Saghir Hussain, Military Secretary to the President. As Saghir received his guest at the airport, he was surprised to see a car from the Prime Minister's Secretariat waiting for General Zia. After his meeting with Mr Bhutto, General Zia told Saghir about his impending promotion and appointment as the Chief of Army Staff.

In 1975, I was posted as Director Military Operations at General Headquarters. In June 1976, I was promoted to the rank of Major-General. Normally, major-generals approved for command are posted to a division first. General Zia asked me to take over from Major-General F. A. Chishti as the Military Secretary. Since I had no previous experience of this work, I requested a command assignment.

Zia said: 'You will enter the Military Secretary's office with a fresh and an open mind, and carry out the reforms without a jaundiced eye,' adding on a personal note, 'I need you in the GHQ for a year or so. Thereafter you may command a division of your choice.'

This left no scope for further argument. Major-General Chishti on promotion went to command 10 Corps with its headquarters located in Rawalpindi.

The government detailed a 'Commission of Inquiry—1971 War' to be headed by the Chief Justice of Pakistan, Mr Justice Hamoodur Rahman, and with Mr Justices Anwarul Haq and Tufail Ali Abdur Rahman as members to:

> Enquire into the circumstances in which the Commander Eastern Command surrendered and the members of the armed forces of Pakistan under his command laid down their arms and cease-fire was ordered along the borders of West Pakistan and India and along the cease-fire line in the State of Jammu and Kashmir.

It was called the Hamoodur Rahman Commission, named after its chairman, and its report is referred to as the Hamoodur Rahman Commission Report. The terms of reference of the Commission were narrow and its proceedings were conducted in a vitiated environment. Mr Bhutto had a motive for putting the blame entirely on others, and for getting himself exonerated. The HRCR has not been made public.

The Hamoodur Rahman Commission should have been given an all-embracing charter, covering all internal and external factors, dating back to 1947, which led to the separation of East Pakistan. However, the evidence of Sheikh Mujibur Rahman held in custody within the country, and of the concerned Pakistani ambassadors serving abroad should have been recorded. This was not done

The debacle of East Pakistan demanded General Yahya Khan's fair trial. This did not take place. Perhaps General Yahya Khan was privy to details about many persons. If driven to the wall, he might have disclosed those facts to incriminate the hidden hands. That risk, it appears, was unacceptable to Mr Bhutto. Major-General M. Rahim Khan, a division commander in East Pakistan in 1971, is of the opinion that Mr Bhutto's motive in establishing the HRC was subjective. He wanted his 'own role and intrigue which were mainly responsible for the national tragedy to be covered up ... under the stamp of a judicial enquiry.'[55]

Has the HRC Report held on record been tampered with, at least in some parts? One newspaper reported that 'about two dozen pages which bore criticism of the role played by the Chairman of the PPP during the 1970-71 crisis had been removed and replaced by an equal number of pages typed out on a similar typewriter, but the contents of these pages were quite different from what the HRC had compiled.'[56] The tampering was detected by an officer who had been detailed by the Commission to authenticate each page of the report after Mr Bhutto had withdrawn the office copy held by it. This officer was kept in wrongful confinement for three days after he had declined to authenticate the fabricated pages. He was released only when Justice Hamoodur Rahman finally told Mr. Bhutto that, 'if the officer was not released immediately, he would have no hesitation in issuing a writ of habeas corpus and make the whole episode public.'[57]

Mystery shrouds Pakistan's lacklustre diplomatic effort during the 1971 war. Mr Bhutto had left for the United Nations on 8 December 1971, announcing that: 'We will not rest, be it today, tomorrow, or a thousand years, till we clear the Indian aggression from the sacred soil of Pakistan.'[58]

By that time India had accorded recognition to the Bangladesh Government (6 December) and the East Pakistan Governor, Dr A. M. Malik, had sent a distress signal to President Yahya Khan indicating that General Niazi had told him that: 'The front in the eastern and western sectors had completely collapsed and that the loss of the whole territory east of Meghna was only a matter of time ... Nothing could move from Chittagong or within the province. As a result all supplies were running short and Dacca would be without food, fuel and oil after seven days. Therefore there would be complete paralysis of life.'[59]

Mr Bhutto's travel plan did not indicate urgency. He reached New York on 10 December after breaking journey en route at Tehran and Frankfurt. From Frankfurt, he telephoned Agha Shahi at New York to update himself with the developments in the Security Council. It took him another three days to address the Security Council. Such a leisurely approach was contrary to the gravity of the situation.

The Soviet Union had tabled a draft resolution before the Security Council on 4 December 1971, calling for a political settlement in East Pakistan which would 'inevitably result in the cessation of hostilities.' This was not accepted by Pakistan.

On 12 December 1971, Mr Bhutto, Agha Shahi, and General N. A. M. Raza (Pakistan's Ambassador to the US) met the US permanent representative at the UN, Mr George Bush (later President of the US). Mr Henry Kissinger and Mr Brent Snowcroft, the latter's deputy (subsequently national security adviser to the US President) were also present. Kissinger stated that 'Pakistan's position in East Pakistan was hopeless and that India had plans to shift the bulk of her troops employed there to the West Pakistan theatre. An intensified war in West Pakistan, said Kissinger, would create serious problems as Pakistan's logistic stamina would be sapped within a few days. America has urged upon the USSR to prevent India from opening a second front in West Pakistan. The presence of the 7th Fleet in the Bay of Bengal, said Kissinger, is a warning to India against escalating war in West Pakistan.'[60]

On 14 December 1971, Poland tabled a draft resolution calling for a peaceful transfer of power to the legally elected representatives of the people in East Pakistan. It suggested a temporary cease-fire, the withdrawal of the Pakistani armed forces to pre-set locations and the simultaneous withdrawal of the Indian armed forces from the eastern theatre of war. Mr Bhutto made his third speech in the Security Council on 15 December 1971. Sobbing, he demanded justice. In a passionate outburst he accused the United Nations of permitting the fall of Dhaka, and told the Security Council, 'impose any decision. Have a treaty worse than Versailles, legalize aggression, legalize occupation ... I will not be a party to it. Why should I waste my time here? I will go back to my country and fight.' He ripped the draft resolution and stalked out saying, 'I will not be a party to your ignominious surrender.'[61] Shahi stayed back in the hall, as Bhutto wanted him to remain there. In terms of time, the Polish effort came too late. By then all the members of the Security Council knew that the collapse in East Pakistan was imminent. The Bhutto act in the Security Council was one of pre-planned showmanship. In his scheme, the army had to be defeated in battle and Mujib removed from the political scene to compel Yahya Khan to hand over power to him. The means employed were irrelevant to Bhutto.

His announcement notwithstanding, Mr Bhutto remained in New York till 18 December 1971, when he was asked by General Yahya Khan to replace him as the head of state.

East Pakistan was lost through a series of errors committed in the entire post-independence period. These had created a sense of deprivation, only partly justified, which was exploited by the ambitious local leadership who misquoted facts and aroused public sentiments for their own vested interests. In the final stages, the ostrich-like approach adopted by the ruling clique hastened the doom. There was neither a Stalingrad in East Pakistan nor was a second front opened in the western theatre at a strategically appropriate early stage. Diplomatically, no initiative was taken in the UN Security Council. An aggressive diplomatic posture from 22 November onwards, supported by a military offensive in the west might have produced a different outcome.

On 5 November 1971, Mr Bhutto had gone to China as a personal representative of the President. His delegation included Air Marshal Rahim Khan and General Gul Hassan Khan. Agency reports from Beijing stated that: 'China has promised Pakistan its support in the event of Indian aggression.'[62] After his return from China, Mr Bhutto, while addressing a meeting at Karachi, said that: 'If India does launch an attack, she will get the worst drubbing of her life . . . China had already helped Pakistan in 1965 war and will fight shoulder to shoulder with Pakistan in case India in her foolishness unleashed her wanton aggression.'[63] Mr Bhutto's statement, coming soon after his visit to China, created a misplaced impression that China might have promised military intervention.

At the UN, Agha Shahi did not receive any such indication. Peerzada maintains that, to his knowledge, China did not give any assurance of physical intervention in war. However, another piece of information creates some doubt: Mr Niaz A. Naik, the Ambassador and Permanent Representative of Pakistan to the European Office of the United Nations at Geneva from 1971 to 1974 was a member of the Pakistan delegation to the UN General Assembly Session in 1971 in New York. Naik recalls that the Additional Secretary Foreign Affairs, Mr M. A. Alvie, telephoned Pakistan's permanent mission at the United Nations in New York. In the absence of Agha Shahi, Naik received the call. Referring to Shahi's telegram, Alvie conveyed the instructions in Urdu. He said, *'Ap Security Council mein janay ke liye koi qaddam na uthaen. Mazeed hidayat ka intizar karen. Aglay chhatees ghanton mein kuch honay wala hai.'*[64] (Do not take any step to approach the Security Council. Await further instructions. Something will happen within the next 36 hours.) The 'thirty-six hours' enigma was also reflected in the signal message sent by President Yahya to the Governor East Pakistan on 11 December 1971. It read: 'Important diplomatic and military moves are taking place by our friends. It is essential that we hold for another 36 hours at all costs.' Whatever was expected did not happen.

There was also the American factor. The publicized movement of three ships of the US Seventh Fleet towards the Bay of Bengal in mid-December created suspense. The American officials stated in Washington on 15 December that the ships were being sent to 'help evacuate Pakistan forces from East Pakistan if a cease-fire was agreed upon.'[65] Perhaps the naval movement was a half-hearted effort to reassure Pakistan and to impress on India that she should desist from attacking West Pakistan. Islamabad had invoked her bilateral treaty with the United States on a personal level but received a negative response.

* * *

Yahya and Bhutto used each other for self-perpetuation in power. Both knew the other's weaknesses and strengths. They were friends and rivals concurrently. Each wanted to eclipse the public image of the other but in such a manner that the blame should lie elsewhere. For reasons of self-interest, neither of them could afford to criticize the other beyond his tolerance limit. It was a tightrope walk for both of them.

Defeated in war, General Yahya earned the wrath of his countrymen. His downfall coincided with Mr Bhutto's rise to power. The shrewd and vengeful Bhutto employed the weapon of public demand to keep Yahya under custody and himself in the power saddle. On 9 or 10 January 1972, the state-controlled Radio Pakistan announced that General Yahya Khan was being put under house arrest. In the words of General Yahya Khan: 'Within ten minutes of the announcement a message was conveyed to me from the President [Bhutto] through a cabinet minister, Mr Abdul Hafeez Pirzada, that the President has ordered my detention for a short while with great regret but purely in my own interest as the people were greatly agitated about East Pakistan.'[66]

General Yahya Khan was kept in the Banni rest-house near Kharian for four months without a detention order being served on him. On 20 April 1972, he was moved to Abbottabad where his movements were restricted to the municipal limits of Abbottabad town for a period of six months under the Defence of Pakistan Rules, 'with a view to preventing him from acting in a manner prejudicial to the security, the public safety and the defence of Pakistan.' On 28 February 1973, another ground was added to the detention order. It read: 'if you (detenu) are not kept in detention it will create commotion and agitation in the public all over Pakistan, seriously endangering the public safety and maintenance of peaceful conditions in Pakistan.' The period of detention was periodically extended and General Yahya's pension was withheld. Mrs Yahya Khan had challenged the detention of her husband on the grounds of its being false, unwarranted, *mala fide*, and in violation of Article 10 of the Constitution of Pakistan.

General Yahya Khan resorted to the legal course as his prolonged detention had caused him financial and administrative hardships. Before his wife filed the writ petition, he had requested that he be shifted to his house in Rawalpindi. Mr Bhutto rejected that request, pointing out somewhat contemptuously that the former President had the means to make himself comfortable. A bureaucratic negative reply was sent to General Yahya Khan. Persisting, General Yahya Khan wrote back to the Ministry, saying that he presumed that his request had been declined personally by President Bhutto. He asked the Ministry to inquire from Mr Bhutto if the verbal understanding reached between him and the President stood cancelled.

The amused bureaucrat dutifully forwarded General Yahya Khan's stinging query to the President's Secretariat. A cornered Bhutto stated that, while no verbal understanding existed between him and the detenu, he would let General Yahya Khan be moved to Rawalpindi, if he so insisted.

On 8 July 1975, Mr S. M. Zafar, advocate, made a statement in the court that the 'petitioner has *adequate basis* for a feeling that it would be worthwhile for her to first approach the executive with a detailed submission about the case of the detenu for redress. Hence the present petition may kindly be allowed to be withdrawn for the *time being.*' The court accepted that prayer. Soon thereafter, General Yahya Khan was shifted to Rawalpindi where he spent the remaining part of his life. A policy of 'live and let live' thus covered up the evidence concerning events that led to the loss of East Pakistan.

* * *

In early 1977, Prime Minister Bhutto enquired from General Zia if the army would be interested in getting military hardware from the

Soviet Union. General Zia replied that so long as the weapons met the operational needs of the army, he was not concerned with the source of their supply. The discussion remained inconclusive. General Zia kept trying to guess the motive behind that question. Mr Bhutto was not the type of person to pose a problem without a reason. Months later, the mystery miraculously cleared up. During Zia's tour of Libya in November 1977, President Moammar Qaddafi disclosed to General Zia that in the closing stages of his rule, Mr Bhutto requested him to convey a message to the Soviet Union about Pakistan's willingness to negotiate a deal with her, involving the use of Pakistan's Mekran coast by Soviet military forces. At that time, Mr Bhutto suspected that the United States was planning to overthrow him. The military overture to Moscow was the result of his frustration with Washington. President Qaddafi communicated Mr Bhutto's message to President Joseph Tito of Yugoslavia with a request that it be conveyed to the Kremlin. This was done. Before any response was received from the Soviet Union, the Bhutto administration fell. President Zia, amazed and amused, made this revelation to some of his colleagues. According to a newspaper report, he also shared this information with three cabinet colleagues and a legal luminary at a reception, just a day before his death.[67]

Under the heading 'Bhutto's Last Gamble', a garbled version of the Bhutto offer was published in a foreign magazine, saying that 'Bhutto was prepared to concede to the Russians Gwadar as a military base and as a springboard for further diplomatic and political offensive in the Persian Gulf.'[68]

ANNEXURE 1

THE AWAMI LEAGUE'S SIX POINTS

Extract from the Awami League manifesto issued at Lahore in February 1966.

Pakistan shall be a Federation granting full autonomy on the basis of the six-point formula to each of the federating units:

Point No. 1   The character of the Government shall be federal and parliamentary, in which the election to the Federal Legislature and to the legislatures of the federating units shall be direct and on the basis of universal adult franchise. The representation in the federal legislature shall be on the basis of population.

Point No. 2   The Federal Government shall be responsible only for defence and foreign affairs and subject to conditions provided in (3) below, currency.

Point No. 3   There shall be two separate currencies mutually or freely convertible in each wing for each region, or in the alternative a single currency, subject to the establishment of a federal reserve system in which there will be regional federal reserve banks which shall devise measures to prevent the transfer of resources and flight of capital from one region to another.

Point No. 4   Fiscal policy shall be the responsibility of the federating units. The federal government shall be provided with requisite revenue resources for meeting the requirements of defence and foreign affairs, which revenue resources would be automatically appropriable by the Federal Government in the manner provided and on the basis of the ratio to be determined by the procedure laid down in the Constitution. Such constitutional provisions would ensure that the Federal Government's revenue requirements are met consistently with the objective of ensuring control over the fiscal policy by the Government of the federating units.

Point No. 5   Constitutional provisions shall be made to enable separate accounts to be maintained of the foreign exchange earnings of each of the federating units, under the control of the respective governments of the federating units. The foreign exchange requirement of the Federal Government shall be met by the Governments of the federating units on the basis of a ratio to be determined in accordance with the procedure laid down in the Constitution. The regional governments shall have power under the Constitution to negotiate foreign trade and aid within the framework of the foreign policy of the country, which shall be the responsibility of the Federal Government.

Point No. 6   The Government of the federating units shall be empowered to maintain a militia or para-military force in order to contribute effectively towards national security.

ANNEXURE 2

PRESIDENT YAHYA'S MESSAGE TO THE GOVERNOR EAST PAKISTAN

TOPSEC. G-0001, 2300 hours, 09 December 1971. From President to Governor repeated to Eastern Command.

Your flash message A-4660 of 9 Dec. Received and thoroughly understood. You have my permission to take decision on your proposals to me. I have and am continuing to take all measures internationally but in view of our complete isolation from each other decision about East Pakistan I leave entirely to your good sense and judgement. I will approve of any decision you take and I am instructing General Niazi simultaneously to accept your decision and arrange things accordingly. Whatever efforts you take in your decisions to save senseless destruction of the kind of situation you have mentioned in particular the safety of our armed forces, you may go ahead and ensure safety of armed forces by all political means that you will adopt with our opponent.

ANNEXURE 3

MESSAGE OF THE CHIEF OF ARMY STAFF TO COMMANDER, EASTERN COMMAND

For Comd from COAS Army.
G-0237, 0910 hours, 10 December 1971. President's signal message to Governor copy to you refers. President has left the decision to the Governor in close consultation with you - as no signal can correctly convey the degree of seriousness of the situation I can only leave it to you to take the correct decision on the spot. It is, however, apparent that it is now only a question of time before the enemy with its great superiority in number and material and the active cooperation of the rebels will dominate East Pakistan completely. Meanwhile, a lot of damage is being done to the civil population and the Army is suffering heavy casualties. You will have to assess the value of fighting on if you can and weigh it, based on this you should give your frank advice to the Governor who will give his final decision as delegated to him by the President. Whenever you feel it is necessary to do so you should attempt to destroy maximum military equipment so that it does not fall into enemy hands. Keep me informed. Allah bless you.

ANNEXURE 4

THE NOTE DELIVERED TO THE ASSISTANT SECRETARY-GENERAL OF THE UNITED NATIONS ORGANIZATION, MR PAUL MARK HENRY, AT DHAKA BY THE GOVERNOR OF EAST PAKISTAN.

A 7107, 10 December 1971

It was never the intention of Armed Forces of Pakistan to involve themselves in an all-out war on the soil of East Pakistan. However, a situation arose which compelled the armed forces to take defensive action. The intention of the Government of Pakistan was always to decide the issues in East Pakistan by means of a political solution for which negotiations were afoot. The armed forces have fought heroically against heavy odds and can still continue to do so but in order to avoid further bloodshed and loss of innocent lives I am making the following proposals. As the conflict arose as a result of political causes, it must end with a political solution. I, therefore, having been authorized by the President of Pakistan to hereby call the elected representatives of East Pakistan to arrange for the peaceful formation of the Government in Dacca. In making this offer I feel duty bound to say the will of the people of East Pakistan would demand the immediate vacation their land by the Indian forces as well. I, therefore, call upon the United Nations to arrange for a peaceful transfer of power and request: 1. An immediate ceasefire, 2. repatriation with honour of the armed forces of Pakistan to West Pakistan, 3. repatriation of all West Pakistan personnel desirous of to returning to West Pakistan, 4. the safety of all persons settled in East Pakistan since 1947, and 5. guarantee of no reprisals against any person in East Pakistan. In making this offer, I want to make it clear that this a definite proposal for peaceful transfer of power. The question of surrender of armed forces would not be considered and does not arise and if this proposal is not accepted the armed forces will continue to fight to the last man.

ANNEXURE 5

TEXT OF SIMLA AGREEMENT
3 July 1972

The Government of India and the Government of Pakistan are resolved that the two countries put an end to the conflict and confrontation that have hitherto marred their relations and work for the promotion of a friendly and harmonious relationship and the establishment of durable peace in the subcontinent, so that both countries may henceforth devote their resources and energies to the pressing task of advancing the welfare of their people.

In order to achieve this objective, the Government of India and Government of Pakistan have agreed as follows:

(i) That the principles and purposes of the Charter of the United Nations shall govern the relations between the two countries.

(ii) That the two countries are resolved to settle their differences by peaceful means through bilateral negotiations or by any other peaceful means mutually agreed upon between them. Pending the final settlement of any of the problems between the two countries, neither side shall unilaterally alter the situation and both shall prevent the organization, assistance or encouragement of any acts detrimental to the maintenance of peaceful and harmonious relations.

(iii) That the prerequisite for reconciliation, good neighbourliness and durable peace between them is a commitment by both countries to peaceful co-existence, respect for each other's territorial integrity and sovereignty and non-interference in each other's internal affairs, on the basis of equality and mutual benefit.

(iv) That the basic issues and causes of conflict which have bedevilled the relations between the two countries for the last twenty-five years shall be resolved by peaceful means.

(v) That they shall always respect each other's national unity, territorial integrity, political independence and sovereign equality.

(vi) That in accordance with the Charter of the United Nations, they will refrain from the threat or use of force against the territorial integrity or political independence of each other.

Both Governments will take all steps within their power to prevent hostile propaganda directed against each other.

Both countries will encourage the dissemination of such information as would promote the development of friendly relations between them.

In order progressively to restore and normalize relations between the two countries step by step, it was agreed that:

(i) Steps shall be taken to resume communications, postal, telegraphs, sea, land including border posts, and air links including overflights.

(ii) Appropriate steps shall be taken to promote travel facilities for the nationals of the other country.

(iii) Trade and cooperation in economic and other agreed fields will be resumed as far as possible.

(iv) Exchange in the fields of science and culture will be promoted.

In this connection delegations from the two countries will meet from time to time to work out the necessary details.

In order to initiate the process of the establishment of durable peace, both the Governments agree that:

(i) Indian and Pakistani forces shall be withdrawn to their side of the international border.

(ii) In Jammu and Kashmir, the line of control resulting from the cease fire of December 17, 1971, shall be respected by both sides without prejudice to the recognized position of the other side. Neither side shall seek to alter it unilaterally, irrespective of mutual differences and legal interpretations. Both sides further undertake to refrain from the threat of the use of force in violation of this line.

(iii) The withdrawals shall commence upon entry into force of this Agreement and shall be completed within a period of thirty days thereof.

This Agreement will be subject to ratification by both countries in accordance with their respective constitutional procedures, and will come into force with effect from the date on which the Instruments of Ratification are exchanged.

Both Governments agree that their respective Heads will meet again at a mutually convenient time in the future and that in the meanwhile, the representatives of the two sides will meet to discuss further the modalities and arrangements for the establishment of durable peace and normalization of relations, including the questions of repatriation of prisoners of war and civilian internees, a final settlement of diplomatic relations.

sd/-
(Indira Gandhi)
Prime Minister
Republic of India

sd/-
(Zulfikar Ali Bhutto)
President
Islamic Republic of Pakistan

CHAPTER 3

Prelude to Intervention

Under the Constitution, the term of the National Assembly was due to expire on 14 August 1977. On 7 January 1977, Mr Z. A. Bhutto announced the holding of early national elections on 7 March that year. The elections to the provincial assemblies were fixed for 10 March. While announcing the general elections, Mr Bhutto said: 'Politicians like to avoid elections as much as generals like to avoid wars, but political battles have to be fought. I hope that the coming elections will be clean and fair.'

That solemn promise made from the podium of the National Assembly was honoured in its breach. The opposition parties protested against the premeditated and massive state-sponsored rigging of the elections under the personal direction of Mr Bhutto. The Model Election Plan, dated 11 April 1976, bore the signature of Mr Bhutto. In July 1978, the Government of General Ziaul Haq of Pakistan issued a *White Paper on the Conduct of the General Elections* held in March 1977. Annexure 1 of that White Paper reads:

<blockquote>
EYES ONLY

I have prepared a scheme for the elections, both central and provincial, for the District of Larkana. This scheme might be of some assistance to you in the preparation of the arrangements we have to work out on a scientific basis for the whole country. You can look at it for your information and guidance. I have no doubt that you may be able to improve on it.

Signed
Prime Minister
11.4.1976
</blockquote>

MR. RAFI RAZA
MINISTRY OF PRODUCTION

The *White Paper* indicates that a comprehensive plan prepared to rig the elections was systematically implemented. The manipulation of the delimitation of constituencies, an essential prerequisite before the actual conduct of polls, was acknowledged by Mr Mumtaz Ali Bhutto, then Minister of Communications in the Federal Government, in a letter dated 11 July 1976, to Mr Zulfikar Ali Bhutto, (Annexure 46 of the *White Paper*). The last paragraph of the letter reads: 'In the meeting on 8th and 9th instant, people have reorganized constituencies, districts, even divisions according to their fancy.'

The *White Paper*, on page 59 records: 'It is rather curious that thinking in the Election Commission [which was legally responsible for delimiting the constituencies] was running parallel to the demarcation plans submitted by the then Prime Minister's Special Assistant.'

The *White Paper* contains documentary evidence indicating misuse of public funds, government transport, and the state-controlled media; provision of firearms to the workers of the ruling party; and the pressure on the civil servants to support the candidature of the Pakistan People's Party (PPP) nominees in the elections. On page 75 it is recorded that 'Mr Bhutto decided in 1976 to resort to large-scale dismissals [of civil servants] as part of his election strategy to break the morale and spirit of services well in time for the general elections . . . 158 persons were served with orders of retirement/termination of service or show cause notices in October 1976.'

The statement of Mr Islam Bahadur Khan, then Commissioner of Quetta, contained in Annexure 66 says that: 'No security of service was guaranteed to the civil servants. Besides, the life and the honour of the individual were not safe and he was denied all the fundamental rights. These were the conditions under which the election staff for 1977 elections and other public servants had to work. There was a state of complete helplessness and insecurity.'

The acts of rigging were country-wide and shameful. The election laws were flagrantly violated; the independence of the Election Commission was compromised; the opposition candidates were kidnapped and forcibly prevented from filing their nomination papers; the nationalized banks were directed to lend financial support to the PPP newspapers through subscriptions, donations, or inflated rates of advertisement; the intelligence services were given their supreme mandate to see that the opposition parties were not allowed to come together—you cannot permit them to unite; a Federal Security

PRELUDE TO INTERVENTION

Force —turned mafia—was created to terrorize and kidnap politicians and disrupt their political meetings; the Income Tax authorities were directed to initiate tax evasion notices to the opposition leaders; and premeditated irregularities were committed by the polling staff appointed through political channels.

Mr Bhutto decided that he should be elected unopposed from his constituency NA 163 - Larkana 1. The PNA nominated Mr Jan Muhammad Abbasi, Amir of Jamaat-i-Islami, Sindh, to oppose Mr Bhutto. Mr Abbasi declined to accept official advice against filing his nomination papers in this constituency. On 17 January 1977, Mr Shahani, Deputy Superintendent of Police, Larkana, whisked him away without any written orders or a warrant of arrest. He was kept in wrongful confinement for the next thirty hours and was released on the evening of 19 January after Radio Pakistan had declared that Mr Z. A. Bhutto had been elected unopposed.

Abbasi moved the Election Commission. The Deputy Commissioner, Mr Khalid Ahmad, attempted to lure Mr Abbasi with a proposal that he (Abbasi) would be elected unopposed from the Nawabshah constituency as a *quid pro quo* for withdrawing his complaint. The adamant Abbasi declined to compromise. The government then hatched a plan to frustrate justice.

Syed Mukarram Sultan Bokhari, a correspondent of the government-controlled Associated Press of Pakistan along with three other correspondents and a sub-editor were coerced by the administration to state that Mr Jan Muhammad Abbasi was present in Larkana on 18 January 1977, and that he had addressed a news conference on that date, whereas in actual fact he was illegally confined on that day at Seri Dak Bungalow. The *White Paper* records that: 'Mr Yahya Bakhtiar [the Attorney General] very tactfully handled the correspondents . . . and persuaded them to file false affidavits. Mr Ghulam Nabi Memon, Advocate General of Sindh, and Mr Mohammad Khan Junejo, Home Secretary of Sindh, were also present and used their influence to obtain the desired affidavit.'[1]

The Election Commission, in its judgment dated 12 February 1977, dismissed Maulana Abbasi's petition. The Commissioner, among other reasons in support of his decision, had relied heavily on the affidavits of these independent gentlemen.

All these 'independent gentlemen', records the *White Paper*, however, disowned their false affidavits in an enquiry subsequently held. Syed Mukarram Sultan Bokhari narrated that on 1 or 2 February

1977, he and his colleagues were summoned by the Election Commissioner to appear before the Election Commissioner at Karachi the next morning. On arrival, he 'was taken to the Sindh High Court building where he was asked by the Attorney General [Yahya Bakhtiar] and the Advocate General [Ghulam Nabi Memon] to change the date of interview from January 17 to January 18 . . . the next day we . . . were provided a typed affidavit and asked to sign the same. A magistrate present there attested our affidavits on the spot.' That the senior law officers and an administrator in the government (Provincial Home Secretary, Muhammad Khan Junejo) were privy to committing acts so low was reprehensible.

Mr Yahya Bakhtiar contested the election to the National Assembly from constituency NA195-Quetta II. The establishment posted local staff in the area, who enjoyed the confidence of the Attorney General. The voting over, the results were withheld. The results, as notified on 21 March 1977, by the Election Commissioner were as follows:

Yahya Bakhtiar (PPP)	18,264
Mahmood Khan (NAP)	16,776
Abdul Wahid (Independent)	8,008
Malik Ghulam Muhammad (Independent)	1,151
Invalid votes	10,993

Mr Yahya Bakhtiar gained the seat by a narrow margin of 1,488 votes in a contest in which the number of votes declared invalid was excessively high—10,993.

What happened in the constituencies of Mr Bhutto and Mr Yahya Bakhtiar happened elsewhere as well.

On 7 March 1977: 'About 30 million voters went to the polls . . . at the end of an extensive, impassioned and acrimonious election campaign conducted for about 42 days by the two main rivals, the ruling PPP and the challenger, the Pakistan National Alliance (PNA).'[2] The election results gave the PPP a landslide victory with 155 seats and the PNA winning a mere 36 seats. The remaining seats went to the independent candidates and some splinter groups.

The PPP's massive success stunned the opponents and surprised Mr Bhutto. He sensed trouble. While addressing a group of senior bureaucrats in the Prime Minister's House, Bhutto said: 'Why have you done this to me?'

The subservient and obliging civil administration had overplayed its hand. Mr Bhutto's success turned into a liability and placed him in an awkward position. The PNA demanded the resignation of the Prime Minister; the dismissal of the Election Commission; the appointment of a fresh Election Commission; and re-conduct of the polls under the judiciary and the army.

The PNA threatened to start an agitation from 14 March in case its demands were not accepted, and declined to participate in the 10 March elections to the provincial assemblies. Air Marshal Asghar Khan, chief of the Tehrik-e-Istiqlal (a party in the PNA) declared: 'We will give it thought whether we should or should not sit in the legislature, as it would serve little purpose.'

Notwithstanding the PNA boycott, elections to the provincial assemblies were held on 10 March 1977, as scheduled. The one-party contest made the election result suspect *ab initio*.

The PNA seized the initiative, launched a country-wide agitation, and demanded fresh elections. The government reacted by arresting prominent PNA leaders. In an address to the nation on 12 March 1977, Mr Bhutto offered to hold a dialogue with the PNA chief, Maulana Mufti Mahmud. The PNA rejected the offer, the terms of which were not clear. This led to an exchange of letters between the government and the opposition. On 17 March 1977, Maulana Mufti Mahmud wrote to Mr Bhutto: 'On 7th March, 1977, the country was subjected to a farce in the name of general elections. On that day a process was adopted in which the administration made every endeavour to subvert the national will and to ensure a new lease of life for a leader and a government which had been overwhelmingly rejected by the electorate ... Your administration once again proved how dishonest it is by announcing that 62 per cent voters cast their votes on 10th March, 1977. A more ridiculous announcement could not be made ... The fresh elections should be held by an administration and agencies enjoying the confidence of the people and the PNA.'

Responding to the letter on 19 March 1977, Mr Bhutto wrote: 'Every day your colleagues and supporters are inciting violence ... Notwithstanding the tone and tenor of your letter, I have already put into action a process which will accelerate the removal of any complaints, backed by evidence, that any party may have, regarding the election results in those constituencies of the National Assembly where such complaints are specific.'

The PNA was an alliance of heterogeneous political parties, hurriedly formed on the eve of the general elections to ease the PPP out of power. It comprised nine political parties, popularly called the nine stars. Their party affiliations ranged from extreme right to left of the centre. Their political philosophy and approach to national issues varied widely. Individually too weak to pose an electoral threat to the PPP, as co-sufferers at the hands of a high-handed Bhutto administration, the parties sank their differences to defeat their common oppressor. The creation of the PNA was thus on the basis of a negative element.

Maulana Mufti Mahmud, the leader of the Pakistan National Alliance, was a man of simple habits, an unassuming personality, and an affable temperament. Despite his moderating influence and persuasive charm, the multi-party PNA was too motley a group to even adopt a joint manifesto. Charisma and flamboyance were not the dominant assets of the PNA leaders. While they easily found fault with any system, their exposure to world affairs was limited and their academic credentials not awe-inspiring. The National Democratic Party leader, Sardar Sherbaz Mazari, described the PNA, of which he was a part, to correspondent Gavin Young: 'The nine-party alliance is grotesquely ill-assorted and, should it win, it is unlikely to hold together for more than six months.'[3]

A pro-PPP correspondent, H. K. Burki, reported: 'Although there are as many as nine "stars" in the opposition alliance, only about half a dozen of those can really hope to twinkle on election day.'[4]

The PNA-launched movement plunged Pakistan into chaos. The agitation spread fast. Violence replaced normalcy. Emotions ran high. City after city witnessed rioting and lawlessness. National life was paralysed. The wheels of industry slowed down. The economy stagnated. Catchy slogans and threatening statements inflamed emotions. From Karachi to Peshawar and from Quetta to Lahore, the people rose in revolt. Acting tough, all the four provincial chief ministers directed their law-enforcing agencies 'To shoot on sight anyone committing violence, arson, looting, damaging property or attempting to disturb the means of communications.' Danger loomed large on the troubled horizon of the country.

Mr Bhutto and the PNA leaders disliked and mistrusted one another beyond measure. In an interview to the BBC Special Correspondent, Andrew Whitley, at Lahore on 13 April 1977, Mr Bhutto called upon the opposition leaders to hold talks 'To prevent the country from slipping into the hands of extremists—rightist and leftist' and warned that 'I would not hesitate to call in the army to restore normal conditions.'

The Attorney General, Mr Yahya Bakhtiar, declared that 'The Prime Minister would be willing to direct the chief ministers of the provinces to seek dissolution of the provincial assemblies so that fresh elections may be held to the provincial legislatures. Should the PNA secure a majority of the votes cast in the four provincial assembly elections taken together, he would be prepared to seek dissolution of the National Assembly so that fresh elections be held for the National Assembly as well.'

The government thus accepted its guilt and looked for a face-saving device to extricate itself from the political quagmire. The PNA wanted a kill. Its General Council rejected the proposal because 'it was entirely irrelevant to the objectives.'

Addressing a press conference, Prime Minister Bhutto ruled out the opposition's demand for fresh polls because 'it would amount to conceding their false charge that I am a manipulator and rigger of elections... I do not want to go down in history as a rigger of elections, which I am not.' He went on to add: 'What the hell is the office of the Prime Minister! I am more concerned about my place in history.'[5]

Mr Bhutto had felt the unease of a wrongdoer. With his eye on posterity, he did not wish to erode his image by accepting the rigging charge. On 30 March 1977, the federal cabinet discussed the aftermath of the elections. Mr Bhutto observed that it was necessary to convince the people that elections had, by and large, been fair. Any misconception put into the minds of the people by the opposition should be removed. He lamented the fact that the PNA had succeeded in establishing a semi-moral basis for their movement; he felt that the main task of the government was to destroy that basis.

The first session of the newly elected Punjab Assembly was held in Lahore on 9 April 1977. The PNA organized a demonstration in front of the Assembly Chambers, terming the session unconstitutional. The administration closed to traffic all the roads leading to the Assembly Chambers. The demonstrators clashed with the police force, causing death and injury to the people. The incident produced a sympathetic response elsewhere and demonstrations and rioting engulfed the country.

Mr Bhutto called General Zia to Lahore on 10 April 1977, and told him that the government would be fair and would keep the door open for negotiations to settle the election problem. While reviewing the prevailing law and order situation in the country, Mr Bhutto stated that, while he would aim to seek a political settlement, the army should prepare a plan for the worst contingency. He did not specify what the worst contingency was. Nor did General Zia seek a clarification on that point. On his return to Rawalpindi, General Zia held a mini conference with some of his Principal Staff Officers (PSOs) in GHQ to which Lieutenant-General Chishti was also invited. The participants came to the conclusion that the government's credibility had been tarnished; the Prime Minister should be apprised of the intensity of public resentment in clear terms, as some sycophants might be sugarcoating their reports; every possible effort should be made to keep the army out of active politics; and the matter deserved a broad-based discussion in GHQ.

On 19 March 1977, in a report submitted to Mr Bhutto, the ISID had assessed that the government had no option other than to hold fresh elections.[6] Many of Mr Bhutto's party men had, of course, thought otherwise.

A conference was held in General Zia's office at GHQ on 14 April 1977. Beside the PSOs, it was attended by the Vice Chief of General Staff, the Director of Military Operations, and the Director of Military Intelligence. It concluded that the elections had been rigged but the extent was unclear due to lack of specific data. It was also their assessment that the government would have won a majority of the seats in a fair election contest. Its eagerness to gain a two-third majority to amend the Constitution led it to commit electoral excesses. The public felt cheated and the PNA had emerged as a victim. Two opinions surfaced. Some officers felt that the government might weather the storm through firm handling and a brave posture. The majority were of the opinion that the government being in the wrong, it would be counter-productive for it to adopt an inflexible approach. It would be more prudent for the politicians to negotiate a package political deal.

Mr Bhutto and General Zia met again in Lahore on 16 April 1977. Zia was told that the worst contingency could soon arise because the PNA's attitude had hardened. Mr Bhutto informed General Zia that he was planning to make an important announcement which, he hoped, would have a soothing effect. While he was prepared to discuss any subject with the PNA, Bhutto said he would not let them tamper with the Constitution. He would neither resign from his post nor hold fresh elections to the National Assembly. The preamble over, the

Prime Minister told Zia emphatically: 'If the worst happens, I will ask the defence services to fulfil their obligations, but will not step aside in favour of any leader in the PNA.' If Mr Bhutto's remark was made in the hope of getting a response from General Zia, he was disappointed. Zia heard him in silence.

On 17 April 1977, Mr Bhutto announced in press conference some religious measures. These included the enforcement of the Shariah (Islamic) Law within six months, the prohibition of alcohol, the banning of all forms of gambling, the closure of bars and night clubs, the preparation of legislation within two months to eradicate corruption, the reconstitution of the Council of Islamic Ideology, and declaring that thenceforth Friday would be observed as the weekly holiday in place of Sunday. A journalist at the press conference stated that the plurality of political parties in the western democratic system created dissensions which were abhorred in an Islamic polity. Mr Bhutto shot back: 'Then make me the Amir [ruler] and abolish the parliamentary system.' This was Bhutto's political philosophy. Power should be wielded by him alone; the mode and the manner of getting it were irrelevant.

A day before announcing the Islamic steps, Mr Bhutto, while a sipping a drink, had told Lieutenant-General Muhammad Iqbal Khan in Lahore that the mullahs were clamouring for an Islamic order in the country and remarked: 'They will get it over my dead body.'[7]

The plan to cash in on the religious sensitivities of the people misfired. The lifestyle of the PPP leadership and their love of worldly glitter and pleasures were well known. Religion was a political gimmick played by a shaky government to regain its balance. Three days later, Mr Bhutto complained to General Muhammad Shariff at Rawalpindi that the PNA agitation had not stopped, despite the Islamic prohibitions announced by him. He stated that he had taken that step on the advice of General Zia, who had anticipated that the agitation would fade away.[8] However, politics, not religion, had initiated the PNA movement. The people demanded fresh and fair polls under a neutral administration.

The top PNA leadership was arrested by the government and the movement slipped into the inexperienced hands of the lower rung leaders. They found it hard to sustain the tempo of the agitation and to keep the government under high pressure. The vacuum in leadership was filled by street power. The people, restive and resentful under the authoritarian rule of Mr Bhutto's revengeful government, joined

69

the movement which took a decisive turn to the right. The arguments were presented thus: Pakistan had been created on the basis of Islam; the people of Pakistan wished to establish an Islamic order in the country; the PPP government should be replaced because it had failed to establish that order. Change had become inescapable because the country had been denied fair elections. Mr Bhutto's government should, therefore, resign and fresh polls be held in the country. The phenomenon of street power defies rational assessment. In an environment of mass hysteria, reason becomes a casualty. Religion is a strong emotive force—easy to arouse and hard to control. The Bhutto administration learnt this lesson the hard way.

In the third week of April 1977, the annual formation commanders' conference was held at General Headquarters. At General Zia's suggestion, the Prime Minister hosted a dinner for the assembled general officers on 19 April. Held at the Prime Minister's residence, the dinner was attended by Mr Aziz Ahmad, the Minister of State for Foreign Affairs, General Tikka Khan, Adviser to the Prime Minister, the Chairman of the Joint Chiefs of Staff Committee, the Chiefs of Staff of the Army, the Navy, and the Air Force, the Secretary General of the Ministry of Defence, the corps commanders, all the PSOs in General Headquarters, and Air Vice Marshal Inamul Haq, Director General Joint Staff. Before the dinner, the Prime Minister held a discussion with a smaller group comprising Mr Aziz Ahmad, General Tikka Khan, General Zia, all the corps commanders, and Major-General Abdullah Malik, the Chief of General Staff. In that meeting, the Prime Minister invited the general officers to individually dilate on the prevailing internal security situation. General Zia stated that the army wished to stay away from active politics, the loyalties of the officers of the rank of brigadier and above were above-board, but the possibility of some junior officers getting carried away by the religious frenzy could not be ruled out. Such an eventuality would be a grave matter. The corps commanders, in their turn, stated that the agitation was directed personally against the Prime Minister, and that a crisis of confidence had developed between him and the PNA. The time factor was against the government, they argued, and advised that a political settlement be reached to end the prevailing crisis. A stone-faced Prime Minister listened patiently and offered only brief comments. After the meeting, the other dinner invitees joined the party. Mr Bhutto was quiet—almost morose—as if under great mental stress. Without mingling with the others, he went into a huddle with

Mr Aziz Ahmad and General Tikka Khan. It was an unpleasant and tense evening. Meanwhile, the law and order situation kept worsening. The 'anti-rigging agitation' turned 'anti-Bhutto' and became violent and emotional. The use of force against the agitators added fuel to the fire. Valuable lives were lost. Property was damaged. The authority of the government kept weakening in the vocal urban areas. On 20 April 1977, the Chief of General Staff, Major-General Abdullah Malik, was summoned to attend a meeting at the Prime Minister's house. Besides the Prime Minister, the meeting was attended by the Federal Ministers Mr Rafi Raza and Mr Abdul Hafeez Pirzada. In that meeting, the Prime Minister indicated that the government was examining the possibility of imposing martial law in Karachi and Lahore. He directed the participants to examine the legal, administrative, political, and military aspects of the proposal and asked them to present their plan to him at 11 a.m. on 21 April.

In a meeting held earlier with the DGISI, Mr Aziz Ahmad and the adviser on national security, Lieutenant-General Ghulam Jilani had advised the Prime Minister against the imposition of martial law and had recommended that he should instead resolve the issue through political dialogue.[9] Jilani's fear was that once the army came in, it might hang around for a long time which would not be good for either side.

The mini martial law option was analysed in a meeting at General Headquarters, with the Chief of Army Staff presiding. It was found unfeasible, as the agitation could be shifted to cities other than Lahore and Karachi. The Prime Minister's meeting held on 21 April was attended by General Tikka Khan, Mr Aziz Ahmad, and the three services chiefs. It was pointed out to the Prime Minister that General Muhammad Shariff, Chairman JCSC, should also have been invited to attend the meeting. Mr Bhutto asked General Zia to apprise the Chairman JCSC of the discussion. Admiral Sharif suggested that it would be better for the Prime Minister to do so personally. A message was sent to General Shariff to meet the Prime Minister. The meeting decided to place Karachi Division and the districts of Lahore and Hyderabad under martial law with immediate effect.

As General Shariff entered the Prime Minister's house that evening, he met Mr Yahya Bakhtiar, the Attorney General, taking the proclamation to the President of Pakistan for his signature. General Shariff read the draft before he met Mr Bhutto, who gave him the rationale behind the move.[10] 'It would be a mistake to impose a mini-martial law,' said General Shariff. 'Should it cover the whole of the country?' enquired the Prime Minister. General Shariff submitted that a resort to martial law would erode the political authority of the government. Besides, it would not achieve the desired aim, as the agitation could spread elsewhere.

The decision to impose partial martial law was undemocratic and unfortunate. The 1973 Constitution was enacted under Mr Bhutto's prime ministership. On that occasion, he had solemnly declared that martial law had been permanently banished from Pakistan. Ironically, the same Prime Minister took recourse to martial law to save his tottering government from collapse through a self-created crisis.

With the imposition of the mini martial law, the Pakistan Army came under added political pressure. Earlier, troops had been employed since March 1977 in aid of civil power on demand by the provincial governments. In the perception of the PNA, the Bhutto government, after 7 March 1977, had no legal standing and, therefore, the army support to it was legally and morally not justified.

For men in uniform, it is always an unpleasant task to fire upon their own citizens. The demonstrators accused the army of siding with the administration. They wanted the troops to support their agitation. Through a postal campaign, many letters were received by the military personnel, urging them not to implement the orders given by an 'illegal' government. The troops were urged to support the popular public demand for enforcing the Shariah Law in Pakistan. The appeal had a psychological impact. Gradually, it started adversely affecting the soldiers who, by tradition, were religious-minded. Some of the military commanders expressed apprehensions that a prolonged exposure of troops to public agitation might erode their military discipline.

Some other developments influenced the soldiers' minds. Two retired service chiefs, Lt. Gen. Gul Hassan and Air Marshal Rahim, then serving as Pakistan's envoys in Greece and Spain respectively, resigned from their posts in protest against the government. The imposition of martial law had also been challenged in the civil courts. This created a legal uncertainty. In early May, Air Marshal (retired) Asghar Khan wrote letters to the three service chiefs, urging them not to obey the unlawful command given by an illegal government. The contents appeared in the Press. In Lahore, some religious zealots, holding copies of the Holy Quran on their heads, marched towards

PRELUDE TO INTERVENTION

the armed police, courting martyrdom. Working under such conditions, the moral pressure on the troops intensified. They started debating the justification of shooting their Muslim brethren, who were demanding the supremacy of Islamic law in the country. Some violent processions in Lahore were fired upon by the troops on duty. It was later discovered that, contrary to military norm, the soldiers had in fact fired bullets in the air. It caused great concern to the military commanders.

The disaffection spread. Three brigadiers, Ishtiaq Ali Khan, Said Muhammad, and Niaz Ahmad, employed on martial law duties in Lahore, succumbed to the inner pressure. Caught between the pull of religion and the military task, they wavered in the performance of their duties and requested to be relieved of their assignments. General Zia dashed to Lahore. As Military Secretary, I accompanied him. At Lahore, we met the three brigadiers, in the company of the corps commander, Lieutenant-General Muhammad Iqbal Khan, and the General Officer Commanding, Major-General Agha Zulfiqar Ali. The officers told General Zia that their conscience forbade them to fire on the protesters agitating against election riggers and cheats. They were retired from military service forthwith.

A disconsolate Ishtiaq complained to the author, years after the episode, that the three conscientious objectors were harshly treated by the army. 'When we declined to pump bullets into the bodies of innocent people,' he said in an injured tone, 'we were prematurely retired. But when Zia staged a coup against the same offender, he himself became the Head of the State. How could a double standard be called fair play?' Ishtiaq should have known the difference between the success and the failure of a coup. The first leads one to the pinnacle of power, the second to the gallows.

As a seasoned tactician, Mr Bhutto employed all means to weaken his adversaries. General Tikka Khan was elected to the Senate on a PPP ticket and given a ministerial appointment to indicate that Bhutto had the support of the military. He asked Air Chief Marshal Zulfiqar Ali Khan, the Chief of Air Staff, to get a press note issued by all the service chiefs reiterating their loyalty to the government. This was unprecedented. Zulfiqar came to GHQ to meet Zia with a draft. They were soon joined by Admiral Sharif. The three service chiefs then took the statement to General Shariff, Chairman JCSC. Shariff opposed the proposal but eventually went along with his three colleagues. The joint statement issued on 27 April 1977 by the Chairman of the Joint Chiefs of Staff Committee and the three service chiefs read:

> While the military code prohibits the soldiers, sailors and airmen to have anything to do with politics, the Armed Forces who belong to the nation have to remain on call to safeguard the country's integrity when threatened on account of external aggression or internal subversion... We wish to make it absolutely clear that the Pakistan Army, Navy and Air Force are totally united to discharge their constitutional obligations in support of the present legally constituted government...

This was active politics, plain and simple, passing a judgement that the present government was legally constituted—an issue disputed by the opposition. The loyalty of the defence services to the country did not need public reiteration. The service chiefs fell victim to the political pressure exerted on them by the government. Their unwise act, defying the military norm, set an unhealthy precedent. Mr Bhutto later used this statement in his trial to establish the legality of his government.

The joint statement was not well received within the army. General Zia sensed the mood and was forced to issue, on 7 May 1977, Command Communication Number 9 to all formations. Some excerpts: 'In the aftermath of National Assembly elections, the country is unfortunately gripped in a frenzy of agitational politics... What is our duty today? We ought to obey the legally constituted government. It is argued that the elections were unfair. Are we in the army justified to pass a judgement? Is there not a legally constituted machinery to adjudicate such issues? Are there not the High Courts and the Supreme Court to judge such allegations? Should the army listen to the processionists to decide what is right or wrong?... Let the army not be the judge regarding the legality of the government'.

The more the military debated the legal status and the rights and wrongs of the government, the more it got sucked into the murky political waters. The Inter Services Intelligence Directorate, in a report, adversely commented on the joint statement issued by the military brass. Mr Bhutto wrote on the margin: 'It was necessary.'

Mr Justice Sajjad Ahmad Jan, the Chief Election Commissioner, took note of the allegations of the rigging of the polls. On 19 March 1977, he requested the government to enable the Election Commission, by a change in the law, to annul the vitiated elections. This placed the government in a quandary. Rejection of the request meant embarrassment.

Acceptance carried a risk. The administration amended the law as requested. Given legal powers, the Election Commission initiated formal hearings in respect of thirteen cases. Six of these cases were decided between 31 March and 20 April 1977. Each of them unseated the previously successful candidate of the ruling party on the ground of widespread rigging. The decisions unnerved the government. On 12 May 1977, the Ordinance was withdrawn. Justice was thus sacrificed at the altar of political expediency. The action further weakened the credibility of the administration.

Mr Bhutto repeatedly met with the military brass in a blaze of publicity to show his control. An experienced politician, he kept his options open. On 13 May he announced in the National Assembly that he would go directly to the sovereign people to seek a vote of confidence as Prime Minister. The Constitution did not contain provision for holding a referendum. Mr Bhutto discussed the referendum proposal with General Zia. An analysis in the GHQ revealed that it was unlikely to satisfy the public demand. Notwithstanding that assessment, the Constitution was amended post-haste in a matter of hours on 16 May, providing for a vote of confidence in the Prime Minister by the people through a referendum. Shah Mardan Shah of Pagara, the acting President of the PNA, rejected the referendum proposal, calling it mere 'eyewash'. It died a natural death.

The government debated the possibility of asking the services chiefs to meet the PNA leaders to achieve a compromise. This proposal was discussed in an exclusive dinner hosted by Mr Bhutto, to which, besides the four military heads, General Tikka Khan and Maulana Kausar Niazi were also invited.

To break the deadlock in the government-PNA negotiations, other mediaries appeared on the scene. The Azad Kashmir Muslim Conference leader, Sardar Abdul Qayyum Khan, shuttled between the government and the opposition leaders in jail to find a common meeting ground. Some friendly Muslim countries offered their good offices for mediation. The special envoy of the Palestine Liberation Organization chief, Mr Yasser Arafat, Mr Hani al Hassan, met the Prime Minister and the PNA Chief, Maulana Mufti Mahmud. Libya, Kuwait, and the United Arab Emirates appealed for a dialogue to find a solution. The Saudi Ambassador in Pakistan, Sheikh Riadh al-Khitab, had a number of meetings with Mr Bhutto and the imprisoned PNA leaders. Both sides agreed to talk without any preconditions. In the ensuing discussions, Mr Bhutto was assisted by two federal ministers, Mr Abdul Hafeez Pirzada and Maulana Kausar Niazi. The PNA negotiating team comprised Maulana Mufti Mahmud (JUI), Nawabzada Nasrullah Khan (PDP), and Professor Ghafoor Ahmad (JI).

On 24 April 1977, Darvesh M. Arbey, advocate, filed a petition in the Lahore High Court challenging the imposition of martial law in Karachi Division and in the districts of Hyderabad and Lahore. This writ petition, 777 of 1977, was heard by a full bench comprising five judges, presided over by the Chief Justice Aslam Riaz Hussain. In a judgment delivered on 2 June 1977, the Lahore High Court declared the act illegal and unconstitutional. Consequently, on 7 June 1977, the Federal Government rescinded its directive issued on 21 April 1977. On the lifting of martial law, 12,900 persons were released from jails.

On 18 June 1977, the Chief Election Commissioner, Mr Justice Sajjad Ahmad Jan, left Pakistan for treatment for two months. As expected, he did not rejoin his post.

The magnitude of the loss of lives and the damage to the national economy remained undetermined. The PNA claimed that over 200 persons died. The government did not contradict that figure. Mr Abdul Hafeez Pirzada, the Minister for Finance, Planning, and Provincial Co-ordination, in an interview stated that 'the country's current economic picture is grim and fiscal 1977-78 will be a hard year ... 60 production [working] days were lost ... and the effects of the agitation on the industrial sector were the worst.'[11]

The export target, set at $1,400 million, was down to $1,050 million. On 14 May, the same minister informed Parliament that 245 banks had been broken open and burnt, and that the Karachi seaport had been rendered ineffective. At one time, the PNA threatened to launch a country-wide 'wheel jam' movement to bring the administration to a grinding halt. This unnerved not only the government but also one service chief. Air Chief Marshal Zulfiqar told his military colleagues in the JCSC meeting that such a development would seriously affect the air force which was already consuming operational reserve fuel for flying, and that too on a reduced scale.

Mr Bhutto suspected a foreign hand behind the agitation. Addressing a joint session of Parliament in Islamabad on 28 April 1977, he alleged in an emotionally-charged voice that: 'they want my blood because I am the symbol and pillar of stability in Pakistan and they want me out'.

Mr Bhutto's accusation was against America. The Prime Minister went on to disclose that 'two officials of a foreign mission did not conceal their glee on the developments in Pakistan in a telephonic conversation on 12 March by observing that "the party is over. He is gone." '

Then, amidst wild thumping of desks, he concluded his speech by declaring 'but gentlemen, the party is not over and it will not be over till my mission is completed for this great nation.' A master of oratory and dramatics, Mr Bhutto surveyed the hall and the jam-packed visitor's galleries, paused deliberately, took a deep breath, raised his voice and thundered: 'I may be a humble person but the Prime Minister's chair that I occupy is very powerful. I cannot be removed that easily.'

The same day, the Minister of State for Foreign Affairs, Mr Aziz Ahmad, told the joint meeting of Parliament: 'there was some circumstantial evidence indicating foreign involvement in the PNA's violent movement to subvert the Constitution.'

On 29 April 1977, the US State Department spokesman, Frederick Brown, said 'We are aware of the allegations made in Pakistan of US interference in the Pakistani political process on behalf of the opposition. These allegations are baseless. The United States has had neither the desire nor the reason to make any effort to support Prime Minister Bhutto's opponents and interfere in the political process in Pakistan and it has not done so.'

On 30 April 1977, at an unscheduled public rally in the Rawalpindi cantonment, waving a two-page letter from the United State's Secretary of State, Cyrus Vance, Mr Bhutto disclosed that the US had offered to discuss, not publicly but privately, whatever grievances Pakistan might have. Again, while talking to newsmen on 10 May 1977, the Prime Minister said: 'There was hard evidence of foreign intervention in Pakistan's internal affairs and that he had informed the United States of Pakistan's readiness for quiet and dispassionate talks with them.'[12]

Pressed by a correspondent for the release of the evidence, Mr Bhutto said: 'It could further deteriorate and spoil relations [with the US]. Secondly, a sovereign government could be under no obligation to put forward the evidence in a court of law.'

Mr Bhutto's confident exterior hid the turmoil which had shaken him from within. The PNA announced a people's long march to the capital city from all parts of the country. The threat unnerved Mr

Bhutto so much that he showed a lack of confidence in the Punjab police which protected his official residence. A large Sindh police contingent was airlifted to Islamabad by the Pakistan Air Force on an emergency basis. It stayed in the city for a while and travelled back to Karachi without being called on to act.

The government accused the PNA of getting financial help from external sources. The allegation was denied by the PNA. In May 1977, this issue was discussed in a cabinet meeting presided over by Mr Bhutto. It was lamented that the intelligence agencies had failed in anticipating foreign intervention. It was not clear how foreign money had entered the country. The intelligence agencies merely provided information, often out of date and without any analysis or forecast. The cabinet discussion revealed that the allegation against the PNA was politically motivated.

According to General Jilani, Mr Bhutto and Mr Aziz Ahmad had put considerable pressure on both the ISI and Intelligence Bureau chiefs to produce evidence to substantiate the alleged unprecedented flow of foreign currencies for the PNA movement.[13] The allegation had been made by some irresponsible party men to curry favour with Mr Bhutto. Both the principal intelligence chiefs told Aziz Ahmad that the allegation lacked substance. According to them, business interests in the country had been donating liberally to keep the PNA movement going. The DGISI and DIB challenged Mr Aziz Ahmad's sources to produce hard evidence and offered the informers up to Rs 2,500,000. Nothing further was then heard by them in this context from the government.

In April 1977, General Zia hosted a courtesy dinner in honour of Mr Henry Byroade, the outgoing ambassador of the United States. Bhutto's advisers called it a mischievous attempt to create a misunderstanding between the Prime Minister and USA. Subsequently, it was termed a fore-warning for the coup. Mr M. Yusuf Buch, Special Assistant to Prime Minister Bhutto (later Pakistan's Ambassador in Switzerland) was one of the dinner invitees. Months after the event, he voluntarily wrote a letter to General Zia and attached to it a statement signed by him. In the letter, he states that there was nothing even faintly conspiratorial about the conversation, which he fully shared between the host and the chief guest. In fact, Mr Byroade told him that the United States had nothing to gain from the downfall of Mr Bhutto. This letter absolves General Zia from the allegation made against him. (The letter is at Annexure 1; the signed statement is at Annexure 2.)

Also attending that dinner were Mr Agha Shahi, the Foreign Secretary, and the Iranian ambassador in Pakistan. Mr Shahi recalls that it was a routine function in which nothing unusual came to his notice.[14] The Iranian ambassador enquired from Mr Agha Shahi if it was true that Mrs Nusrat Bhutto had gone to Tehran and Mr Bhutto was planning to join her there soon. Mr Shahi expressed his ignorance of the matter and apprised Mr Yusuf Buch of the query raised by the ambassador.

The Government-Opposition talks began on 3 June 1977. The PNA negotiating team comprising Maulana Mufti Mahmud, Nawabzada Nasrullah Khan, and Professor Ghafoor Ahmad, who were freed from jail. The dialogue, starting on an optimistic note, soon faced hurdles. The pro-government correspondent, H. K. Burki, reported that 'at the end of fourth round of discussions which lasted two and half hours at the PM's house today, the Government - PNA dialogue has run into difficulties about some of the details of the package deal.'[15]

By 15 June 1977, the major difficulties had been overcome. An accord was reached on the basic issues and a two-man subcommittee was formed to work out the details. It was declared that fresh elections would be held in October 1977. It was a moral victory for the PNA.

With the talks delicately poised, the government sprang a surprise. On 16 June 1977, it was suddenly announced that Mr Bhutto would be visiting some Islamic countries in view of an urgent development. The four-day tour was to take him to Saudi Arabia, Libya, Kuwait, United Arab Emirates, Afghanistan, and Iran.

Mr Bhutto did not take the PNA into confidence about his projected foreign tour. The sudden announcement created irritation and Mr Bhutto's motive became suspect. The opposition felt cheated and hardened its attitude because of the delaying tactics adopted by the government. When the talks finally recommenced in late June 1977, the PNA presented amendments in the previously agreed draft. A surprised Mr Abdul Hafeez Pirzada expressed strong reservations, saying that 'he was neither authorized nor was he willing to accept the PNA draft as the Government-PNA accord under a take it or leave it threat.' Notwithstanding the rhetoric, the discussions continued in a climate filled with hostility and doubt.

The delay in arriving at any agreement put pressure on General Zia and the corps commanders. They were fearful that the prevailing polarization might cause a crack within the army. This apprehension was frequently expressed by General Zia to his PSOs at GHQ. The corps commanders periodically met General Zia. The meetings were held in the Army House to which the Chief of General Staff from GHQ was invariably invited. This was a departure from routine as the formation commanders' meetings, to which all the PSOs were invited, were customarily held in GHQ. The exclusion of PSOs was hard to explain. After each meeting, General Zia gave the gist of the discussion held with the corps commanders to the PSOs. He usually stressed the fact that the army was the right arm of the government and would not become a party to the dispute. General Zia kept the Prime Minister apprised about the corps commanders' conferences and the views expressed by them. On some occasions, he met the Prime Minister along with the corps commanders and the Chief of General Staff. This was a deviation from the custom of service. Besides, it amounted to politicizing the corps commanders.

The corps commanders told Mr Bhutto candidly and frankly—so General Zia informed his PSOs—that the agitation was unlikely to be suppressed by coercive methods; that elections had been rigged on a large scale; that the agitation was directed against the Prime Minister's person; that a crisis of confidence existed between the government and the PNA; and that the government should find a political solution. They informed the Prime Minister that the army had tried hard to stay away from politics, despite provocations and intimidation, and in the process, had gained time for the government to negotiate a political settlement.

On 20 June 1977, General Zia expressed his apprehension to the Prime Minister that, if the agitation did not end, it could erode the army's discipline and cause divisions in its ranks. This would be a disaster for the army and for the country. Mr Bhutto sensed the mood. Employing his charm, he said, 'you are my brother and I trust you.' He asked General Zia not to get unduly worried as the government did not plan to employ the army in a hurry again. He went on to confide that he had taken 'other measures' to deal with the PNA agitation. That statement rang an alarm bell in General Zia's mind. It flashed back to the report he had received of PPP workers being armed for a direct confrontation with the PNA agitationists. The prospects of the eruption of a civil war alarmed Zia. He informed the

Prime Minister that, as a routine measure, the army had done contingency planning to deal with the law and order situation. Mr Bhutto enquired when such a plan would be implemented. 'Whenever the government felt that the situation had gone out of their control,' replied General Zia.

With a smile on his face, Mr Bhutto said: 'This time, I will deal with the situation politically.' General Zia enquired if he had agreed with the PNA to hold the elections soon. Mr Bhutto replied: 'If elections are held as a result of the Government-PNA accord, and if the PNA wins in those elections, the army should intervene and impose martial law in the country.'

Stunned by the unsolicited mischievous advice, Zia replied: ' In that eventuality there would be no justification for the army to intervene.' Mr Bhutto suddenly brightened, as if he had been waiting for just such an opening. He said with confidence: 'Don't worry. I will give you the justification. My brain is your power.' The remark surprised General Zia still further.

With Bhutto's words ringing in his ears, General Zia returned to GHQ, and narrated this conversation to a small group of general officers including myself. He was amazed at how the mind of the head of the government worked. Nearly two years after the event, General Zia narrated this conversation to Mr Abdul Hafeez Pirzada who called on him on 4 March 1979 to seek clemency for Mr Bhutto. Mr Pirzada made no comment.

The negotiations kept dragging on through the month of June. The elusive accord contained rough edges. Neither the draft agreement nor the changes proposed in it by the PNA were released to the Press. Maulana Kausar Niazi gives the text of the accord which was handed over to the PNA by the government on 12 June 1977.[16] His book does not disclose the final approved version of the accord. Two points contained in the draft agreement aroused controversy. One pertained to the trial of the National Awami Party (NAP) leaders in a special court at Hyderabad. The second concerned the recall of the army to the barracks in the province of Balochistan where it had been deployed in the anti-insurgency operations.

The NAP was banned, under an order passed by the Supreme Court of Pakistan, for indulging in anti-state activities. The top office-bearers of the party were under trial in Hyderabad in a special court. The Prime Minister enquired from General Zia if the PNA demand to abolish the special court and to withdraw the cases against

81

those under trial be accepted. After discussing the issue with the corps commanders and the PSOs, General Zia recommended to the government that the law be allowed to take its course.

The question of the recall of the army to barracks in Balochistan came under discussion when General Zia and the corps commanders met the Prime Minister towards the end of June 1977. Mr Bhutto informed the general officers that the PNA had demanded an immediate withdrawal of troops from the troubled area. General Zia stated that the PNA leadership might be underrating the hurdles involved. The Prime Minister asked General Zia to explain the position to the PNA leaders. A meeting was arranged. As General Zia began to speak about the insurgency, Maulana Mufti Mahmud and Nawabzada Nasrullah Khan interrupted, saying that they were not interested in the general's assessment because the problem was political in nature. General Zia stated that he would only express his professional advice on the military aspects of the issue. Nasrullah Khan insisted that they were not interested in the military view. General Zia said, 'you may spit at me if I make an incorrect statement.' General Shariff intervened to say that while the political decision would be taken by the political masters, it was the responsibility of the military to advise the government about the military point of view.

While narrating this incident to the PSOs, General Zia observed that the gulf separating the government and the PNA was wide and their suspicions about each other were grave.

(Throughout this chapter, as indeed elsewhere in the book, the terms corps commanders and PSOs have been used. The corps commanders at that time were: Lieutenant-General Muhammad Iqbal Khan, Lieutenant-General Sawar Khan, Lieutenant-General Faiz Ali Chishti, Lieutenant-General Ghulam Hassan Khan, Major-General Jahanzeb Arbab (acting corps commander) and Major-General Ghulam Muhammad (acting corps commander). The PSOs working in the GHQ were: Major-General Abdullah Malik, Major-General Muhammad Riaz, Major-General Jamal Said Mian, Major-General Rahimuddin Khan, Major-General Saeed Qadir, and myself.)

There appeared a flicker of light at the end of the political tunnel. The nation heaved a sigh of relief when the newspapers of 3 July 1977 reported the successful completion of talks. The daily *Dawn* splashed the news in these words:

> The Government and the PNA negotiating teams after a marathon ten-and-a-half-hour session, announced agreement on the draft of

PRELUDE TO INTERVENTION

their accord on June 15. However, the position continues to be uncertain and confusing.

Maulana Kausar Niazi and Professor Ghafoor Ahmad, spokesmen for the government and PNA respectively, told newsmen that 'their points of difference had been sorted out and the draft agreement evolved on the basis of PNA's revised draft was expected to be finally signed in a day or two, *after approval by the PNA Central Council.*' (Emphasis added)

The significance of the catch-words 'after approval by the PNA Council', was taken lightly by the government. It believed that the PNA Council was honour-bound to approve the agreement arrived at by its negotiating team. This was not to be so. The hawks in the PNA Council—Air Marshal Asghar Khan and Begum Nasim Wali Khan—took exception to some of the agreed items and proposed nine amendments before it could be signed. This put the negotiated accord in jeopardy.

At 7 p.m. on 3 July 1977, Mr Bhutto telephoned General Muhammad Shariff to apprise him that, despite his best efforts to reach a fair settlement, the government-PNA negotiations had broken down because of the extreme intransigence of the opposition.[17] Two hours later, he spoke over the telephone to Admiral Sharif and gave him a similar impression.[18] The following morning, a pro-government newspaper stated: 'The PNA seems to have backtracked on the settlement. It is now refusing to state whether it has endorsed or rejected the agreement its negotiating team reached with the government.'[19] Air Marshal Asghar Khan, while 'speaking for himself' said: 'It would be a mistake to consider that an accord had been reached.' He indicated that, 'lawyers representing diverse components of the Alliance were in disagreement over the settlement arrived at between two negotiating teams.' The same paper in its editorial on 4 July 1977 said:

> ... then began this meeting of the PNA Central Committee on Saturday night and there ... bitter differences have come to the surface ... why had the negotiating team agreed to amendments in the PNA draft?

One member of the PNA negotiating team said: 'Nawabzada Nasrullah Khan, PNA Vice President, said that nine points given by PNA to Prime Minister Bhutto last night were not new points and these did not amount to reopening settled issues.'[20] He added that the claim that all the matters were settled was not correct.

83

The government took the opposite view. The Prime Minister discussed the nine points with his colleagues in a cabinet meeting and issued a firmly worded statement declaring that, 'after the accord had been reached between the government and the PNA, it cannot be reopened. This is just not done.'[21]

It was past midnight when the cabinet meeting ended. Immediately thereafter, the Prime Minister held a press conference. While apologizing for calling the gentlemen of the Press at such an odd hour, Mr Bhutto said 'in the cabinet meeting held, there was a sharp difference of opinion... My colleagues had not differed with me so much during the past five and a half years as they did now. If the PNA had its difficulties, I too have difficulties of my own.' He concluded the press conference by saying, 'there are many Tarzans sitting in my party.'[22]

The truth was buried under a heap of confusion worse confounded by deliberately planted lies. A Karachi-based newspaper reported: 'The Prime Minister said if the PNA wanted to raise further points after reaching a final settlement, the government had more right to do so, not as tit for tat because it was the government which had given concessions. There could be no double standards, one for the PNA and another for the government.'[23]

Nawabzada Nasrullah Khan addressed a press conference on 4 July 1977. Commenting on that statement, Salamat Ali wrote: 'Nawabzada claimed that he and his two colleagues had submitted to the Prime Minister last night nine points that constituted slight amendments in the language and proposals given by the government. He asserted that they had been submitted only because PNA lawyers considered them necessary to remove certain lacunae.'[24]

The 'Tarzans' of the PPP and the 'hawks' of the PNA won the day. An accord virtually clinched was aborted due to a crisis of confidence. A historic opportunity to reach a settlement was lost because of mutual mistrust.

Professor Ghafoor Ahmad's book, *Phir Martial Law Aa Gaya, (And Then Martial Law was Imposed*) indicates that some PNA leaders doubted Mr Bhutto's sincerity in implementing any agreement reached with the opposition. The politics of hatred and doubt so clouded political sagacity and the negotiating skill of the two sides that, in the final analysis, trivial issues prevailed over matters of substance.

Without being explicit, Professor Ghafoor Ahmad blames the hawks within the PNA for adopting a negative approach. He narrates a statement made by Maulana Mufti Mahmud about his conversation with Begum Wali Khan held in the presence of Sardar Sherbaz Mazari. The narration is quoted verbatim: 'The car started moving. En route, the Begum [Mrs Nasim Wali Khan] told Maulana Mufti Mahmud that Mr Bhutto could no longer be trusted on the issue [holding of elections]. Do not sign an agreement with Mr Bhutto she told Maulana Mufti Mahmud. Let martial law be imposed because only such a step would guarantee the holding of elections within 90 days. Maulana Mufti Mahmud enquired from her if she had consulted Khan Wali Khan on the subject. She replied in the affirmative saying that his opinion was the same. Mufti Mahmud differed with her assessment. Earlier, Asghar Khan [Air Marshal] had also expressed identical views. He was also of the view that the imposition of martial law was conducive to the holding of elections.'[25] The persons named in the narration did not contradict these contentions in any subsequent statements.

The PNA leaders slept on the night between 4 and 5 July 1977 with a firm conviction that the accord had not been finalized. This was the end of democracy, given the kiss of death by the feuding political leadership.

I later asked Lieutenant-General Ghulam Jilani Khan (the then Director General of Intelligence) whether the intelligence agencies and the government had anticipated a military take-over. Jilani, an honourable person with a cold logical mind but a warm heart, gave some details. His assessment is reproduced here, even at the risk of some repetition: 'In the early stages of the PNA agitation, the army stood solidly behind the Bhutto government. However, a perceptible change was discernible from the time the Head of the Government started meeting the corps commanders frequently. This was the beginning of their involvement in politics, and was indicative of the government's weakness. The corps commanders were frank and open in expressing their viewpoint before the Prime Minister, as well as the cabinet. At one stage, while emphasizing the need for an early political settlement with the PNA leaders, the corps commanders said that, in the event of the government's failure to resolve the present crisis, they may perforce be obliged to exercise a military option. The mention of a "military option" had caused the intelligence antennae to be raised by the two principal intelligence agencies. Although they had both been discreetly following the overt and covert activities, including the meetings held in the COAS House, yet it might be acknowledged that, by its very nature and by necessity, a military coup is a hush-hush affair, the details of which are kept a closely-guarded secret. While the intelligence agencies can make a reasonably accurate assessment about its possibility, it is extremely difficult to predict its exact timing and date. Things can be made even more difficult, where, as in our peculiar circumstances, a COAS himself decided to strike!'

Jilani went on to recall that, 'From mid-April 1977 onwards, the Attorney General Yahya Bakhtiar used to hold daily law and order conferences in Rawalpindi, in which the army was represented by Lieutenant-General F. A. Chishti. As the government's position kept weakening, there came about a visible change in the tone and tenor of Chishti's conversation: he was more authoritative, firm, and assertive. This did not escape the notice of the "I" men. After the conference of 2 July Rao Abdul Rashid, the new Director Intelligence Bureau, and myself both concluded that the army's patience was exhausted and it was planning some action at any time. We met Mr Bhutto together on 3 July and apprised him of our fears and assessment based on our observations and analysis. By then, there had also been reports of some opposition party leaders encouraging/conniving with the military for a possible take-over to end the agony. After listening to both of us, Mr Bhutto, in our presence, spoke to each of the corps commanders on telephone individually. In a subtle manner, he enquired from them if all was well and whether anything unusual was happening! Mr Bhutto was no wiser after the conversation and there ended the matter.'

Jilani confirms what General Zia had disclosed earlier to his close colleagues. Bhutto did speak to the corps commanders. All of them, except one, in turn telephoned General Zia and apprised him of their talk with the Prime Minister that afternoon. Jilani went on to add that: 'At this point in time, the Prime Minister had rendered himself too weak and too isolated to act firmly. He kept on delaying matters till it was too late. In response to a call received by me at 02:30 a.m. on 8 March 1977, I had told Mr Bhutto that he might himself take the initiative and consider negotiating a settlement with the opposition, even if it amounted to holding fresh elections. On 19 March I submitted a paper to the Prime Minister in which I had concluded that Mr Bhutto had no option other than to hold general elections afresh.

PRELUDE TO INTERVENTION

There were of course many of his detractors, cronies, and near and dear ones, who had been counselling him otherwise. In his pensive mood, he would say that the situation arising out of the PNA's boycott of the elections was nothing short of a Greek Tragedy; at times, he would say wistfully that he should have done what King Amanullah and Ataturk had done to the *mullahs*! He was too arrogant and proud to come down and accept defeat, or let his position or power be weakened in any way. He kept on hedging and dilly-dallying, and in the process lost considerable ground and time. Rather than trusting people, and finding a political solution through the medium of negotiation and reconciliation, he kept on looking elsewhere for solace and escape. Disenchanted, many of his close friends had left him for other pastures! He blamed the USA for his misfortunes, and accused her of pumping in huge sums of money.

'After the PNA's boycott, at first he tried to browbeat and intimidate the opposition; he used the police and paramilitary forces, and later the army to crush the PNA movement. In the process, even the women were beaten up and disgraced by the "Nath Force" [women's police force]. Against all advice, he amended the Constitution and imposed martial law in some of the major cities; against all advice, he started meeting the corps commanders directly and thus dragged them into politics; he would rather hold a referendum than face the real issue; he tried to take the PNA off the hook by holding out the bait of Islamization, declaring Friday as a weekly holiday, imposing prohibition, banning races, etc. These were all survival gimmicks. He often used to say that he was the master of timing. He wasted three months before he came to grips with the issue. It was not till 3 June that the government held its first meeting with the PNA leaders. But just as the talks made some headway, he suddenly decided to go abroad on 17 June, to visit some countries, leaving the unresolved issues to his lieutenants. By the time he returned, the cooks had spoiled the broth, and there was a deadlock. The talks were resumed in the midst of allegations and counter-allegations, proposals and counter-proposals, and agreements and disagreements. The army too had reservations about the Hyderabad Tribunal, and its own withdrawal from Balochistan. There were hardliners on both sides who tried to rock the boat at every step; Mustafa Khar and Dr Ghulam Hussain of the PPP were sabre-rattling; the PNA too had its detractors, who would rather demonstrate street power, or even prefer a martial law, than trust Mr Bhutto. There being no apparent let-up in the attitude of the warring leaders, the COAS, who had earlier in the evening of 4 July attended a cabinet meeting, in his wisdom finally decided to exercise the military option just as Mr Bhutto was finishing his Press conference at 0030 a.m. on 5 July. Till then, no one had any notion of the "H" hour. Within an hour or so of General Zia's decision, troops started reaching their destinations. Reconciliation, accommodation, and tolerance among the quarrelling politicians could have saved yet another setback to the process of democracy in Pakistan.'

Jilani first learnt about the army action at night from Mr M. A. K. Chaudhry, Secretary Interior, who rang him up about the presence of soldiers outside the house of Mr Masood Mahmud. After the military take-over, Jilani himself was shifted to the Ministry of Defence. His successor was Major-General Riaz Muhammad and, on his demise, Lieutenant-General Akhtar Abdul Rahman was appointed DGISI.

Did a cornered Bhutto think of sacking Zia? In response to this question, Jilani said that, 'Even if the Prime Minister had "spotted" his next man [as the COAS] and there was perhaps a "dark horse" around, by the time things precipitated during the course of the antigovernment agitation, he was too weak, too isolated and unsure of himself to contemplate opening yet another front. He was intelligent enough to have assessed from the corps commanders' views that the army enjoyed unity of command. If he had not reduced himself to impotence and had still retained a modicum of manoeuvrability and initiative, the time for him to act was perhaps on 3 July, when the two intelligence chiefs had together apprised him of the imminent threat. Having heard his "I" chiefs, the least that Mr Bhutto might have done in the interest of the continuance of a democratic process was to have signed the agreement with the PNA leaders either on that very night or on the following day at the latest. Alas, his destiny was set on a different course. Not that Mr Bhutto did not know, and not that he was not told what was coming by more than one source, but I believe that a time comes to every ruler when he sees what he wants to see, and hears what he wants to hear.'[26]

In July 1977, Edward Behr asked General Zia: 'How and when did you decide the time had come to take this step [impose martial law]?'[27] General Zia replied: 'I am the only man who took this decision and I did so at 1700 hours on 4 July after hearing the press statement which indicated that talks between Mr Bhutto and the opposition had broken down. Had an agreement been reached between them, I would certainly never have done what I did.'

ANNEXURE 1

TEXT OF MR M. YUSUF BUCH'S LETTER TO GENERAL ZIA

3 November, 1977

My dear General M. Zia-ul-Haq:

I have just read the despatch in *Times*, London of today headlined: "Mr. Bhutto implicates United States in plotting his overthrow." The following excerpt from it is of particular interest:

> As an indication of General Zia's involvement in such a conspiracy, Mr. Bhutto said the Chief of Staff had given a farewell reception for the retiring envoy of an unnamed power. General Zia did, in fact, arrange a farewell reception last April for Mr. Henry Byroade, the American Ambassador.
>
> Mr. Bhutto stated: 'I was still in Lahore (in April) when the Foreign Office informed me that despite my strict instructions that no senior official or minister could give receptions and banquets without the prior permission of the Foreign Office, the respondent (General Zia) had not bothered about these standing instructions by giving a lavish reception to the departing ambassador.'
>
> He said that his Interior Secretary had regarded General Zia's reception as a 'signal for the coup.'

I realise that the national situation has now reached a stage where you would find it hardly worthwhile to expend any attention, far less feeling, on this matter. I also firmly believe that it would be ludicrous that this incident be dwelt upon in any manner whatsoever or turned into an issue before any court, civil or military, or in any trial, secret or open. The same applies to any discussion in the press.

Nevertheless, knowing as I do know, honest truth, whether historical or contemporary, is easily distorted. I feel it to be my moral obligation to put on record my own clear recollection of this reception and the relevant circumstances. This obligation becomes greater because you had kindly invited me to the dinner and nothing transpired at it beyond my hearing or observation.

I am, therefore, appending a signed statement regarding what happened at the dinner. Without being presumptuous, I feel you may wish to keep it for use at some future time when you would like to piece the story of these fateful days together.

With my profound respect and warmest regards.

                                            Yours sincerely,
                                            SIGNED
                                            M. Yusuf Buch

ANNEXURE 2

TEXT OF THE SIGNED STATEMENT OF MR M. YUSUF BUCH

Mr Henry Byroade was the Ambassador of the United States in Pakistan from 1974 to 1977. For a long period earlier, the United States had sent no diplomat of his seniority to head its Embassy in Pakistan. During his tenure, he was personally popular and well spoken of by the Foreign Office and even by the Prime Minister. This personal good feeling withstood the several serious differences or difficulties in relations between Pakistan and the United States, particularly with regard to the supply of arms and the nuclear reprocessing plant project.

Mr Byroade's departure from Islamabad coincided with the onset of the national crisis in Pakistan in March, 1977. This element of coincidence is important because Mr Byroade had indicated to all who knew him in 1976 that, whether or not there would be change of administration in Washington in November, he planned to retire from diplomatic service and could not stay at his post beyond March/April 1977.

He gave a farewell reception in early April at which those who were invited and attended included the then Finance Minister, Mr Abdul Hafeez Pirzada, Chief of Army Staff, General M. Zia-ul-Haq, Secretary General (Defence), Mr Ghulam Ishaq Khan, many other secretaries of the Federal Government and myself. I had a conversation with General Zia-ul-Haq for a few minutes during which he expressed sincere gratitude to the Almighty that the situation in the country had not deteriorated to such a degree as to call for any painful measures.

Some days later, on 9 April, Mr and Mrs Byroade called on me and my wife to say good-bye and had an informal supper at our house. During his conversation on this occasion, Mr Byroade repeatedly emphasized that the United States had 'nothing to gain' from the downfall of Mr Bhutto. He expressed the hope (with some warmth and feeling) that something could be done to save the situation for Mr Bhutto. He had, he said, advised his Embassy as well as the State Department not to attach any importance to Mr Bhutto's animadversions (in the speech he made after taking the oath as Prime Minister in March 1977) about the Carter administration's concern with human rights. 'We' (meaning the United States) 'are sold on Bhutto'... these were his words. I am certain that he was not dissimulating; at an informal, social occasion, he could have easily turned the conversation to other lighter subjects. I reported the substance of what he said to Mr Bhutto orally.

Two or three days afterwards, General M. Zia-ul-Haq gave a reception and dinner to say farewell to Mr and Mrs Byroade. The reception was attended by not only some senior army officers but also a large number of secretaries of the Federal Government and the ranking members of the diplomatic corps in Islamabad. The dinner that followed was graceful but by no means 'lavish' in the sense of a champagne-and-caviar affair—at that time, prohibition had not yet come into effect, yet only non-alcoholic drinks were served. It was attended, among others, by the then Foreign Secretary, Mr Agha Shahi; the Foreign Office was, therefore, not uninformed of the dinner.

The host and hostess had graciously placed my wife and myself at the centre table along with themselves and the two guests of honour. There was nothing even faintly conspiratorial about the conversation shared by the six of us. The host, General M. Zia-ul-Haq, made a careful after-dinner speech. A notable feature of his remarks was that he made it clear diplomatically that his gesture was one of friendship to Mr Byroade personally and carried no implications about the state of relations between Pakistan and the United States.

After the dinner, when taking leave and conveying my thanks to the host, I briefly asked him what could be done to save a fast deteriorating situation. General Zia-ul-Haq's answer left no doubt in my mind that at that time he was not contemplating any military option in the sense of an ouster of the civil administration.

If, as alleged, the reception and dinner had been 'the sign for the coup', General Zia-ul-Haq would not have bothered to invite me to it. I was Special Assistant to the Prime Minister at that time and General Zia-ul-Haq could have had no knowledge that I had incurred Mr Bhutto's displeasure by my expressed views regarding the conduct of elections in March 1977 and the imperative of fresh, honest, unimpeachable polls. This displeasure was known only to those, besides myself, who had heard Mr Bhutto say that he would never 'give' me the assignment at the United Nations which I had asked for more than a year earlier.

Lastly, when an international plot develops regarding the internal affairs of a country, it does not require dinners or banquets as its signal. If anything, it would dispense with them so as not to awaken any attention or rouse any suspicion.

Signed
(M. Yusuf Buch)

3 November 1977

CHAPTER 4

The Military Option

March through July 1977, as the country was in turmoil with the anti-Bhutto agitation, President Fazal Elahi Chaudhry remained a silent spectator and virtually twiddled his thumbs. The Constitution did not permit the Head of State to act except on the advice of the Prime Minister. The President's helplessness during the national crisis disclosed a lacuna in the Constitution. The division of power between the President and the Prime Minister was unrealistic.

With the legal status of the parliament in dispute, the government's moral authority to rule compromised, and the government-PNA dialogue having reached a deadlock, a political impasse ensued. The army was frequently used to bail out the administration. Some opposition leaders and the public demanded the imposition of military rule. The political failure was an invitation to an extra-constitutional measure and the Chief of Army Staff intervened.

At 6:30 p.m. on 4 July 1977, Lieutenant-General F. A. Chishti and Major-General Riaz Muhammad arrived at my residence, unannounced, in a private car. Pleading urgency, they took me to the Army House. A relaxed Zia told us that the military contingency plan—Operation Fair Play—was to be implemented that night. 'The government and the PNA have agreed to disagree,' said General Zia, adding, 'There is no light at the end of the negotiating tunnel. The corps commanders agree with my assessment.'

As the clock started ticking towards the appointed hour, an air of uncertainty and expectation filled the room. Those present gazed at one another in silence.

General M. Ziaul Haq summoned his Principal Staff Officers (PSOs) and selected directors at General Headquarters to meet him in his office at 11 p.m. on 4 July 1977. When the invitees inquired about the agenda for discussion, Brigadier Khawar Latif Butt, Personal Secretary to General Zia, had a stock reply: 'No preparatory work is needed for the meeting.'

The unusually late hour of the meeting and its purpose gave rise to speculation. Most invitees guessed that it was connected with the ongoing government-PNA negotiations. The quick-witted Khawar received the arriving officers with a smile. While waiting for the army chief, we sipped tea, cracked jokes, and talked on a variety of subjects in the best tradition of a happily-knit team.

'I am sorry to call you at an odd hour but it could not be helped,' said General Zia. Explaining the background of the Government-PNA negotiations, he stated that the Prime Minister had told him of the wide gulf which separated the points of view of the two groups. He and the corps commanders had urged upon the Prime Minister to negotiate a political settlement of the dispute. A flicker of hope appeared on 3 July 1977, but it turned out to be an illusion. The PPP and the PNA accused each other of being insincere and unreliable. Personal ego and party considerations outweighed the national interest. In the meantime, said General Zia, both sides had equipped their workers with lethal weapons. This could lead to civil war. During the last few months, said General Zia, he had tried to keep the army out of politics. Any split in the army on regional, ethnic, or political lines could jeopardize the security of the country. The failure of the negotiations had been disclosed to the Press that day by Nawabzada Nasrullah Khan. Under the circumstances, said General Zia, he had reluctantly concluded that, in order to save the country from a bloodbath, it was the responsibility of the army to act, separate the warring politicians, restore peace and tranquillity, and hold just and fair elections. For that purpose, he had decided to put the country under martial law. General Zia informed his audience that earlier that evening he had directed Lieutenant-General Faiz Ali Chishti, Commander 10 Corps, to implement his orders. That process was about to commence. The discourse was heard in an agonized silence.

A brief discussion ensued. It was not known till then what specific orders had been issued to Lieutenant-General Chishti and how he was implementing them. A consensus emerged on three issues: one, the Constitution should not be abrogated; it could be kept on hold to be resuscitated at the time of lifting of martial law. Secondly, the duration of the martial law should be short. Thirdly, the people should elect their representatives through a fairly-held ballot. The meeting also discussed the contents of General Zia's proposed address to the nation the following day. I was asked to draft the speech.

THE MILITARY OPTION

At the time when the PSOs assembled at General Headquarters, Lieutenant-General Faiz Ali Chishti directed the local brigade commander, Brigadier Imtiaz Ullah Waraich, to implement the plan. This involved taking the designated politicians into custody and ensuring the security of some installations. The plan of action was simple. Its success depended on its secrecy during the planning stage and its speedy implementation. Lieutenant-General Chishti was ably helped by his Chief of Staff, Brigadier Muhammad Aslam Shah, and a handful of junior officers who were given the unpleasant task of arresting politicians. Chishti arrived at General Headquarters around 2 a.m., 5 July, and disclosed the names of those persons who had been taken into custody. By 2:15 a.m., Operation Fair Play had been substantially implemented. Some details:

Those taken into custody from the PPP were:

1. Mr Zulfikar Ali Bhutto
2. Mr Abdul Hafeez Pirzada
3. Maulana Kausar Niazi
4. Mr Mumtaz Ali Bhutto
5. Mr Hamid Raza Gilani
6. Sheikh Rashid
7. Mr Ghulam Mustafa Khar
8. General Tikka Khan

The PNA leaders arrested were:

1. Maulana Mufti Mahmud
2. Air Marshal (retired) Asghar Khan
3. Syed Mardan Ali Shah (Pir Pagaro)
4. Nawabzada Nasrullah Khan
5. Professor Ghafoor Ahmad
6. Mr Sherbaz Mazari
7. Maulana Shah Ahmed Noorani

The bureaucrats taken into custody included:

1. Mr Rao Abdul Rashid
2. Mr Masood Mahmud, Director General Federal Security Force
3. Mr Waqar Ahmad, Cabinet Secretary
4. Mr Akram Sheikh, Director, Federal Investigation Agency

5. Mr Muhammad Raza, ex-Deputy Director, Federal Security Force

The operation was carried out without a bullet being fired. Mr Abdul Hafeez Pirzada's servant was slapped before he confirmed his master's presence in the house. The door was broken open as loud knocks failed to bring a response from inside. A surprised and shocked Pirzada was found in his study. Regaining his composure, he enquired about the safety of Mr Bhutto and any split in the army. He wanted to go upstairs to get some cigarettes and his slippers. The officer arresting him did not wish to take a chance. He gave him his own packet of cigarettes and escorted him out.

The party that arrested Mr Pirzada was also to pick up Maulana Kausar Niazi. There was no response from the house, despite repeated ringing of the doorbell and knocking. A soldier climbed up to the first floor and contacted Maulana Kausar Niazi. He came out after changing his clothes, appearing shocked and surly. On request, he provided a pair of slippers for Mr Pirzada.

Mr Mumtaz Ali Bhutto asked no questions. He collected some medicines and accompanied the arresting officer.

Mr Rao Abdul Rashid, a retired police officer serving as the Director Intelligence Bureau, when arrested enquired, 'Which army has taken over?'

Some difficulty was experienced in locating the house of Mr Hamid Raza Gilani. The Aabpara Police Station provided a guide to identify the residence. At the time of his apprehension, just before dawn, he gave the impression that he was waiting to be picked up.

It took time to locate Mr Ghulam Mustafa Khar. He was missing from the Punjab House in Rawalpindi where he was reportedly staying. From the Punjab House, two guests of Mr Ghulam Mustafa Khar took the party to the residence of Mr Mustafa Khar's brother, Mr Arbi Khar, in Islamabad. The lady of the house informed the group that Mr Mustafa Khar was at the residence of his other brother, Mr Rehmani Khar, in Islamabad. The servants of that house were uncooperative. As the arresting officer tried to break open the door, Mr Rehmani Khar peeped out through the window and quickly disappeared. The party entered the house to find Mr Rehmani Khar having a telephone conversation. He froze as the officer put his hand on his pistol. Mr Rehmani Khar took the group to the State Bank Guest House from where Mr Ghulam Mustafa Khar was

THE MILITARY OPTION

arrested. His immediate inquiry was: 'What about Abdul Hafeez Pirzada and Mumtaz Ali Bhutto?' When informed that they had already been arrested, he relaxed in a sofa chair, took a deep breath and said: 'Thank God the devils have reached their destiny. I do not mind if you people even kill me now.' He said goodbye to his wife and accompanied the officer.

General Tikka Khan created a scene. As an adviser to the Prime Minister, his son Captain Tariq was his aide. The officer told Tariq that he had a message to deliver personally to General Tikka Khan. Tariq returned from his father's bedroom saying that the message be given to him and that he would not permit others to enter the bedroom. He was removed from the house. The officer then met General Tikka Khan, to face a barrage of questions: 'Who are you? Why have you entered my room without my permission? Who has sent you here?' The officer told him that he had been sent by his commander. 'Who is your commander?' Tikka enquired. The General insisted that he would not accompany the officer unless he first spoke to the Chief of Army Staff. Permission was denied. The General started thinking aloud: 'You can't arrest me like this. I am the father of this army which I have served for forty years. You cannot do that.' The officer told him that, notwithstanding his personal regards for him, he was determined to carry out his orders. General Tikka Khan calmed down, changed his clothes, and accompanied the officer.

Syed Mardan Ali Shah (Pir Pagaro) readily accompanied the officer who went to his residence to arrest him.

Air Marshal Asghar Khan was asleep. When told that he was being taken into custody, he checked the identity of the officer before accompanying him to the place of detention.

Professor Ghafoor Ahmad asked for the identity of the officer and wanted his warrant of arrest to be shown to him.

Nawabzada Nasrullah Khan, who was staying in Islamabad, asked no questions. He got ready within minutes, after changing and taking some luggage with him. Maulana Mufti Mahmud, who was picked up from his residence in a mosque in Rawalpindi City, took a few minutes to accompany the officer who had approached him for his arrest.

Mr Sherbaz Mazari, who had been staying in the MNAs' Hostel, Islamabad, was located at the residence of Sardar Shaukat Hayat in Islamabad. He was initially somewhat aggressive, but soon became normal, even jovial.

Maulana Shah Ahmad Noorani was taken into custody from the MNAs' Hostel, Islamabad. He changed his clothes before accompanying the arresting officer.

The arrest of the civil servants was uneventful. Mr Waqar Ahmad appeared surprised and enquired: 'Why, what has happened?' On getting the details, he said: 'I am happy. This was the only answer to the tense circumstances prevailing in the country.' His wife and children, sleeping in the adjoining rooms, remained unaware of his arrest. He left a note with his servant for his wife, reading: 'I am going to a cabinet meeting.'

Polite and respectful to them, the officers brought the arrested persons to an officers' mess in Chaklala, Rawalpindi. They were lodged in the bachelor officers' quarters, which had been kept vacant by Chishti, were allowed free access to each other, and were well looked after. Barring Air Marshal Asghar Khan, the other internees were barely equipped with the items of daily use. These were collected from their respective residences the following morning. Maulana Shah Ahmad Noorani requested the services of a barber to get his beard trimmed. He was obliged. Mr Sherbaz Mazari had himself shaved by the same barber. The detention was a benign affair.

General Zia kept all the corps commanders informed. He then telephoned General Muhammad Shariff, Chairman Joint Chiefs of Staff Committee, Admiral Muhammad Sharif, Chief of Naval Staff, and Air Chief Marshal Zulfiqar Ali Khan, Chief of Air Staff, and informed them of the ongoing operation. Admiral Sharif remarked: 'Well done.' Air Chief Marshal Zulfiqar heard the news and made noncommittal remarks. General Shariff felt sorry that this ultimate step had become inevitable. He wished the army well.

Brigadier Khawar called the Military Secretary to the President, Brigadier Saghir Hussain Syed, and the Military Secretary to the Prime Minister, Major-General Imtiaz Ali, to GHQ. Saghir, in his usual exuberant mood, arrived promptly. General Zia asked him to enquire from the President if it would be convenient for him to continue to perform the duties of the Head of State. Saghir inquired if he should disturb the President immediately or wait for him to wake up at his normal time, mentioning that the President was an early riser. It was getting close to 3 a.m. already. He was told to let the old man rest till his normal time. A couple of hours later, a bubbling Saghir returned to General Headquarters and told General Zia that President Fazal Elahi Chaudhry would not decline the request if the offer

THE MILITARY OPTION

was personally made to him by the Chief of Army Staff. Saghir was directed to arrange a meeting with the President in the early part of the morning.

Glum and agitated, Imtiaz complained that, soon after midnight, he had observed the movement of troops close to the Prime Minister's House. He made vain attempts to determine the cause of the abnormal happening. His soldier's instinct compelled him to investigate. He donned his uniform, came out of his house, and was soon met by a junior military officer. The officer respectfully told him that he would not permit any person, including him, to move around. This annoyed Imtiaz. He enquired from Zia about the personal safety of Mr Bhutto and was relieved to hear that the ex-Prime Minister and his family members would be safe. He was asked to convey that assurance to Mr Bhutto.

General Zia personally spoke to the ex-Prime Minister. The telephone system of the Prime Minister's House had intentionally not been disconnected. Mr Bhutto came on the line promptly, indicating that he was already awake. Addressing him as 'Sir', General Zia informed him that the political deadlock reached in the parleys between the government and the PNA had created a threat to national security. In the absence of a political agreement, he had reluctantly decided to exercise the military option and assume control of the country. Mr Bhutto neither contested that statement nor made any observation. He was informed that in order to defuse the prevailing tension, he and some of his PPP colleagues were being taken into custody for a short period. The PNA leaders were also being detained. General Zia said: 'You may not be as comfortable under detention as you are in your present house, but we will try our best to make life as easy for you as possible. You would be shifted to the Government House, Murree, tonight, where you would enjoy all the administrative facilities which are available in that house.'

General Zia concluded his statement by indicating that martial law would be lifted after holding free and fair elections and he was confident that the Prime Minister would return, with a fresh mandate from the people. Mr Bhutto thanked General Zia for talking to him personally. He enquired if his move to Murree could be delayed for a while and he be permitted to remain in the Prime Minister's House, along with his family members. General Zia acceded to that request. He went on to inform Mr Bhutto that during his stay in Murree, his Military Secretary and his aides would remain in attendance on him.

The general officers present in the office, after listening to the conversation, told General Zia that he had been too generous. Zia replied that the former Prime Minister deserved some special consideration. 'Besides,' he said, 'one should act with grace and style.'

Two of Mr Bhutto's children left Rawalpindi for Karachi on the morning of 5 July 1977. He himself was shifted from his residence to the Government House, Murree, at 4 p.m. on 5 July. His wife left for Karachi the same evening.

The Secretary of the Ministry of Law was directed to enquire from the Chief Justices of all the four Provincial High Courts if they would agree to become the Acting Governors in their respective provinces. He contacted them in the early hours of the morning. All of them accepted the offer. They were requested to meet General Zia in Rawalpindi on 5 July 1977.

It was time to go public. The Director of the Inter-Services Public Relations (ISPR), Colonel T. H. Siddiqui, was summoned to GHQ. He arrived, accompanied by Major Siddiq Salik. They were asked to prepare a press note for release to the media. It was too late for the morning newspapers to carry the news. A brief statement was sent to Radio Pakistan, Rawalpindi, just before the morning broadcast.

Stunned by its content, the Director of News would not permit its broadcast without first checking its authenticity with Mr Ijlal Haider Zaidi, Director General Radio Pakistan. Ijlal was no wiser either. As a good bureaucrat, he got confirmation from General Zia himself before giving the green signal to Radio Pakistan, Rawalpindi, to announce the news.

The concluding part of the 6 a.m. news bulletin said: 'The armed forces of Pakistan have taken over the administration of the country this morning. It has been announced by a military spokesman that top political leaders belonging to the PPP, including the former Prime Minister, Mr Zulfikar Ali Bhutto, and PNA leaders have been taken into temporary protective custody.'

On 5 July 1977, General Zia met Mr Ghulam Ishaq Khan, Secretary General of the Ministry of Defence, and promoted him to the rank of Secretary-General-in-Chief with the rank of a cabinet minister. He asked him to formulate a plan to run the administration at the federal and the provincial levels for the next few months.

General Zia also met Mr Justice Yaqub Ali, the Chief Justice of Pakistan, and informed him that he did not plan to abrogate the

THE MILITARY OPTION

Constitution. The Chief Justice suggested the formulation that 'it might be held in abeyance.' General Zia accepted that advice.

General Zia had an early morning meeting at the Presidency with President Fazal Elahi Chaudhry. Brigadier Saghir was in attendance. Zia apprised the President of his reasons for the military intervention. He told him about his plan to hold elections after three months and requested him to keep occupying his high office to enable him to benefit from his experience and wisdom. The President accepted the offer and enquired if he had consulted some legal expert. General Zia replied that he had briefly met the Chief Justice of Pakistan who had been helpful. The President reacted sharply. With a broad smile and in a humorous tone, he passed some unsavoury remarks about the person which are best omitted, and said that it might not be prudent to accept the advice given by Mr Justice Yaqub Ali at face value. The President suggested that legal opinion might be obtained from someone else. He pointedly expressed the view that a three-month framework for holding elections was optimistic.

The President had less than kind words for Bhutto. He briefly analysed the causes of Bhutto's downfall and said that 'Bhutto had concentrated too much power and authority in himself. He destroyed all the state institutions and kept sycophants around him.' He advised General Zia: 'Pick your team with great care.'

Saghir clearly recalls the President's advice given to General Zia on political matters in these words: 'PPP has an important role to play in the domestic politics. Do not destroy this party. It is true that some leaders with controversial integrity and dirty habits have joined it. Such persons should be legally disqualified from holding public office for a prolonged period of time. Cleanse it up, but keep it in being. As for the future, select your close team carefully. You may choose half a dozen honest and dedicated people and give them the task of preparing a plan to salvage the country.'[1] General Zia learnt that, under the thin veneer of amity between the President and the former Prime Minister, there existed a thick layer of dislike, if not hatred. Zia thanked the President and promised to remain in touch with him.

All the political internees spent the day in the officers' mess at Chaklala. Apprehensive, nervous, and shaken, the PPP leaders generally stayed aloof. On the other hand, the PNA internees were visibly cheerful. Some of them, expecting to be arrested by the Bhutto administration, had heaved a sigh of relief when the army personnel knocked at their doors on 5 July.

Chaklala was a temporary abode. In the evening of 5 July, 1977, the PPP internees were taken to Abbottabad, a hill resort in the NWFP. The PNA leaders were shifted to the serene hill station of Murree. Pir Pagaro was released. While in custody, the jocular Pir was in a talkative mood, supporting the military take-over. He predicted an early breakup of the PNA, as, in his assessment, Mr Bhutto's removal from power had 'removed the cohesive force which created it.' In the next election, assessed Pir Pagaro, while no single party was likely to gain a clear majority, the Muslim League and the Jamaat-i-Islami would fare better than other political parties. He was critical of Mr Mumtaz Bhutto for starting a hatred campaign against the settlers and *mohajirs* in Sindh. He forecast the break up of the PPP and disclosed that some PPP MNAs and MPAs in contact with the PNA were willing to change their political affiliations. Pir Pagaro remarked that Mr Bhutto had committed atrocities on the people and, when released, he would need an armed escort to move out of his house in Larkana.

In the afternoon, the three Governors-designate, Mr Justice Aslam Riaz Hussain (Punjab), Mr Justice Abdul Kadir Sheikh (Sindh), and Mr Justice Abdul Hakim Khan (NWFP) met General Zia. Justice Khair Baksh Marri, the Governor-designate of Balochistan, could not reach Islamabad because he missed the incoming flight from Quetta. Before meeting General Zia, the three Chief Justices had met the Chief Justice of Pakistan, whom they found tight-lipped and evasive.

My draft of General Zia's address to the nation in English, a maiden attempt at speech-writing, lacked bite, as I kept groping for populist phrases. Mercifully, General Zia decided to speak in Urdu, the national language of the country. A professional writer, Major Siddiq Salik, drafted the speech with rhythm, flow, and promises inserted in the text. It was ready just in time to be simultaneously broadcast and telecast on the electronic media.

Throughout the day, media correspondents kept asking 'who imposed martial law?' They got the answer when General Ziaul Haq, the Chief Martial Law Administrator and the Chief of Army Staff addressed the nation at 7 p.m. The twenty-minute address was one of the shortest speeches that the General made during the eleven years and forty-four days that he remained at the helm of the affairs in Pakistan. Some excerpts: 'I want to make it absolutely clear that I neither have any political ambitions nor does the army want to be detracted from its profession of soldiering. I was obliged to step in to fill the vacuum created by the political leaders. I have accepted this challenge as a true soldier of Islam. My sole aim is to organize free and fair elections which would be held in October this year. Soon after the polls, power will be transferred to the elected representatives of the people. I give a solemn assurance that I will not deviate from this schedule.'

The solemn assurance was short-lived. The elections remained elusive. The street power, which had paved the way for Zia's rise to authority, had weakened the ineffective political system still further. There was no serious and organized challenge to Zia's prolonged rule. After two postponements, elections were finally held at the federal and the provincial levels in February 1985. The promised three-month time schedule was extended to one hundred and two months.

In his address, General Zia termed the martial law government 'interim', in which President Fazal Elahi Chaudhry would remain the Head of State. A four-member Military Council was formed to assist the President in the discharge of his national duties. The Military Council was to deal with undefined 'important administrative matters' and comprised of the Chairman, Joint Chiefs of Staff Committee, and the Chiefs of Staff of the Army, the Navy, and the Air Force. Other salient points of the address were:

a. The civil courts were to keep functioning as before.

b. Martial Law Orders and Martial Law Regulations, if and when issued under unavoidable circumstances, could not be challenged in any court of law.

c. All agreements, commitments, and contracts signed by the outgoing government would be honoured.

d. The composition of the Interim Government was:

(1) The Chief Martial Law Administrator was the Chief Executive.

(2) The Federal Secretaries were to continue to head their respective ministries and departments.

(3) The Chief Justices of the Provincial High Courts would be Acting Governors of their respective provinces.

(4) The Provincial administrations would be headed by the Provincial Martial Law Administrators, and the Provincial Secretaries would continue to hold charge of their respective departments.

The same day a Proclamation was issued stating that:

a. The Constitution of the Islamic Republic of Pakistan shall remain in abeyance;

b. the National Assembly, the Senate and the Provincial Assemblies shall stand dissolved;

c. the Prime Minister, the Federal Ministers, Ministers of State, the Speaker and the Deputy Speaker of the National Assembly and the Provincial Assemblies, the Chairman and the Deputy Chairman of the Senate, the Provincial Governors, the Provincial Chief Ministers and the Provincial Ministers shall cease to hold office;

d. the President of Pakistan shall continue in office, and

e. the whole of Pakistan will come under martial law.

Much to the dismay of freedom lovers, Pakistan had once again fallen into the pit of martial law.

The fate of the country might have been different if, after the 1971 elections, Mr Bhutto had become the leader of the Opposition. But an out-of-power Bhutto did not suit his psyche. He had once remarked sarcastically that he was 'no Clement Attlee', a reference to Winston Churchill's deputy in the British War Cabinet. Mr Bhutto's rise to power in what remained of Pakistan had created hopes and expectations in the public mind. He had started on his mission with gusto and introduced a number of reforms at a quick pace. He once proudly remarked: 'If you Americans think Franklin Roosevelt had an amazing first hundred days, watch us.'[2]

For a person who had risen to power so dramatically, his fall from it was no less sudden. In a short spell of under six years, power corrupted Mr Bhutto. His lust for it was all-embracing. He was a master politician—ruthless, unforgiving, unscrupulous, and ready to sacrifice ethics to achieve his ambition: absolute power. The scion of a feudal family, Mr Bhutto believed that he was born to rule over others. For him, loyalty was a one-way street—others should follow him without reservations. He despised criticism, indulged in vendetta, and hounded friends and foes who crossed his line.

Tragically, Mr Bhutto brought about his own downfall. He weakened the judiciary, terrorized the bureaucracy into submission, destroyed state institutions, and disbelieved in the concept of loyalty of the opposition to the country. For him, democracy meant his staying in power. The means employed to achieve that end were irrelevant: any process that kept him in power was democratic. He relied heavily on a few hand-picked police officers, who succeeded in turning the country into a police state. This was the beginning of the end for Mr Bhutto. The rigged elections ignited the suppressed passions. The people rose against his high-handed policies. Mr Bhutto lost his credibility and, consequently, power. In the process, the country once again missed an opportunity to keep moving on the democratic path.

* * *

The military planners took no chances. Despite Mr Bhutto's low popularity graph, small contingents of army troops were deployed on 5 July as a show of force. They were, however, not used and were soon withdrawn.

The imposition of martial law was silently approved by the people of Pakistan as was evident from their conduct. The agitation came to an instant end and normalcy replaced chaos and unrest in the cities. The labour force went back to work; the wheels of industry started turning again; students returned to their classes; market-places hummed with activity. The administration regained its confidence and the law-enforcing agencies heaved a sigh of relief. The change came about without the use of force. Many people felt relieved. A section of the intelligentsia argued that General Zia had violated Article 6 of the Constitution—an act of treason. It foresaw a legal battle in the courts.

The removal of the PPP from power vindicated the position of the PNA. It felt elated. Some of its leaders started considering themselves taller than their actual stature. True, the public had risen to protest against the rigged elections. The PNA movement provided them a convenient platform to give vent to their feelings. The demonstrators were all anti-Bhutto, but all of them were not necessarily pro-PNA. The PNA leadership lost sight of this aspect.

The urge for political survival had inhibited Mr Bhutto from accepting the guilt of holding rigged elections. The imposition of martial law removed the pressure from the PPP, albeit temporarily. It felt that, with the passage of time, public hostility against it would subside, the PNA might disintegrate, and its prospects in the elections would brighten.

The civil servants, the police, the banks, the semi-autonomous establishments, and the administrative machinery in the public sector felt that they would be able to exercise more freely the power and authority that had been denied to them because of the political pressures and compulsions which had been imposed on them by the party in power. For these reasons, the imposition of martial law, despite being a draconian step, had an easy and acceptable start.

The promulgation of martial law was commented upon by the national Press. One newspaper called it 'A Bridge over an Abyss'.[3] A government-controlled newspaper published an editorial under the heading 'Corrective Interlude', and projected the military take-over as a patriotic action.[4] The editorial of a right-wing daily, captioned 'Determination and Promise of a Soldier of Islam', said: 'the mutual differences and personal animosity between the two sides were so intense and distrust of one another was so great that even after the categorical announcement of a consensus, the attending parties were as far apart as on the first day of the dialogue.'[5]

The editorial of the PPP newspaper said: 'General Zia's announcement that "the survival of the country lies in democracy alone" is heartening, for no other system of governance can lend stability to Pakistan and keep it united.'[6]

A weekly publication with socialist leanings commented: 'the two main contenders for power, thus, share the responsibility for creating, and then refusing to resolve Pakistan's worst—and, in a sense—its most meaningless crisis.'[7]

The weekly *Afrasia*, in its issue of 16-23 July, said in an editorial: 'Allah had heard the supplications of crores of helpless and oppressed human beings. The blood of men, women and children has brought dividends, and a cruel, wayward and corrupt ruler, who had become a curse for the nation, has been swept down from the pinnacle of power to the lowliness of the dust below.'

Political leaders, other than those of the PPP, did not hide their jubilation on the eclipse of Mr Bhutto from power. Pir Pagaro declared that if the armed forces had not taken this step, the resultant situation would have been so explosive that gory clashes would inevitably have sundered the nation, and the macabre plan of the former government, which had armed its party men to the teeth, would have succeeded.[8]

In a message sent from protective custody in Murree, Maulana Mufti Mahmud said that, with the promulgation of martial law, the ominous clouds of tribulation, that had cast their dark shadow on the nation, had blown away and the reasons given by General Zia (for imposing martial law) were convincing.[9] Air Marshal (retired) Asghar Khan said on the BBC: 'General Ziaul Haq had done well to take a timely step to intervene. He had saved the country from impending disaster.'[10]

Mian Tufail Muhammad, Amir of the JI, hailed 'the sincere and well-meaning views expressed by the Chief Martial Law Administrator.' Begum Nasim Wali Khan (NDP) called the *coup* a ray of hope'.

Bilateral relations with all countries remained undisturbed. The exit of Mr Bhutto did not raise political ripples in the country. General Zia assumed control without ado and fanfare. The changeover was generally accepted, at home and abroad, as an inevitable and a necessary evil. All the Pakistani ambassadors serving in different countries remained at their posts. Some comments appearing in the foreign press on the internal developments in Pakistan are quoted below to illustrate the international media reaction.

The Daily Telegraph said: 'Mr Bhutto, Pakistan's only outstanding politician, must shoulder the blame. The opposition were a poor lot, but he could have handled them better.'[11]

The Times editorial read: 'When generals take over government they are usually eloquent about their desire to get back to barracks. Often they do not go ... Meanwhile, the Pakistani people seem so far to have taken the military decision with complacence .... General Zia has started on a course which, like war itself, does not always go according to plan.'[12]

The Daily Mirror reported: 'Mr Bhutto, Pakistan's too powerful Prime Minister has been defeated by his own huge election victory ... But

Bhutto's road to democracy was harsh and autocratic. Zia is not a comic opera figure riding a paper tiger. He heads one of Asia's most powerful war machines.'[13]

Lewis M. Simmons wrote: '. . . Ultimately, the army decided to seize control rather than see its ranks shattered by internal dissent. Except for the bond of Islam, only the army holds Pakistan together. Had the handful of recent resignations by senior officers spread, civil war would have been the most likely outcome.'[14]

The Los Angeles Times editorial read: 'It was not so much the ambitions of the generals as it was the quarrelsome blundering of the politicians that led to this week's restoration of military rule in Pakistan.'[15]

A British leftist weekly reported in its editorial: 'Few tears are likely to be shed over the political demise of Zulfikar Ali Bhutto . . . A man of great intelligence and ability, he [Bhutto] increasingly came to rely on the methods of repression in order to preserve his own personal predominance.'[16]

The Baltimore Sun in its editorial of 8 July 1977 said: 'The arrogance of the deposed Prime Minister Zulfikar Ali Bhutto undid him in the end.'

The Statesman of Delhi wrote: 'By all accounts, the military coup in Pakistan has been greeted there with a sense of relief.'[17]

'Bhutto and Pakistan on Grim Trial' was the heading of the editorial published in another newspaper. Excerpts: 'Mr Bhutto combined arrogance and authoritarianism with a vainglorious, but not untalented demagogy, and these made a most dangerous political combination.'[18]

And, finally a lament by Mr Bhutto about himself: 'There has been a noticeable erosion in the credibility of the deposed Prime Minister, who boasted the other day that "My crime is that Pakistan has not produced a leader of my calibre" and "the Himalayas would weep the day I relinquish my office." '[19]

Verse 18 of Surah Luqman in the Holy Quran reads:

And Swell not Thy Cheek
(for Pride) at Men,
Through the Earth;
For God Loveth not
Any Arrogant Boaster.

CHAPTER 5

Voyage of Discovery

On 6 July 1977, General Zia asked me about the functioning of the Chief Martial Law Administrator's (CMLA) Secretariat during the 1969 martial law. The organizational structure was explained to him. Who should be his Principal Staff Officer for martial law work was his next question. I suggested the name of the Adjutant General, Major-General Muhammad Riaz. General Zia felt that Riaz did not possess any experience of martial law work. 'You had worked in the previous martial law,' said General Zia, adding, 'How about you roughing it out for the next three months in addition to your present assignment?' I hesitated, but Zia had already decided. In the Pakistan Army, officers are not consulted about their appointments. My reluctance was influenced by the division of the country under the Yahya regime. I had no heart to carry the stigma of involvement with yet another martial law—in any capacity. The norms of military discipline prevailed and General Zia carried the day.

General Zia wished to establish the proposed CMLA Secretariat anywhere except in the ex-Prime Minister's office block. 'I would not like to work in that office,' he said firmly. There could have been two reasons for this reluctance: either the inconvenience involved in changing an office for a mere three-month period did not suit him or he might have been superstitious.

A bare-bones organization for the CMLA Secretariat was established with the Chief of Staff as the senior-most officer to the CMLA. After a quick search, two small adjacent houses on Firdousi Road, Rawalpindi, were hired, and the Secretariat was established in them. The bedrooms, converted into offices, were small and crowded. There was no place to seat visitors. Security arrangements were inadequate. Office facilities were minimal. The working environment was uncomfortable. A ninety-day countdown being at the back of one's mind, such shortcomings were accepted and inconveniences ignored. All eyes were focused on 18 October, the date fixed for the general elections.

A three-tier organization was created to run the affairs of the state. The three components were:

A. *The Military Council* consisted of the Chairman, Joint Chiefs of Staff Committee (JCSC), and the Chiefs of Staff of the Army, the Navy, and the Air Force. Its meetings were invariably attended by Mr Ghulam Ishaq Khan, the Secretary-General-in-Chief, and by the Chief of Staff (COS) to the CMLA.

B. *The Martial Law Administrators' Conference* was attended by the martial law administrators of all the four provinces, the Chairman JCSC, the Deputy/Vice Chief of Army Staff, the army generals holding cabinet posts in the Federal Government, the Director General of Intelligence, Major-General Mujibur Rahman (while serving in the Ministry of Information), members of the Election Cell (while it functioned), and the COS to the President. The Brigadier (Martial Law) attended and kept notes. Till late 1979, these meetings were held in General Headquarters and the Principal Staff Officers also took part. Thereafter, the venue was shifted to the CMLA Secretariat and the PSOs did not participate.

C. *The Council of Secretaries* was later replaced by a Council of Advisers and, still later, by the Federal Cabinet.

The first few meetings of the Military Council highlighted its inadequacy. The Chief of Naval Staff, Admiral Sharif, supported General Zia's policies. The Chief of Air Staff, Air Chief Marshal Zulfiqar, a Bhutto supporter, adopted an ambivalent posture. The Chairman of the JCSC, General Shariff, despite being senior to General Zia, gave him unflinching respect, which the latter deserved as the Head of the Government. On his part, General Zia reciprocated by asking General Shariff to chair the meetings. The atmosphere was congenial, with decisions taken unanimously. However, the members were placed at a disadvantage. They did not have access to information and statistics needed to make a meaningful contribution to the decision-making process. Besides, the concept of joint responsibility ran counter to that of autocratic rule. It soon became obvious that, despite its symbolic political value, the Military Council was destined to wither away. Gradually, its meetings became less frequent and it soon became a dormant body. It was neither formally disbanded nor was a conscious effort made to revive its functioning. Its slow death was a case of good riddance.

The Martial Law Administrators Conference was a perennial policy-making organ which took major policy decisions on all matters of substance. These meetings were normally held one day before the cabinet meetings, at an interval of four to six weeks, except when some urgent business demanded an early session. Towards the middle of 1984, and more significantly after the referendum of December that year, the frequency of holding the MLAs' Conference decreased appreciably. The President increasingly preferred to discuss important issues with the Governors concerned individually, rather than dealing with them in the open full house.

The ambassadors accredited to Pakistan were briefed about the imposition of martial law. The United States' Ambassador suggested to General Zia that Pakistan's ongoing nuclear programme be downgraded. The unsolicited advice was the beginning of vigorous pressure exerted by America against Pakistan's nuclear research and development effort. Ambassador Arthur Hummel and his successors in Islamabad took time to learn that, on the nuclear issue, Zia would not compromise.

Lieutenant-General Ghulam Hassan Khan, the CMLA's Adviser on National Security, had his office in the former Prime Minister's Secretariat. He reported that the office record in Mr Bhutto's office was being burnt under the orders of Major-General Imtiaz Ali. He proposed that the office be sealed off to preserve the historic documents. To his dismay, the suggestion was not accepted. In the words of General Zia: 'Our tenure is limited and the goal clear. We do not have the time to dig into history.'

Much to the delight of the wrongdoers, bonfires continued destroying the truth. By the time the Prime Minister's Secretariat Office record was eventually taken over, it was too late—a part of the national archives and the documentary evidence of the deeds and the misdeeds of policymakers had been reduced to ashes. A part of our national history was lost forever.

Imtiaz confessed to the author in 1977 that, after holding a Stocktaking Board, 'the old, surplus and unwanted files and letters had been destroyed by burning, as a lot of trash had accumulated over the years.' The 'old and unwanted trash' might have been an invaluable source of inside information for historians. To a question as to why this surplus material was not destroyed while Bhutto was in power, Imtiaz gave an unconvincing reply that the rush of work had prevented a cleansing effort.

General Zia's first press conference held on 11 July 1977 was a fiasco. With blazing searchlights and clicking cameras focused on him, he delivered sermons on religion, ethics, and morality in a monotone. His answers were neither brief nor crisp. His media experts blundered in exposing him to the spotlight without adequate homework. General Zia disclaimed any political ambition and advised the Press not to overplay his personal image. He criticized the policy of victimization and witch-hunting of political opponents and gave an assurance that he would not amend the Constitution and would hold elections within ninety days. He claimed that the joint press statement of 27 April 1977 was issued by the services chiefs 'to strengthen the hands of the government and inject indirectly sanity in the minds of the opposition.' He called Mr Bhutto, 'a very tenacious fighter and a great politician—a man with a great sense of history.'

On 15 July 1977, General Zia went to Murree to meet the detained political leaders. Lieutenant-General Chishti and I were also present. Maulana Mufti Mahmood's meeting with General Zia was arranged at Headquarters 12 Division. He came alone and requested that Nawabzada Nasrullah Khan and Professor Ghafoor Ahmed should be allowed to join the discussion. The request showed the difficulty of leading a loosely-knit alliance. Both the gentlemen soon arrived. The three PNA leaders were jubilant about the fall of the previous government. Hatred of Bhutto was writ large on their faces and imbued their conversation. They confessed that Tehrik-i-Istiqlal and Jamiat-i-Ulema-i-Pakistan were likely to opt out of the PNA. Maulana Mufti Mahmud termed the detention of the PNA leaders unjust. By arresting them, he complained, the aggressors and victims had been equated. General Zia told them that they would soon be set free to enable them to prepare for the forthcoming elections. The meeting took place in a relaxed atmosphere. Maulana Mufti Mahmud invited General Zia to have lunch with them. He accepted the offer.

At the lunch-table, the PNA leaders expressed confidence that they would win the elections by a wide margin. General Zia told Air Marshal Asghar Khan, who had joined us for lunch, that his letter to the military commanders inciting them against the Bhutto government was an act of sedition for which he could face trial. Air Marshal Asghar Khan, however, felt that he had committed no wrong by writing that letter.

The author, General Khalid Mahmud Arif.

General Muhammad Ziaul Haq.

Zulfikar Ali Bhutto.

Zia, as Colonel Commandant, greeting Bhutto, the Colonel in Chief of the Armoured Corps, at Kharian on 1 November 1974

Bhutto reviewing the Passing Out Parade at the Pakistan Military Academy, Kakul, on 18 November 1976.

VCOAS Arif greeting President and COAS Zia during a visit to Corps Headquarters, Multan, on 25 February 1986.

The author with President Ziaul Haq and the Minister for Finance, Ghulam Ishaq Khan, at the Presidency in Rawalpindi.

VOYAGE OF DISCOVERY

In the afternoon, General Zia, General Chishti, and I drove to the Punjab Governor's House in Murree to meet an immaculately dressed but visibly depressed Mr Bhutto. As we entered the lounge, General Zia enquired from Mr Bhutto if he would like to meet him alone or in the company of the others. Mr Bhutto answered, 'Let General Chishti be present.'

The Zia-Bhutto meeting covered a wide range of issues. Mr Bhutto, outwardly calm and congenial, was inwardly a worried person. While hiding his bitterness, he had some unsolicited advice to offer. 'Do not withdraw the Hyderabad conspiracy case, do not pull back the troops from Balochistan, do not trust the PNA leadership, and keep General Yahya Khan interned for his own safety,' was the gist of advice given by Mr Bhutto to Zia.

The military option might have been necessary, stated Mr Bhutto, but the future was more important. 'It is for you to plan it well and while doing so, if you need any help, you can count on my support. Once the dust settles down,' said Mr Bhutto, 'we could run the country together.' He pointed out that the military intervention had constitutional implications and hastened to add that he knew how to overcome them. The legalities need not cause any worry, he emphasized again. Answering a Bhutto query, General Zia indicated that the detained politicians would be set free within days. Bhutto complained that while the PNA interned leaders enjoyed the advantage of staying at one place, his PPP colleagues, kept in Abbottabad, were not available to him for consultation. General Zia acceded to his request that they be moved to Murree. Zia also told Mr Bhutto that he had intervened reluctantly, was determined to remain neutral, and would hold fair elections on schedule. Thereafter, 'I will revert to the barracks leaving the field free for you to manage the affairs of the state as you consider appropriate,' said Zia.

The shifting of the detained PPP politicians from Abbottabad to Murree was not without a mini drama. While in Abbottabad, Mr Ghulam Mustafa Khar had requested Lieutenant-General Chishti that he be lodged separately from the other detained PPP colleagues. On his way to Murree, Khar met Chishti at Rawalpindi, ostensibly to seek permission to meet his wife. There was a hidden motive behind the halt: Khar sought an interview with General Zia.

General Zia met Mr Khar in his office at GHQ in the presence of Chishti and myself. Mr Khar's main attempt during the meeting, which lasted over an hour, was to win General Zia's confidence by portraying himself as an injured person—once liked, but lately out of favour with Mr Bhutto. While claiming to be an ardent PPP worker and an admirer of Mr Bhutto, he bitterly criticized him for falling under the evil influence of political opportunists. As a consequence, Khar had faced suffering and persecution, left the party, and later rejoined it, only to strengthen Mr Bhutto's hands. Despite Khar's sacrifices, Mr Bhutto remained cool towards him. The mighty errors made by Mr Bhutto, leading to his own downfall, were the result of his autocratic style and of faulty advice, said Khar. Being a founder member of the PPP and a party confidant, he was privy to many secrets. But he believed in placing the country before everything else—including his party, claimed Mr Khar.

Mr Khar had carefully rehearsed his performance. He said enough to indicate that he could be trusted by the administration, without saying so in clear terms. He used the politician's technique—a glib tongue and ambiguity—to keep his options open.

General Zia saw through Khar's double talk. 'How could a person whose loyalty to his own political benefactor was suspect be trusted by others?' said Zia after the interview. Mr Khar's image remained questionable in Zia's mind.

On 15 July 1977, Mr Justice Mushtaq Hussain was appointed as the Chief Election Commissioner. His name was suggested by the Attorney General, Mr S. Sharifuddin Pirzada. The Chief Election Commissioner took up his assignment with vigour. A committee was formed under his leadership, to frame the election rules. Its members were Mr Justice Nasim Hasan Shah, the Attorney General, and an eminent advocate, Mr A. K. Brohi.

All the arrested PPP and PNA leaders were released on 28 July. General Zia met them in Murree on that day, before they were set free. He cautioned them not to inflame public tempers during the pre-election campaign. Mr Bhutto requested a neutral and just administration during the election and once again took the initiative to tell General Zia that he knew how to handle the constitutional aspects of the military take-over. The other PPP leaders who briefly met General Zia after the Bhutto-Zia *tete-a-tete* complained that the print media was maligning Mr Bhutto.

With the release of the leaders, limited indoor political activity was permitted from 1 August. On 2 August, the Chief Election Commissioner announced the election schedule. Polling for the National

Assembly and for all the Provincial Assemblies seats was to be held simultaneously on 18 October 1977. The PNA agitation had visibly shaken Mr Bhutto. While in custody in Murree, he showed his anxiety. On the eve of his release, he made two requests to the CMLA. Firstly, he requested to be allowed to retain his personal weapons for 'family and emotional considerations.' On the imposition of martial law, all weapon-holders had been directed to deposit their personal weapons in their respective police stations. His second request was that a police guard be provided at his residence, as he was apprehensive about the security of his family members. Both the requests were accepted.

The three weeks of detention provided an unplanned opportunity to the army authorities to observe the lifestyle of the PPP and the PNA leaders at close quarters. Though incarcerated, they were treated as state guests and looked after with meticulous care and consideration. As a group, the PNA leaders led a simple life. Their first love was politics. The quality of cuisine served to them remained high on their discussion list. The PPP leaders were no less interested in political matters. Many of them enjoyed their pre-dinner drinks. A more exclusive group watched pornographic video films after dinner. These items of pleasure were procured through the obliging lower staff. They were recovered from them during a search by the security elements deployed on duty and were consequently confiscated. Such was the life the distinguished guests lived while in custody.

Mr Bhutto was an expert in paying a backhanded compliment. While leaving the Punjab Governor's House, he pointedly thanked a junior army officer on security duty for 'all you have done for us.' The young officer kept wondering if the remark was a compliment or a rebuke.

* * *

General Zia was suddenly catapulted to a position of high visibility. Commanding the army under the shadow of a charismatic and populist Head of the Government was a low-profile job. With Mr Bhutto out of power, and with General Zia at the helm of national affairs, the eyes of the masses were suddenly focused on him. A relatively obscure soldier overnight came into extreme prominence, enjoying total and unchecked authority. His word was law. People at home and abroad were keen to learn more about him. His actions and statements received wide coverage. He started with a plus to his credit. His 5 July address to the nation was down-to-earth and straightforward. The national malaise identified by him was accepted even by his critics. The time-frame given by him for putting the country back on the rails of democracy was appreciated. His subsequent assurances not to deviate from that schedule won him respect. His statement that he had no political ambition was accepted at face value. He was seen as a military professional, a technician, God-fearing and religious, calm, relaxed, and competent, a person who had intervened reluctantly in the national interest, whose sincerity was above-board, and who was expected to keep his word. General Zia's exposure to the public enabled the observers to watch his performance and assess the person hidden in him—the real Zia, hitherto unknown.

Zia was born on 12 August 1924, into a non-military, middle-class, religious family residing in the city of Jullundur in East Punjab, India. His school days were uneventful. His early education completed, his father gathered the resources to get his son admitted to St Stephen's College, New Delhi. Zia used to fondly recall his stay in that alma mater, which groomed him for adult life. While in college, he fasted during the month of Ramazan and regularly offered prayers five times a day as ordained in Islam.

The Second World War interrupted young Zia's academic career. He left his studies in the fourth year of college to join the Indian Army. After the completion of his military training at the Officers' Training School, Mhow, India, he was granted commission on 12 May 1945 and was posted to 13 Lancers, then serving in Burma. This was a former horse cavalry unit which, on mechanization, had been re-equipped with tanks.

Second Lieutenant Zia was soon in trouble. On Eid day, he visited the Junior Commissioned Officers of his unit in their mess in his native dress. In those days, the British-prescribed custom of military service demanded all officers to wear European clothes when outside their places of residence. By wearing the national dress, even on a religious occasion, Zia had committed an 'un-officer-like crime.' His commanding officer, an Englishman, was furious. Such an irregularity from a youngster made a mockery of military discipline and had tarnished the image of his unit. The act could not go unpunished. As an admonishment, Zia was posted to another unit—6 Lancers. He served briefly in Malaya and Java, and at the end of the Second World War returned to India along with his unit. In August 1947, at the birth of Pakistan, Lieutenant Zia was posted to the Technical Training Wing of the freshly raised Armoured Corps Centre at Nowshera. He subsequently commanded the Boys' Wing located at Cherat. There, he introduced a system by which the first parade every morning was preceded by recitation by a recruit trainee from the Holy Quran.

Zia married Shafiqa, a cousin, at Lahore on 10 August 1950. The couple developed an enviable understanding and comradeship which matured fast and remained firm to the end. Their union produced five children—two sons and three daughters. Zain, the youngest child, was born with a congenital deformity. The darling of her father, she was hard of hearing and had a speech defect. So strong was her hold on him that her demands—fair or unfair, possible or impossible—were orders to Zia which he could not refuse. The child was as adorable as she could be moody and insistent. Zia could not upset her. At times she demanded almost the moon and got it too, notwithstanding the personal and official hurdles in the way.

In September 1950, Zia joined the Guides Cavalry. In his decade-long stay in this unit he developed a lifelong close understanding and friendship with some of his brother officers. In their hours of leisure, they met and recalled with nostalgic pleasure the time spent together in yesteryears. Despite his elevation in life, Zia talked to them on equal terms. On their part, they gave him due respect.

Zia graduated with credit from the prestigious Command and Staff College, Quetta, in 1955, where he was later assigned as an instructor. His performance in the course earned him important staff assignments in his subsequent military life. He served as a Brigade Major in an armoured brigade, General Staff Officer 2 (Major) in the Military Operations Directorate at GHQ, General Staff Officer 1 (Lieutenant-Colonel) in an armoured division, Assistant Adjutant and Quarter Master General (Lieutenant-Colonel) in an infantry division and Colonel Staff in an armoured division. He commanded a tank regiment—22 Cavalry—an armoured brigade, an armoured division, and a corps. He became the Chief of Army Staff at the age of 52.

Zia assumed command of 22 Cavalry under peculiar circumstances. This unit had had a lacklustre performance under a commanding officer who had earned the ire of a demanding Major-General Gul Hassan. Zia, then serving as a staff officer with General Gul Hassan, was posted to command 22 Cavalry. Accepting the challenge, he soon brought that unit to such a state of professional excellence that it became the envy of the formation. Zia's performance proved the point that no unit is bad. It is the officers, in particular the commanding officer, that make it so.

Promoted to Brigadier in 1969, Zia commanded 9 Armoured Brigade. Within months, he went on a deputation to Jordan where he served for two years. At that time, King Hussein had problems with Syria and the Palestinian Liberation Organization. Zia helped the Jordanian land forces in their military operations—a task which he seldom discussed.

Zia commanded 1 Armoured Division (1972-5) with gusto. His style was direct, personal, and, at times, unconventional. His weekly meetings were marathon sessions, held in a frank and cordial atmosphere. A patient listener, Zia took copious notes, picked up ideas, allowed free discussion, formulated a hectic training schedule, and seldom minced his words—whether in praise of good work or criticism of a fault. Never at a loss for words, he summed up the meetings and the after-exercise critiques in a leisurely manner. The time factor had little relevance with him. Punctuality was not his hallmark. A stickler for neat and meticulous work, Zia liked lucidly-made presentations and well planned written effort. A flaw would upset him. He would read the drafts carefully and sign them only if they were error-free and cleanly typed.

Zia's visitors encroached on his time. He did not show the door to those who entered his office. His military secretary was always on tenterhooks, attempting to fix appointments for those held on his ever-expanding waiting list. He usually slept after midnight. After his pre-dawn prayers, he would sleep again for a couple of hours and start his public work at about 10:30 a.m. Frequently, he was a little tense in the morning. He would give long instructions to his personal staff for the day and express annoyance on minor matters. An hour later, he would be a different person—pleasant and receptive. As the day, progressed his cheerfulness returned to him fast. His idiosyncracy for excellence drove his staff crazy. There was a contradiction in his personality: while he demanded clockwork perfection from others, he did not operate by a set system himself.

Zia handpicked his military secretary and aides with care. He had a fatherly attitude towards them and treated them as a part of his family. His military secretary, as in charge of his personal affairs, held an unenvious appointment. In many matters Zia would not bother about rules and regulations and failed to draw a distinction between public and personal expenditure. Loyalty demanded that his military secretary point out the omission—an act that could draw ire. At times, he would show anger if his personal staff acted in a style which was not to his liking. Such pressures unnerved them. Three successive military secretaries requested me to get them posted out, as they felt that they had lost the confidence of the President. One of them recalled that, while absorbed in major policy matters, he would suddenly remember some minor issue like the menu for a dinner, the gifts for a guest, or the shabby dress of a police constable standing on the roadside. He called Zia 'the king of trivia'.

Endowed with considerable stamina, Zia could keep awake all night without showing signs of fatigue. He slept well during travel and could doze off while sitting in a chair. He collected books, read them sparingly, and hated file work. To put it mildly, his official mail was always in arrears and it needed a constant herculean effort to convince him to devote a part of his time to clearing his piled-up desk. So frustrating was the experience of cajoling or goading him to do so that, after failing in my repeated attempts to correct the situation, I decided to quit in sheer exasperation. In February 1979, as COS, I wrote to the President thus:

> Because of other commitments, disposal of official mail is given a low priority by the President resulting in considerable delays. This generates criticism against the efficiency of CMLA Secretariat which hurts my professional pride. Since I have failed to correct this situation, I respectfully request that the President may be graciously pleased to relieve me of my present appointment.

General Zia's Personal Assistant, Taj, who typed the draft, stood motionless when I signed the paper. 'Please don't leave the President. It will isolate him,' pleaded Taj with palpable sincerity. Touched by his loyalty, I did not submit the letter to General Zia. Apart from the emotional appeal of a dutiful subordinate, another factor influenced the change. Mr Bhutto's case was in a crucial stage. My exit at that juncture might have created an erroneous impression in the public mind of a split in the military hierarchy.

Quick in making promises, Zia was sympathetically disposed towards those who sought his attention and help. He honoured his pledges at his leisurely convenience and liked the applicants to keep reminding him occasionally. Generous by nature, he spent public funds without reservation to provide relief to the needy people. Some people took undue advantage of his financial liberalism, causing him embarrassment when the false pretexts of their requests were detected.

Zia was a family man. Under his visibly firm exterior lay a kind heart pulsating with love and affection for his family. When away from home, Zia would call his wife every night. When that was not possible, he would write long letters to her. Shafiqa and Zia were a loving couple—humble, smiling, and hospitable. Both were affable and charming, and put their visitors instantly at ease. Many of Zia's actions concerning his relatives and close friends had the hand of his wife behind them. She generally stayed aloof in other matters of statecraft.

A devout Muslim with a sense of mission, Zia worked hard for the consolidation of the Islamic *Ummah*. He was a broad-minded person whose personal life had been free of scandal. He believed in pan-Islamism. While he practised his faith, he did not impose his belief on others. Zia was affectionately called a 'maulvi' (religious teacher) by some of his old and close friends. It was a matter of faith with him to preach Islam and see an Islamic polity emerge in Pakistan. He felt that intellectual liberalism had eroded the moral fibre of the permissive western society. He considered Islam a strong shield to avoid such a decay in the Muslim world.

On issues of substance, Zia did not compromise. While he listened to a broad cross-section of views—pleasant, hostile, or unpalatable—with patience, humility, and ease, he usually acted on the dictates of his own head and heart.

In his early adulthood, Zia had been an excitable and irritable man: a wrong act would touch a raw nerve and cause a surge of temper. He unburdened himself by using unprintable foul language. On one occasion, he demoted an officer on the spot. With the passage of time, a transformation occurred. Age, experience, and responsibility mellowed him. He became tolerant and understanding beyond measure.

In March 1979, the Military Council recommended that the award of Nishan-i-Imtiaz (Military) be conferred on General Zia, 'in recognition of his outstanding contribution to the enhancement of professionalism and efficiency of the Army.' While being grateful for the trust and confidence shown to him, Zia declined to accept the offer 'for obvious reasons'. ' Let my work,' he wrote on the file, 'be better judged by posterity.'

Zia had no respect for time. Punctuality was not his forte—except in the case of prayers and diplomatic engagements. So pronounced was this quality that one wondered how he survived in the army service and rose to the top. This contradiction defies a rational explanation. Perhaps he was just lucky.

Zia was allergic to changing those of his household staff who had earned his affection. Some grew too big for their boots and misused the name of their boss, seeking their own advantage. A soldier valet of Zia had served beyond service limits. Durrani, the Military Secretary, suggested that he be retired, pointing out that at times he behaved like a devil. Zia agreed. Weeks later, a day before the person was to retire, Zia told Durrani, 'I would rather live with an old devil than a new one. Get the valet's retirement order cancelled.'

Zia talked to dignitaries and his visitors with ease and grace. A pleasant conversationalist, he quickly developed an equation with others. It always fascinated him to learn how some leaders had managed to stay in power for long periods of time. He enquired of the secret of the longevity of their rule from the Presidents of Romania, North Korea, and Nigeria, and the Prime Minister of Singapore.

In political talk, there is usually a gap between rhetoric and reality. Zia practised this successfully. Guided by his sixth sense, he could anticipate developments and made plans to meet them. His style of work was personal and centralized. One of his close subordinates harshly commented that he administered the country as if he was commanding a unit in the army. National institutions were weakened during his rule.

On 31 October 1984, Zia was presiding over a meeting in the Governor House, Peshawar, when news about the assassination of Mrs Indira Gandhi was received. While flying back to Islamabad, he told his military staff on board that God Almighty had taken care of all those persons who had harmed Pakistan.

Brigadier Mahmud Ali Durrani, Zia's Military Secretary for over three years, listed Zia's most striking qualities as humility, patience, coolness under pressure, affection for the poor people, and a deeply religious approach.[1] He reflected for a while when asked about Zia's main weaknesses. His reply was procrastination, hypocrisy, and a lack of high intellect. Zia's main achievements as assessed by him were a successful foreign policy towards the USA and India, his Afghan policy, spreading the popularity of Islam (despite the emergence of 'isms'), and the economic stability given to the country. He quoted

Zia's main failures as the Sindh situation, weakening of the political system, the personality cult, erosion of civil and military institutions, and his tendency to push matters under the carpet. Durrani was asked to name three persons who might have contributed most to damaging Zia's image. He chose to list Mr Muhammad Aslam Khattak and Lieutenant-Generals Refaqat and Hamid Gul. He was asked to name three individuals who might have conspicuously assisted Zia in prolonging his rule. He named Mr Ghulam Ishaq Khan for steering the economic and financial policies and giving unqualified support, and Lieutenant-General Ghulam Jilani Khan for governing the biggest province (Punjab) from the mid-1980s onwards and leaving it behind fairly tranquil. The third name quoted by him is better omitted.

If General Zia was being discovered by his critics and admirers, he was himself aghast to see the ugly face of the hitherto little known Bhutto administration. Mr Bhutto's authoritarian style and revengeful nature had put a tight lid on the entire spectrum of Pakistan's political and administrative life. Many unpleasant truths were swept under the carpet as a matter of state policy. The instances of oppression, and misuse of authority had remained a state secret. Bhutto's fall suddenly removed the lid of secrecy. Immediately, the bits and pieces of the hitherto suppressed truth and acts of terror started surfacing everywhere, painting a grim, ugly, and pathetic picture of the past. A few state-sponsored acts of violence and police excesses are narrated to illustrate the point.

The Liaquat Bagh Case

In 1973, the Opposition parties formed a United Democratic Front (UDF). UDF announced the holding of a public meeting on Pakistan Day, 23 March, at Liaquat Bagh, Rawalpindi, to be addressed by a number of Opposition leaders. Mr Bhutto, perennially short of tolerance, did not relish the idea of the Opposition projecting their programmes to the people and criticizing his government. A plan was prepared to disrupt the UDF meeting, using state power. According to the President of the UDF, the Pir of Pagaro: 'Lakhs of people gathered for the meeting were fired upon with rifles and automatic weapons. Incendiary and tear-gas shells were thrown at the crowds. Men in the uniform of the Federal Police and the PPP Guards were seen firing at innocent, unarmed and peaceful people.'

The Pir of Pagaro disclosed at a press conference on 24 March that, before the meeting, he received a telephone call from the Governor of the Punjab advising him not to attend it. He declined to oblige. He was then requested by the Governor to delay his arrival at the venue of the meeting by at least half an hour. The Governor also promised police protection for him. At 2 p.m., the Opposition leaders, Pir Pagaro, Chaudhry Zahur Elahi, Khan Abdul Wali Khan, Sardar Shaukat Hayat Khan, Professor Ghafoor Ahmed, and Mr Ajmal Khattak were present on the dais. As the meeting commenced, it was fired upon from different sides of the ground. As a consequence, eleven persons died and eighty were wounded. The government blamed the National Awami Party for causing the disturbance. The charge was refuted by, among others, the former Governor of the North-West Frontier Province, Arbab Sikandar Khan Khalil who said: 'It was inconceivable that a party would disturb its own public meeting by resorting to firing on the people who had come to hear its leaders.'

The former Governor of Balochistan, Mr Ghaus Bux Bizenjo at a press conference at Lahore said that the meeting had been disrupted by the government and the police.[2] The use of automatic weapons and incendiary shells pointed towards the involvement of the police as these weapons were not in the possession of common people. A case registered in the police station the same day remained 'under investigation' till martial law was declared in July 1977. The Opposition alleged that the plan had been hatched by the government itself, in which its higher leadership was involved.

The Dalai Camp

Mian Iftikhar Tari and Chaudhry Muhammad Irshad, ministers in the Punjab Government, were supporters of Mr Ghulam Mustafa Khar, the former Chief Minister and Governor of the Punjab. In subsequent years, Mr Khar fell foul of Mr Bhutto. In sympathy, Tari and Irshad left the government and resigned from the PPP. Mr Bhutto, hating non-conformists, disapproved of the voice of dissent in or outside his party. The administration turned against Tari and Irshad. The name of Mian Muhammad Aslam, another party dissident, was added to the list. The cases of these three victims of terror were commented upon by Amnesty International in its report on Pakistan for the year 1976 in these words:

Chaudhry Mohammad Irshad was arrested on 6 October, 1975. His arrest at Gujranwala was witnessed by his younger brother, Chaudhry Mohammad Nawaz, and Mr. Z. A. Bajwa, a member of the National Assembly. In an affidavit presented to the Lahore High Court on 5 November, 1975, Raja Mohammad Afzal Khan, advocate, stated that he had seen Mr. Irshad in Dalai Camp, a military detention camp in Azad Kashmir. The government have denied any knowledge of his arrest. Another missing member of the Provincial Assembly allegedly abducted is Mian Iftikhar Tari. On October 10, 1975, Mr. Tari was granted interim bail before arrest after claiming that his renunciation of membership of the Pakistan Peoples' Party placed him in immediate danger of arrest. On October 15, he was taken from his home and has not been heard of since that date. Raja Mohammad Afzal Khan, who had also made a statement about the other missing MPA, claimed in the court that he had seen Tari in Dalai Camp, Azad Kashmir.

The sudden disappearance of the politicians became a mystery. The federal and the provincial governments disclaimed their arrest or custody. They were illegally abducted by the Federal Security Force (FSF), brought to the police lines in Islamabad, and were transferred to the custody of the Deputy Inspector-General of Police, Azad Kashmir, who secretly lodged them in the Dalai Camp in Azad Kashmir. This camp was chosen for the illegal detention because Azad Kashmir was outside the legal jurisdiction of Pakistan's courts. While inside the Dalai Camp, the inmates were subjected to physical and mental torture. Both the gentlemen were quietly released on 6 July 1977, one day after the Bhutto administration fell. Months later, they narrated the stunning stories of the atrocities committed on them to the people of their country in a televised programme.

The Bhutto influence removed, their release spurred into action the hitherto blocked process of law. The pending writ petitions in the Punjab High Court were revived, together with the related contempt proceedings and that of unlawful confinement. Some officers of the FSF were convicted of contempt of the High Court. The court found Mr Masood Mahmud, the Director General of the FSF, guilty of 'the gravest contempt, unparalleled in the annals of legal history.' The judgment went on to read, 'The extent of damage done to this court and to the judicial process will be apparent from the fact that, since October 1975, the proceedings in the *habeas corpus* petition and in one contempt petition remained pending in this court. The Provincial Government, through its two Deputy Secretaries, denied that it had anything to do with it. On behalf of the Federal Government, the Deputy Attorney-General denied the implication of the FSF'.

The Death of Six Hurs

The Pir of Pagaro, the spiritual leader of the Hurs in Sindh, was a political opponent of Mr Bhutto. The Prime Minister's Chief Security Officer, Mr Saied Ahmad Khan, prepared an anti-Hur contingency plan to demolish the Pir's influence by subduing his followers. A strategy of indirect approach was used to tame a political foe. Saied wrote to Mr Bhutto on 15 May 1973: 'A number of prominent followers and khalifas of the Pir are involved in one form or another for violation of land reforms. They have not been effectively and speedily dealt with. This aspect may be examined and effective measures taken to give a stunning blow to such of them as are recalcitrant and still continue in their anti-government activities.'[3]

On 17 May 1973, Mr Bhutto 'approved' the proposal. Mr Saied Khan and Jam Sadiq Ali, a minister in the Sindh cabinet, then conducted the anti-Hur operation.

The White Paper on the Performance of the Bhutto Regime, Vol III, gives the details: 'On October 5, 1973, one Mr Ali Bakhsh Junejo, an active member of the People's Party in Sanghar district and a close associate of Jam Sadiq Ali was murdered in Sanghar town by some unidentified men. On the following day, six Hurs, namely Mehbub Sinjhrani, Umaid Ali Sinjhrani, Jan Mohammad Sinjhrani, Hanzo Bahnejo, Syed Ali Sher and Dadan alias Allah Dad Wadho, went to attend the court of Mr Imdadullah Unar, the District Magistrate, Sanghar, where proceedings under the Goonda Act were pending against them. The District Magistrate handed them over to police custody, but in the record they were allegedly marked absent and non-bailable warrants were issued against them. The next hearing of the case was fixed for October 17, 1973. They were allegedly confined in the lock-up of the Sanghar police station. During the night they were taken out, handcuffed and driven out in a van, escorted by a police party, towards Kanan Mori of Ban Wah. Jam Sadiq Ali, Mr Imdadullah Unar, and Mr Ghulam Shabbir Kalyar, the Superintendent of Police, followed them in two other vehicles. On reaching Kanan Mori, the detained persons were boarded off and reportedly shot dead, under the false cover of an encounter with the police.'[4]

In August 1977, the Federal Investigating Agency (FIA), under instructions from the government, registered a case relating to these murders. In the challan (charge sheet) Jam Sadiq Ali was shown as an absconder whom the trial court later declared a proclaimed offender. The judgment announced by the trial court on 18 November 1981 resulted in the conviction of some accused persons.

Soon after 5 July 1977, Jam Sadiq Ali sought permission from the MLA Sindh, Lieutenant-General Jahanzeb Arbab, for a short visit to Saudi Arabia to perform *Umra*. The ruse worked when the unsuspecting Jahanzeb Arbab, with the approval of General Zia, granted permission. Jam Sadiq Ali stayed abroad in self-exile in London for the next eleven years. On his return to Pakistan in 1988, he was granted bail before arrest by the Sindh High Court. The Benazir government promptly appointed him as an adviser in the Sindh Government, a post he considered low for his high calibre. He bided his time to avenge the slight. A shrewd politician, he quickly patched up differences with the Pir of Pagaro.

Jam Sadiq Ali parted ways with the PPP when President Ghulam Ishaq Khan appointed him the caretaker Chief Minister of Sindh in 1990. In the elections held that year, he won his seat as an independent candidate. He was elected leader of the House and became the chief executive of the province of Sindh—a post he held till his death on 5 March 1992. Under his chief ministership, the government of Sindh dutifully filed an application before the Sindh High Court in October 1991, seeking withdrawal of the case against Jam Sadiq Ali (in the Hur murder case). The court granted that permission. As a person, Jam was a steadfast and obliging friend. Cunning, mercurial, and revengeful, he dealt with his political opponents with no holds barred and extensively employed the coercive apparatus of the state to keep them on the run. Jam's rule in Sindh was an unmitigated horror in which a reign of terror was let loose against the PPP. He once quipped that he did so to give the PPP leaders a feel of their own policies.

Other Cases

In the Bhutto era, some prominent personalities died in mysterious circumstances. The causes of their deaths remained undetermined because of the 'inability' of the police to trace out the culprits. The opposition criticized the government's failure to unearth the culprits. Two cases drew considerable public ire. One pertained to the murder of Dr Nazir Ahmad in his clinic in Dera Ghazi Khan on 8 June 1972. The other concerned the murder of an outspoken opposition leader, Khawaja Muhammad Rafiq, while participating in a political procession in Lahore on 20 December 1972. The mystery remained unresolved.

A significant characteristic of the Bhutto government was the persecution of political dissidents through the abuse of the vast statutory powers assumed by the executive in the name of 'state security.' Some were harassed by fabricating cases of common crime against them. An Amnesty International mission which visited Pakistan in mid-1976 found that Chaudhry Zahur Elahi, a member of the National Assembly, and his family members were facing 130 charges. According to the Amnesty report: 'forty-seven of these charges were against Zahur Elahi personally, among which some were registered as criminal cases, including stealing a buffalo.'

Chaudhry Zahur Elahi was arrested on numerous occasions. On 12 February 1976, the Punjab High Court issued an order to the Inspector-General of Police to produce Zahur Elahi before the court and to ensure that he was not moved outside the court's jurisdiction without the consent of High Court. Disobeying the order, Mr Zahur Elahi was taken to Karachi to face three other cases pending against him there. By adopting such tactics, the executive branch frustrated the functioning of the judiciary and undermined its independence.

Dossiers

In April 1976, a National Documentation Centre was established to compile dossiers on all important political personalities. The rationale written in the words of the prefatory note to the dossiers reads: 'It is hoped that for working purposes the material contained in these dossiers will be of some use at the time when the nation is going to the polls.'

Volume III of the *White Paper On The Performance Of The Bhutto Regime*, issued by the Government of Pakistan in January 1979, sums up the dossiers in these words: 'The pen pictures make very depressing reading. The details are unsavoury and sordid. A sizeable majority of National and Provincial Assembly members, in the fold of Mr Bhutto's party, are revealed as licentious, lecherous and harbourers of criminals, goondas and smugglers. At least a dozen of them have been shown to be sexual perverts. One minister is said to have smuggled narcotics on an outward journey on an official visit; another to have made advances to an air hostess on the return flight after leading a delegation overseas. Ministers are reported to have received commissions abroad. Some Assembly members are stated to have been beaten up when they attempted to pick up a girl student.'

Many pieces of information contained in the dossiers, prepared with painstaking care and a sadistic pleasure, giving insight into the personal lives of political leaders, are unprintable.

The Witch-hunt

During the East Pakistan crisis, Mr Bhutto represented Pakistan's case in the United Nations Organization. The brief for the delegation contained information on defence matters. Lieutenant-Colonel Mukhtar Ahmad Khan accompanied the delegation. On return from New York, Mr Bhutto became the President and the CMLA. The ambitious Mukhtar, taking advantage of his acquaintance with Mr Bhutto, requested an intelligence appointment, to serve his benefactor in an independent assignment. On his retirement from the army in 1975, he was inducted in the Intelligence Bureau and assigned the task of preparing dossiers on senior army officers. In this he was assisted by a number of selected military and police officers serving in the Intelligence Bureau. They had their tentacles spread out in cantonments to keep an eye on the activities of the military officers. Mukhtar pieced together facts, fiction, and rumours, and submitted juicy reports to please Mr Bhutto. His appointment undermined the time-tested intelligence system which Bhutto trusted on a selective basis. The charter of responsibilities of the Intelligence Bureau precluded military intelligence work. Such a job fell under the purview of the Inter-Services Intelligence Directorate. By creating a parallel system, Mr Bhutto eroded institutions for transitory gain, and played one intelligence agency against the other. Besides the IB, Mr Saeed Ahmad Khan and Mr Masood Mahmud were also assigned the task of keeping the activities of the armed forces under check.

It may be recalled that, on 5 July 1977, Mr Masood Mahmud, the Director General of the FSF, was arrested. He was kept in the custody of the FIA, in a 'safe house' in Islamabad. The FSF was a dreaded and detested organization. It had earned notoriety for clandestinely committing acts of violence and terror. The government then attributed those misdeeds to the opposition. While in the custody of the FIA,

Mr Masood Mahmud expressed grave apprehensions about his own safety to Lieutenant-General F. A. Chishti. Himself a police officer, he confessed to being mortally scared of the police force. Lieutenant-General Chishti detailed a senior staff officer from his own headquarters to bring him to Chaklala. As this officer entered the FIA's safe house, Mr Masood Mahmud fell to his knees and begged to be kept in the safety of an army environment. Chishti lodged him in an officers' mess at Chaklala.

A few days later at a dinner held at the CMLA's house, Chishti told General Zia that Mr Masood Mahmud wanted to make a confessional statement in the murder case of Nawab Muhammad Ahmad Khan and desired that I should accompany him to meet the detained officer. General Zia agreed.

Chishti introduced Mr Masood Mahmud to me and asked him to repeat his request. Mr Masood Mahmud stated that Mr Bhutto had pressurized him to commit serious offences which he dared not resist for fear of retribution. 'I did not possess the moral courage to refuse,' he said, 'because I was mortally scared of the vindictive nature of Mr Bhutto.' After taking a deep breath, he said, 'The Prime Minister made life hell for those who did not fall in line with his desire. I feared for my safety and the honour of my family.'

These misdeeds started weighing heavily on his mind and he wanted to make a clean breast of them. Given the services of a stenotypist, he dictated a long statement in which he implicated Mr Bhutto and himself on many charges, including the murder of Nawab Muhammad Ahmad Khan. His revelations stunned those who read his statement.

Soon after the promulgation of martial law, Mr Ahmad Raza Kasuri, the son of the late Nawab Muhammad Ahmad Khan, started demanding fresh investigations into the case of the assassination of his father. In August 1977, the FIA unearthed sufficient incriminating evidence against three officers of the FSF to justify their arrest. They confessed their guilt before a magistrate and implicated others. Those netted accused yet others who were also arrested. The expanding net tightened the noose around the neck of the former Prime Minister, Mr Bhutto. He was arrested on 3 September 1977.

The decision to rearrest Mr Bhutto was a tragic, painful, and difficult one. Some would call it a vendetta to malign the image of a fallen populist hero. Many motives could be attributed to it. It might be beyond the comprehension of others that a person occupying a position so high could stoop so low as to order the murder of a fellow citizen—even a political opponent.

The trial of the former Prime Minister on the charge of murder was a shameful stigma. Mr Bhutto's personal reputation apart, the image of the country was at stake. Mr Bhutto's conviction would not be pain-free either for him or for the country. On the other hand, if the charge against him was aborted by the court, the government would be hard put to to justify the allegations of victimization and malice.

Mr Bhutto had his admirers and his critics. The latter would argue that justice should follow an even course. All the accused should face a fair trial and their innocence or guilt be established in a court of law. Let the courts convict or acquit him. Should he escape trial merely because of his high status in society? So ran the argument.

The FIA and the public prosecutors felt that the available incriminating evidence justified a trial in a court of law. In their assessment, justice had been denied in the past by hushing up the case at the investigation stages. Should the error be perpetuated by shirking responsibility? The law was allowed to take its normal course.

Released from detention in Murree, Bhutto had fast regained his confidence and adopted a defiant attitude. The PNA agitation had been relegated to history. The fragile unity of that alliance was in jeopardy. Mr Bhutto had a new whipping-boy—the man who had imposed martial law. He lashed out at its legal validity to put Zia on the defensive. 'Offence is the best defence' became his approach.

The PPP violated the restrictions imposed on indoor political activity. On 6 August Mr Bhutto was received at Multan by a large, vociferous, and rowdy group of his party workers. His public address was harsh and insulting to the leaders of the other political parties. Two days later, when Mr Bhutto arrived at Lahore, the PPP workers disrupted the airport security arrangements, entered the airport forcibly, and attacked some of the non-PPP political leaders. Maulana Shah Ahmad Noorani, Mr Javed Hashmi, and Mr Hanif Ramay were insulted and subjected to indignities. The local administration advised Mr Bhutto to exercise restraint. He took that advice as a sign of the government's weakness.

On 11 August, Mr Bhutto's procession at Peshawar became disorderly. The police used tear-gas to disperse the crowd. Mr Bhutto threatened to boycott elections if fair polls were not promised.

On 19 September, a group of students of the Sindh People's Students Federation broke into the examination centres in Sukkur and tore up candidates' answer sheets. They forcibly took 150 examinees to Rohri, where they stoned trains and damaged a bookstall at the railway station.

Commenting on the adverse law and order situation, the weekly *Zindagi* observed (18 September 1977): 'Violations of the restrictions continue and the sparks of confrontation and clashes keep turning into flames. Human blood is spilled. This is a manifestation of organized *goondaism*. As soon as the political process was allowed, weapons began to be publicly brandished.'

Addressing his party workers in Islamabad on 26 August, Mr Bhutto said: 'If I am forced and handcuffed, I will certainly raise issues of a fundamental nature.' The implied threat to Zia indicated that Mr Bhutto's patience was running out and apprehension was getting the better of him.

On 30 August, four retired judges, B. Z. Kaikaus, Bashiruddin, Muhammad Sadique, and A. R. Changez of the High Courts, issued a joint statement demanding the trial of Mr Bhutto and his accomplices in a court of law, 'for committing crimes against the people of Pakistan.'

The Muslim League leaders, the Pir of Pagaro and Chaudhry Zahur Elahi, met General Zia on 30 September and requested the postponement of elections, the former suggesting a five-year delay. A few days earlier, on 25 September, the Central Council of the PNA had met at Quetta. Professor Ghafoor Ahmad states: 'A majority of the PNA leaders felt that the elections should be postponed. This group included Air Marshal Asghar Khan, Maulana Shah Ahmad Noorani, Mian Tufail Muhammad, Begum Nasim Wali Khan and Chaudhry Zahur Elahi . . . lacking unanimity, the PNA decided to reiterate its demand to complete the process of accountability before holding the elections. The PNA would remain silent if the martial law authorities decided to postpone the elections.'[5]

The PPP was divided on the election issue. Its top leadership demanded that the polls be held. Some of its prominent leaders felt otherwise. Lieutenant-General Chishti states: 'On the same afternoon [September 28] [Mr Ghulam Mustafa] Khar, [Mr Ghulam Mustafa] Jatoi, [Maulana] Kausar Niazi, Mr Mir Afzal [Khan], Mr Hamid Raza Gilani and Mr Noor Hayat Noon met the Election Cell and recommended that the elections be postponed and no new date given.'[6]

The arrest of Mr Bhutto hurt the PPP. His wife and daughter, becoming increasingly emotional, used the election platform to inflame public sentiments. Miss Benazir Bhutto told a party rally in Okara on 29 September 1977: 'the five rivers will flow with blood if Mr Bhutto is hanged.'

A day later, Begum Nusrat Bhutto thundered in a public meeting in Nishtar Park, Karachi: 'A revolution will engulf the country if the path of democracy is blocked.' Earlier, she had declared: 'Zia will be retired if PPP wins the election.'[7]

Pressure tactics is a legitimate weapon in politics. It is best employed with finesse and subtlety. The outcry of the Bhutto ladies harmed their own cause. Their provocative rhetoric, at a time when the trump cards were in Zia's hands, displayed their lack of experience in the game of power.

It was suggested that the PPP should be banned and debarred from participating in the October polls. This view did not find favour with the government as it would have impaired the credibility of the elections, besides appearing partisan. The PPP's violent election campaign was designed to win sympathy votes. It aroused a lurking fear: the prevailing tension and acrimony could plunge the country into a crisis once again, from which martial law had ostensibly just taken it out. Under the circumstances, would elections usher in an era of peace? Many people felt otherwise.

July through September, the administration faced another handicap. The prospect of a PPP success in the elections made people, including the bureaucrats, hesitant to divulge details of the excesses committed by the Bhutto administration—the fear of retribution was too strong and pervasive. Nevertheless, it was a period of discovery. Every now and then, some ugly, suppressed facts surfaced. These concerned a wide range, such as the denial of civil rights, the systematic destruction of the institutions of the state, the misuse of the national exchequer, the employment of the law-enforcing agencies to subvert democracy and to terrorize the opposition. Pakistan, a democratic country, had been turned into a single-party fascist state, ruled by an autocrat. The numerous instances of the political, administrative, legal, constitutional, and financial excesses committed by the Bhutto government emitted a foul smell and painted a grim picture of the state of affairs. Their disclosure brought about a perceptible change in General Zia's views about the person he had toppled. Mr Bhutto, whom he had called a 'tenacious fighter and a great politician' not too long ago, was now called, 'an evil genius and a Machiavelli', who had let loose a 'reign of terror' in Pakistan and who was 'totally devoid of principles'. The transformation was total. This was a parting of the ways.

Another factor came into play. The arrest of Mr Bhutto and his exposure as a wrongdoer created a personal animus between him and General Zia. Both started hating and fearing each other. Known for his vindictive nature, Mr Bhutto was expected to hold an eternal grudge against Zia for harming his reputation and image. The risk was not acceptable to General Zia. He wanted the trial of Mr Bhutto completed before the elections were held.

That desire was influenced by a historic reality. A conspiracy case against Sheikh Mujibur Rahman was withdrawn by Ayub under political pressure, with tragic consequences. Any post-election government could succumb to similar pressure in respect of Mr Bhutto. To convert an alleged murderer into a political hero was a denial of justice. General Zia wanted the Bhutto case to be decided by the courts.

On 1 October 1977 in a radio and television address to the nation General Zia said: 'After much deliberation I have come to the conclusion that to hold the elections on 18 October in the present circumstances would be inviting a worse crisis.'

The country was back to square one. The factors which influenced the decision to postpone the elections were:

1. To prevent Mr Bhutto's trial becoming an election issue.

2. The discovery of the gross misuse of the instruments of state power by the Bhutto government and the time needed to take such cases to their logical conclusions.

3. The PPP revival.

4. To complete the process of accountability of the violators of the law and rules before holding the elections.

5. To give time to the political parties, as requested by them, to prepare for the elections.

6. To create a tension-free environment for the conduct of polls.

General Zia had said on 1 September 1977: 'As a nation we will have to evolve a political system that suits us. The Muslims have one

God, one Prophet, one Book; how can you have two hundred leaders ruling you? You have got to have one Ameer [ruler]. In my humble opinion, for Pakistan, the presidential form, which is closer to the Islamic ideology, is the most suited one.'

Had power started intoxicating Zia? Did he plan to prolong his rule by exploiting religion? Was the Bhutto nemesis at work? General Zia's critics attributed personal motives to the postponement of the elections.

The issue of elections was discussed in an MLAs Conference, which recommended their postponement. In that meeting, General Zia gave no indication that the postponement of elections was a ruse to prolong his rule. While his preference for an Islamic polity was well-known, this was not the reason for delaying the polls. By and large, the Bhutto factor and the reluctance of other political parties to face the electorate influenced the government decision.

The election postponement question was also discussed in an informal meeting of the Military Council. In that meeting, Admiral Sharif and Mr Ghulam Ishaq Khan supported the proposal. General Shariff had learnt before the meeting that the MLAs Conference had already taken a decision to postpone the elections. He participated in the deliberations without expressing his bruised feelings that the Military Council was being used as a rubber-stamp body. General Shariff's posture in the meeting—dignified and military-like—gave an impression of aloofness. He showed no sign of rancour then or thereafter and kept laying emphasis on military solidarity in his words and deeds.

General Zia had commanded a division under General Shariff in 2 Corps. Their mutual relationship had always been official and businesslike. Their social contacts were few. Shariff suspected, without a tangible reason, that his presence in service might some day cause an irritation in their mutual relationship. He decided to pre-empt that possibility. A couple of months later, he expressed a wish to seek retirement for personal reasons. General Zia requested him to complete his normal tenure of three years in his assignment in which he was due to serve till March 1979. General Shariff was adamant and General Zia reluctantly agreed to his retirement in February 1978.

General Shariff parted with grace and never looked back. Known to be a strict disciplinarian in the Army, he was every inch a soldier—upright, forceful, and correct. Above all, he was a gentleman.

Gist of Various Meetings

Throughout the twelve summers of his rule, General Zia had a long line of daily visitors. During the early months of his administration, I attended such meetings and kept notes. This was a taxing, unproductive, and boring business which kept me away from my enormous quantity of daily mail, which required considerable time to clear. Here are some excerpts from the notes I took:

7 July 1977

Sardar Abdul Qayyum Khan

1. The Azad Kashmir government may be dissolved, a caretaker administration established under a neutral person, and fresh elections held.

2. Elections in Azad Kashmir be held on the basis of the previous, unanimously accepted Constitution, under which the President was to be elected by a direct vote.

3. My party is not linked with any political party in Pakistan. During the PNA agitation our association with it was merely on a philosophical plane.

8 July 1977

Mr A. K. Brohi

1. I apprehended Pakistan's breakup and prayed to Allah to give me strength to serve my motherland. When you called me for today's meeting, my wife told me that my prayer had been accepted. I place my life at your disposal.

2. You have risked your life by imposing martial law. The forces dismantled by you may start clandestine activities to bring about a counter-revolution. Be watchful.

3. The imposition of martial law might be challenged in a court of law. This is not so important because, in the final

analysis, political considerations will outweigh legal necessities. Your action can be well defended.

4. Do not trust the administration which had supported the previous government. Agha Shahi and Ghulam Ishaq Khan were the exceptions. The bureaucrats will give limited loyalty to you as your tenure is short.

5. You have started with a considerable bank balance to your credit. With the passage of time, it will decrease. You have to devise ways and means to replenish the stock and give injections to retain vitality.

6. Issue 'white papers' on the failure of the Bhutto administration. Highlight the sinking economic plight of the people. Do not overemphasize religion. This complex issue will defy a settlement in a ninety-day time-frame.

7. Do not make a reference to the Supreme Court to seek legal cover for the military take-over. Besides showing a weakness, the onus of providing proof will fall on the government. Let others file a writ. The case can be defended well.

8. Our courts are responsive to public opinion. Do not trust the lawyers but consult the previous chief election commissioners on matters of law and rules.

9. Bhutto's land reforms were a fraud. The important PPP leaders had gifted their lands to the children who are yet to be born to escape the reach of law.

10. A presidential form of government is preferable for Pakistan.

11. Future elections should be held on the basis of a legal framework which may be prepared.

11 July 1977

Mr Justice Hamoodur Rahman (Former Chief Justice of Pakistan)

1. I had held martial law illegal in the Asma Jilani Case. In a grave emergency a *de facto* martial law can be imposed. It

becomes legal if the people in general and the courts recognize it.

2. The failure of the political system indicates that the martial law will remain in force for a long time.

3. It will be desirable that the legality of martial law be recognized by the courts before elections are held. If Bhutto wins the next election, may God help you and your colleagues.

4. Politics in Pakistan is based on expediency. It is not clean. Parliamentary democracy is unlikely to work in the country. Bhutto was thinking on these lines. For our politicians, personal interest takes priority over national needs.

5. Even without rigging the elections, the PPP would have returned to power with an adequate majority.

6. Bhutto manipulated the Constitution to satisfy his personal vendetta. The fifth amendment was made to oust Justice Iqbal from the office of the Lahore High Court. The sixth amendment was designed to grant extension to Justice Yaqub Ali.

7. Justice Mushtaq Hussain enjoys a good reputation.

8. Bhutto is fully accountable for the brutalities committed during his tenure as the Prime Minister.

1 August 1977

Mr Aziz Ahmad (Minister of State in the Bhutto administration)

1. Military rule has tarnished the image of Pakistan. Foreign powers consider the country politically unstable.

2. The administration is against the PPP. The impartiality of the government, as claimed by you, should also be visible.

3. Pakistan should never yield under the American and the French pressure to give up the building of a reprocessing plant in the country.

Mr Yusuf Khattak (Muslim League)

1. Mr Bhutto had crippled the Muslim League in the North-West Frontier Province by doling out millions of rupees as bribes. We should merge this party with its Pagara group faction—a process in which Chaudhry Zahur Elahi can play a role.

2. PNA, a heterogenous group, is likely to disintegrate. There is no real difference between Wali Khan's NAP and Mufti Mahmood's JUI. If one is a Hindu, the second is a Sikh. Wali Khan is another Sheikh Mujibur Rahman. His heart does not pulsate for Pakistan.

Air Marshal (Retired) Asghar Khan (Tehrik-i-Istiqlal)

1. Fear of Bhutto kept the PNA united. He maligned his opponents.

2. Major-General Imtiaz, Mr Bhutto's Military Secretary, and Mr Munir Hussain, Chief Secretary NWFP, exerted undue pressure on the NWFP administration to favour PPP during the elections held in March 1977.

6 August 1977

Chaudhry Zahur Elahi (Muslim League)

1. Mr Bhutto should be tried for his criminal acts in a court of law. He attempted to get me murdered.

2. Corrupt politicians and officials should be prevented from fleeing the country.

Mr Rafiq Bajwa (Jamaat-i-Islami)

1. The Western democratic system cannot provide the foundations of an Islamic society. An Islamic system can only flow from an Islamic Constitution. Our present Constitution is not Islamic.

2. Enforce an Islamic Constitution before reverting back to the barracks.
3. There is no concept of the Western-style opposition in Islam.

Mr Hanif Ramay (Former Chief Minister, Punjab)

1. The first requirement should be to create an Islamic society based on the principles of social and economic justice. Islamic punishments should be introduced thereafter.
2. Bhutto in power had committed serious malpractices.

10 August 1977

Lieutenant-General Gul Hassan Khan (Former Chief of Army Staff)

1. I resigned from the post of ambassadorship but did not return to the country, fearing arrest by the vindictive Bhutto.

2. It is untrue that I was instrumental in bringing Bhutto to power. On 20 December 1971, I met Mr Bhutto at his request in the Punjab House, Rawalpindi. He told me that he had just become the President of Pakistan. With tears in his eyes, he asked me to take command of the Pakistan Army. I needed some time to reflect, but he forced the pace as he was to address the nation that day. I accepted the offer on four conditions which Mr Bhutto readily accepted. The conditions were:

    a. To seek an early return of the Pakistani prisoners of war from India.

    b. The Army should not be deployed on internal security duties. Police force be used on such tasks.

    c. The government will not interfere in the internal working of the Army.

d. I would retain my existing rank and would not be promoted.

3. Bhutto, a damned liar with a crooked mind, excelled in playing one person against the other. He once asked me if I had promised Mr Ghulam Mustafa Khar the appointment of the Governor of Punjab for life. I told him that as the Chief of Army Staff I had no business or authority to make such an irresponsible offer. 'Khar told me so,' said Bhutto. A year later Mr Bhutto asked Air Marshal Rahim Khan, Pakistan's ambassador in Spain the same question with the only difference that Rahim's name had been inserted and mine deleted. Bhutto's purpose was to create a wedge between Rahim and me.

12 August 1977

Mr Ghaus Bakhsh Bizenjo (under trial in Hyderabad Jail)

1. The two-nation theory ran out its course with the creation of Pakistan.

2. Pakistan's four provinces are rich in their respective history, culture, language, and heritage. The country is composed of four brothers who should live in harmony by removing mutual suspicions and creating a binding trust.

3. Balochistan and Pakistan are inseparable. Their interests and destiny are common.

(After his release from custody, Mr Bizenjo met General Zia to thank him for the withdrawal of the Hyderabad Conspiracy Case. During the course of his discussion, he talked of his aging car and surprised his host by requesting the government to provide one to him. General Zia obliged. A new Mercedes car was presented to him in June 1978.)

Khan Abdul Wali Khan (NAP, under trial in Hyderabad Jail)

1. Bhutto branded me a traitor for his personal political motives. I am unjustly accused of opposing the establishment

of Pakistan. We had in fact presented an alternative plan for the freedom of the Muslims of India.

2. I am neither a secessionist nor I have ever talked of Pakhtunistan.

3. You have dissolved all the tribunals except the Hyderabad tribunal. This may create doubts in the minds of the people of Balochistan and the NWFP. This may encourage the extremists to exploit the issue.

29 August 1977

Mian Tufail Muhammad (Jamaat-i-Islami)

1. If Mr Bhutto is taken to the court, he will challenge the validity of military rule.

2. The beneficiaries of the Bhutto administration continue to rule the roost. The police force, the lateral entrants in the civil service, and the administration are infested with personnel inducted by the PPP.

3. The March 1977 elections were a slaughter-house for Mr. Bhutto. He planned to create an East Pakistan (1971) like crisis in Pakistan—particularly in Sindh.

4. The Chief Justice of Pakistan, Mr Justice Yaqub Ali, is a PPP nominee.

5. The government should issue a 'white paper' to expose the misdeeds of the PPP regime.

30 August 1977

Mr Justice Qadeer Ali

1. Mr Bhutto had politicized the judiciary. Remove those judges who were appointed for political considerations.

2. You are riding a tiger. Do not trust the politicians.

31 August 1977

Mr Muhammad Ayub Khuhro (Former Chief Minister of Sindh)

1. You have done well by imposing martial law and exposing Mr Bhutto. In my long political life, he is the most crooked person I have met. Complete the process of accountability of the political leaders before elections are held. Mr Bhutto is no saviour of Sindh though he has favoured some people by giving them job opportunities.

2. In July 1958 Governor-General Iskandar Mirza with the help of General Muhammad Ayub Khan imposed martial law to forestall the elections planned to be held in February 1959. His plan was to remove Ayub Khan within three months of the imposition of martial law and replace him with Mr Qizilbash as the Prime Minister of Pakistan. Ayub pre-empted him.

2 September 1977

Maulana Kausar Niazi (PPP)

1. The PPP has been facing an internal struggle with Sheikh Rashid leading the leftist group and I the rightist elements. I was accused, within the party, of being pro-Islam. Pakistan needs a leadership imbued with the thinking of Islam as a progressive and modern religion.

2. The PPP is not all bad, though it is not a clean party. With some pruning, it could become an asset to contest elections. Moderation, not extremism, should be our political philosophy. I joined PPP on the request of Mr Bhutto to uphold the cause of Islam and *musawat-e-Muhammadi* [Islamic justice]. It should be kept as a political party.

3. Mr Bhutto indulged in character assassination of the PPP members by collecting incriminating data about them and blackmailing them to keep them under check.

4. I do not visualize public disturbances in case Mr Bhutto is arrested. In such an eventuality, he has nominated Sheikh Rashid to become the Chairman of PPP.

30 September 1977

Chaudhry Zahur Elahi (Muslim League)

1. The PPP leaders should be debarred from participating in the elections. The completion of a process of accountability deserves priority over the conduct of polls.
2. Mr Bhutto's trial in a civil court has weakened the PNA. Some of its components feel that the vacuum created by the Bhutto exit should be filled by them.
3. Mr Bhutto had kept the PPP together through arm-twisting. Many of his party members including Abdul Hafeez Pirzada and Maulana Kausar Niazi are not loyal to him.
4. Many PPP leaders have amassed wealth outside the country.

5 October 1977

Khan Abdul Wali Khan (NAP)

1. Elections are merely a means to an end. Your decision to postpone elections is appropriate.
2. Mr Bhutto and Pakistan cannot co-exist. He is a criminal, a murderer of democracy, an unscrupulous politician who has corrupted all national institutions. He indulged in cheap politics and befooled the simple people by making the false and impractical slogan of *roti, kapra aur makan* (food, clothing, and shelter).
3. Mr Bhutto once told me that the domination of Punjab could only be broken if Pathans and Balochis got united against it. For this reason, he maliciously kept the Army—

mostly comprising of Punjabi manpower—engaged in the internal security duties in Balochistan. Bhutto also indicated that the interests of the smaller provinces could not be protected by Punjab. He told me that he would ensure that the prisoners of war did not return from India for at least two years to break the spinal cord of Punjab.

4. The judiciary in our country looks towards the executive branch for guidance.

5. Mr Bhutto did not follow the Constitution. He created a crisis of confidence. He should be tried in a military court.

6. Mr Bhutto told me that the Shah of Iran and the army generals were against the withdrawal of troops from Balochistan.

7. The Bhutto strategy was to keep everyone engaged in one crisis or the other so that he may establish himself as the master of ceremonies (to solve the crisis).

8. You are the first Head of the Government in Pakistan to call my father, Khan Abdul Ghaffar Khan, a patriot. I am grateful to you.

(Khan Abdul Ghaffar Khan, the Red Shirt leader, was an insistent old man. Called the 'Frontier Gandhi' by his admirers, he spent many years in detention. In the closing years of his life, while he did his politicking in Pakistan, he mostly lived in self-exile in Jalalabad, Afghanistan. He wrote frequently to General Zia, complaining on one minor issue or another. His failing health worried him. In 1978, he requested government assistance to visit the Soviet Union for medical treatment. Moscow maintained a diplomatic silence on that request. When reminded to send a reply, the Soviet Ambassador in Islamabad told a Foreign Office official in a humorous vein that the ailing Ghaffar Khan might next wish his son Khan Wali Khan and then Mrs Nasim Wali Khan to visit him in Moscow. The Government of Pakistan might conclude that 'Pakhtunistan' was being discussed in the Kremlin. He pleaded for help to prevail on the 'old man' to drop his request. Pakistan's ambassador in Kabul conveyed the diplomatic regret to Khan Abdul Ghaffar Khan. Back came a counter-demand: 'In that case, send me to China for treatment.' China did not relish the proposal and asked to be excused. Eventually, he went for treatment to an East European country of his own choice. After his death Ghaffar Khan was buried in Jalalabad as he wished.)

12 October 1977

Khan Abdul Qayyum Khan (Muslim League—Qayyum faction)

1. Pakistan should have a presidential form of government.
2. Under the circumstances, the postponement of elections, due on 18 October 1977, was justified.

Mr Khurshid Hassan Mir (Pakistan Jamhoori Party)

1. Retain the parliamentary system with enhanced power given to the president and adequate checks and balances.
2. If the presidential form of government is to be adopted, abolish all the four provinces and divide the country into divisions of manageable sizes.

13 October 1977

Maulana Mufti Mahmud (JUI)

1. Ban the PPP by making a reference to this effect to the Supreme Court.
2. Disband the Hyderabad Tribunal.
3. The military officers convicted in the Attock Trial Case (1973) may be released and their sentences be remitted.

Nawabzada Nasrullah Khan (Pakistan Democratic Party)

Ban on political activity may be lifted and a time-frame for holding elections be indicated.

Air Marshal Asghar Khan (Tehrik-i-Istiqlal)

1. The numerous problems faced by the country cannot be solved in a short period of time. Do not consume your energy on settling minor issues.

and in December 1977

2. The Muhammad Ahmad Khan murder case is unlikely to arouse public sentiments against Mr Bhutto because it is a private case. The government should initiate cases against him and others. Mr Bhutto should be tried in a military court.

3. By our (politicians') actions, we forced you to step in and clamp martial law; therefore, we have a stake in your administration.

4. The political parties should face the PPP politically to bring about its demise.

August 1977

Haji Maula Bukhsh Soomro

Mr Bhutto suffers from an inferiority complex concerning his maternal parentage. He treated his mother with considerable contempt and harshness. With tears flowing from her eyes, she once told my wife, 'May God's curse be on my son.' My wife was astonished to hear such harsh words from a mother regarding her own son. It is my conviction that his mother's cries will not go unheard. I have a hunch that Mr Bhutto will be punished by Almighty Allah in this world for maltreating his mother.

Mr Aslam Khattak and Mian Jamal Shah (Muslim League)

Mr Bhutto fabricates lies to pitch one friend against the other. He once told Mr Mumtaz Bhutto that I (Aslam Khattak) had reported to him that Mumtaz Bhutto was an agent of the Shah of Iran. This was an utter falsehood.

4 February 1978

Nawabzada Nasrullah Khan (PDP) and Mian Muhammad Tufail (JI)

At a dinner hosted in honour of the participants of the political leaders meeting held that day, Nawabzada Nasrullah Khan and Mian Tufail said that martial law should either be enforced effectively or lifted. They also proposed that the process of accountability be decided through military courts. General Zia reminded them that they had been publicly demanding initiation of the accountability cases in the civil courts. The two leaders, along with Begum Wali Khan, stated that the martial law authorities should take their own decisions and need not worry about the statements made by the political leaders.

CHAPTER 6

The Political Juggernaut

The postponement of the October 1977 elections created a credibility gap between the words and deeds of General Zia. His critics called it an act caused by his PPP phobia. Mr Bhutto's trial, they argued, was meant to tarnish his image to favour his political opponents. General Zia, the hitherto reluctant ruler, having tasted power, was no longer reluctant to rule. His actions earned him ire. Addressing a press conference at Tehran he said: 'What is the Constitution? It is a booklet with ten or twelve pages. I can tear them up and say that from tomorrow we shall live under a different system. Is there anybody to stop me? Today, the people will follow wherever I lead. All the politicians, including the once mighty Mr Bhutto, will follow me with their tails wagging.'[1]

This outburst put him in the political dock. The concluding line of the same statement was seldom quoted, which read: 'But is that good for the country? No, I have no political ambition personally.' General Zia might not have had political ambitions in September 1977. He decidedly developed them soon thereafter.

The Central Committee of the PNA met in Lahore on 8 October 1977. While conspicuously avoiding criticizing the postponement of elections, it urged upon the government to complete the process of accountability speedily and demanded the announcement of a fresh election date. The PNA statement, conciliatory in tone, tacitly approved the government decision. In practice, it supported the government policy and extracted concessions from it.

The Pir of Pagaro (Muslim League) said in a statement that the postponement was necessary to create a peaceful environment for the conduct of polls. Professor Ghafoor Ahmad (Jamaat-i-Islami) expressed unhappiness that the CMLA had not taken the political parties into confidence before taking this decision. Chaudhry Zahur Elahi (Muslim League) expressed satisfaction that the elections had been postponed. Mr Yusuf Khattak (Muslim League) congratulated the CMLA on his 'patriotic, courageous, and timely action.' Khan

Abdul Wali Khan (National Awami Party) declared that accountability and chastisement of the former rulers were more important than any other issue. He felt that Bhutto and Pakistan could not co-exist. The need of the hour, he said, was 'to destroy Bhuttoism'.

Others publicly supporting the postponement included Khan Abdul Qayyum Khan (Muslim League—Qayyum Group), Mr Muhammad Ayub Khuhro from Sindh, Arbab Sikandar Khan from NWFP, Messrs Nabi Bakhsh Zehri and Ali Muhammad Jogezai from Balochistan, and Allama Aqeel Turabi, a prominent Shiite leader. Mr Bhutto called the postponement an act without justification.

The public mood was reported thus: 'Reaction around the country so far appears to have been calm. Campaign flags, posters and banners have disappeared from the streets but no incidents have been reported.'[2]

On 20 September, Begum Nusrat Bhutto challenged the validity of the imposition of martial law in a constitutional petition filed in the Supreme Court of Pakistan. On 10 November 1977, the Supreme Court announced its judgment in which it validated the imposition of martial law on the ground of the 'doctrine of necessity.' *The de facto* government of General Zia thus became *de jure* as well.

A process of consolidation was started by the government. Political survival demanded firm control of the state administration. The CMLA Secretariat was expanded. It was shifted from its improvised offices on Firdousi Road to the premises of the former Prime Minister's Secretariat.

From 6 July 1977 till 22 March 1984, except for a couple of weeks' interregnum, I was the Chief of Staff (COS), first to the CMLA and later to the CMLA-cum-President. In that capacity, I participated in all meetings of the cabinet, and the Military Council, the Defence Committee of the Cabinet, and the Afghan Cell, and was privy to the policies covering Pakistan's domestic life and her relations with foreign countries. The spectrum covered was wide and varied, in effect, all embracing. It included internal developments, foreign affairs, nuclear policy, election schedule, policies of the state, and martial law work. The summaries submitted by the federal ministries to the CMLA Secretariat were mostly endorsed by me, with only a few more important cases going to the CMLA for his orders.

The Zia-Arif team worked in harmony, with the former placing confidence in his COS and trusting his judgement. Zia delegated total responsibility for handling office work to me, and I took decisions within the overall policy framework. During this seven-year association, in not even a single case was the decision given by me subsequently reversed by the President. We knew each others' minds well. General Zia was a gracious senior. While introducing me to his visitors, he would say on many occasions that 'Eighty per cent of my work is performed by Arif.' Such remarks caused embarrassment, but they depicted the President's generous nature. On my part, I gave complete loyalty to my senior.

At times, our opinions on the subjects under discussion differed. We exchanged views, examined the choices available, consulted specialists and other colleagues on the issues. General Zia, a patient listener, encouraged discussion to an extent which many others in his position would not have permitted. He respected the conviction of those who disagreed with his own assessment. He knew that, once a decision was taken, it would be implemented, in letter and spirit, without disclosure of the internal debate which had taken place.

When the two of us agreed to disagree, it was the President's prerogative to have the last word. If the views were hard but unacceptable, Zia would appear to defer the final decision. He would then quietly convey it directly to the person or the agency concerned without routing it through the staff channels.

Autocratic rule is essentially a one-man performance. The advisers assist the decision-maker but the person on centre-stage is the one who alone enjoys the final authority. General Zia's team members knew the limits of their responsibility. On substantive matters, he had the final say. Whereas he was accommodating on some issues, he could be unyielding and rigid on others. On major policy matters, he was guided by the dictates of his conscience.

I usually accompanied General Zia during his foreign tours and participated in the inter-state negotiations; but normally I stayed at the headquarters during his travels within the country.

Visitors to the Secretariat included friends, acquaintances, critics, and strangers. They raised a variety of questions. Some had grievances against the administration; others needed help. They complained that the bureaucratic system was corrupt, inefficient, lethargic, and willing to accept grafts. Claiming to be aggrieved parties, the complainants desired that cases be decided in their favour. If a case was settled in favour of an applicant, he invariably took it as a matter of right. When a decision went against him, I usually lost a friend.

The appointment I worked in generated immense pressures in which all movements, acts, words, and decisions came under the focus of the watchful eyes of the bureaucrats, the politicians, the information media, and the people of Pakistan. Seven years in a position of high visibility is too long a time to hide oneself or escape from public criticism. There was no dearth of critics. Double-edged praise was lavished in private and in public. I was variously termed 'the man next to General Zia; more powerful than what his appointment indicates; a person to be watched; and the *de facto* Prime Minister of the country.'

Some visitors injected sugar-coated remarks in a jovial manner with meaningful smiles on their faces. There were admirers, hypocrites, critics, and sycophants, all claiming to be well-wishers. Such were the environmental realities of work. In addition, professional jealousies surfaced.

Statecraft is a fascinating and frustrating experience. Public administration is a rough business in which political problems defy a mathematical solution. It needs a political approach, based on compromises, to reach amiable settlements. Those who govern invariably develop techniques to handle the problems faced by them. No country is problem-free. Many of her rulers learnt the hard way that Pakistan was not an easy country to govern. The Zia administration was no exception.

Political and administrative troubleshooting is a difficult process. A good government anticipates issues and evolves workable plans to deal with events to avoid being surprised and overtaken by them. Our approach was to assign specific tasks to a small team to prepare a plan of action. The recommendations of the kitchen cabinet were then discussed in a larger group or in the cabinet. While evaluating administrative matters, Mr Ghulam Ishaq Khan, the Minister for Finance, and I usually formed part of the kitchen cabinet. Other persons were co-opted on a case-to-case and need-to-know basis.

Troubleshooting for the political and the martial law work was assigned to a Governor. In many cases, Lieutenant-General Fazle Haq, Governor of the NWFP, and I jointly carried out studies on such problems. The study group's recommendations were then discussed in the MLAs' Conferences. On occasion, General Zia modified the action plan, marginally or substantially. The decisions taken in the MLAs' Conferences were implemented by the Governors without reservation. The teamwork was healthy.

Dr Zbigniew Brezenski, the National Security Adviser in the Carter Administration, visited Pakistan officially in February 1980. He enquired from an American diplomat posted in Islamabad: 'What is the status of General Arif in the Pakistan administration?' The diplomat replied: 'He roughly enjoys the same position as you do in the US Administration.' Dr Brezenski smiled wistfully and said 'In that case, he must be an unpopular person.'

A military staff officer should shun personal publicity, work quietly, run a happy team, create a congenial atmosphere free from doubts and tensions, and act as a shock absorber between the head of government and heads of provincial governments. He must give decisions fairly, impartially, and quickly, radiate confidence, remain cool and balanced under stress, protect the legitimate interests of all concerned, contribute fully in providing an efficient administration, and, through his words and deeds, enhance the image of the country. The people should judge him by a performance yardstick. This is a tall order. All human beings possess an ego. They like publicity and projection of their performance. It is often difficult to resist the temptations which surround them. Many of them fall prey to the worldly advantages which are theirs for the asking. The more difficult the task in hand, the more necessary it becomes to sacrifice personal convenience. The higher one rises in life, the more demanding are the restrictions placed on him. I make no evaluation of my own performance in the Zia administration, leaving it to posterity to pass judgement.

The government-controlled television and radio networks were instructed not to project the COS even when he participated in public events. I neither issued any press statements, nor granted interviews to any media correspondents; I declined all invitations to social or business functions organized by the public and private sector organizations. On two occasions, the President offered me the status of a minister of the federal government. The offer was declined.

In the previous spells of martial law, the Warrant of Precedence was amended to give an enhanced position to the martial law functionaries over others. President Zia was prevailed upon by me not to make such a change. It irritated some status-conscious senior military officers who found nothing wrong in displaying their authority in public. Some felt that at times it was necessary to do so.

It was decided that in military functions the warrant of precedence in respect of service officers would be followed, based on their military seniority. Some governors (three stars) felt that, inside their own provinces, they should have protocol preference over four-star generals. On one occasion, Lieutenant-General Fazle Haq, Governor of the NWFP, did not attend the passing-out parade at the Pakistan Military Academy, Kakul, because General Muhammad Iqbal, the Deputy Chief of Army Staff, was to be given protocol preference over him. For similar reasons, Lieutenant-General Rahimuddin Khan, the Governor of Balochistan, declined to attend a function held at the Staff College, Quetta, in which General Sawar Khan, the Vice Chief of Army Staff, was to be seated at the head of the front row. President Zia, the chief guest, was seated on the dais.

In July 1977, the CMLA Secretariat inherited a system of issuing permits for the purchase of cars. The market value of cars being high, each permit had a premium of approximately Rs 25,000 to Rs 30,000. The permits issued to the lucky influential persons by the previous government were frequently sold by them. That system was scrapped. Also discontinued was the use of the intelligence secret funds by the Secretariat of the Head of the Government.

Let this narration give way to events of greater public importance. A brief description of the following subjects may be of interest.

1. The Federal Cabinets.
2. The Election Cell.
3. The President's Resignation.
4. The Hyderabad Conspiracy Case.
5. The Process of Accountability.
6. The Emergency in Balochistan.

The Federal Cabinets

After 5 July the federal secretaries in charge of their respective ministries *ipso facto* formed the federal cabinet under the title 'Council of Advisers', presided over by the CMLA. Similar arrangements were made in the provinces under the respective MLAs. It was an emergency measure designed to work for three months.

Once the elections had been postponed, the formation of a federal cabinet became a necessity. On 14 January 1978, a Council of Advisers was formed. It comprised bureaucrats, military officers, technocrats, and a few persons with political backgrounds. The advisers enjoying the powers and status of federal ministers were:

> Mr Ghulam Ishaq Khan, Secretary-General-in-Chief, Finance, Provincial Co-ordination, and Planning.
> Mr A. K. Brohi, Law and Parliamentary Affairs, Religious and Minority Affairs.
> Lieutenant-General F. A. Chishti, Establishment, Kashmir Affairs, and Federal Inspection Commission.
> Mr Ghulam Mustafa Gokal, Shipping, Ports, and Export Promotion.
> Lieutenant-General (Retired) Habibullah Khan, Industries and Production.
> Air Marshal Inamul Haq, Interior.
> Mr A. G. N. Qazi, Finance, Economic Affairs, Statistics, Water and Power, Agrarian Management.
> Mr N. A. Qureshi, Railways.
> Mr Mahmud Ali, Housing and Works, Chairman, National Council of Social Welfare, Environment, and Urban Affairs.
> Sardar Maula Bakhsh Soomro, Commerce and Political Affairs.
> Mr Muhammad Ali Khan of Hoti, Education.
> Dr Amir Muhammad, Food, Agriculture, Co-operatives and Livestock.
> Mr Sharifuddin Pirzada, Attorney General.
> Mr Agha Shahi, Foreign Affairs.
> Rear-Admiral R. M. Sheikh, Petroleum and Natural Resources.

The two legal luminaries in the cabinet, Brohi and Pirzada, were professional rivals and not the best of friends. With Brohi as the Adviser for Law and Pirzada as the Attorney-General, their official relations were anything but smooth. Mr Pirzada, a sharp-witted shrewd operator, met General Zia soon after the portfolios were announced on 14 January and offered to resign if the appointment of Mr Brohi as Adviser for Law implied a lack of confidence in him. He was satisfied when General Zia told him that he and Brohi enjoyed equal status and that, as Attorney-General, Pirzada would report directly to him.

Mr Brohi had expressed a desire to become an Adviser for Foreign Affairs in addition to holding the portfolio of law. He did not press his request when told that Mr Agha Shahi had been earmarked for that slot. The Brohi request leaked out. Mr Agha Shahi enquired from me if Mr Brohi had requested some ministry other than that of law. He was assured that the allocation of the ministries made to the advisers was final.

The term 'adviser' turned out to be an inappropriate choice. It created psychological problems at home and frequently needed one to explain that the advisers were in fact federal ministers. The experience failed because a cabinet of non-political individuals did not inspire public confidence.

The political parties were invited to form a broad-based national government. This invitation aroused a mixed response. The PPP had already been alienated. The PNA was internally divided on the issue. Some political leaders were ambivalent, supporting the idea in private but lacking the courage to say so in public. The Muslim League (Pagaro Group) was eager to join the government but the PNA was a drag on it.

On 25 June 1978, General Zia declared in a broadcast to the nation that he had dropped the idea of forming a national government. On 5 July 1978, a 22-member Federal Cabinet comprising of 17 ministers and 5 ministers of state was announced. It included 5 Muslim Leaguers appointed on the basis of individual merit. The cabinet members and their portfolios were:

> Mr Ghulam Ishaq Khan, Finance, Planning, and Provincial Co-ordination.
> Mr A. K. Brohi, Law and Parliamentary Affairs.
> Lieutenant-General F. A. Chishti, Establishment, Kashmir Affairs, Federal Inspection Commission.
> Mr Fida Muhammad Khan, Housing and Works.
> Mr Ghulam Mustafa Gokal, Shipping, Ports, and Export Promotion.
> Lieutenant-General (Retired) Habibullah Khan, Industries and Production.
> Mr Mahmoud A. Haroon, Interior.
> Lieutenant-General Ghulam Hassan Khan, Petroleum and Natural Resources.
> Major-General Jamal Said Mian, States and Frontier Regions.
> Mr Gul Muhammad Khan Jogezai, Water and Power.
> Mr Muhammad Khan Junejo, Railways.

Mr Muhammad Ali Khan of Hoti, Education, Culture, and Tourism.
Mr Mohyuddin Baluch, Communications.
Mr Sharifuddin Pirzada, Attorney-General.
Khawaja Muhammad Safdar, Food Agriculture, Co-operatives, and Livestock.
Mian Zahid Sarfraz, Commerce.
Chaudhry Zahur Elahi, Labour, Manpower, Local Government, and Rural Development.

The ministers of state were:

Mr Hamid D. Habib.
Mr Javed Hashmi.
Mr Mahmud Ali.
Mr Agha Shahi.
Begum Viqarunnisa Noon.

The cabinet formation coincided with the first anniversary of the 1977 martial law. Soon thereafter, two ministers, Haroon and Pirzada, and the Chief Election Commissioner, Maulvi Mushtaq, voluntarily submitted their undated resignations to the author with the remarks that Zia could enter the dates whenever he lost confidence in them.

The unity of the PNA came under stress. Air Marshal Asghar Khan's Tehrik-i-Istiqlal quit the Alliance on 10 November 1977. Jamiat-i-Ulema-i-Pakistan started exerting its individuality and met the Election Cell as a separate entity. The National Democratic Party was not in favour of joining the government. The Muslim League was keen to do so. The Jamaat-i-Islami was also inclined to do so. The PNA Chief, Mufti Mahmud, faced a dilemma. He wanted the Alliance to survive because, individually, its component parties were too weak to defeat the PPP in a fairly contested poll.

The PNA leadership occasionally met General Zia and the Election Cell and discussed the possibility of joining the government. The frequency of such contacts increased after the conviction of Mr Bhutto on 18 March 1978. On 22 March, a PNA delegation, composed of Maulana Mufti Mahmud, Professor Ghafoor Ahmad, and Chaudhry Zahur Elahi indicated to the Election Cell its willingness to join the government. Despite a series of meetings, the modalities could not be agreed upon. Zia formed the federal cabinet on 5 July 1978, with some Muslim League ministers. The Muslim League's inclusion in the cabinet could have caused a split in the PNA. At its meeting held on 3 August 1978 in Rawalpindi, the PNA decided to join the government. The PNA parties haggled over details. Each wanted a large share of the cabinet cake and preferred to nominate its own representatives. The issue was settled with General Zia selecting the ministers through mutual consultation with the party leaders. The allocation of cabinet seats and portfolios to each political party was the next hurdle. The party demands were heavy. The CMLA had already promised some ministries to the non-PNA ministers and he desired a consensus on the allocation of other ministries. Nawabzada Nasrullah Khan asked for three cabinet posts for his tiny Pakistan Democratic Party (PDP). His colleagues smiled at his insistence. The CMLA offered him two cabinet seats. He demanded one more. The pleasant atmosphere suddenly became tense. There was a hushed silence. General Zia's patience ran out. He looked around and said, 'Well, I will be unfair to others if I accept your demand. I have stretched myself to the limit. It is for you to take it or leave it.' Nasrullah accepted the offer but declined to join the cabinet himself. Nasrullah had spent his political life in opposition, finding faults in every administration. He did not wish others to make him the butt of their criticism.

The previous cabinet resigned on 23 August 1978. The same day, a new cabinet with the PNA ministers included in it was sworn in. The ministers in the new cabinet were:

Mr Ghulam Ishaq Khan, Finance and Planning.
Mr A. K. Brohi, Law and Parliamentary Affairs.
Mr Fida Muhammad Khan, Housing and Works.
Mr Ghulam Mustafa Gokal, Shipping, Ports, and Export Promotion
Mr Mahmoud A. Haroon, Interior.
Haji Faqir Muhammad Khan, States, Frontier Regions, Northern Areas, and Kashmir Affairs.
Chaudhry Rehmat Elahi, Water and Power.
Mr Muhammad Khan Junejo, Railways.
Mr Muhammad Ali Khan of Hoti, Education, Culture, and Tourism.
Mr Mohyuddin Baluch, Communications.

Khawaja Muhammad Safdar, Food, Agriculture, and Co-operatives.
Mian Zahid Sarfraz, Commerce.
Chaudhry Zahur Elahi, Labour and Manpower.
Mr Iftikhar Ahmad Ansari, Religious and Minority Affairs.
Professor Ghafoor Ahmad, Production.
Mr Muhammad Zaman Khan Achakzai, Local Government and Rural Development.
Mr Ali Ahmad Talpur, Defence.
Mr Mahmud Azam Farooqi, Information and Broadcasting.
Mr Subuh Sadiq Khan Khoso, Health and Population.
Mr Muhammad Arshad Chaudhry, Science and Technology

Mr Sharifuddin Pirzada was sworn in as Attorney-General later, as he was away from the country at the time

The ministers of State were:

Mr Mahmud Ali.
Mr Javed Hashmi.
Mr Habib D. Habib.

Mr Agha Shahi was Adviser to the CMLA.

A significant feature of the cabinet was the absence of military personnel from it. The induction of a purely civilian cabinet was designed to inspire public confidence in it. Simultaneously, indoor political activity was permitted and the CMLA announced 1979 as the election year.

Many of the fresh inductees lacked ministerial experience. Some of them were inadequately groomed to handle state work. During the cabinet meetings, such ministers mostly detailed their secretaries to make presentations. Individually, they were simple and well-meaning persons, neither desirous of learning the rules of business nor caring much about them. This apathy brought them into conflict with the bureaucrats who, by tradition, followed the safe administrative path, littered with rules and regulations. The bureaucratic attitude irritated the ministers. They complained that their staff created hurdles in the performance of their ministerial functions. Three incidents will illustrate the point.

1.   A federal minister undertook a tour of the province of Sindh. He demanded that the concerned heads of the

divisional and district administration should accompany him to take down orders which he might like to issue on the spot. The provincial government declined to oblige the minister and he felt insulted. This was quoted as an act of 'the lack of co-operation by the civil servants who wanted the civilian cabinet to fail.'

2. One minister sent instructions to a deputy commissioner asking him to provide public funds in cash and to disburse the money to the persons to whom the minister might be pleased to provide relief during his tour of the district. The DC refused to oblige.

3. Most ministers were keen that the postings and transfers of civil servants in their own home districts should be made with their prior approval. Their demand was opposed by the provincial administrations.

In the cabinet meetings, much time was spent in discussing minor issues. The ministers complained that their visits to the provinces were resented by the provincial administration and the quality of transport provided to them on such occasions was below their status. They pointed out that the provincial MLA held conferences to coincide with the itinerary of federal ministers, which prevented the provincial secretaries from attending on them. They apprehended that the MLAs were hesitant to meet them. The provinces maintained that it was not possible for them to disrupt their pre-arranged meetings at short notice to meet some visitors from Islamabad. They accused the federal ministers of interfering in the local and provincial administration.

The grievances originated from a dichotomy. While the cabinet functioned at the federal level, the provinces were governed directly by the MLAs through the provincial secretaries. The PNA was keen to induct cabinets in the provinces. General Zia supported this demand. The provincial MLAs wanted to judge the performance of the federal cabinet before adopting that model in the provinces. This was a lame excuse. In fact, the MLAs, possessive about their respective provinces, preferred to administer them without political interference and were hesitant to share power. The CMLA was faced with a dilemma. He could not fully explain to his ministers the real motives of his MLAs and yet he had to carry his cabinet team with him. He adopted a wait and see policy, hoping that the passage of time might defuse the issue.

The release of the PNA workers during the anti-Bhutto agitation of March through July 1977 became a bone of contention. The provinces were prepared to release all such persons, except those who had been convicted by the courts of law on charges of a non-political nature. The PNA ministers maintained that the previous government had cooked up charges against their party workers. Finally, the unexpired portion of the sentences of the convicts were remitted and those detained without trial were set free.

The Brohi-Pirzada undercurrents of tension also surfaced. On 30 November 1978, Mr Brohi wrote a strong note to the President on the 'considerable misunderstanding touching and concerning the constitutional and legal status of the Attorney-General.' He raised four points:

1. The Attorney-General should not be a member of the federal cabinet.

2. In cases involving the government, the Attorney-General could only appear for the government and not as a law officer of the court.

3. The Attorney-General was under the administrative control of the Law Division. The Ministry of Law seriously objected to any reference being made directly or indirectly to the Attorney-General by the federal government except through the Law Division.

4. The Attorney-General had created virtual chaos in the handling of legal problems by the administration.

I wrote on the Brohi note: 'Should the President be pleased to accept the version of the Ministry of Law, the Attorney-General is most likely to resign. I am not sure if this is the game.' Zia saw through the problem. Both the ministers stayed, but eventually Mr Brohi left the cabinet and was accommodated elsewhere.

The PNA remained in the government from 23 August 1978 to 21 April 1979. During this period, President Daoud was assassinated in a *coup d'etat* in Kabul, Afghan refugees started migrating across the Durand Line into Pakistan. The Shah of Iran left his country, never to return again. Inside Pakistan, steps were taken to establish the

Shariah courts and to introduce Islamic laws; President Fazal Elahi Chaudhry resigned; and Mr Bhutto was executed.

On the occasion of Pakistan Day, 23 March 1979, General Zia declared his intention of holding general elections in the country in December 1979. His critics remained sceptical. One was reminded of a biting remark made by Mr David Frost on the BBC in 1970. Commenting on the elections announced by the then President, General Yahya Khan, he commented acidly: 'General elections will soon be held in Pakistan. Which General is going to win?' Nine years later, Pakistan faced the same problem with different actors.

In April 1979, the cabinet ministers were told that those wishing to participate in the election would be required to resign from their ministerships about three months before the polling date. Surprised, the ministers argued that, in a democracy, the cabinet stayed in power when elections were held. President Zia reminded them that during the Bhutto-PNA negotiations, the PNA itself had demanded that the government should resign before elections to demonstrate its impartiality. General Zia enquired if it would be morally correct for the PNA to renege on its own stand on the issue. Cornered, one of them said; 'If we have to resign around August, why not do so now? It would give us more time to prepare for the elections.'

Others endorsed that view. The federal cabinet resigned on 21 April 1979 and a new cabinet was installed. It comprised of military officers and those persons who did not wish to participate in the forthcoming elections.

The Election Cell

In July 1977, an Election Cell was created with Lieutenant-General F. A. Chishti as its chairman and Major-General Jamal Said Mian and Major-Generals (Retired) Rao Farman Ali and Ihsanul Haq as its members. Chishti enjoyed Zia's total confidence. In addition to commanding 10 Corps and being chairman of the Election Cell, he had two tenures of assignment as a federal minister where, at one time, he held charge of three ministries. Azad Kashmir also came under his purview. He was called the strong man of the Zia administration. The Election Cell met the leaders of the political parties, discussed their suggestions, and conveyed their ideas to General Zia. The politicians meeting it were aware of Chishti's equation with Zia. Normally, its meetings were held in Rawalpindi. When it met in other cities, its tour programme was announced in the Press in advance, to enable the political leaders to establish contact with it. Those who met the Cell belonged to all political parties, including a segment of the PPP. The charter of responsibility of the Election Cell covered the entire spectrum of political activity and its recommendations were made either orally or in writing.

In October 1977, the Election Cell mooted an idea that a Deputy Chief Martial Law Administrator be appointed. Chishti and Farman made this proposal in the MLAs Conference but it evoked a lukewarm response from other participants. The two kept repeating the proposal in the conferences held subsequently, with others not visibly taking serious note of it.

Martial law is an indivisible one-man rule. The Chief Martial Law Administrator draws his strength from his power-base, the army. Only the person who commands the Pakistan Army can successfully impose martial law. And he alone can administer the country under its label. The Chairman of the Joint Chiefs of Staff Committee and the Chiefs of Staff of the Navy and the Air Force lacked the means and the clout to perform this task. Seen in this context, the Deputy CMLA had to be a person from the army if he was to replace the CMLA on a permanent basis, in an emergency situation.

The chairman and members of the Election Cell argued that their object was to prevent confusion in the country in the event of Zia's sudden death or incapacitation. General Zia enjoyed the discussion but wilfully refrained from commenting on the proposal. He fully understood the motivation of the proposers and sensed equally well the implied intention. He finally intervened, saying, 'I appreciate the anxiety of the sponsors. They need not worry too much. The seniority structure in the army is clearly defined and well understood by everyone. Should something happen to me, the line of command is unambiguous. Keep praying.' The hint was too obvious to miss. The issue was never raised again.

Mr Ghulam Mustafa Khar of the PPP met the Election Cell frequently, saying that he had access to some important documents lying in the United Kingdom which implicated Mr Bhutto in several misdeeds. He requested permission to go abroad to fetch those documents. Chishti and the other members of the Election Cell made a request in an MLAs conference that Mr Khar be allowed a short visit to London. Some of the participants expressed serious doubts about Mr Khar's truthfulness and reliability. The members of the Election

Cell in general and Chishti and Farman in particular pleaded that their judgement in the matter be trusted. The two Generals confidently said; 'Mr Khar would return to Pakistan whenever required on three days notice.' That optimism was not shared by their colleagues sitting around the table. General Zia approved the Election Cell's recommendations. Mr Khar and his family left for London. He stayed abroad for the next eleven years in self-imposed exile and bitterly opposed Zia's rule, creating embarrassment for his benefactors in the Election Cell.

On his return to Pakistan in 1987, Mr Khar was arrested. After release from jail on bail, he issued a press statement, saying; 'I do not forget a helping hand given to me. I am grateful to Chishti and Farman for facilitating my departure from Pakistan in 1977. They both were aware that I would not return in a hurry.' Chishti and Farman did not make a public comment on this statement.

The performance of the Election Cell followed an uneven course. Starting on a high note, its utility and effectiveness decreased with the passage of time. After remaining dormant for a while, it was revived again in 1979. It ceased to function after its chairman, Lieutenant-General Chishti, retired from military service in March 1980. In the eyes of some critics, its performance was suspect. Professor Ghafoor Ahmad writes: 'This cell played the role of creating hurdles in the way instead of making elections a certainty.'[3]

The President's Resignation

President Fazal Elahi Chaudhry was to complete his five-year tenure of office in September 1978. On 10 August 1978, in a letter addressed to General Zia, he expressed his wish to retire on the completion of his period of assignment. General Zia requested him to continue holding his high office. The President reiterated his desire to quit. General Zia followed up his discussion with a letter addressed to the President on 12 August 1978, in which he said, 'while noting the President's desire to relinquish the Office of President on the expiry of normal term, I once again request that you may be pleased to reconsider your decision in the larger good of our country. If the President so desires we may discuss the matter again towards the end of this month.'

The President was adamant and resigned on 19 September 1978. General Zia then accepted the advice of Mr Sharifuddin Pirzada that he become the President, in addition to his responsibilities as the Chief Martial Law Administrator. Mr Fazal Elahi Chaudhry's exit from the government was a non-event in Pakistan. Some blunt comments appeared in foreign Press. *The Economist* said: 'Even habitual sycophants have stayed silent about the new President.'[4] Another view was: 'In this context, it will not be wrong to say that General Ziaul Haq's self appointment as the President of Pakistan is like a man marrying a woman with whom he has been living for so long that everybody took her as his legally wedded wife. His move seems to provide a *de jure* basis to what had long been accepted as a *de facto* reality.'[5]

Mr Fazal Elahi Chaudhry was a lawyer turned politician with more experience in politics than in law. He had remarkable foresight in sensing the public mood and anticipating political trends. He joined the PPP at the opportune time and became the titular head of state, performing ceremonial functions. As the President of Pakistan, in August 1973, he issued a political statement without taking the Prime Minister into confidence. Mr Bhutto promptly addressed a stiff letter to him pointing out that 'the Head of the State would be better advised not to make statements of a political character, whether in the context of internal problems or of external relations.'[6] Mr Fazal Elahi Chaudhry, hamstrung by the constitutional tilt towards the Prime Minister, meekly replied that 'I agree entirely with your views on the subject and I intend to abide by them in all my public pronouncements.'[7] Thereafter, throughout his tenure he was a nonentity as a President, unsure of himself, and subservient to the Prime Minister. Mr Bhutto's disrespect to the President is also disclosed in a widely circulated harsh letter, written by Mr Waqar Ahmad, the Cabinet Secretary, to the secretaries and others officials on 19 December 1974, directing that 'no ministry or department or provincial government should in future deal directly with the President's Secretariat on all such matters and should send any such request to the Prime Minister's Secretariat—addressed to the Secretary to the Prime Minister—who will examine the requirements of protocol before giving clearance.'

The President remained a silent spectator when the country faced serious turmoil following the rigged elections held in March 1977. The martial law of July 1977 might have been avoided if the distribution of constitutional powers between the President and the Prime Minister had been balanced and not lopsided as was the case. The President could play no constitutional role in averting the crisis.

Mr Fazal Elahi Chaudhry had no policy differences with General Zia. Their mutual personal relationship was cordial. Both met frequently and exchanged views on national affairs. General Ziaul Haq respected him for his age and experience, and for the valuable advice he occasionally gave.

The Hyderabad Conspiracy Case

The left-leaning National Awami Party (NAP) had been accused by the Bhutto government of anti-state activities. Mr Bhutto and the NAP leader, Khan Abdul Wali Khan, were arch political antagonists. Frequently, Mr Bhutto used to castigate Khan Abdul Wali Khan and his father, Khan Abdul Ghaffar Khan, for opposing the creation of Pakistan. Khan Abdul Wali Khan blamed Mr Bhutto for the breakup of Pakistan in 1971.

In 1947, Khan Abdul Ghaffar Khan mooted a vague theme of 'Pakhtunistan' (land of the Pakhtuns), without specifying its details. The proposal was rejected by the people of the North-West Frontier Province when they decided to join Pakistan. In that referendum, the Red Shirts (NAP) had abstained from voting. This theme was subsequently projected by Afghanistan, chilling her relations with Pakistan. At one stage, the Soviet Union came to support Afghanistan on the issue of the Durand Line. The Transfer of Power documents (published by the British Government in 1977) reveal that the idea of 'Pakhtunistan' had first been floated by the British Governor of the NWFP.

Paragraph 2 of a confidential letter written by Sir Olaf Caroe, Governor of NWFP, to Sir John Colville, Governor of Bombay, on 22 May 1947, reveals that:

2. The interesting local development in the political fields is that my Ministry and Abdul Ghaffar Khan have started propaganda on a theme which I advised them to take up some months ago: that of a Pathan national province under a coalition if possible, and making its own alliances as may suit it. When I put it to them then, they professed what amounted to fury at the mere suggestion. There is a good deal in the theme itself, and the appeal is a far more constructive one than that of Islam in danger. The switch-over has probably come too late, but to my mind it is a strength, and not a weakness, that Pathanistan cannot subsist financially or otherwise on its own legs. The weakness is that the Pathans have hitherto been

too divided among themselves to set up a stable state, and where they have ruled, they have ruled as conquerors of alien populations. They themselves have always been in a state of anarchy right through history until we came and put them in order (Afghanistan is not really a Pathan state at all).[8]

This letter depicts colonial treachery. Having failed to prevent the creation of Pakistan, the British, in collusion with the Hindu-dominated Indian National Congress, wished to stab the newborn state in the back.

The Bhutto administration had made a reference to the Supreme Court of Pakistan against the NAP. After hearing the case, the Supreme Court held the NAP guilty and the party was banned. The government arrested the top office-bearers of the NAP, lodged them in the Hyderabad Jail, and put them on trial under the Criminal Law Amendment Special Court Act of 1976. Because of the place of the trial, it assumed the name of the 'Hyderabad Conspiracy Case'. The trial commenced in 1975. Initially, nine persons were charged. The number of the accused subsequently increased to 92. The prosecution cited 445 prosecution witnesses. By January 1978, the evidence of 30 prosecution witnesses had been recorded. General Zia was asked at a press conference held on 14 July 1977 if all the political detenues would be released. His reply was: 'Incidentally, we have decided to dispense with all the special tribunals, except the one at Hyderabad. That is of a different nature.'

Before the year was out, General Zia went to Hyderabad and met Khan Abdul Wali Khan, Mr Khair Bakhsh Marri, and Mr Ataullah Mengal who were facing trial in the Hyderabad Conspiracy Case. Events then moved fast. Mr Ataullah Mengal was sent for heart surgery to the United States of America at government expense. Khan Abdul Wali Khan was shifted to the Combined Military Hospital, Rawalpindi, ostensibly for medical treatment. While in Rawalpindi, he met the CMLA twice, once alone and on the second occasion (12 December 1977) along with his wife, Nasim Wali Khan. I was present on both the occasions. Khan Abdul Wali Khan was very critical of Mr Bhutto's high-handed vindictive policies. 'Bhutto is a viper,' he told General Zia, adding that, 'He will bite you hard if you do not crush his head.' Months later, with Mr Bhutto facing trial, Wali Khan's views about him remained venomous. In a mischievously jocular manner he once said to General Zia: 'There are two corpses and a solitary grave.

If the Bhutto body is not buried first, you may be the one to lead the way.'

Commenting on the Hyderabad conspiracy case, Khan Abdul Wali Khan maintained that he had ideological differences with the Balochi leaders facing trial with him. 'Our visible unity is no more than skin-deep,' adding that, 'even this has been forced on me because the government had made me a co-accused with them in the joint trial.' Wali Khan maintained that the case, being politically motivated, should be withdrawn. A perusal of the prosecution case indicated that the trial had started with inadequate preparatory work and it was being conducted at a leisurely pace on an *ad hoc* basis. It was decided to end the agony. On 1 January 1978, the Hyderabad tribunal was dissolved. All persons under trial in that case were granted a general amnesty in the interest of 'national unity'. While announcing the decision, General Zia said: ' The underlying purpose of this step is to start a new chapter of life for national unity based on a system of dialogue, love and Islamic traditions and to forget the bitterness of the past for the wider interests of the country.' He called Khan Abdul Wali Khan and his father, Khan Abdul Ghaffar Khan 'patriotic Pakistanis.'

The dissolution of the Hyderabad tribunal and the release of Khan Abdul Wali Khan and others caused speculation. Was General Zia playing a cat and mouse game with the politicians of Pakistan? Was it an attempt to strengthen the unity of the PNA which was decomposing? Was the release of the secularist Wali Khan an attempt to counter the power of the fundamentalists in the PNA? Was it to woo the two smaller provinces—the NWFP and Balochistan? Was Mr Wali Khan being used as a trump card against Mr Bhutto, or was it a sincere attempt to bury the ill will of the past and make a new effort towards a better future? In my estimation, General Zia's decision was genuinely motivated by considerations of national unity and security. No doubt it had a bearing on the ongoing dialogue with Afghanistan, a subject discussed in Chapter 12.

After his release from jail, Khan Abdul Wali Khan spoke with vehemence. He called for the elimination of 'Bhuttoism' before general elections were held. He pleaded that Mr Bhutto be given the same treatment which the latter had meted out to him. He demanded that accountability of the politicians should precede the elections.

The possibility of General Zia being politically motivated in quashing the trial is a factor which can not be ignored. With Bhutto facing trial and the PPP opposing the government, Zia needed the moral support of as many politicians in the country as possible. If such a thought struck him or influenced his decision, he did not share his feelings with his colleagues. To be fair, it must be stated that basically it was Zia's initiative which ended the trial. Some of his team members questioned the wisdom of doing so, but eventually went along with him.

The Process of Accountability

The legal system being slow and cumbersome, the ninety-day period was inadequate to complete the process of accountability. The magnitude of the irregularities committed and the cases of gross misuse of state power and corruption which came to light surprised the government. Time and effort were needed to take the process of accountability to its logical conclusion. Many politicians (except those in the PPP) and a sizeable section of the national Press demanded that accountability should precede elections. The daily *Dawn* recorded: 'Frequent demands have been made for the quick removal of past irregularities and for instituting martial law enquiries into wide-ranging accusations of graft, nepotism, personally or politically inspired victimization and squandering of public wealth.'

The daily *Nawa-i-Waqt* said: 'It is a matter for the Martial Law authorities to ponder whether it was enough to publish the black deeds of those who, while being members of the Assemblies or holding important offices, had been guilty of malpractice and misappropriation of national wealth, and had also been playing with the life and honour of their political opponents. Is it not necessary to take stock of their doings and punish those against whom adequate evidence has come to light?' The *Morning News* had this to say: 'The misdeeds of the elected representatives have landed the nation in a vicious cycle of corruption. A rat race ensues that tramples all the finer values of life and pushes into the background the higher national objectives. The root cause of this evil is indeed the elected representative.'

A two-tier accountability plan was prepared. This involved the publication of a series of White Papers covering selected areas of the previous government's activities. Secondly, the assets and the performance of those who had held high public appointments were scrutinized to ascertain the allegations of the misuse of the national exchequer for personal gains. The task of compiling the White Papers was taxing. Those guilty of acts of commission or omission had taken care to cover up their misdeeds. Most bureaucrats were uncooperative in the investigative work, some because of their own involvement, and others for fear of retribution against them in the future. At times, some source provided a clue about a misdeed. The ministry concerned would dutifully send a heap of files to the CMLA Secretariat, without committing itself on the issue. With time, effort, and prodding, hidden facts started surfacing. While some irregularities were unearthed, a lot more remained undetected.

A senior civil servant undertook to compile the *White Paper on the Performance of the Bhutto Regime*. He addressed a letter to the ministries seeking details of the irregularities. Soon, the bureaucratic instinct got the better of him. He telephoned the recipients of his letter, urging its return to him in original. He wrote a brief narration in which the emotional content outweighed the facts. Eventually, the *White Papers* were written by a group of dedicated persons. The 'Performance' series was compiled by professional writers with known integrity and character. *Volume IV*, for instance, dealing with the economic policies of the Bhutto regime was put together by a banker. The bulkiest of the *White Papers*, relating to the conduct of the 1977 general elections, was pieced together by a talented Pakistani who willingly undertook the assignment when contacted, without bothering to discuss the terms of his engagement. On completion of his work, he refused to accept any remuneration, in cash or in kind, on the plea that his contribution was part of his attempt to put the historical record straight. Such selfless persons are hard to find in a society in which money makes the mare go. May God compensate him for his difficult work. The *White Papers* were issued in the following volumes:

A. **White Paper on the Conduct of General Election in March 1977**, issued in July 1978, covering 405 pages, and an additional 1,044 pages reproducing documents in the form of annexures.

B. **White Paper on the Performance of the Bhutto Regime, Volume I**, issued in January 1979, covering Mr Z. A. Bhutto, his family, and associates.

C. **White Paper on the Performance of the Bhutto Regime, Volume II**, issued in January 1979, covering *Treatment of Fundamental State Institutions*. These included the parliament, the executive, the judiciary, andthe administration.

D. **White Paper on the Performance of the Bhutto Regime, Volume III**, issued in January 1979, covering *Misuse of the Instruments of State Power.*

E. **White Paper on the Performance of the Bhutto Regime, Volume IV**, issued in January 1979, concerning *The Economy.*

F. **White Paper on Misuse of Media**, issued in April 1978.

The process of accountability of the erring individuals commenced with the promulgation of Martial Law Regulation No. 21. It required all the former members of the Senate, the National Assembly and the four Provincial Assemblies to declare their assets. The declarations made by them were scrutinized by a Scrutiny Board to assess if the assets and the properties held by them were within their declared sources of income. No further action was taken in respect of those individuals whose declarations were found in order. The cases of those persons who could not justify their assets were sent to a Commission of Inquiry, composed of a military officer and a civil magistrate for a detailed examination. The accused had an opportunity to personally explain his case and provide evidence in support of his claim. The Commission of Inquiry gave a decision of guilty or not guilty in each case. The cases for those found not guilty were dropped. Those found guilty were declared ineligible to contest public elections for a period of seven years. The former public representatives who were found to have either amassed wealth or were guilty of serious charges could face a trial in a military court. The process was lengthy. The projected period of seven years disqualification was fixed to debar those found guilty from participating in two national elections. As it turned out, the elections were delayed for so long that, in most cases, the punishment of disqualification became meaningless. The accountability process brought to the fore the badly eroded moral fibre of the society. The general pattern that emerged was distasteful and sickening. Instances of greed, corruption, lust for worldly pleasures, and the desire to get rich overnight through any means were found in abundance.

The Emergency in Balochistan

As indicated elsewhere, the internal security situation in the province of Balochistan had taken a serious turn and Mr Bhutto's government had directed the army to restore peace in the affected areas. By the time Mr Bhutto's government fell, the back of the insurgency had been broken, the army had made a network of roads in the hitherto inaccessible areas, the government writ had been re-established and the insurgency was reduced to minor sporadic incidents in some remote areas. In the process, casualties were suffered on both sides, the size of the military presence in the affected areas had steadily grown, and sufficient intelligence was collected about the insurgents and their links with elements inside and outside the country. Some insurgent leaders took shelter in Afghanistan which provided moral and material assistance to them to keep their activities going in Pakistan. There was evidence of the involvement of the Soviet Union and India to keep Balochistan destabilized. Iran expressed anxiety and hinted that she would not remain an idle spectator if the internal situation kept deteriorating. She donated a few utility helicopters to Pakistan to deal with the insurgents. The Shah did not relish the idea of a 'Greater Balochistan', incorporating parts of Balochistan, Afghanistan, and Iran in it. Such a proposal had been floated by the Soviet intelligence agency.

The internal situation in Balochistan had a history behind it. In 1972, the PPP formed the government at the federal level and in the provinces of Punjab and Sindh. The NAP formed coalition governments in the provinces of the North-West Frontier and Balochistan. This was a cause of irritation to Mr Bhutto who considered the NAP governments as hurdles in his exercise of total and unchecked authority in the country. The federal government exchanged pinpricks with the NAP governments, and their relations were anything but smooth. A minor law and order situation in Balochistan developed into a major confrontation in which Mr Bhutto dismissed the democratically elected ministry. In protest, the NAP ministry headed by Maulana Mufti Mahmud in the NWFP also resigned. This led to a chain reaction. The Baloch tribes in Balochistan felt offended at the dismissal of their elected government headed by Sardar Ataullah Mengal. In accordance with their traditional tribal style of expressing their resentment and anger, their men left their homes, took up positions on the hills, and started sniper firing at the vehicles which plied the roads. The federal government felt that its writ was being questioned. Having failed to exert its authority through the civil law and order agencies, the situation was handed over to the army to bring it under control. A large number of Marri tribesmen on the order of their sardar—Khair Bakhsh Marri—migrated to Afghanistan.

About this time, and in full view of the world media, a large quantity of arms was recovered from the Iraqi Embassy in Islamabad. Contrary to the advice given to him by the ISID, Mr Bhutto ordered the raid prematurely and did not allow more time to actually ascertain the final destination of the Iraqi arms.[9] He was obviously in a great hurry to draw political mileage out of this event. Accordingly, the ever-ready Mr Saied Ahmad Khan took charge of the operation and concocted a story that the arms were being sent to Sheroff (Sher Muhammad Marri), Mr Khair Bakhsh Marri, and other dissidents in Balochistan.

While the army was engaged in Balochistan, Mr Bhutto started wooing the members of the provincial assemblies of Balochistan and the NWFP by adopting a carrot and stick technique. Through a process of inducement, coercion, and graft, he used his charm and high-handed techniques and succeeded in winning over the members in the provincial assemblies and eventually establishing PPP governments in Balochistan and NWFP. It was possible for him to break party affiliations because the political institutions in the country were fragile and it was not an uncommon phenomenon for political leaders to change their political parties and loyalties, mostly in search of greener pastures.

The army toiled hard in Balochistan. In the process, it arrested a large number of dissidents whose interrogation revealed that the control of the sardars over their respective tribes was firm, and that tribal loyalties were strong and durable. By and large, the arrested dissidents refused to divulge information about their sardars, either because of their loyalty towards them or for fear of retribution, or both. In a tribal society, retribution is quick and severe. The tribesmen are intelligent, hardy, and nimble-footed; they are sharp-shooters and know the mountainous terrain of their area like the back of their hands. They conducted ambush operations with a remarkable success rate. Most of them were illiterate, and had spent their lives in the rugged mountains and the barren valleys with scarce water resources. Their sardars were demigods whose decisions were final and unquestionable for them. Mr Bhutto tried to do away with the Sardari system through legislative and administrative measures. By and large, the old barriers did not break in practice.

The insurgency enabled the army to gather intelligence about the customs and traditions of the area and the root cause of the prevailing lawlessness. While the internal unrest was exploited by the external powers, in essence it was administratively mishandled and politically created and exploited by the government itself. It became a matter of ego and prestige for Mr Bhutto to settle the issue through the force of arms on terms dictated by him. Equally, it became a matter of self-respect and honour for the tribes. They did not wish to succumb to pressure and surrender their traditional freedom and rights.

The problem in Balochistan was essentially political, economic, and psychological in nature. While the military had restored a temporary peace, a political action plan was needed to win over the hearts of the people and provide them better economic opportunities. The Zia administration reversed the Bhutto approach. All military operations in Balochistan were ended, troops were withdrawn from the area, a general amnesty was granted to all dissidents, and all those who had suffered were given monetary compensation. The decision produced immediate healthy results and peace returned instantly to the hitherto troubled area.

ANNEXURE 1

Z. A. BHUTTO'S LETTER TO PRESIDENT FAZAL ELAHI CHAUDHRY

Camp Hyderabad
29th August 1973

My dear President,

I have read with interest the statement which has been issued from the Presidency today answering some criticism in certain quarters about your recent pronouncements. While I appreciate the point made in your statement, I would suggest that, in order to inspire among our people a healthier respect for the Constitution and create a public awareness of the norms and practices of parliamentary democracy established in other countries, the Head of the State would be better advised not to make statements of a political character, whether in the context of internal problems or of external relations. This invests the Head of the State with a sanctity which is most important for Pakistan, particularly at the present stage of its political evolution.

Yours sincerely,

(Signed)
Zulfikar Ali Bhutto

Mr. Fazal Elahi Chaudhry,
The President,
Presidency,
Rawalpindi

ANNEXURE 2

PRESIDENT FAZAL ELAHI CHAUDHRY TO Z. A. BHUTTO

September 7, 1973

My dear Prime Minister,

I am grateful for your letter of August 29, 1973 regarding statements of a political nature by the Head of State. I anticipated some problems in this regard myself and had hoped to discuss the implications with you immediately after the inauguration. Unfortunately your preoccupation with the disastrous flood situation has not made this possible. May I state that I agree entirely with your views on the subject and intend to abide by them in all my public pronouncements.

There are some other aspects of this problem on which I would welcome your views but these can wait till your return to Rawalpindi.

Yours sincerely,

(Signed)
Fazal Elahi Chaudhry

Mr Zulfikar Ali Bhutto
Prime Minister of Pakistan
Camp Karachi.

CHAPTER 7

Verdict of Guilty

'I sentence Zulfikar Ali Bhutto, Mian Muhammad Abbas and Ghulam Mustafa to death. I also sentence Arshad Iqbal and Rana Iftikhar Ahmad to death. All these five accused shall be hanged by the neck till they be dead.'

So read the judgment in the criminal case number 60 of 1977, decided on 18 March 1978 by a full bench of the Lahore High Court, comprised of five judges. The judgment was unanimous. The full bench comprised of the following:

    Mr Justice Mushtaq Hussain, Chief Justice.
    Mr Justice Zakiuddin Pal.
    Mr Justice M. H. S. Qureshi.
    Mr Justice Gulbaz Khan.
    Mr Justice Aftab Hussain.

The judgment was written by Mr Justice Aftab Hussain to which all the other four judges had appended: 'I agree.'

Mr Z. A. Bhutto had held the office of the Prime Minister of Pakistan from 14 August 1973 to the night intervening 4 and 5 July 1977. Earlier, he was the Chief Martial Law Administrator and the President of Pakistan from 20 December 1971 to 14 August 1973.

On the night between 10 and 11 November 1974, at 12:30 a.m. Mr Ahmad Raza Kasuri, a member of the Opposition in the National Assembly of Pakistan, was returning to his house in Lahore in his car after attending a wedding in the city. He was driving the car himself. His father, Nawab Muhammad Ahmad Khan, was occupying the other front seat of the car. His mother and another lady were sitting in the rear. As he was negotiating a bend in the road, the car was suddenly fired at with automatic weapons. As a result of that attack, Nawab Muhammad Ahmad Khan received serious injuries. He was rushed to a hospital where he died after a few hours. The same night, a First Information Report (FIR) was registered by Mr Kasuri at the police station and the name of Mr Z. A. Bhutto was indicated as a suspected accused. The police officer tried to persuade Mr Kasuri not to mention the name of the Prime Minister in the FIR. However, on his insistence it was recorded. The police investigation failed to trace the alleged murderers. Significantly, the enquiry did not extend to the Federal Security Force (FSF), despite the fact that the ammunition used was found to be 7.62 mm calibre—a type used by the FSF. The police filed the case as untraceable on 1 October 1975, after obtaining instructions from the PPP government of the Punjab. The dependents of the deceased kept complaining that the case was hushed up by the government for ulterior motives.

Mr Ahmad Raza Kasuri was a founding member of the Pakistan People's Party, and had been elected on the ticket of that party as a member of the National Assembly in the elections held in December 1970. In his testimony in the trial court, Mr Kasuri said: 'The relations between Mr Bhutto and me cooled down and became strained after I found that Mr Bhutto was power-hungry.'

He was the only member of the PPP who went to Dhaka to attend the session of the National Assembly scheduled to be held on 3 March 1971. He did so against the advice of his party, as he felt it was 'in the interest of the integrity and solidarity of the country' to do so. Mr Bhutto had publicly threatened that 'Whosoever would go to Dacca, his legs would be broken and whosoever would be going to Dacca would be going on a single fare.'

From that day onward, Mr Kasuri's relations with Mr Bhutto had become estranged and 'serious differences' arose between them. The relations deteriorated further, Mr Kasuri said, 'I did not sign or vote in favour of the Constitution of Pakistan of 1973 since I considered it an instrument of tyranny which could only perpetuate one-man rule.'

In a privilege motion moved in the National Assembly on 29 November 1974, Mr Kasuri listed fifteen attacks made on his life between the period from May 1971 to November 1974. Mr Kasuri maintained that the assault on his car on 11 November 1974 was made as a result of a conspiracy hatched on the orders of Mr Bhutto to kill him. The firing resulted in the death of his father, while he escaped unhurt.

Victoria Schofield, Benazir Bhutto's friend and her successor as the President of the Oxford Union, records: 'But apparently one of the most crucial turning points, according to Kasuri's testimony and documents, came in June 1974, a few months before the murder, when

Bhutto was addressing the National Assembly. Always proud of the 1973 Constitution, he referred to the fact that it was unanimously adopted. An interruption came from the Assembly. It was Kasuri. He objected because, he said, he wished to put the record straight. Nine members of the National Assembly had not signed the Constitution, he protested, himself being one of them. Bhutto found this an unnecessary irritant. The nine members who had not signed the document were considered not to have opposed the Constitution but to have abstained. But Kasuri insisted. Bhutto lost his temper. "You keep quiet," he said. "I have had enough of you. Absolute poison." They argued. "Virtually a parliamentary scuffle took place," stated Kasuri. Bhutto concluded this episode by exclaiming, "I have had enough of this man. What does he think of himself?" Kasuri and the Prime Minister reconciled after the murder but this reconciliation was apparently only skin-deep.'[1]

In the words of Mr Kasuri during his testimony: 'I made a temporary peace as a matter of political strategy. I simply maintained a posture of affiliation with the party as a measure of expediency and self-preservation because I knew I was a marked man.'

The Federal Security Force was created as a civil task force of the federal government, ostensibly to assist the civil administration and the police in the maintenance of law and order, and, to quote Mr Bhutto, to enable 'a civilian government to avoid seeking the assistance of the armed forces in dealing with its responsibilities and problems.' The FSF was commanded by a police officer, Mr Masood Mahmud. At the time of its raising, the manpower was recruited from ex-soldiers and ex-policemen in a state of confused hurry. Many of them were later found to have been retired on disciplinary grounds from their previous services. The FSF was managed entirely by police officers.

The nucleus of the FSF was created in October 1972. In June 1973, Parliament passed an Act which authorized the raising of the FSF. It was equipped with rifles, automatic weapons, and rocket launchers. Plans were prepared to issue tanks and helicopters to the FSF. Mr Bhutto's government fell before these measures could be implemented. The FSF had its own intelligence cell. A Secret Service Fund was placed at the disposal of its Director General. In fact, the FSF was a mini parallel army. It was used to harass the Opposition. It committed state-sponsored acts of terrorism and sabotage which were dutifully attributed to Bhutto's opponents by the government-controlled information media. The FSF earned notoriety during the PNA's antigovernment agitation in 1977. It was accused by the Opposition of operating against its authorized charter of responsibilities and had become a weapon of terror to browbeat and silence those who dared to differ with Mr Bhutto.

After the deposition of Mr Bhutto on 5 July 1977, a committee was established under the chairmanship of Major-General S. R. Kallue to examine the performance of the FSF and make recommendations for its reorganization. The committee was informed by the Director (Operations and Intelligence) of the FSF that five truckloads of handwritten notes and documents were destroyed by burning under the direction of the former Director General. The committee's report said: 'The extent to which the organization went to keep people in line with the ruling party includes all forms of threats, coercion, intimidation, attempts to murder, arson, disrupting meetings, economic and administrative squeeze and illegal confinement.' The committee recommended the disbandment of the FSF. The recommendation was implemented.

In July 1977, the Federal Investigation Agency (FIA) was directed to assist the Kallue Committee in assessing the performance of the FSF. During the course of its investigation, FIA detected hard evidence implicating the FSF in the 11 November 1974 murder in Lahore. Two employees of the FSF were arrested. On interrogation, they confessed their participation in the commission of the offence. The links provided by them widened the net. More arrests were made, in which additional evidence was unearthed. The evidence implicated Mr Masood Mahmud, the Director General of the FSF. It may be recalled that Mr Masood Mahmud, while held in custody in Headquarters 10 Corps, had written a confessional statement accepting his crime and taking the plea that he had acted on the orders given to him by Mr Bhutto. The incriminating evidence was too strong to be ignored. Mr Bhutto was arrested on 3 September 1977, on the charge of the murder of Nawab Muhammad Ahmad Khan.

Mr Bhutto's arrest raised the question of his trial. A panel of prosecution lawyers meticulously scrutinized the heap of evidence pieced together by the investigators. After an indepth analysis they concluded that sufficient evidence was available to proceed against the accused persons. The prosecution case was complete. On legal merits, a trial was warranted.

There was a moral angle to the case. An innocent citizen had been gunned down in cold blood by a state agency. It was a premeditated, brutal murder, allegedly carried out on the orders of the head of the government. This revelation was as startling as it was painful. Those who govern are required by the Constitution to protect the lives of their fellow citizens. In a democratic polity, it is inconceivable that they should employ the state apparatus to eliminate their political opponents. The prosecution evidence also showed that the police agencies had acted half-heartedly at the investigation stages in 1974-5. They were either guilty of wilful neglect or of professional incompetence, or both. The incident had been swept under the carpet for nearly three years. Justice demanded that it should see the light of day.

No less compelling were the political overtones. It was rare for a prime minister to be privy to a murder and still more rare that he be tried for such a heinous crime. It was highly unusual for a person occupying such an exalted position to commit an act so low. Bhutto had his critics. He also had his admirers, well-wishers, and political followers. His involvement in a criminal case would stun some and enrage others. His trial, howsoever fair it might be, was expected to raise a political storm. Ulterior motives would be attributed to it. The government would face pressure. It involved a risk. Was the risk worth taking?

Justice outweighed all other considerations. Human life is sacrosanct. Its wilful destruction is an abominable and deplorable act. Mr Bhutto was accused of murder. Justice demanded that his innocence or guilt be proved in a court of law. The trial was on.

There were other charges against Mr Bhutto. These pertained to the misuse of secret funds, misappropriation of public money for personal use, and gross misuse of state power for personal and political ends. These cases were not pursued, as the murder charge was far more heinous and serious. The *White Paper* issued by the government contained the details of these charges.

More than one option was available on the mode of the murder trial. The prevailing environment and the political requirement both demanded a speedy disposal of the case. It was a legal and political necessity that the trial should not only be fully fair, it should also appear to be so to all impartial observers. One option was to hold the trial in a military court. That was a speedy course of action but had a serious disadvantage. A military trial might have given rise to objections that

VERDICT OF GUILTY

the accused did not get a fair deal. The sceptics might have called it a kangaroo court. It could be argued that the prosecution evidence was weak and it might not have resulted in conviction, if the trial were held in a civil court.

The case was tried in a regular civil court and in accordance with the normal civil law of the land. The charges were not framed under any martial law regulation or order. The possibility of holding the trial in camera was considered and rejected. The government felt it had nothing to hide from the public. The case was eventually heard in the premises of the Lahore High Court in Lahore in the presence of the members of the Press and the public.

Mr M. Anwar, an advocate of Lahore, was appointed as the special public prosecutor. He was an eminent jurist, excelling in criminal law. He was assisted by a competent team of lawyers: Mr Ejaz Hussain Batalvi, Mr Fazal Hussain, and the staff of the FIA, which had investigated the case. During the trial, Mr Anwar died of a heart attack. His place was taken by Mr Ejaz Hussain Batalvi.

The prosecution story was simple. Mr Bhutto desired to eliminate Mr Ahmad Raza Kasuri, who had become a constant source of political irritation to him. He directed Mr Masood Mahmud to do the needful. An assassination plan was prepared. It was implemented under the direction of Mr Masood Mahmud, employing FSF personnel and resources. In the murderous attempt, Mr Ahmad Raza Kasuri miraculously escaped, while his father, travelling in the car with him, was hit by bullets which killed him.

In September 1977, the prosecution team met General Zia and apprised him of the available evidence in the case. He was told that the evidence was sufficient to seek conviction in any court of law. There was one weak spot. Only one of the prosecution witnesses, Mr Masood Mahmud, had received direct orders from Mr Bhutto for the commission of the offence. His evidence was of vital importance for the case of murder to be established. General Zia was told that Mr Masood Mahmud had confessed his own incriminating role and would be an asset to the prosecution case if he was made an approver. Zia was reluctant. He was of the opinion that Mr Bhutto and Mr Masood Mahmud, being co-sharers in the crime, deserved to face trial along with the other conspirators. The FIA did not wish to weaken its case. Zia reluctantly agreed to grant a pardon to Mr Masood Mahmud when he made a request to that effect. Mr Masood Mahmud became an approver in the case.

Bhutto was arrested from his residence at Karachi on 3 September 1977. He was flown to Lahore and lodged in a bungalow. Peeved by his arrest, Mr Bhutto threatened the investigation staff and adopted an uncooperative attitude. Consequently he was transferred to Kot Lakhpat jail. Under the law, he was to face trial in the province of the Punjab—the venue of the crime with which he was charged. On 13 September, Mr Justice Samdani of the Lahore High Court granted bail to him because of some 'contradictions' in evidence. Three days later, Mr Bhutto was detained under a martial law order.

The trial commenced on 11 October 1977, at Lahore. Mr Bhutto pleaded not guilty to the charges levelled against him. He blamed the presiding judge, Mr Justice Mushtaq Hussain, of having a personal bias against him. Prime Minister Bhutto had had Mushtaq superseded for the office of the Chief Justice of the Lahore High Court. Bhutto also stated that the Central Executive Committee of the PPP, presided over by him, had criticized Mushtaq in respect of some statements made by him in his capacity as the Chief Election Commissioner in August 1977. Mr Justice Mushtaq stated that he had no animosity against the accused.

Mr Bhutto was defended by a panel of senior counsel led by the former Attorney General, Mr Yahya Bakhtiar, who had a greater standing in politics than in the legal profession. A well-meaning person with firm views, he had developed the art of losing the sympathy of his audience by his emery style oratory. Tolerance was not one of his virtues. Political loyalty weighed heavily in his appointment as the defence counsel.

The defence strategy was to prolong the trial and generate a feeling of sympathy in support of the accused. Mr Yahya Bakhtiar obtained frequent adjournments 'to prepare the case', and consumed excessive time in cross-examining the witnesses. His closing address was lengthy and acrimonious. The time gained was used for building up public opinion at home and abroad against the trial.

The defence counsel claimed that the case was politically motivated and had a weak legal basis. Knowledgeable Bhutto supporters confessed that the quality of defence counsel themselves left something to be desired. Mr Bhutto's biographer writes: 'Hayat M. Junejo, an extremely capable criminal lawyer . . . was dropped as he refused to fight the case on any basis other than its legal merit . . . D. M. Awan was inarticulate, often ill-prepared and on several occasions was admonished by Bhutto himself for failing to argue coherently.'[2]

The defence counsel established a less than smooth relationship with the court. Periodically, the court was castigated for being partial. Such accusatory remarks generated heat during the trial. If Mr Yahya Bakhtiar and Mr Bhutto were abrasive and excitable, Justice Mushtaq was not the judge to tolerate any uncivil behaviour in his court. An ugly incident took place on 17 December 1977. Mr Bhutto was tense in the court because on the previous day his wife and his daughter had sustained minor injuries while witnessing a cricket match at the Qaddafi Stadium, Lahore. Mr Bhutto asked his counsel, Mr Awan, to request the court for a slight adjustment in the court hours to enable him to receive news about the welfare of his family. The counsel failed to make the submission. As the court was about to rise, Mr Bhutto harshly swore at his counsel and said in a loud enough voice: 'Damn it, why don't you address the court?'

Justice Mushtaq took exception to the language used. Mr Bhutto tendered an apology, explaining that he was in a disturbed state of mind. Mushtaq replied: 'We don't care.'

'I have had enough,' said Bhutto.

The Chief Justice looked into Mr Bhutto's eyes and enquired: 'Enough of what?'

Mr Bhutto shot back, 'Of your insults.'

A surprised Justice Mushtaq turned red in the face. Controlling his temper he ordered the police officials: 'Take this man away until he regains his senses.'

The trial proceedings, witnessed by local and foreign observers, received wide publicity. Some foreign journalists stayed for weeks and covered the court deliberations on a regular basis. They also interviewed a cross-section of political leaders (mostly belonging to the PPP), speculated widely, and wrote copiously on the political implications of the trial. Their dispatches generally favoured the underdogs.

Some foreign lawyers and members of human rights groups also visited Pakistan. Mr Ramsey Clark, the former US Attorney General was one of them. His request to meet Mr Bhutto in jail was not accepted as it might have given a political colour to a criminal case. Unhappy at the rejection of the request, he came to believe that the prosecution evidence 'would not support a verdict of guilty'.

The International Federation of Human Rights was represented at the trial by a French lawyer, Monsieur Etienne Jaudel who found 'anomalies' in the case. Another French lawyer, Monsieur Robert

Badiner, after a short visit made a characteristic remark that 'History will judge the judges.'

The courtroom was invariably full with visitors. The evidence was heard in rapt silence. The Press reported all the details; nothing remained hidden. As the trial progressed, the facts came to the fore. The admirers and the critics of Mr. Bhutto speculated and wondered about the outcome of the case. Held on a day-to-day basis, the trial was spread over a period of five months. Those agonizing months were full of hope and fear. The time of decision finally came. On 18 March 1978, the courtroom was packed to capacity. The hearts of the accused persons and the visitors probably beat faster than normal when the judges, attired in wigs and their flowing robes, entered the courtroom at the appointed time. All eyes were focused on the judge who announced the judgment in a measured tone. It read:

> ... All the offenses which the accused are charged with are thus proved to the hilt. It is also proved that the conspiracy to murder Ahmad Raza Kasuri did not end with the death of Nawab Muhammad Ahmad Khan but continued even thereafter. He [Mr Bhutto] has been hurling threats as well as insults on us and at times had been unruly. In addition, he has proved himself to be a compulsive liar. . . . the principal accused [Mr Bhutto] is the arch culprit having a motive in the matter. He has used the members of the Federal Security Force for personal vendetta and for satisfaction of an urge in him to avenge himself upon a person whom he considered his enemy. For his own personal ends he has turned those persons into criminals and hired assassins and thus corrupted them.

In a unanimous decision, all the five accused were awarded capital punishment by the court. They had the right to appeal. All the convicted persons filed appeals against the judgment of the Lahore High Court in the Supreme Court of Pakistan. Keeping in view the sensitivity and importance of the case, the appeals were heard by the full court of nine judges comprising Chief Justice Anwarul Haq, Mr Justice Qaiser Khan, Mr Justice Waheeduddin Ahmad, Mr Justice Muhammad Akram, Mr Justice Dorab Patel, Mr Justice Muhammad Haleem, Mr Justice Ghulam Safdar Shah, Mr Justice Karam Elahi Chauhan, Mr Justice Nasim Hassan Shah.

On 30 June 1978, Mr Justice Qaiser Khan retired from the court on attaining the age of superannuation. Thereafter, the hearing was continued with the remaining eight judges till 20 November 1978, when Mr Justice Waheeduddin Ahmad, a patient of hypertension and diabetes, suffered a cerebro-vascular accident which seriously impaired his eyesight, speech, and general physical activity. The hearing of the case was adjourned till a medical board decided that the ailing judge had unfortunately been incapacitated, 'with a strong likelihood that residual neurological damage may be left permanently.' He did not participate in the court proceedings any further. The criminal appeals were therefore decided by the remaining seven judges.

On 17 May 1978, an elegantly dressed Bhutto travelled in a police van from Kot Lakhpat Jail to Lahore airport. An army helicopter brought him to the Dhamial base at Rawalpindi. The early morning journey was smooth and uneventful. A police van with an escort waited for him at the Dhamial helipad. It was the same type of vehicle in which he had travelled in Lahore in the morning. As Mr Bhutto alighted from the helicopter, the police officer requested him to move towards the police van. His mercurial temperament suddenly got the better of him. Without any provocation, Mr Bhutto became emotional. Talking loudly in an angry mood he said: 'Is this transport worthy of a prime minister? I refuse to travel in it. I can't take such an insult.' A few moments later, he calmed down, sat in the police van, and was escorted away. He was lodged in the district jail, Rawalpindi, as prisoner number 3183.

The Supreme Court gave personal hearings to all the five convicts, including Mr Bhutto. These hearings started on 18 December 1978. Mr Bhutto's address to the court lasted several days. He was well-prepared for the occasion. He spoke at length about the entire spectrum of his life. This included his roots in Pakistan; his days at Christ Church College, Oxford; his twenty years experience in the National Assembly of Pakistan; his respect for his faith, which was a matter between him and his God; his achievement of hosting the Second Islamic Summit Conference in Lahore in 1974; the immense services he had rendered for the country; the enforcement of prohibition in Pakistan, and the introduction of many Islamic measures in 1977 by his government; changing the name of the Red Cross Society to the Red Crescent Society; the decision of the National Assembly to declare Ahmadis as non-Muslims; and the hardships faced by him in the jail due to the *mala fides* of 'a sick and depraved regime'. Mr Bhutto's lengthy statement also covered his favourite subject—the prevailing geo-strategic environment. He saw a void in Pakistan at a time when the country was precariously poised. He foresaw a crisis brewing in the subcontinent.

The Supreme Court allowed Mr Bhutto complete freedom to express his views without interruption, even though he mostly dilated upon issues which were irrelevant to the case. Only once did the Chief Justice remind him: 'This is all interesting, but would you like to come to the point?'

He did. Mr Bhutto pleaded that the case against him was 'a tissue of lies—a bad novel—a concocted story.' In a voice charged with emotion, he said: 'It is all a fantasy. No conspiracy—it was all the figment of a malicious imagination of a sick mind.'

Taking strong offence at being called 'a compulsive liar' in the High Court judgment, Mr Bhutto felt peeved. He called it an unfair remark. He contended that his reputation, his political career, the honour and the future of his family and that of Pakistan were involved in this case. He asked for justice.

Mr Bhutto showed profound gratitude for being heard patiently in the Supreme Court. Expressing unqualified confidence in the Court, he said: 'I am in your hands.' At one time while addressing the Court, Mr Bhutto said: 'Thank God, I have been allowed to say something. You have done me this favour and you have given this right to me. You can even hang me now.'

Mr Bhutto with a shrewd mind, command over the language, and oratory skills tempered with emotion, made a lucid impressive submission. He took full advantage of the fact that, under the law, the statement of a convict was neither made under oath nor could it be subjected to cross-examination.

The remaining four co-convicts also addressed the court. Their submissions were brief and to the point. They pleaded that they merely obeyed the orders given to them by their superiors as they could not have dared to disregard them. They incriminated Mr Masood Mahmud and Mr Bhutto, and pleaded for mercy.

The hearing was over. The judges retired to reflect on the evidence and write their judgment.

The Supreme Court announced its judgment on 2 February 1979. The main judgment, spread over 825 pages, dismissing all the appeals, was written by Chief Justice Anwarul Haq, with whom Mr Justice Muhammad Akram, Mr Justice Karam Elahi Chohan, and Mr Justice Nasim Hassan Shah agreed. Mr Justice Muhammad Halim, Mr Justice

G. Safdar Shah, and Mr Justice Dorab Patel disagreed with the majority view.

Chief Justice Anwarul Haq in his judgment said: 'I am left in no doubt that the prosecution has fully succeeded in establishing its case ... There is absolutely no support for the contention that the present case was politically motivated, or was the result of international conspiracy ... The cumulative effect of all this oral and documentary evidence is to establish conclusively the existence of motive on the part of appellant Zulfikar Ali Bhutto; and the existence of a conspiracy between him, approver Masood Mahmud, approver Ghulam Hussain and appellants Mian Mohammad Abbas, Ghulam Mustafa, Arshad Iqbal and Rana Iftikhar Ahmad ... It is a pity to find that from the very beginning the appellant (Mr Bhutto) entered upon his trial with an initial bias ingrained into him against the Court (Lahore High Court) and as the prosecution evidence involving him began to pour in, he instead of defending himself, became more and more defiant and indulged in scurrilous and scandalous attacks on the Court. He was thus responsible for having created tension....'

As to the sentence, he went on to say: 'This was a diabolic misuse of the instruments of state power as the head of administration. Instead of safeguarding the life and liberty of the citizens of Pakistan, he set about to destroy a political opponent by using the power of the Federal Security Force, whose Director General occupied a special position under him. Ahmad Raza Kasuri was pursued relentlessly in Islamabad and Lahore until finally his father became the victim of the conspiracy, and Ahmad Raza Kasuri miraculously escaped. The power of the Prime Minister was then used to stifle proper investigation, and later on to pressurize Ahmad Raza Kasuri in rejoining the PPP. All these facts go to show that there are no extenuating circumstances in favour of the appellant, and the High Court was accordingly right in imposing the normal penalty sanctioned by law for the offence of murder as well as its abetment.'

The Supreme Court dismissed the three appeals by a majority decision of four to three, and the sentences recorded by the High Court were upheld and confirmed except for a minor variation.

In his dissenting judgment, Mr Justice G. Safdar Shah expressed the view that certain statements of Masood Mahmud, being in the nature of hearsay, were not admissible in evidence. Besides, this approver was not a reliable witness. He also felt that the existence of a criminal conspiracy between Zulfikar Ali Bhutto and Masood Mahmud had not been proved.

Disagreeing with the majority view, Mr Justice Dorab Patel did not consider Masood Mahmud a reliable witness and stated that his evidence required stronger corroboration needed in this type of murder case, based on the evidence of an approver.

The third judge, Mr Justice Muhammad Haleem, while agreeing with Mr Justice G. Safdar Shah, expressed the view that the case against Bhutto and Mian Abbas had not been proved, but since the other appellants had confessed to the crime, there was no doubt with regard to their guilt.

All the convicted persons filed review petitions before the Supreme Court. These were heard by the full court and were unanimously rejected by all the seven judges, including the three judges (Haleem, Safdar Shah, and Dorab Patel) who had earlier disagreed with the majority view. It was a sad and a shameful day for the people of Pakistan. The head of their elected government was convicted on the charge of murder by the highest civil court in the country.

The legal battle was over. The necks of the five convicts were in the noose. Under the Constitution, only the President of Pakistan had the authority to commute their sentences. Would General Zia exercise his discretion? This was the question which was widely speculated on.

A reflective reading of history reveals its hidden ifs and buts. The wisdom of hindsight raises many questions. The delaying tactics adopted by Bhutto's counsels unnecessarily prolonged the trial. In the process, two out of the original nine Supreme Court judges, who comprised the full bench, were no longer on the bench when the four to three split judgment was announced in February 1979. The judgment might have been different if those two judges had still been on the bench at the time of decision.

From his death cell, Mr Bhutto managed to smuggle out some papers which were later compiled and published in India as a book titled 'If I Am Assassinated'. This is a piece in his self-defence, in which he curses his stars for all his ills. His motive in writing the book and the authenticity of its contents will continue to be doubted and debated in the future as well.

CHAPTER 8

The Tragic End

At four minutes past 2 a.m. on 4 April 1979 Mr Zulfikar Ali Bhutto breathed his last. He was hanged to death in the district jail, Rawalpindi. By a coincidence, the hanging site was located a couple of hundred yards away from his seat of power, the luxurious house of the Prime Minister, which had been occupied by him since December 1971. It is not for human beings to comment on such contrasts. Verse 26 of *Surah Al-Imran* in the Holy Quran reads:

> 'O Lord of all dominions,
> You give whom it pleases You the kingdom,
> and You take away the power from whosoever You will;
> You exalt whom You please and debase whom You will.'

Mr Bhutto, deeply conscious of his place in history, was a successful populist leader. In the emotionally charged political climate of Pakistan, the Bhutto era is yet too close for any one to speculate on his place in history. Will he be acclaimed for his charisma and intelligence, or censured for his authoritarian and brutal rule, and denial of liberty to those who dared to differ with him? Will he be praised for lifting the sagging morale of a nation defeated in war and for creating a political awakening in the masses, or criticized for systematically destroying the institutions of the country? Will he be credited for giving a Constitution to Pakistan or blamed for violating the letter and spirit of the same Constitution? The list could be long. This is not the place to discuss his strengths and weaknesses. He was a human being who had his virtues and failings. With the passage of time, objectivity will replace emotionalism, the fog will disperse, and his appropriate place in history will be determined by unbiased observers and historians. For the present, he has gone down in history as the first elected Prime Minister of Pakistan who was sentenced to death by the Supreme Court of the country, for the murder of a political opponent whom, as the Chief Executive of Pakistan, it was his duty to protect.

It is a matter of academic interest whether Mr Bhutto's fate could have been different if his legal, political, and media experts had adopted a different operational strategy during and after his trial. On the legal plane, the defence effort was to prolong the trial, adopt a defiant attitude, put the judges and the courts under political pressure, and accuse the administration of digging out a 'trumped up' charge against Mr Bhutto. The defence laboured hard to give a political colour to a criminal case. The attempt misfired.

Mr Bhutto committed a political error. The rigged elections had tarnished his image and credibility. His arrest split the PPP. The nomination of Mrs Nusrat Bhutto as the acting Chairperson of the PPP, during the period when Mr Bhutto was in custody, was resented by the party diehards as an undemocratic act. It turned the party into family property and started a political cult. Some PPP leaders left the party in protest. Some weak-kneed members sulked but remained in the party fold. A third group went abroad into self-exile to distance itself from the tragic scene. Yet others were silently happy over Bhutto's ordeal. They saw their own political rise in Bhutto's eclipse. Such internal divisions weakened the PPP. It turned into a group of dedicated workers without a far-sighted and dynamic leadership. The party popularity graph dipped low. Its street power diminished. Bhutto's trial and execution proved that point.

Strangely, Bhutto's strategy was naively simplistic. He depended excessively on external support to save his life. After his conviction in the High Court, a major effort was launched in foreign countries on his behalf, urging their governments to request the government of Pakistan to show leniency in the case. The action plan prepared with meticulous care was implemented at two levels. PPP workers and sympathizers living abroad were rallied to hold protest meetings on selected occasions. The main target areas were the USA, Canada, England, Denmark, and Holland. An organized attempt was made to win over the sympathy of the foreign Press corps, eminent legal journalists, law institutions and universities, and prominent writers in Europe and America.

The more taxing and confidential high level work was performed exclusively by the Bhutto family members. This involved establishing contacts with the governments in Iran, the United Arab Emirates, Libya, England, and the United States. For this, the policy guidelines were prepared in Pakistan and sent to the Bhutto family members abroad for implementation.

THE TRAGIC END

It is not the intention here to question the *modus operandi* of the Bhutto strategy. A course of action was adopted to achieve a desired goal. The end result failed to justify the expectations. This teaches us a lesson. External crutches, whether in the field of economy, defence, or diplomatic support, are inherently a poor substitute for internal strength. External help is a bonus—it cannot replace internal power. Over-reliance on others is a self-defeating process. The Bhutto family learnt this lesson at considerable cost.

In the assessment of the 'save Bhutto' strategists, the key to their success was President Jimmy Carter. He alone, in their view, possessed the economic, diplomatic, and other leverage which could pressurize General Zia to save the life of Mr Bhutto. All efforts were thus directed to urge upon the US President that he exercise his immense influence to achieve that end.

The guidelines were provided by Miss Benazir Bhutto to her brother, Mir Murtaza Bhutto, living abroad in self-exile. On 26 March 1978, in a long handwritten letter, she sent comprehensive instructions to him. Copies of her letters were obtained during a search of Bhutto's papers. These are quoted at length to illustrate the Bhutto family's viewpoint. On the conduct of the trial, Miss Benazir said:

> Don't tell the other children, but the Supreme Court will most probably rubber stamp Maulvi Mushtaq's judgement and they will try to carry it out immediately so as to make the foreign pressure impossible (let our foreign friends know this). Therefore, all our efforts have to be made now.... TIME IS OF THE ESSENCE.

The advice to Mir Murtaza continues:

> It would be productive if you could go to America and through the Kennedys, Galbraith, Kissinger, Nelson Rockefeller, George Bush (and) Devek Rock get something done.... Galbraith and Kennedy can put you in contact with the 'reasonable' senators. George McGovern should be thanked.
>
> *Approach to Senators etc*: ... you can say, 'you may be thinking why I came to meet [you].' They will say, 'why come to us when you hold us responsible and have attacked us in the trial, in the courts and in other cases?' The answer is, the reason we have come to you is because you are responsible for the destabilization of Pakistan and for the perpetuation of the martial law. It is only logical, and indeed moral, that we request you to put right the terrible wrong. It is your moral responsibility. If you act on this moral responsibility you should win the abiding goodwill of the

people of Pakistan. It might also help remove the strong suspicion in the minds of our people that you are behind this despised regime.

This regime, due to its colossal blunders, and its defective and archaic policies will not last. Sooner or later it will collapse. Its repression has been senseless. The land of the pure has been turned into a land of lashes. The subcontinent is not Latin America or Africa where military dictatorships are the order of the day. The subcontinent has had a long history of the right to vote and of democracy. It has had a tradition of a freedom struggle. In India the people rejected Indira Gandhi because she imposed civilian dictatorship for 19 months. In Pakistan the people overthrew the dictatorship of Ayub Khan. Another mass movement in Pakistan will lead to bloodshed and disruption... If the junta does not hold elections, there will either be a mass movement or another coup d'etat. Another coup executed by charlatans who have not the slightest idea of the art of politics or the ability to govern a complex country like Pakistan, would precipitate the 'balkanization' of Pakistan, and set into motion a train of fissiparous tendencies in India as well.

After you meet as many as Senators as possible, through Galbraith, Kennedy and any others, then contact the Iranian Ambassador in Washington, Ardeshir Zahidi and get him to introduce you to other Senators. *American pressure is vital.* [Emphasis added.] ... But we must not let the Americans think we have weakened.... that is in our mutual interest that American pressure be exerted to the appeal and to the early holding of the general elections. Both of us speak from a position of strength but our strength is more durable. The people of Pakistan are with us. General Zia will go in time. Now is the time for us to open a new chapter as suggested by Vance [the Secretary of State] last April. Let them take the first step. But let there be no delusion that the PPP can be crushed. Begum Bhutto is the accepted leader already. Should she be disqualified, then the people of Pakistan during the election campaign and during her Sindh tour in February have demonstrated that they will accept her as their leader. These are the general lines for you to develop. If the Americans tell us to completely stop attacking them, tell them we will stop completely when they bring about a new situation. In the absence of a new situation it is unreasonable to expect us to stop.

We brainwash the Senators so they can appeal on their own. McGovern did. More importantly, tell Jimmy Carter to appeal as such a step is in the American interests. *Jimmy's appeal will be the decisive one.* But the motion must be set now as he [General Zia] may try to forestall foreign pressure by immediately carrying out the sentence within hours of the Supreme Court judgement.

THE TRAGIC END

Miss Benazir's strategy as advised to her brother was: 'Please do not let the press know whom you are meeting. News has just come over the teleprinter that you met Gaddaffi. Please be very careful. Please do not take Khar [Ghulam Mustafa Khar] to America. He must not know your contact.'

Four days later, some more instructions were sent. Some excerpts from Miss Benazir Bhutto's letter to Mir Murtaza Bhutto, written on 30 March 1978:

> I hope Sheikh Zayyad has given you a contact in London for sending the messages to him. The Sheikh has been a superb friend. We must take him into confidence over the fact that they wish to execute Papa (God forbid) within hours of the Supreme Court judgement. The Sheikh has very good relations with Iran and Saudi Arabia. Iran and Saudi Arabia have good relations with U.S. Therefore, if His Highness would be kind enough to ask both Iran and Saudi Arabia to put pressure on Jimmy Carter to ask for the commutation of the sentence on humanitarian grounds (or services to the world) as soon as the Supreme Court announces the judgement. If Carter is pressurized, his Ambassador can call on Zia as soon as the sentence is confirmed by the Supreme Court, to commute it. Iran and Saudi Arabia have a lot of pull with America. Perhaps Sadaat can help here too. Discuss the point with the Sheikh's man in London. I am sure he has given you a contact there. Kubah may ask Greece and France to put pressure in a diplomatic but forceful way on Jimmy. Please let me know by sending a letter through Frederick about all your activities. Please don't take Khar, Tariq, Poncho, Osman or Najeeb or any others into confidence about the American or Arab offensive mentioned in the letter. The less they know the better. But Khar must be tricked into believing that we tell him everything. Khar is a big trickster but this time you must be the bigger trickster. I believe you met the Chinese Ambassador and the Russian Ambassador. I hope the Chinese are putting the heat on Zia. If it is possible, please see the Chinese Ambassador and request him in a dignified manner to ask the U.S. to intercede and commute the sentence. The Chinese also carry weight with the Americans. If the Russians want to help, they can really put tremendous pressure on Zia—perhaps they can put pressure on the Americans too. Much depends on the influence America, Saudi Arabia and Iran exert on Zia. However, do you think our friends will launch a diplomatic offensive even after the Supreme Court or do you think they feel that they have done their best and there is no more they can do? If all our international friends do not immediately swing the diplomatic machinery for commutation

after the announcement of the Supreme Court decision, we may be in trouble. If the Arabs cut off all the economic aid, it can exert big pressure on Zia.

The pressure should be exerted whether it is done quietly or publicly. Moreover, American intercedence is crucial. It is here that Iran, Saudi Arabia and China can play a role besides the direct pressure they can put on Zia. If they threaten to cut off all the economic aid, what can Zia do? France can also pressurize Jimmy and your American trip will be our internal pressure on Jimmy. But please be very quiet about these activities as any leakage is counter-productive. Please do not confide in Tariq. He tells his mother who tells Roedad [Secretary Interior] who tells Zia.

P. S. Try not to get photographed with Khar. It has an unfavourable reaction here.

General Zia's views on the issue of clemency were publicly stated by him. In reply to a question asked by a press correspondent, he had said unambiguously: 'If the Supreme Court says "acquit him," I will acquit him, if it says "hang the blighter," I will hang him.'[1]

The Bhutto lobby misread Zia's statement as a political gimmick, played at a time when pressures on him had not yet reached a climax against the death sentence. An adversary should be respected. The Bhuttos underestimated Zia's capacity to resist foreign interference in Pakistan's domestic affairs.

The Muhammad Ahmad Khan murder case frequently came under discussion in the cabinet meetings. The cabinet did not debate the facts because the case was *sub judice*. During those deliberations, the ministers complained that the trial received excessive publicity in the local Press. They criticized the external publicity wing of the government for not having effectively rebutted the slanderous campaign launched against Pakistan by a section of the Press in some foreign countries, particularly in England and in the United States of America.

The media's interest in the case was logical and justified. The persons under trial included the former head of the government and the penalty of conviction was heavy. The wide Press coverage of the trial in Pakistan had a healthy effect. It silenced critics who were surprised to see the degree of freedom enjoyed by the Press during martial law.

The trial over, the Pakistan government started receiving appeals from foreign countries. These were appropriately couched in diplomatic language, requesting clemency on humanitarian grounds. The validity of the trial and its legal details were not questioned by the appeal-makers. Their requests took the added precaution of saying that they did not wish to interfere in the internal affairs of Pakistan. Their appeals for mercy, they pointed out, were motivated by their sentiments of friendship with Pakistan.

About thirty clemency requests were received. It was emphasized in them that Zia's image would be enhanced if he converted the sentence of death into a lesser punishment. The Soviet Union and China sent appeals. So did Chancellor Helmut Schmidt, President Giscard d'Estaing, UN Secretary General Kurt Waldheim, Mr Yasser Arafat, and Mrs Indira Gandhi. President Carter was against the implementation of the sentence. The US House of Representatives passed a clemency resolution saying that the commutation of the sentence would be a statesmanlike and humane gesture. The Muslim countries who approached General Zia included Saudi Arabia, Iran, Turkey, the United Arab Emirates, Kuwait, and Qatar. Some countries sent special emissaries who pleaded for compassion and mercy. One Muslim country expressed its willingness to grant political asylum to Mr Bhutto if he was expelled from Pakistan. The Prime Minister of India, Mr Morarji Desai, declined to intervene, saying that he did not wish to interfere in Pakistan's internal affairs. The British Prime Minister, calling Zia 'a very wise man,' felt that an approach beyond the strict application of law would be more beneficial to Pakistan.

Whereas clemency requests were received in respect of Mr Bhutto, no such concern was shown by the world at large about the fate of the other four convicts, sentenced to death in the same case. This occasioned a comment from General Zia that it was a 'trade union activity,' in which politicians were seeking to save a politician's life. While many countries expressed anxiety, none gave even a hint of straining bilateral relationships, of raising the issue in any international organization, or of withdrawing their ambassador in protest if the sentence was carried out. This caused no surprise as the case was purely an internal matter.

It may be recalled that Mr Fazal Elahi Chaudhry, the President of Pakistan, had retired in September 1978. At that time Mr Bhutto had been convicted by the Lahore High Court and his appeal was under consideration in the Supreme Court of Pakistan. Mr Bhutto's conviction had placed Mr Fazal Elahi Chaudhry in a quandary. The pressure started tearing him up from within. As a shrewd lawyer cum politician, he anticipated the impending developments in the case. He apprehended that, as the Head of State, he might have to deal with the mercy petition of Mr Bhutto if the review petition in his case was dismissed by the Supreme Court. He was well aware of the Constitution, under which the President was legally bound to accept the advice given to him by the Head of the Government—General Zia. For understandable reasons, he did not wish to earn the stigma of taking his own party chairman to the gallows. Buckling under such mental pressure, he chose the right time to quit his office. In so doing, he avoided facing an awkward situation.

A weak personality, rendered even more ineffective by a slanted Constitution, Mr Fazal Elahi Chaudhry remained a puppet President for over five years. In that glorified position he was virtually the highest paid 'prisoner' in the country. During the anti-Bhutto agitation, someone wrote on the walls of his official residence: *'Sadar Fazal Elahi Chaudhry ko reha karo'* (Release President Fazal Elahi Chaudhry.)

On 12 February 1979, the former President addressed a letter to General Zia seeking clemency for Mr Bhutto. He wrote:

> The implementation of death sentence passed by the Supreme Court of Pakistan, on the former Prime Minister, Mr. Zulfikar Ali Bhutto, is a matter of great concern not only for Pakistan but for the international community as well. Nationally, it threatens the independence, integrity and sovereignty of the motherland and internationally it is bound to aggravate, beyond the point of no return, instability in an area of extreme strategic importance to the economy and politics of the whole world... with the situation in the neighbouring countries being what it is, Pakistan is in danger of being engulfed in a very unhappy predicament. Any event with some political and emotional content can trigger off the process. The execution of Mr. Zulfikar Ali Bhutto can provide much more than a detonation.

Mr Fazal Elahi Chaudhry recommended leniency on the ground of 'the peculiarities in the judgement' which, in his assessment, were 'too glaring and solid to be ignored.' He elaborated his viewpoint by stating that: 'The lesson of history is that in criminal cases the extreme penalty imposed by courts of law, that has social, political, regional,

THE TRAGIC END

national and international overtones, can be best dealt with by remission or commutation. The courts as a matter of policy and practice do not take notice of such matters which are best left to the executive government for any appropriate action.'

The former President's premature appeal (the case was *sub judice*), leaked to the Press, might have been a sincere effort, or an attempt to rehabilitate his image with Mr Bhutto.

The law and order situation in Pakistan generally remained quiet and stable. Throughout the course of the trial and the hearing of the appeal, the people remained inquisitive but peaceful. Some sporadic incidents of local violence occurred in bigger cities, but there was no countrywide movement. One person each tried to immolate himself in the cities of Lahore, Gujranwala, and Faisalabad. Some of them were hired for the act. Unfortunately, one of them died of the self-inflicted burns. Students of Jamshoro University set three vehicles and a police station on fire. A few shops, public buildings, and banks were attacked in Larkana and its telegraph office was set ablaze. Minor incidents of violence took place in Nawabshah and some other towns in Sindh and in the cities of Gujranwala and Multan in the Punjab. In all cases, the local administration restored normalcy quickly.

Most of the political parties, other than the PPP, adopted a wait-and-see policy. In private meetings, many politicians bitterly criticized Mr Bhutto for humiliating and torturing his political opponents and cautioned General Zia about his vindictive nature. Such loaded advice was self-serving. They expected to gain political advantage if Mr Bhutto was removed from the scene. While the blame for his execution would fall on Zia, the chances of their coming to power would be enhanced.

Not surprisingly, the views of these very politicians in public were different. Most of them observed a meaningful silence on the court verdict. On the question of the grant of clemency, they took shelter behind the Constitution, under which the prerogative lay exclusively with the President of Pakistan. The PPP leaders argued that since the Supreme Court had given a split verdict, there was a justification for the grant of a lesser punishment to the convicts.

The Muhammad Ahmad Khan murder case came under discussion in the MLAs conferences. In these meetings, the internal security situation in all the provinces was discussed threadbare and preventive measures were decided on for maintaining peace in the country.

A Joint Security Committee under the chairmanship of the Secretary Interior was formed for crystal-gazing into the law and order situation in the country in the event of the Supreme Court convicting or acquitting Mr Bhutto. It consulted the federal intelligence agencies and the provincial governments.

A Committee on Public Affairs was also formed for a similar purpose. Presided over by Lieutenant-General Sawar Khan, Governor of the Punjab, it had six federal ministers as members. They were Mr Mahmoud A. Haroon, Mr Ghulam Ishaq Khan, Chaudhry Zahur Elahi, Professor Ghafoor Ahmad, Mr Muhammad Arshad Chaudhry, and Haji Faqir Muhammad Khan. This committee examined the report of the Joint Security Committee. Its recommendations, which were of an administrative nature, were conveyed to the provincial governments.

The administrative machinery in all the provinces was put on alert in February 1979. The political atmosphere being emotionally charged, it was considered prudent to take pre-emptive measures and to act with firmness to maintain peace and tranquillity. Such steps paid dividends. Many acts of lawlessness were prevented and contained.

The rejection of the appeal in the Supreme Court was discussed in an MLAs Conference attended by the four Governors, the Chairman of the Joint Chiefs of Staff Committee, the Deputy Chief of Army Staff, Lieutenant-Generals Chishti and Ghulam Hasan, the Director General of Intelligence, Major-General Mujibur Rehman, then serving in the Ministry of Information, and the Chief of Staff to the President. The conference was given details of the clemency messages received from foreign countries. The Governors and the Director General of Intelligence analysed the internal situation. The implications of the review petition being accepted or rejected by the Supreme Court, and the options in the event of its rejection were discussed. These were to implement the sentence, to convert it into a lesser punishment, or to keep the decision pending for the post-martial law government to take. The request made by a foreign government to grant political asylum to Mr Bhutto was discussed and rejected.

The deliberations lasted several hours. A consensus emerged that this case should be treated at par with other criminal cases of a similar nature and that all the convicted persons deserved equal treatment. The President listened patiently but did not give a decision. The debate—a contingency planning experience—remained inconclusive, as the case was *sub judice*. General Zia stated that he would consult the federal cabinet and the services chiefs before taking the final decision. Another MLAs' meeting was to be held thereafter.

The unanimous rejection of the review petition of all the five convicts on 24 March 1979 by the full bench of the Supreme Court completed the legal process of the case. The trial had taken over seventeen months to complete. The convicts had one last course open to them: they could file a mercy petition. Under Article 45 of the 1973 Constitution, it was the prerogative of the Head of State to accept or reject it. The Constitution empowered the President to grant mercy even if no mercy petition was filed.

The President met the services chiefs. Their views on the grant of clemency were identical to those expressed by the participants in the MLAs conference. They recommended that the court decision be upheld.

A special unscheduled cabinet meeting, without the attendance of bureaucrats, was held to ascertain the views of the federal ministers. The Cabinet considered the rejection of the review petitions by the Supreme Court. It criticized those countries which had meddled in the internal affairs of Pakistan and unanimously recommended that the supremacy of the law be upheld and the order passed by the Supreme Court be implemented. The President thanked the cabinet members for expressing their views freely and candidly. He informed them that their advice would help him in taking a final decision.

Immediately after the conclusion of the cabinet meeting, the President met all the cabinet members in smaller groups in his office—each group comprising ministers from one particular political party. I was present in all the meetings. The President told each group that the decision concerning the fate of Mr Bhutto was an important matter, and by way of abundant caution, he thought it prudent to once again consult his cabinet colleagues in their respective political party groups. It was necessary to do so, said the President, as some ministers might have been reluctant to express their views openly and fully in the presence of their colleagues from other political parties, notwithstanding their affiliation with the PNA. Without exception, every minister reiterated his earlier view, recommending that the court sentence be carried out.

The Jamaat-i-Islami ministers told the President that the cabinet recommendations had been clear, unanimous, and unambiguous, and that there was no need to summon them separately again in party groups. Some ministers spoke with an emotive approach. One of them felt that the crime committed by Mr Bhutto was so heinous that he deserved to be hanged more than once. Chaudhry Zahur Elahi made a personal request. He asked the President that the pen used to reject the mercy petition might be gifted to him as a souvenir.

A section of the Press carried inspired stories. These were based on planted disinformation that the convicts would be executed within hours after the Supreme Court decision was given. Such sensationalism, totally inaccurate, was based either on ignorance of the legal process of law or on deliberate mischief. The critics ignored the fact that the trial was held under the civil law of the land by the superior courts. Any apprehension that the government, which had consistently allowed the legal course to prevail, would act otherwise after the rejection of the review petition, was a figment of the imagination of an unsound mind.

After 24 March, events moved at a rapid pace. An MLAs Conference was held. It was attended by all the regular participants. The Chief of General Staff, Major General A. S. F. Lodhi, attended by special invitation. The conference was informed about the views expressed and the recommendations made by the cabinet and the service chiefs. All the alternatives available were once again critically analysed. The prevailing view was that a state-sponsored unmitigated act of terrorism deserved no mercy and the convicts should suffer for the crimes committed by them. A single voice suggested another angle. It stated that, while on merit Mr Bhutto deserved to be punished, it might be politically prudent to let the mercy decision be taken by the post-election government. This argument did not find favour. A period of prolonged suspense, others felt, would be against the national interest. The conference recommended the rejection of all the mercy petitions submitted by or on behalf of the convicts.

The date and place of execution, and the location and mode of burial were also debated. After examining various options, it was decided that, if the mercy petitions were rejected, the executions should be made in accordance with the normal procedure. The burials should take place in daylight, preferably in the ancestral graveyards of all the convicts. The dates of the execution were to be decided after completion of the administrative arrangements.

Since Mr Bhutto was lodged in the district jail, Rawalpindi, it was administratively convenient to carry out the execution there. The co-ordination of the burial arrangements in this case came under the purview of the government of Sindh, as the family graveyard of Mr Bhutto was located at village Garhi Khuda Bakhsh in the province of Sindh. The plan, tentative in nature, was to be kept confidential. The Governors concerned were authorized to divulge details to the implementing agencies on a need to know basis.

On 31 March 1979, Begum Shahrbano Imtiaz, the stepsister of Mr Bhutto, personally submitted a mercy petition to the Military Secretary to the President in Rawalpindi. Earlier, a similar mercy petition had been submitted by Sahibzada Farooq Ali (PPP) on 29 March 1979. On 30 March 1979, Mian Muhammad Yasin Wattoo, acting Secretary General, PPP, also submitted a mercy petition. Its concluding paragraph read: 'The Central Executive Committee of PPP therefore urges the President to exercise his powers under Article 45 of the Constitution of the Islamic Republic of Pakistan and to remit or commute the sentence of Chairman Zulfikar Ali Bhutto.' Some other mercy petitions were also received by the government of Punjab.

The submission of the mercy petitions, though a normal phenomenon, was in contrast to the oft-repeated statements made by the Bhutto family that no mercy petition would be filed. The case containing the mercy petitions 'of the condemned prisoner Zulfikar Ali Bhutto son of Sir Shah Nawaz Bhutto' was submitted to the President for his decision by the Ministry of Interior on 1 April 1979.

The summary for the President pointed out that 'while dismissing the review petition, the Supreme Court has made the observation that "although we have not found it possible in law to review the sentence of death on the grounds urged by Mr Yahya Bakhtiar, yet these are relevant for consideration by the executive authorities in exercise of their prerogative of mercy." While commenting on this issue, it was stated in the summary that "It has been contended in the mercy pleas that the observations of the Supreme Court on the quantum of sentence constitutes a recommendation for commutation of death sentence and that such recommendations have always been honoured by the executive." The contention is misconceived and erroneous. According to the guiding principles, the recommendations of the court to the executive to consider the question of commutation of death sentence is not binding and is not meant to be honoured in every case but is to be considered keeping in view the facts and circumstances of each case and even in such cases the scope of interference by the executive is of a very limited character. In view of the finding of the Supreme Court on the quantum of sentence, the advice of the Law Division and our views, no case for commutation of death sentence appears to have been made out.'

While analysing the political implications, the summary read: 'This is an unprecedented case which has caused deep concern at home and has generated a lot of interest abroad. The general reaction, particularly in USA and Western Europe, to the execution of the sentence would be strong and adverse and would cause aversion and do immense damage to the image of Pakistan abroad. According to the guiding principles "cases in which there are special or political considerations are to be dealt with on the merit of each case." It may sometimes be necessary to take account of the public opinion and to commute the sentence in deference to a widely spread or strong local expression of public opinion lest the execution should arouse sympathy for the murderer than otherwise.'

It was prayed in one mercy petition that Mr Bhutto be granted clemency on humanitarian grounds. On this request, the Law Division said: 'Legally it is humane to kill the killer, more so when he is found so by the superior-most court. In fact the authority that allows merciful commutation etc. of a sentence is merciless to the deceased, his heirs and his relatives. Mercy, remission or commutation is negation of justice, and the justice is not only to be done to the killer who is surviving because of legal formalities but is also to be done to the deceased who cannot be heard but whose soul looks for justice—the revenge—death for death, and that in fact is the humanitarian consideration.'

General Zia read the summary carefully. In his considered judgement, the ends of justice demanded that the rule of law override other considerations. Three fatal words put the seal of death on Mr Bhutto's life. Late in the evening of 1 April 1979, while working in the austere drawing-room of his modest house, he wrote: 'Petition is rejected.'

The countdown for the execution began. I accompanied General Zia to Karachi to attend a meeting held in the Governor's office. Beside the Governor, Lieutenant-General S. M. Abbasi, it was attended by Major-Generals Jahan Dad Khan, Abdullah Malik, and Mahmood Aslam Hayat, all serving in Sindh. They explained the burial arrangements and the security measures proposed for the occasion. It was decided with Governor Abbasi separately that, subject to other considerations, the execution be carried out on 3 April 1979.

All the members of the MLAs' Conference were verbally informed of the fateful date.

Before narrating the events which followed, a small digression may be in order. Mr Justice Safdar Shah was on the Supreme Court Bench which heard the Nawab Muhammad Ahmad Khan murder case. He had earlier retired as Chief Justice of the Peshawar High Court on 31 October 1976. In July 1977, he approached Mr Sharif uddin Pirzada, the Attorney General of Pakistan, and explained to him his personal financial difficulties. The Attorney General brought his request to the notice of Mr Justice Anwarul Haq, Chief Justice of Pakistan, who recommended to the President that the retired judge be appointed a judge of the Supreme Court. General Zia approved that proposal. Mr Justice Safdar Shah thus became a judge of the Supreme Court.

By tradition, the judges of the superior courts in Pakistan follow a conservative approach in the performance of their duties. They avoid personal projection and follow the dictum that judges speak about the cases through their judgments. Mr Justice Safdar Shah was an experienced judge. It was expected that he would follow the customary judicial tradition in the Nawab Muhammad Ahmad Khan murder case. He was one of the three dissenting Supreme Court judges at the level of appeal. There was nothing unusual about it. The honourable judges were known to give their judgments in accordance with their conscience and the legal merits of the case as assessed by them. But the matter did not end there. Two days after the rejection of the review petition, Mr Justice Safdar Shah told media correspondents that the Supreme Court observations on the Nawab Muhammad Ahmad Khan murder case and the arguments of the defence counsel, Mr Yahya Bakhtiar, presented during the course of the trial, could not be disregarded by the executive while deciding the question of implementing the death verdict. Such a public pronouncement, made by a trial or reviewing judge, was unprecedented in the judicial history of the country. His impartiality became suspect. Mr Justice Safdar Shah went a step further. He also told the Press reporters that all the seven judges of the Supreme Court held a similar view. The mystery deepened further. Was he authorized by his brother judges to speak on their behalf? The answer to this question was given in a Press release issued by the Supreme Court on 29 March 1979. It reads:

> The attention of the Chief Justice of Pakistan and the remaining five judges constituting the Bench which dismissed Mr. Zulfikar Ali Bhutto's

review petition against the appellate judgement of the Supreme Court dated the 6th February 1979 has been drawn to some remarks reported in the press today as having been made by Mr. Justice G. Safdar Shah, in relation to certain observations contained in the order made by the learned judge to the BBC correspondent and two others whom he came across while walking on a road in Islamabad. It is not the practice of the Superior Court to issue statements explaining the import of their judgement or orders, or of any observation contained therein, as they speak for themselves. Whatever Mr. Justice G. Safdar Shah has said reflects his personal views only and he had no authority to speak on behalf of the other members of the Bench. As the remaining judges would not like to depart from this settled practice, they would refrain from making any comments on this behalf.

It is the faith of all Muslims that in matters of life and death, as indeed in all others, God's will prevails. The life span of living creatures can neither be shortened nor prolonged by human beings. As stated earlier, Mr Bhutto's execution was fixed for 3 April 1979. Providence willed otherwise. The meteorological forecast for the morning of 3 April 1979, indicated that flying conditions would be unfavourable for transporting the body by air from Rawalpindi to the place of burial. The execution was, therefore, postponed by twenty-four hours. All the members of the MLAs' Conference were so informed verbally.

Between 24 March and 3 April 1979, Mr Bhutto met eighteen visitors in his prison cell. They included his two wives, one daughter, some other relatives, and his counsels. Mrs Nusrat Bhutto and Miss Benazir Bhutto were the last of his visitors whom he met jointly for nearly four hours from 11 a.m. to 3 p.m. on 3 April 1979. On their arrival at the jail gate, the two ladies inquired from the Deputy Superintendent (Jails) if this was their last meeting. They were given an affirmative reply. On their request, they met Chaudhry Yar Muhammad, the Superintendent of the Jail, who informed them that the mercy petitions filed in the case had been rejected and Mr Bhutto would be hanged to death the next morning. He also told them that this would be their last meeting with Mr Bhutto. The two ladies then went inside the jail to meet Mr Bhutto. Shortly thereafter, the Jail Superintendent went to Mr Bhutto's cell and informed him, in the presence of his wife and daughter, that he would be executed the next morning. Not showing any sign of nervousness in the presence of his wife and daughter, Mr Bhutto put up a brave face throughout the long

THE TRAGIC END

meeting. Begum Nusrat Bhutto remained tense but calm. Miss Benazir broke down several times. She sobbed and wept on a few occasions. After their meeting, both the ladies were escorted back to the Sihala Camp Jail where they had been lodged since their detention. They came under immense emotional stress when bidding farewell to their beloved husband and father, whom they were not destined to see again. The three ashen-faced persons stood for a few moments looking at one another, motionless and speechless. Their parting was painful and difficult. It was a touching scene. They faced those torturous moments calmly. Mr Bhutto sat down when the two ladies left. The Sihala camp authorities took measures to prevent them from communicating with any person outside the improvised jail till the next day. Soon after arrival in the camp Jail, Begum Nusrat Bhutto wrote a letter to the President. Its text is reproduced below:

Sihala Camp
April 3rd, 1979

Dear Mr President:

My husband's eldest sister made a mercy appeal to you on March 31st, 79, but I have been informed that it has been rejected. I believe my husband is to be executed at dawn. I would appreciate it if you will please give me some time today to have some talks with you. I realize, as President you are a very busy person, but as far as the time is so very short, hence I hope you will kindly meet me today. If you cannot give me the time with you, please authorize some one else to meet me on your behalf today. I shall be grateful to you.

Yours Sincerely,
(signed)
Nusrat Bhutto

Major-General Saghir Hussain Sayed, the Deputy Martial Law Administrator, Rawalpindi, met Begum Nusrat Bhutto and Miss Benazir Bhutto the same day. They pleaded for a stay of the execution. No other matter of substance was discussed between them. Saghir found Begum Nusrat Bhutto shaken, morose, and tired. Wailing and hysterical, Miss Benazir Bhutto used undignified language during the conversation.

* * *

Mr Bhutto, a populist leader gifted with charm and charisma, played on the psyche of the masses and spoke to them in a language that aroused their emotions. A feudal by birth, inheritance, and conviction, he followed a two-track policy in politics. On the one hand, he espoused the cause of the poor, and on the other, he gathered around him landlords with immense wealth and vote-winning influence. Such was his *modus operandi.* He was glib-tongued and effective. His brilliance was surpassed only by his cunning. Mr Bhutto annoyed his friends and foes by his arrogance, his stiff-necked approach, and insulting behaviour. Democratic norms decayed under his dictatorial rule. His administration relied heavily on a few police officials of dubious distinction. They tried hard to convert the country into a serfdom. Mr Bhutto in power was different from Mr Bhutto out of power. Out of power, he had demanded justice and fair play for all. In power, he rigged the elections and denied justice to others. His prolonged trial gave ample chance to his admirers to demonstrate their strength through political activity, if they so wished. Most of them were conspicuous by their absence. When Mr Bhutto's sun of power started setting, they maintained a safe distance from him on one pretext or another, and watched him facing the ordeal alone.

The terse and matter-of-fact official press note issued on 4 April 1979 read: 'Mr Zulfikar Ali Bhutto was hanged to death at 2 a.m. this morning in Rawalpindi District Jail... The dead body was flown in a special aircraft from Rawalpindi and handed over to the elders of the family who buried him after *namaz-i-janaza* [funeral prayers] in the ancestral graveyard at Garhi Khuda Bakhsh near Nau Dero, Larkana at 10:30 a.m. in accordance with the wishes of the family. The funeral was attended by relatives, including his two uncles, Nawab Nabi Bakhsh Bhutto and Sardar Pir Bakhsh Bhutto, his first wife Sherin Amir Begum, friends and residents of the area.'

Thus ended the life of a person who once claimed to be 'the only sacred cow in Pakistan'.

During Mr Bhutto's detention in Rawalpindi, the jail premises were well guarded. Some intelligence reports had indicated a plan of a commando-type operation against the Rawalpindi jail to free Bhutto and whisk him away from the country, ostensibly with the help of a foreign power. The jail security measures were improved, although such a raid did not appear plausible. In Pakistan, the police force is

THE TRAGIC END

not equipped with automatic weapons. An army contingent was located outside the jail to reinforce the jail police. As a matter of policy, it was given high visibility to deter any escape attempt. The jail administration did not come under the purview of the army troops. This responsibility remained exclusively with the superintendent of the jail.

Mr Bhutto's execution stunned the country. While a pall of gloom and shock prevailed, the people generally took the announcement calmly. Some instances of protests and disturbances took place, but no rivers of blood flowed as some prophets of doom had predicted earlier.

Many stories subsequently appeared regarding the final hours of Mr Bhutto's life. Some were highly fanciful and attempted to construct a legend around him. Others were crude concoctions. I consider it a moral obligation to set out the authentic facts regarding Mr Bhutto's tragic end, known to me by virtue of the position I was holding at the time.

Mr Bhutto was kept under continuous but unobtrusive observation on the last day of his life, from the time he was informed about his execution, to safeguard against any rash act which he might commit. This provided details of his behaviour in the closing hours of his life.

Mr Bhutto's wife and daughter stayed with him till 3 p.m. on 3 April 1979. At 6:30 p.m., the Superintendent of the Jail, accompanied by a witness, went to Mr Bhutto's cell. They found him on the floor, leaning against the wall. He was asked whether he would like to write or dictate his last will and testament, as he was to be executed the next morning. Mr Bhutto indicated his preference for writing it down personally and was provided writing materials. He complained that the written orders about his execution had not been shown to him. The Superintendent informed him that they had been received but that, under the rules, condemned prisoners were not entitled to see the papers. Mr Bhutto expressed a desire to meet some more relatives as well as Mr Abdul Hafeez Pirzada. He was told that time did not permit any more interviews. He then asked for a shaving kit. During that conversation, he looked normal and displayed no undue anxiety. The Superintendent stayed with him for nearly thirty minutes. After he left, Mr Bhutto stood up and stumbled while taking the first step. He then shouted for Abdul Rahman, the *mushaqqati* (attendant) and asked for hot water for shaving, saying, 'I do not want to die like a bearded *mullah.*'

Mr Bhutto sipped a cup of coffee at 7:27 p.m. and shaved. He had another cup of coffee at 8:05 p.m. Then, suddenly, his confidence gave away. He looked around blankly, cried like a child, and begged forgiveness from Abdul Rahman, 'as I will soon be hanged.' Then he kept scribbling on a piece of paper between 8:15 p.m. and 9:40 p.m. He appeared mentally preoccupied and disturbed. He started arranging and rearranging his things on the table and repeated this process a few times. At 9:55 p.m. he brushed his teeth. His conduct then became increasingly less rational. At 10 p.m. he started sweeping his cell with a piece of paper held in his right hand. He regained his composure once again and, while lying on the bed and resting against the wall, he kept writing something between 10:10 p.m. and 11:05 p.m. He once inquired from the head warden how much time was left before his execution.

Mr Bhutto then burnt all the papers written by him and called upon Abdul Rahman to clean the cell. Ashen-faced, he stretched himself on his bed, closed his eyes, and appeared to be sleeping.

At 11:59 p.m. the Deputy Superintendent of the jail came to the cell and addressed Mr Bhutto but received no response. He informed the Superintendent on the telephone, who arrived along with a jail doctor and the magistrate, Mr Bashir Khan. The doctor examined Mr Bhutto and declared him medically fit. The magistrate shook Mr Bhutto's arm, introduced himself and inquired whether he had written any will. Mr Bhutto, physically weak but mentally alert, replied in a low voice: 'Will . . . will be written in the books.'

The jail doctor was once again asked by the Superintendent to examine Mr Bhutto. After a thorough examination, the doctor declared Mr Bhutto medically fit and stated that he was in a state of shock due to the impending execution.

At 1:45 a.m. on 4 April, the Superintendent, along with a magistrate, the jail doctor, and the jail stretcher-bearers, entered the cell. They found Mr Bhutto lying motionless in bed. The magistrate inquired if he wished to make any will. In a weak and somewhat incoherent voice Mr Bhutto said: 'I had tried but my thoughts were so disturbed that I could not do it and I have burnt it.' He was then asked if he would like to walk or be carried to the place of execution. There was no response from him. After a pause he said: 'I pity my wife

Prime Minister Zulfikar Ali Bhutto arrives by helicopter and waves to the cheering crowds at Dir on 10 July 1974.

Zulfikar Ali Bhutto's coffin is unloaded from a helicopter for transfer to an ambulance at Garhi Khuda Baksh on 4 April 1979.

Prime Minister Zulfikar Ali Bhutto addresses a public meeting at Quetta on 2 August 1974.

Funeral prayers being offered for Zulfikar Ali Bhutto in his ancestral village.

Prime Minister Muhammad Khan Junejo, accompanied by top military brass, arrives at the Race Course Ground, Rawalpindi, for the *bara khana* on 23 March 1986.

President General Ziaul Haq pins a decoration on the author at the investiture ceremony at the Presidency on 23 March 1987.

Presidents Ziaul Haq and Jimmy Carter with the Pakistani delegation on the lawns of the White House in October 1980.

THE TRAGIC END

left the jail.' It was a tragic sight, an anti-climax to the vibrant and exuberant life of Mr Bhutto.

Raising his voice, the magistrate again inquired if he wished to make a will. Mr Bhutto mumbled that he would like to dictate. He was then not in a mentally alert state to think coherently as the time set for the execution was fast approaching. The Superintendent once again asked Mr Bhutto if he would like to walk or be carried. Since there was no reply, he ordered his men to lift Mr Bhutto. As four persons lifted him from his bed, Mr Bhutto said: 'Leave me, leave me.'

He was carried to the courtyard by the four persons, where he was put on a stretcher, handcuffed, and taken towards the scaffold. Mr Bhutto appeared incapable of walking the distance from the cell to the scaffold. He did not speak *en route*. The stretcher was placed near the hang house (the place of execution) and Mr Bhutto was helped to get off it. He stood up with the help of the jail staff who assisted him to climb up the few steps. He stood alone unaided at the scaffold. As the noose was fitted around his neck and a hood placed on his head, Mr Bhutto mumbled: 'Remove it, remove it.'

There was a hush of silence in the gloom-filled April night. The Superintendent, the jail doctor, the magistrate, and a few others on duty stood motionless, witnessing the final act. As the clock struck two, the lever was pulled. The wooden planks instantly parted. A few minutes later, the doctor on duty pronounced Mr Bhutto dead. May God bless his soul.

Mr Bhutto's body was bathed in accordance with the prescribed religious rites and placed in a coffin inside the jail premises. It was then taken to the Islamabad Airport where an air force aircraft was kept ready. As the coffin was being placed inside the aircraft, someone standing there remarked: 'Even in his death, Mr Bhutto's body is being transported in the VIP version of C-130.'

After a flight of about forty minutes, the aircraft developed a fault and had to return to Islamabad. The coffin was shifted to a standby aircraft which promptly took off. It reached Jacobabad at 7:20 a.m., from where the body was transported to Garhi Khuda Bakhsh in a waiting helicopter. The body reached Garhi Khuda Bakhsh at 8:10 a.m. It was then carried in an ambulance and handed over to the relatives of the deceased and to the civil authorities. The body was then taken to the *haveli* of Mr Muzaffar Khan Bhutto. The *namaz-i-janaza* was held near the old mosque at 9:20 a.m., and was attended by nearly 300 persons. At 9:40 a.m., the body was carried to the family graveyard adjacent to the mosque. The burial was completed by 10:30 a.m.

For reasons of religious sensitivity, Muslims prefer an early burial of their dead. Transporting Mr Bhutto's mortal remains to his grave involved a long journey successively using an aircraft, a helicopter, and then an ambulance as the means of conveyance. It was a time-consuming process. In addition, it was considered advisable to complete the funeral ceremony in the early and cool part of the day to avoid inconvenience to the mourners. For these reasons, the time of the execution was kept early by the competent authority, the Government of the Punjab. Mr Bhutto's body was photographed and his burial filmed.

On 4 April, Miss Benazir Bhutto wrote a letter to the Deputy Martial Law Administrator, Rawalpindi, requesting permission for her mother and herself to attend the *soyem* of her late father at Garhi Khuda Bakhsh on 6 April 1979. The request was accepted. The two ladies left Islamabad at 7 a.m. on 6 April by a special aircraft and, after a visit to Garhi Khuda Bakhsh and Larkana, returned to Rawalpindi the same day.

It will be debated by historians to what extent, if any, Mr Bhutto himself paved the way for the sad end he met. In 1965, the British High Commissioner in Pakistan reported to London in an official dispatch that 'Bhutto would destroy himself . . . and was born to be hanged.'[2]

* * *

The case file pertaining to the mercy petitions of the remaining four convicts in the Nawab Muhammad Ahmad Khan murder case— Mian Muhammad Abbas, Ghulam Mustafa, Arshad Iqbal, and Rana Iftikhar Ahmad—was received in the CMLA Secretariat from the Ministry of Interior soon after the execution of Mr Bhutto. All the four condemned persons belonged to the erstwhile Federal Security Force. This Force had committed some acts of terrorism and sabotage and, on that account, some of its former members were facing trial in different courts of law. The Ministry, of Interior had not indicated if the evidence of the four convicts was required in any other cases then under trial or under investigation. The mercy petition file was returned to the Ministry seeking this confirmation.

The Ministry of Interior took a few weeks to get the facts checked from the provinces and the agencies concerned. During this period, a whispering campaign started that the four convicts, all of Punjabi domicile, were being considered for grant of clemency. There was no truth in that speculative disinformation. The question of delay in the disposal of the four mercy petitions was raised by a participant in the MLAs' Conference. General Zia looked towards me to explain the reason, which I did. A question was asked if there were plans to commute the sentences of those convicts to lesser punishments. A firm negative reply put the doubts to rest.

In July 1979, the Ministry of Interior resubmitted the file, indicating that none of the four convicts was a witness in any other case. The President rejected the mercy petitions without showing any hesitation. On 24 July 1979, Mian Muhammad Abbas and Ghulam Mustafa were hanged to death in the District Jail, Rawalpindi. The same day, Arshad Iqbal and Rana Iftikhar Ahmad went to the gallows in Faisalabad and Lahore jails. Thus ended a gory drama which put an ugly blot on the fair name of the country.

The story did not end with the execution of the five convicts. Lieutenant-General Faiz Ali Chishti made a disclosure which caused me anguish and surprise. In his book, he has said: 'I think it was in July 1978, when we were holding a session of the Election Cell, that I was informed that the relatives of one of the four co-accused in the Kasuri case, along with their lawyer, Irshad Qureshi, wanted to see me. . . . I met them in the presence of other Election Cell members, General J. S. Mian, General Farman and General Ihsan. They asked me what would happen to the co-accused if they told the truth in court. . . .I told them to tell the truth fearlessly, as required by Islam and to have faith in Allah. On this, General Ihsan asked why they were worried, since General Ziaul Haq had already given an assurance to the prosecution that nothing would happen to any of them if they told the truth. General Ihsan also said that this pledge given by Zia was also known to MLA General Iqbal, A. K. Brohi and the late Barrister Anwar, as well as the COS General Arif.'[2]

What lured an unnamed relative of an unnamed accused to approach Chishti has not been disclosed. And in what capacity did he and his colleagues grant the interview to the person if the Election Cell was not concerned with the Nawab Muhammad Ahmad Khan murder case? The Election Cell meetings in Rawalpindi were held in Chishti's office in Headquarters 10 Corps—a well-guarded office where a military sentry stood day and night. The person who met the generals must have received someone's approval to enter the premises.

The concluding sentence of the passage lists the persons who were allegedly aware of a 'pledge' made to some co-accused persons. Those were Mr A. K. Brohi, Mr M. Anwar, and Generals Iqbal, Jamal Said Mian, Farman, and Ihsan. The first two are no longer alive. On 30 May 1990, I wrote letters to Generals Iqbal, Jamal Said Mian, Farman, and Ihsan requesting them 'to confirm the authenticity of the statement' attributed to them.

Despite verbal reminders, J. S. Mian did not answer the letter. Farman sent a non-committal reply, indicating that he did not remember the exact words used. General Muhammad Iqbal Khan in his reply dated 1 July 1990, said: 'My comments on the extracts, to the extent concerning me, are: a) False, and b) Malicious.'

Major-General Ihsanul Haq Malik's reply was not that brief. He wrote on 11 June 1990 in these words:

> I do not know that 'General Zia-ul-Haq had already given an assurance to the prosecution that nothing would happen to any of them if they told the truth.' I do not know of any 'pledge' given by General Zia. Hence I could not have said that such a pledge was given in the presence of anybody. I never discussed this aspect of the case with General Zia-ul-Haq in the presence of General Iqbal, A. K. Brohi, Mr. Anwar or yourself. General Chishti is a gentleman and a very good friend. If he says that I did say what he asserts I did, then I must not have been telling the truth at that time. Either it is a lapse of memory on the part of General Chishti or for some reason I made up a completely false story. It is not my normal habit.

General Zia is dead. It is the author's moral obligation to narrate that he did not give any hint of making any promise to any co-accused.

Mr Bhutto's culpability took him to the gallows. His death removed him from the political path of Zia. It can be debated whether Zia's action was politically motivated. No evidence is available to substantiate such an allegation. However, there is no doubt that Zia and Bhutto had become irritants for each other from the time Bhutto was arrested on the murder charge.

CHAPTER 9

From the Pinnacle

Coinciding with the execution of Mr Bhutto, a pre-emptive Operation Sweep was launched throughout the country to round up history-sheeters and suspects whose names were on police records. Some die-hard PPP activists were also detained. The whole operation was conducted by the respective provincial administrations to pre-empt agitation in the post-execution period. The public reaction was milder than expected and those arrested were soon released.

Two days before Mr Bhutto's execution, his houses at Karachi and Larkana were searched. A scrutiny of the photocopies of a mass of classified and unclassified government files and documents recovered revealed that Mr Bhutto had developed an elaborate system to preserve records, presumably for his memoirs. His death robbed him of the chance of using them. That making photocopies of classified official documents for personal use was prohibited under the law of Pakistan was a different matter. Bhutto always considered himself above the law.

Mr Bhutto wrote remarks generously on the official papers submitted to him. Some of the orders endorsed by him were brutally bold —even incriminating—and these were used against him during his trial. The prosecutors presented them in the court to prove Bhutto's personal involvement.

One top-secret official document recovered from his house during the search had a history behind it. As narrated in Chapter 2, the Hamoodur Rahman Commission had determined the causes of Pakistan's defeat in the Indo-Pakistan War of 1971. One complete set of all the volumes of the report was kept by Mr Bhutto in the Prime Minister's Secretariat. This highly sensitive and classified document was in the custody of Major-General Imtiaz Ali, the Military Secretary. All the remaining copies of the report had been destroyed by burning under the orders issued by the government.

After the fall of the Bhutto government, Major-General Imtiaz Ali handed over the record held in his personal charge to Brigadier Muhammad Younas, who worked in the CMLA Secretariat. During the handing over-taking over process, one volume of the Hamoodur Rahman Commission Report was found to be missing. Imtiaz explained that, on the orders of Mr Bhutto, the missing volume was given by him to Mr Ghulam Mustafa Khar. No receipt was held on record to support that transaction. After some time had lapsed, Imtiaz said, he requested Mr Khar to return the borrowed volume. Mr Khar claimed that he had already handed it over to Mr Bhutto. Between the trio—Imtiaz, Khar, and Bhutto—one volume was thus lost, misplaced, or stolen.

One of the reasons for searching the Bhutto residences was to locate that missing report. It was recovered from his house, tucked away in a small hidden steel vault embedded in a wall, with its front covered by a large-size wall mirror. The immured cabinet was detected when the mirror was removed from the wall. The vault contained not only the wanted document but also photocopies of scores of its pages. How many of the photocopies might have been distributed to unauthorized persons or agencies would never be known. The entire seizure was recorded and signed by a magistrate on duty who had accompanied the search party.

Bhutto's execution polarized the country. While many of his arch critics maintained a diplomatic silence on his execution as a matter of political expediency, his admirers felt cheated and stunned. The prevailing political climate was emotionally charged. The sporadic instances of disturbances soon subsided but under the surface of an uneasy calm, lingering bitterness persisted. The PPP was enraged and its desire for retribution became the dominant theme in politics. Zia became a symbol of its hatred and a target of its revenge. He was perhaps a marked person.

The Bhutto tragedy created a wave of sympathy for the PPP. Some faint-hearted leaders, who had been sitting on the fence, started eulogizing the services of the dead leader in an effort to rejoin the PPP bandwagon. The Bhutto ladies, keeping the party reins firmly in their hands, saw through their game. The renegades were either suspected of duplicity or accepted in the party fold but kept on the sidelines.

The PPP strategy was to cash in on public sentiment to gain sympathy votes whenever an election should be held. It employed the slogan of 'Bhuttoism' to put General Zia on the defensive. A policy of defiance, abuse, and threats was adopted. Revenge became the war cry of the party.

The threat of violence polluted the political atmosphere. The government desired an issue-oriented election campaign, not one dominated by emotions. The PPP felt otherwise. An atmosphere charged with emotional frenzy was not propitious for holding of elections, due in November 1979.

The hanging of Bhutto closed the door for political dialogue, and Zia and the PPP became bitter rivals. If Zia was an enigma to the Bhutto ladies, he in turn abhorred the idea of the PPP returning to power. He publicly stated that, elections being the means to an end, should show 'positive results'. It implied that, to him, a PPP government was no longer acceptable. Zia told his colleagues that the misdeeds of the Bhutto government were so many and so grave that it would be folly to return power to the PPP after the lifting of martial law.

Zia did not regret his decision about Bhutto, which he felt was legally and morally correct. To him, justice outweighed political considerations. Despite this, the ghost of Bhutto haunted him. The PPP cry of revenge created a security problem for Zia which led him to prolong his rule.

Slowly but surely, Zia started believing that he was the best person to rule the country. Many of his sycophantic visitors praised him lavishly and urged him to keep guiding the country through a difficult period.

Postponement of the elections for the second time put Zia on the mat. His credibility, previously suspect, nosedived. When pressed to indicate a fresh election date, he refused to be baited. The postponement of the elections raised some political dust but the peace was not disturbed. The political parties in the country were too weak and divided to pose any serious threat to Zia's government.

With elections on the backburner, it was time to consolidate his power base. General Zia was in no hurry to hold elections, but he also faced the pressures and disadvantages of running the administration without the people's participation. The allegation of being a non-elected ruler weighed heavily on him. He wanted a way out, short of going to the polls. The MLAs Conferences suggested the formation of a broad-based political government, headed by a politician, preferably from Sindh, the province of Mr Bhutto. Mr Ghulam Mustafa Jatoi emerged as a consensus candidate. General Zia agreed, albeit reluctantly. Mr Jatoi responded positively to the government's overtures. In February 1980, he met General Zia at the Army House in Rawalpindi. Lieutenant-General S. M. Abbasi, the Governor of Sindh, and I were also present. General Zia, carefully avoiding the word, 'Prime Minister', invited Mr Jatoi to join the government in an 'important capacity.' Mr Jatoi indicated his willingness. When General Zia explained the parameters of co-operation, Mr Jatoi interjected to say that, 'I might not be of much help, if I joined the government alone.' Mr Jatoi felt that he could form a team of like-minded persons from the PPP and other parties to serve the country. Zia agreed that, 'a mutually acceptable group of persons with good reputation could administer the country till the lifting of martial law. That government should also speed up the process of the Islamization of laws.'

Mr Jatoi expressed a desire to take Begum Nusrat Bhutto into confidence because, as he put it, 'It is better that she hears it firsthand from me, rather than hearing a garbled version from others.'

General Zia did not object. Mr Jatoi enquired if he could discuss the matter with Mr Ghulam Mustafa Khar. Reacting sharply, General Zia said: 'I would not like Mr Khar to be associated.' Not pressing the point further Mr Jatoi told General Zia that as he had planned to perform *Umra*, they could meet again after his return from Saudi Arabia. It was decided that a separate meeting be held between Jatoi, Abbasi, and myself to settle details. The following day, the three of us met and prepared an agreed framework for forming a government.

After performing *Umra,* Mr Jatoi went to Dubai where he met Mr Ghulam Mustafa Khar who had flown in from London to meet him. A report on the Jatoi-Khar contact was with Zia before the former returned to Pakistan. General Zia felt hurt that Mr Jatoi had betrayed his confidence, and he decided to distance himself from him. The proposal of associating Mr Jatoi with the government was not processed any further.

In March 1980, General Sawar Khan was appointed VCOAS and was succeeded by Lieutenant-General Ghulam Jilani Khan as the Governor of Punjab. Earlier, General Muhammad Iqbal had succeeded General Muhammad Shariff as the Chairman, JCSC.

In March 1980, Lieutenant-Generals Chishti and Ghulam Hassan retired from the Army. General Zia offered ministerial assignments to both of them. Ghulam Hassan accepted with gratitude. Chishti reminded Zia, 'You had said earlier that we would go together.' 'While I am stuck till elections,' replied Zia, 'the army train must keep moving to create promotion opportunities for the junior officers.'

Chishti declined to be a minister after retirement on the plea that he did not feel justified in holding that post once he was no longer in military service. On the eve of his retirement, Chishti developed a grudge against General Zia which he showed in subsequent life. He considered himself qualified for further promotion. Zia liked him, but, in his assessment, Iqbal and Sawar—both senior to Chishti— deserved promotions no less.

In March 1983, Generals Muhammad Iqbal Khan and Sawar Khan completed the three-year tenure of their assignments as Chairman Joint Chiefs of Staff Committee and the Vice Chief of Army Staff respectively. They were given one year's extension each. Similar extensions were granted to the service chiefs of the Pakistan Air Force and the Pakistan Navy. When the extended tenures of Generals Muhammad Iqbal and Sawar Khan were nearing completion, General Zia was once again faced with the question of appointing their successors. At that time, out of the serving Lieutenant-Generals, three had been promoted to their present ranks after having been superseded earlier. Lieutenant-General Akhtar Abdul Rahman was one of them. Among the fresh general officers, the senior-most was Lieutenant-General S. M. Abbasi, the Governor of Sindh. Abbasi had an unpleasant meeting with General Zia in the President's office in Rawalpindi, when told that he would be retiring. A bruised and bitter Abbasi accused General Zia of backtracking on an unsolicited promise made to him earlier, indicating that his next assignment would be as Chairman JCSC with the rank of a four-star general. While Abbasi was in the President's office, I was asked to join the meeting. I found the atmosphere tense and the faces of both the generals serious and glum. The President briefly narrated the gist of their conversation, adding that Abbasi felt let down and hurt. He concluded his remarks by indicating the date of change-over of the Governor of Sindh. I escorted Abbasi out of the President's office. With bitterness writ large on his face, Abbasi criticized General Zia for using senior officers and then dumping them after they had served his purpose. By nature, General Abbasi was quiet, sober, and an introvert. His outburst and the anger indicated how grievously hurt he felt.

In early 1984, the President selected General Rahimuddin Khan as the Chairman Joint Chiefs of Staff Committee, and myself as the Vice Chief of Army Staff. He asked for recommendations on the appointment of his next Chief of Staff. I told him that I would hate to be accused of exploiting my position to seek personal advantage. Zia responded by admitting that, 'command opportunities had been denied to you in the past because of my preference to retain you as my Chief of Staff.' 'Even then,' I said, 'by way of abundant caution, you may consult others on my promotion.' 'Whom do you suggest?' enquired Zia. 'Some intelligence agency' was my reply. With a smile, he said, 'I have done that in my own style.' He explained his style by saying, 'I had asked Akhtar who should replace Sawar.' Then after a short pause, he looked at me and said, 'Akhtar offered himself for the post,' adding, 'I think he is alright where he is.'

I proposed the name of my deputy, Major-General Malik Abdul Waheed for the post of Chief of Staff, mentioning his qualities of sincerity, fairness, and incorruptibility. The President accepted my advice.

I became Vice Chief of Army Staff on 23 March 1984. Before assuming that appointment, I asked General Zia if there were any subjects on which I should not give a decision without consulting him. General Zia, while expressing confidence in me, said, 'I trust you, Arif, and do not wish to place any impediments in your way. Take your decisions as you deem proper. I wish you luck.' I thanked the President and promised to keep him posted on important matters.

Movement for the Restoration of Democracy

In February 1981, twelve opposition political parties, an assorted group of right, centre, and left, had formed a 'Movement for the Restoration of Democracy' (MRD). Besides the PPP and the NDP, the remaining constituent parties of the MRD were tiny in size, regional in nature, and essentially splinter groups of the bigger parties. Differences on their political philosophy notwithstanding, they united to demand an end to military rule. The MRD was largely kept alive by a responsive Press, giving coverage to its drawing-room meetings.

The MRD declared its intention of holding protest rallies against the government on Pakistan's independence day, 14 August 1983.

To pre-empt the agitation, the government announced a three-tier election plan on 12 August. It involved holding of local, provincial, and national elections over the next eighteen months.

Zia's political opponents termed the announcement of the election schedule a gimmick for prolonging one-man rule. Some parties threatened to boycott the elections. Others opposed them, unless they were held on conditions demanded by them. Notwithstanding such tactics, the announcement had a dampening effect on the projected agitation.

The MRD movement in Sindh, launched under the guidance of Mr Ghulam Mustafa Jatoi, soon took a regional turn when it adopted a catchy slogan that Sindh faced a 'sense of deprivation'. The theme, chosen to play upon the sensitivities of the poor people, alienated other provinces. The allegation was factually unsustainable. An assessment carried out by the federal government revealed that Sindh had more than its fair share of representation in the federation and in the departments which came under its control. Nearly 60 per cent of the national industry was also located in that province. Statistics showed that, whereas the province held appointments in excess of its quota, wide disparities existed within the province. The better educated urban areas absorbed most of the job opportunities which caused frustration and a sense of neglect in the less educated rural interior.

The movement started with some momentum, persisted for a while, but failed to spread beyond some parts of the interior of Sindh. The parochial slogan did not get a sympathetic response in the urban areas of Sindh. The other provinces remained largely unaffected.

The weakly planned movement was inexpertly launched. Mr Jatoi was arrested. His son went into hiding, crossed over to India, and emerged in London. The MRD leadership fell into the hands of inexperienced low-level workers, who lacked the capacity to lead. From the noble slogan of restoring democracy, the movement took an anti-social turn. Public buildings were burnt; railway lines were uprooted; banks were looted; canals were breached. Roads became unsafe for travel; dacoits and miscreants took advantage of the disturbed conditions. As the law and order situation took a turn for the worse, public hostility turned against the anti-social elements. It was left to the law-enforcing agencies to restore order, which they did.

Mr Jatoi was suspect, even within the fold of his own party. The PPP accused him of hobnobbing with the government and manoeuvring his own arrest to improve his declining public image. His son's escape to India gave rise to speculation that the movement was Indian-inspired. The government exploited such weaknesses to regain the initiative.

The PPP had sensed the mood of the people. When the people in the other provinces, particularly in the Punjab, kept aloof from the agitation in Sindh, the PPP gradually distanced itself from the MRD, without making a formal break. Foreseeing elections and knowing that the minor parties would become an election drag, it took the decision to ditch the MRD at a suitable time. The PPP tested its popularity during the local bodies elections. In theory, it boycotted those elections. In reality, the party candidates contested them with great vigour under the name *Awam Dost* (Peoples' friends). Benazir Bhutto drew large crowds initially, but the public euphoria soon subsided. The MRD had served the purpose of the PPP, which no longer cherished the idea of sharing power with the splinter groups. MRD started eroding from within.

As stated elsewhere in the text, elections were held in the country in 1985. In these elections, candidates were prohibited from using the platform of any political party during the pre-election campaign period. The MRD boycotted these elections to protest against the ban on political parties fielding their party candidates. In reality, many MRD members, including those in the PPP, participated in the elections as candidates. The elections over, Prime Minister Muhammad Khan Junejo formed the federal government. The MRD adopted a two-track approach towards the Junejo government, accusing it of being 'an extension of martial law', while negotiating with it when necessary.

The death of President Zia in August 1988 removed the last veneer of unity. The MRD had outlived its purpose and was soon in disarray. It suffered its clinical death when its component parties disagreed on the issue of the distribution of tickets for the November 1988 elections. Some diehard MRD leaders took refuge behind platitudes, saying that the 'MRD was not an alliance. It was only a movement'. Mr Rao Rashid (PPP) called it an 'unnatural alliance.'

The MRD leadership could not ensure the security of information of their own action plans. The government usually remained one step ahead of their agitational activities. One of the top political leaders in their fold actively co-operated with a national intelligence agency. The MRD was thus paralysed from within.

India's War Hysteria—1983-1984

Within Sindh, the MRD agitation involved violence in politics and lust for easy money. Often, abductions for ransom were carried out by those who enjoyed the political patronage and protection of the big landlords. The military intervened, restored a measure of order, and brought the situation under control—but not without a price. Ugly scars were left on the face of national unity. India fished in Pakistan's troubled waters. The Sindh dissidents found a safe haven across the Indo-Pakistan border. The Indian support, initially covert, soon became overt. Mrs Indira Gandhi threatened that India could not remain indifferent to the cause of the people of Sindh. A 'Sindhi Sammelan' (Seminar) was held in New Delhi under the chairmanship of the President of India. In that seminar, a member of the Indian Parliament belonging to the ruling party demanded that Sindh be absorbed in the Indian motherland. Pakistan's diplomatic protest brought the official reply that the individual had expressed his personal views. In Pakistan's perception, India had unholy designs against her. The Indian Chief of Army Staff, General K. Sunderji, met Major-General Nishat Ahmad of the Pakistan Army in late 1986. The two general officers had once attended a military course together in the USA. Sunderji told Nishat that if Pakistan could help the Sikhs in the Indian Punjab—an allegation denied by Pakistan—India too possessed a 'Sindh card.' He added that India had not exploited that card yet.

From late 1983 onwards, Mrs Indira Gandhi created war hysteria. She saw clouds of war on the clear Indo-Pakistan horizon and issued threatening statements without any provocation. At that time, the Sikhs in the Indian Punjab were demanding freedom. Some visiting Indian Opposition leaders warned Pakistan that a cornered Mrs Indira Gandhi was looking for an excuse 'to teach Pakistan a lesson'. In their assessment, she planned to externalize her own internal failures. Pakistan played her diplomatic cards well. President Zia declined to be provoked and made conciliatory statements. Zia had learned diplomacy fast. He had no intention of involving Pakistan in a multi-directional threat. While playing it cool with India, he wanted to fully concentrate on the Afghanistan problem.

In June 1984, the Indian Army attacked the Golden Temple, the holiest shrine of the Sikhs, located in Amritsar. As a consequence, in October 1984, Mrs Indira Gandhi was assassinated by a Sikh. A prominent Opposition leader in India told General Zia in late 1984 that the Indian misadventure against the Golden Temple had averted an Indo-Pakistan war.

Contact with India

The Indian defence and military attache in Islamabad, Brigadier D. K. Khanna, met me in the GHQ during a routine courtesy call. He was asked to convey to the Chief of Army Staff in India, General A. S. Vaidya, that the two armies could assist their respective governments in keeping the border conflicts and tensions under control. Simultaneously, Pakistan's military and defence attache in New Delhi was directed to take up this issue with the Army Headquarters, India. The attache, Brigadier Z. I. Abbasi, called on the Indian Army chief.
A letter received from General Vaidya, dated 8 June 1984, read: 'You would always find us meeting you more than halfway in any steps which may help in normalization of relations and building goodwill between the peoples of our two countries.'
At about the same time, the Indian Foreign Secretary, Mr M. Rasgotra, while on a visit to Pakistan, met the author. Through him, two proposals were sent to the Indian Army chief. General Vaidya wrote again on 3 July 1984, saying: 'Shri M. Rasgotra has conveyed to me your suggestions for keeping the border tension-free and informing each other about movement of troops to the border. As I have written to you, we have always been keen to avoid tension on our borders with all our neighbours. I would like to assure you again that we will only be too happy to reciprocate any steps taken in this direction. I am also agreeable to your suggestion for providing advance information regarding movement of troops close to the border. The modalities for this can be evolved by our Directors of Military Operations, who already have a direct telephone link. On our part, we had already taken a positive step by keeping you informed of recent moves in Punjab, through Ministry of External Affairs.'
In a reply to General Vaidya dated 24 July 1984, I wrote: 'I am happy that we both agree in principle on two issues: to keep the border tension-free and to provide advance information to each other about movement of troops ... Perhaps the time has come for us to develop regular contacts at some agreed levels to promote better understanding. Some time ago, the Government of Pakistan had made some concrete suggestions in this regard to the Government of India. You will find us responsive to any practical measures that can help to generate light by removing the cobwebs of suspicion and doubt.'
No reply was received to the last proposal. On the first two issues, some progress was made. The Directors General of Military Operations

of the two countries telephoned each other on a few occasions. The movement of troops close to the border was at times reported to the other side and the sector commanders across the Line of Control between Azad Kashmir and Indian-occupied Kashmir met to discuss the local pinpricks. No progress was, however, made on the contentious issue of the Siachen Glacier.

Surrounded by lofty mountains, perennially covered with snow, and void of vegetation and human habitation, the 72 kilometre long and 2 to 3 kilometre wide Siachen Glacier area is located at an altitude of 15,000-23,000 feet above mean sea level in the north and northwest corner of the disputed state of Jammu and Kashmir. Swept by high speed blizzards in winter, and riddled with deep and treacherous snow-covered crevasses, human survival here is a hazardous task. During the Kashmir liberation struggle (1947-8), fighting did not erupt in this area because of the absence of civil or military population located here. Under the UN aegis, India and Pakistan ended hostilities in Kashmir in January 1949 and a Cease-fire Line Agreement was signed. The demarcation of the Cease-fire Line was completed up to the terminus point NJ 9842 (edge of the Siachen Glacier area) 'on the basis of factual position as of July 27, 1949.' The demarcation beyond the terminus point was left to be done subsequently, and has not yet taken place. The Siachen Glacier area thus remained free from the troops of either country. This status quo was not disturbed during the Indo-Pakistan wars of 1965 and 1971.

In early 1984, in blatant violation of the Cease-fire Line Agreement 1949, the Line of Control Agreement 1972 (negotiated after the 1971 war), and Simla Agreement 1972, Indian troops infiltrated into the Siachen Glacier area and occupied some high passes. This created an untenable security situation for Pakistan which also established its military presence in the region. Pakistan lodged a protest with India against the intrusion of her forces into the disputed territory. This led to negotiations. On the conclusion of the fifth round of talks between the defence secretaries of India and Pakistan held in Islamabad, an agreement was reached. This was announced in a press conference jointly addressed by the two defence secretaries on 17 June 1989. Some details. 'There was agreement by both sides to work towards a comprehensive settlement, based on redeployment of forces to reduce the chances of conflict, avoidance of the use of force, and the determination of future positions on the ground so as to conform to the Simla agreement and to ensure durable peace in Siachen area.'[1]

A day later, India reneged. Mr Rajiv Gandhi, who had become the Prime Minister of India after the assassination of his mother, apprehended that the Siachen Agreement might cost him the votes of militant Hindus in the elections then due in his country.

Army Command Structure

After 5 July 1977, statecraft consumed most of General Zia's time. Army work took a back seat. This had adverse consequences. In mid-1978, Lieutenant-General Muhammad Iqbal was appointed Deputy Chief of Army Staff. He found his assignment irksome, with the limited powers delegated to him. Additionally, the Corps Commanders-cum-Governors in the provinces acted oddly. During his visits to the military formations, General Iqbal was at times not received on arrival by the corps commanders who were supposedly engaged elsewhere on gubernatorial duties. It eroded the military discipline and created undercurrents of unease. The situation was corrected by appointing full-time military governors in three provinces. Balochistan remained the exception, where Lieutenant-General Rahimuddin Khan kept the governor's post in addition to commanding 2 Corps virtually in absentia. Its headquarters was located in the distant city of Multan. Many eyebrows were raised in the army because of his relationship with General Zia—Rahimuddin's daughter was married to Zia's son.

In March 1980, the rank of Deputy Chief of Army Staff was elevated to that of a four-star general and the appointment was redesignated as Vice Chief of Army Staff. General Sawar Khan was given that appointment. The vice chief was authorized 'To exercise and perform all the powers and functions vested in the Chief of Army Staff under the law, rules, regulations, orders and instructions for the time being in force.' The vice chief was allowed all facilities 'as authorized to the Chief of Army Staff for so long as COAS holds the office of the President.'

In the letter of law, the vice chief, *ipso facto*, enjoyed total authority, power, and facilities as allowed to the army chief. In practice, it varied on a person to person basis, depending on the degree of understanding which existed between President Zia and the vice chief.

The Political Structure

To make fundamental changes in the political structure—political parties, the election system, and the form of government—became an obsession with General Zia. In the early period of his administration, this issue occasionally came up for discussion but was not seriously debated. With elections postponed the second time, he took a plunge into this hornet's nest. By this time, his growing Islamic impulse impelled him to dismantle the Westminster model superficially imposed on an eastern culture by an alien western power. There were nearly eighty political parties in Pakistan, of which hardly ten were meaningfully functional. The remainder were minor groups with some nuisance value but without much public support.

Critical of the 1973 Constitution, General Zia felt that the parliamentary form of government neither suited the psyche of the people of Pakistan nor promoted the concept of Islamic unity. In his view, the presidential form was much better suited to Pakistan's requirements.

Ideas were frequently floated to provoke discussion on some controversial issues and to assess public reaction. The questions raised pertained to the minimum age and qualifications of the voters, the honesty and the piety of the candidates, the mode of filtering the candidates through a pre-election selection process, the desirability of having an opposition, the need for reducing the number of political parties in the country, the possibility of the Election Commission scrutinizing the source of income of the political parties and their manifestos, the advantages and disadvantages of the joint or the separate electorate systems, the usefulness of a system of proportional representation, and the possibility of a woman being head of state and head of government in an Islamic state.

It was also proposed in the MLAs' conference that a military council be formed as a crisis management body to deal with any future political impasse. Such a council could consist of the prime minister and the leader of the opposition, the chief ministers of the four provinces, and all the defence services chiefs along with the Chairman of the JCSC. In addition it was also discussed whether the judicial system based on Anglo-Saxon laws should be replaced with a rule of law based on *Shariah*. The issue was what changes needed to be made to the 1973 Constitution to make it responsive to the needs of the time.

Such questions raised bitter controversies, inflamed emotions, and divided the people. The Zia administration gave prominent coverage to Islamic scholars and religious teachings on the state-controlled electronic media. A corresponding reduction in the entertainment programmes brought protests from viewers. One viewer sought help from the Information Secretary over the telephone to get his television put right. The bureaucrat advised the caller to consult a TV mechanic. 'No technician can help me,' lamented the person, 'only you can help because a *maulvi* is stuck to my television screen.'

The religious groups and the Rightist parties supporting General Zia on his Islamization process had a limited vote catching ability. The secular political parties opposed Zia's programme of action on philosophical and technical planes. They did not approve of a dictator making changes in the Constitution. The law gave this authority to Zia but they did not wish him to exercise it. General Zia felt differently.

General Zia kept his critics and opponents guessing. His legal advisers compiled a heap of recommendations concerning electoral and constitutional matters. He kept his decisions well-concealed and announced them when it suited him to do so. The constitutional changes finally made were derived from a number of sources—the earlier constitutions of Pakistan, the Indian constitution, and those recommended by his legal and religious advisers.

On constitutional matters, General Zia played a waiting game with his team-mates. A clever tactician, he discussed the proposals with them on umpteen occasions, but took care not to disclose his final decision. The art of statecraft was learnt by Zia very quickly.

Power addicted Zia. There was a pinch—the more he wielded authority, the more it created the feeling of guilt in him that he was not an elected president. He wanted the stamp of public legitimacy on his rule, without facing the risk of an election. That such an endorsement would provide a further tenure in high office was also an attraction. General Zia felt, and his colleagues agreed with him, that he should preside over the transitional period of change-over from martial law to a democratic order. But he kept postponing the fateful date on one pretext or another. When pressed to announce the election schedule, he once confessed that, before taking a decision, he had to take into consideration many factors like the future of the country and his subordinates. The remark indicated a fear psychosis deep within.

The Presidential Referendum—1984

The martial law administrators' meetings frequently discussed the future political action plan for the country. The question of holding national elections and the desirability of a referendum were analysed. While two or three members favoured the idea of a referendum, the majority was against such a proposal. This group advocated the holding of general elections and transfer of power to the elected representatives. The proposal for holding of a referendum appealed to the President.

The President's military colleagues were united in urging the President to make up his mind quickly and to opt for one of the several alternatives available to him. The modalities could easily be worked out, but the difficulty was that he would not say what he wanted. Irrespective of their views and approach, it must be said that the participants were all sincere and had genuinely felt that power must be transferred to the elected representatives, whether elected on a party basis or a non-party basis. The important thing was to lure the President to take the bait. In due course of time, the politicians would in any case be reverting to the multi-party system.

A difference of opinion existed on the conduct of polls. While the majority favoured holding them on a party basis, the President, along with two or three members, felt that they should be held on non-party lines. In the absence of a consensus, many committees were formed to examine the problem and suggest a suitable methodology. Except for one committee all the others recommended holding of elections on a party basis. The National Assembly, composed of members nominated by the government and called *Majlis-e-Shoora*, also recommended such a course. The President, however, remained averse to holding party-based elections.

In the fall of 1984 the deadlock was still unresolved. In the MLAs' meeting held on 6 November 1984, elections and a referendum were discussed once again. This time, a compromise was reached. It was agreed that a referendum would be held as a prelude to holding general elections. The aim of the referendum was to elect General Muhammad Ziaul Haq as the President of Pakistan for a further period of five years after martial law was lifted. After considering some formulations, the framing of an appropriate referendum question was left to the legal experts. It was further agreed that the referendum proposal should be placed before the cabinet for its approval.

The cabinet approved the holding of the referendum in its meeting of 16 November 1984. The Minister for Law, Mr Sharifuddin Pirzada, opposed the proposal on the plea that, in the light of the Supreme Court ruling in the Nusrat Bhutto case, there was no legal requirement for seeking a vote of confidence from the people. Subsequently, he went along with the majority view.

The referendum plan was finally announced by the President on 1 December 1984, fixing 19 December 1984 as the date for holding it. On 2 December, an MLAs' meeting was held to make administrative arrangements and to evolve a publicity plan. The President was to visit important cities and towns, campaigning and explaining the purpose of the referendum, and seeking votes. His tour took him to the Punjab (8 - 11 December), Sindh (12 - 14 December), Balochistan (14 - 15 December), and the NWFP (16 - 17 December 1984). The turnout of people during the campaign meetings was heavy. The local administration ensured that.

According to the prevailing election rules, the showing of the National Identity Card at the time of voting was not compulsory. The MLAs and the federal cabinet recommended that the rule be followed for the referendum voting as well. Disagreeing with that recommendation, General Zia, in his address to the nation on 1 December 1984, announced that the production of the National Identity Card would be mandatory while voting. Later, during his election tours in the provinces, he realized that many people in the rural areas did not possess identity cards, a factor which would reduce the turnout of voters. While still on his campaign, the President directed his COS to have the condition of identity cards re-examined in consultation with the Chief Election Commissioner, the Ministry of Law, the Interior Secretary, and the Vice Chief of Army Staff. Consequently, a meeting was held on 17 December 1984. After examining the issue, the committee came to the conclusion that a change in law at that belated stage would raise doubts about the fairness of the referendum results. It suggested that no change be made in the rule. The President was unhappy at the recommendation. He altered the rule and announced the withdrawal of the identity card condition.

It was decided that a cell should be established to oversee the referendum arrangements and provide administrative support to the Chief Election Commissioner on demand. It was proposed that the cell should to be created in the Joint Staff Headquarters. General

Rahimuddin Khan, the Chairman of the Joint Chiefs of Staff Committee, opposed the use of the military headquarters for election work. A compromise was made—the JSHQ provided the staff (Lieutenant-General Syed Refaqat), who created a cell in the CMLA's Secretariat. The President felt greatly assured after his success in the referendum. A discernible change appeared in his attitude and style of work. He gradually sidelined the MLAs' meetings. Their frequency decreased and issues of substance somehow lost their importance and urgency. The elections were due soon but they no longer appeared a priority matter. The governors, keen to discuss election matters with the President, received a lukewarm response from him. On one occasion, Generals Jilani and Fazle Haq, the Governors of the Punjab and the NWFP respectively, virtually forced a meeting on General Zia. It remained inconclusive.

The referendum was held on 19 December 1984, in which General Zia, the only contesting candidate, received a vote of confidence from the people. The turnout of voters, according to official figures, was over sixty per cent. The question put to the voter was: 'Do you endorse the process initiated by the President of Pakistan, General Muhammad Ziaul Haq, for bringing the laws of Pakistan in conformity with the injunctions of Islam as laid down in the Holy Quran and Sunnah of the Holy Prophet (peace be upon him) and for the preservation of the ideology of Pakistan; and are you in favour of the continuation and further consolidation of that process and for the smooth and orderly transfer of power to the elected representatives of the people?' Every voter was required to answer 'yes' or 'no'.

In his address to the nation on 1 December 1984, General Zia had said: 'If the majority of the electorate responds to this question in "YES", it will be taken to mean that the people of Pakistan have expressed confidence in the present government, have endorsed its policies and have elected General Muhammad Ziaul Haq [as President] for the next five years.' After the referendum, General Zia started distancing himself from his military colleagues.

The referendum was called a fraud and a subterfuge to prolong one-man rule in the country. The critics claimed that the question put to the electorate was mischievously framed to achieve a 'positive result' by playing on the religious sensitivities of the people. Many of the illiterate voters might have been unaware of what they were voting for. They claimed that the turnout of the voters was not more than twenty to twenty-five per cent.

Legalities apart, the referendum did not provide a seal of legitimacy to Zia on the moral plane. The criticism irritated and embarrassed him. He was hard put to to explain why, if a referendum was justified at all, had a straight question not been put to the voters: 'Do you elect General Zia as the President of Pakistan for a further period of five years?'

General Elections—1985

In 1977, the army was reluctantly sucked into the vortex of power because the self-seeking politicians had made a mockery of democracy. Once on the tiger's back, General Zia could not get off it. Despite some good work done by the Zia administration, his prolonged military rule is hard to defend. A faulty democratic system with its in built checks and balances is, in the long term, better than a seemingly benign one-man rule, in which the process of accountability has no place. Zia's colleagues, including this writer, share the blame for not holding elections much earlier than they were actually held. For them, it was not difficult to argue with Zia, and they did, frequently and forcefully. But it was not easy for them to rid Zia of his obsession with fundamental issues. They had their limits. Zia was psychologically opposed to the western concept of democracy and looked for an Islamic order, which continued to evade his grasp.

On the question of elections, General Zia faced an ideological barrier. He considered that the parliamentary form of government, based on the multiplicity of political parties, was not consonant with Islam. He argued that the Muslim *ummah* constituted one indivisible group and any attempt to create divisions in it on the basis of political, national, ethnic, linguistic, or any other considerations, was against the spirit of Islam. His orthodox religious advisers opposed the parliamentary form of elections *ab initio,* and pleaded that Islam advocated the election of only one *Amir.* In their view, the presidential form of government was closer to the concept of Islam. In the performance of his functions, the *Amir* could appoint consultants from among men of piety and righteousness. Strongly leaning towards such views, General Zia was an advocate of the pan-Islamic concept.

The logic of the orthodox religious scholars did not convince many of General Zia's other colleagues. They considered the election process neither repugnant to Islam nor separable from a democratic order. His attempts to reach a consensus failed, as the gulf separating the two views was too wide to bridge. He constituted a number of committees to examine the issue. He met Muslim scholars from home and abroad. Committees and individuals submitted a plethora of recommendations. They usually agreed on the basics and differed on the specifics. Those consulted by the President included the Council of Islamic Ideology; Maulana Zafar Ahmad Ansari; Mr Muhammad Asad, author of *Principles of State and Government in Islam*; Dr Hameedullah, author of *Muslim Conduct of State*; Mr A. K. Brohi; Mr Justice Muhammad Afzal Cheema; Dr Al'Maroof Dawalibi, Adviser for Religious Affairs in Saudi Arabia; Professor Zarka of Jordan; and a group of scholars from Saudi Arabia and the Al-Azhar University, Cairo. His military and cabinet colleagues discussed the recommendations made by various sources, without reaching a consensus.

The recommendations of such committees had earlier resulted in 1982 in the formation of a *Majlis-e-Shoora* (consultative assembly). It was composed of persons nominated by the President on the basis of recommendations made by the provincial governors. The *Majlis-e-Shoora* was composed of political personalities, religious scholars, technocrats, and persons representing trade, industry, and the media, and included some women members. As a body, it neither filled the vacuum caused by the absence of elected assemblies nor came up to public expectations. The lack of a public mandate and the absence of authority to enforce its decisions made it a superfluous organization. Notwithstanding the calibre of its members, and despite some useful contributions made by it, the *Majlis-e-Shoora* failed to make an impact.

There was another psychological barrier. General Zia was averse to political parties contesting the elections. Some of his military colleagues and other advisers shared his views that elections be held on a non-party basis to avoid the tension created by a party-based electioneering process. It meant that every candidate canvassed for himself without using the platform, the slogans, and the resources of any political party to project his candidature. This was a new and untried approach. Those advocating it felt that elections held on the basis of political parties might polarize the country. Their argument appealed to the President.

The proposal for non-party elections was strongly advocated by a political activist, Raja Munawwar, who was introduced to General

Zia by the Punjab Governor, General Sawar. Raja Munawar, ex-PPP, enjoyed government hospitality for a long time and impressed Zia with his arguments. Many of Zia's colleagues were much less impressed by his logic, and attributed ulterior motives to him. Zia once asked Munawwar to explain the concept to the MLAs. Knowing the general officers' reservations about the person, Zia advised them in advance not to ask any questions after the presentation. Apart from other considerations, Zia sensed in the non-party election system a mechanism to dilute the power of the PPP. He also felt that assemblies formed by such a process might be more pliable.

There was a vocal lobby among the President's military colleagues which felt that politics is to a nation what blood is to a human body. It recommended the holding of elections on a party basis. It was of the conviction that political parties were the *sine qua non* of any democratic political system and the two were not separable. It argued that the mode of party-based elections, being familiar to the voters, should be retained. It held the view that, irrespective of the mode of its election, a democratically elected parliament could not operate on non-party lines. The President did not share this view and felt that the members elected on the basis of their personal popularity and strength would like to retain their independent status in the parliament even after the elections. The lobby members then suggested a compromise: they proposed that, as a one-time exception, elections may be held on a non-party basis, but political parties be revived immediately on the completion of the election process, and that the parliament should function on party lines. The President rejected the proposal.

There was a division among the President's advisers. Some supported non-party-based elections, an idea forcefully opposed by others. The more the concept of party-based elections was discussed, the more the President distanced himself from it. In one MLAs' meeting he showed his annoyance by saying, 'I don't know why Fazle and Arif are so much fascinated by the party-based elections.' In mid-1983 the issue was discussed in a MLAs' meeting held at Nathiagali. General Zia, spending a weekend in Murree, invited General Jilani, the Governor of the Punjab, to travel with him during the drive from Murree to Nathiagali. En route Zia tried to win over Jilani's support for non-party elections. During the meeting held the following day, General Zia started reading a paper in a favour of non-party-based elections, stating that it had been prepared by 'a friend.' To withhold the name was an unusual practice. He had hardly read a page or two when there was an interruption. One participant guessed aloud the name of the author. The irresistible Fazle Haq remarked, 'This habitual sycophant lacks scruples. He could simultaneously prepare equally convincing documents in favour of and against any proposition if a person in authority so directed him.' Zia took that outburst sportingly.

It was also proposed to General Zia that a pragmatic course open to him was to either form a party of his own or to accept the leadership of one of the existing political parties. The Pir of Pagaro had repeatedly offered General Zia the presidentship of the Pakistan Muslim League. General Zia stated that, temperamentally, he could not adjust himself to leading a political party. The political system demands compromises and accommodations. After having wielded total power for so long, it would have been difficult for General Zia to share it with others.

Elections for the National Assembly were held on 25 February 1985. Three days later, elections for the four provincial assemblies took place. All these elections were held on a non-party basis.

Nomination of the Prime Minister

Under the amended Constitution, the President was to nominate one of the members of the National Assembly as the Prime Minister of Pakistan. The nominated member was required to obtain a vote of confidence in the National Assembly within sixty days. It was unanimously agreed that it would be advisable to elect the first post-martial law Prime Minister from one of the smaller provinces because President Zia was a Punjabi and the bulk of the defence services human resource came from the provinces of the Punjab and the North-West Frontier province.

The MLAs' conference, after considering many names from amongst the elected members of the National Assembly, selected Mr Illahi Bukhsh Soomro and Mr Muhammad Khan Junejo, both from Sindh, in that order of preference. The President seemed to agree with this recommendation. It was also suggested that the President might stay above politics and propose both the names to the members of the National Assembly in an unofficial meeting, giving them the option of selecting their leader from the two. The President desired that the modalities of implementation be left to him.

At 3 p.m. on 18 March 1985, a small exclusive meeting was held in the President's office. It was attended by Mr Ghulam Ishaq Khan, Sahabzada Yaqub Khan, General Rahimuddin Khan, myself, and Major-General Malik Abdul Waheed. The President apprised the group of the recommendations made by the MLAs' conference and asked for comments. The group endorsed the MLAs' views. Soomro was preferred to Junejo.

The President then met the Pir of Pagaro and disclosed both the names to him. The Pir of Pagaro pleaded that the President should propose only one name, and, being a well-wisher of the Pakistan Muslim League, he should propose the name of Mr Muhammad Khan Junejo. President Ziaul Haq, disregarding the advice of his colleagues, agreed with the Pir of Pagaro. He then played a gimmick with his staff.

On the evening of 19 March 1985, the President told his COS, Major-General Waheed, that instead of nominating one candidate for the prime ministership as decided earlier, he would recommend three names to the National Assembly members (in informal meetings), who would then elect one of them by vote. He directed that a ballot paper be printed for the voting process with three letters in the Urdu alphabet one for each of the three candidates. The Printing Corporation Press at Islamabad worked overnight to print the required ballot papers. Special envelopes were prepared and a procedure for voting was evolved.

On Wednesday, 20 March, the President met the newly elected members of the National Assembly in groups of their respective provinces. The first group, at 2:30 p.m., was from the province of Balochistan, followed by the members of the provinces of the NWFP, Punjab, and Sindh. The President told his staff that he would make a brief statement to each group of provincial MNAs. The ballot papers would then be issued to the MNAs to exercise their choice. The COS to the President and his Military Secretary, Brigadier Mahmud Ali Durrani, attended the meetings with the required number of ballot papers in their possession for distribution amongst the MNAs. While addressing the first group of MNAs of Balochistan, the President surprised his staff by suggesting the name of Mr Muhammad Khan Junejo as the next Prime Minister. After the President's pep-talk, two of the MNAs requested that the National Assembly be allowed to elect its own leader and the members should not be influenced in favour of Mr Junejo. They argued that Mr Junejo, a staunch follower of Pir of Pagaro, would create problems for the President.

The President then met the remaining MNAs in their provincial groups and made similar statements. From each group, some members raised objections similar to those made by the Balochistan MNAs. The ballot papers remained unused.

The meetings with the MNAs over, the President met Mr Muhammad Khan Junejo in his office in the President's House at 8 p.m. the same evening. The COS was also present. Warmly greeting Mr Junejo, Zia congratulated him on his election to the National Assembly and said, 'I have decided to nominate you as the Prime Minister of Pakistan.' The disclosure caused no surprise to Mr Junejo. The Pir of Pagaro and the MNAs had already spilled the beans to him. Without a shadow of emotion appearing on his face, Mr Junejo heard General Zia in an unconcerned manner. Without expressing a word of thanks, he said abruptly, 'Mr President, when do you plan to lift the martial law?' Shocked at the lack of elementary courtesy shown to him, General Zia kept his cool and said casually: 'Martial law is now in your support. It will help you to settle down in your high appointment. I will lift it whenever you are in control of the situation.' The relationship between the President and his nominated Prime Minister started on an icy note.

The newly elected parliament held its inaugural session on 23 March 1985. While addressing the parliament, the President emphasized the point that, as its members were elected on a non-party basis, they should keep functioning without political parties. That unsolicited advice was untimely. The mood of the House was different. Political parties were soon revived. General Zia lost the political initiative, and the credit for the revival of political institutions and a democratic order was claimed by Prime Minister Junejo. In his very first speech on the floor of the House, Mr Junejo said that democracy and martial law were incompatible. Later in the year, on 14 August 1985, while addressing a huge public meeting at Lahore, Mr Junejo declared that martial law would be lifted before the end of the year. Junejo had taken prior permission from General Zia for making that announcement.

In the first session of the National Assembly, General Zia formally nominated Mr Muhammad Khan Junejo as the Prime Minister of Pakistan. The National Assembly gave him a unanimous vote of confidence.

The country remained under martial law for a further period of nine months. The draconian law was lifted thereafter but Mr Junejo continued to be castigated by the opposition as the quasi-military prime minister.

The Power Tussle

Mr Junejo did not wish to become a puppet prime minister. He wished to follow the Constitution which clearly defined the powers of the head of government. A difficulty arose about the trappings. Mr Junejo was as much interested in the ceremonial splendour of his appointment as he was in the exercise of power. He considered those ceremonial trappings a public manifestation of the exercise of power by him. Besides, Junejo was obsessed with the desire to demonstrate his legitimacy as an elected prime minister—not merely a nominee of the President. This created ripples of turbulence between him and General Zia almost from day one. Initially, the differences remained submerged beneath an apparently serene surface, but they were too strong to be hidden for long.

Mr Junejo, a former minister in the provincial and federal cabinets, was well versed in the system of public administration. His political and spiritual attachment to the Pir of Pagaro was his strength as well as the weakness. Temperamentally, a soft-spoken and an unassuming person, Mr Junejo was down-to-earth in his dealings. He was a stickler in his official dealings, spending much of his time on trivial matters.

In his thought, actions, upbringing, and behaviour Mr Junejo vastly differed from Mr Bhutto. Junejo's humility was a contrast to Bhutto's arrogance. If the former had a down-to-earth approach to life, the latter rode high and had an exaggerated opinion about himself. Bhutto, well-read, sharp, eloquent, and mischievous, was in a class different from Junejo. There were two things common between them: both belonged to Sindh and both became prime ministers. The similarity ended there.

Unlike many of his contemporaries, Mr Junejo was steadfast in his political affiliation. He never changed his political party—an uncommon phenomenon in Pakistan's political history.

Mr Junejo's nomination as the head of government provided him with a unique opportunity to go down in history as having become a

Prime Minister of Pakistan without having to undergo the pains of leading a political party through a tough election process. The prime ministership was an unexpected but welcome gift. He seized the opportunity and claimed that he had accepted the offer to expedite the lifting of martial law. The Zia-Junejo honeymoon was short-lived. While General Zia found power slipping from his grasp, Mr Junejo found himself politically hamstrung by the label of being the hand-picked nominee of an autocratic ruler.

Mr Junejo faced a dilemma. He had convinced himself that the public would consider him a handicapped prime minister unless he possessed the authority, perquisites, and trappings equal to those enjoyed by the former Prime Minister, Mr Z. A. Bhutto. He adopted a quietly persistent approach to get his demands accepted. The pinpricks caused irritation between the President and the Prime Minister. Mr Junejo desired the services of a military secretary and an aide-de-camp. General Zia quoted the example of many countries to indicate that such trappings were reserved only for the head of state. 'I must have them because Bhutto had them,' was the reply. Such a staff had served Mr Bhutto when he became the President and the Chief Martial Law Administrator in 1971. He retained the facility on assuming the office of the prime minister in 1973 because there was no check on him. Mr Junejo was not impressed with this argument and General Zia grudgingly yielded.

The Inter-Services parade, held on 23 March each year in the capital, started a controversy. Mr Junejo was keen to review the parade along with the President and to arrive at the parade ground riding in the imperial style horse-driven carriage in the company of General Zia. 'Prime Minister Bhutto had done so before,' he said. 'Two wrongs do not make a right,' said General Zia firmly. The President reviewed such a parade in his capacity as the supreme commander of the armed forces. A video tape of the Indian Republic Day parade was shown to Mr Junejo to see for himself the position occupied by the prime minister of that country on such an occasion. Mr Junejo made a counter-proposal. If the President reviewed the parade on 23 March, the Prime Minister would be the chief guest at the flag-hoisting ceremony on 14 August, Independence Day. The deal was made.

A divergence of views emerged on issues of substance. General Zia felt that the National Assembly, elected on a non-party basis, should function without forming political parties. Mr Junejo thought, and rightly so, that it would be impossible to deal with 237 members in their individual capacity. Finally, the Prime Minister's views prevailed, but, before this happened, General Zia faced a setback in the National Assembly on the issue of the election of the Speaker.

Khawaja Muhammad Safdar was the President's choice for the speaker's post. The Prime Minister was reluctant, but did not propose another name. The members sensed the split. One group proposed the name of Mr Fakhar Imam (a former Zia minister) for speakership. Fakhar declined to respond to a telephone call from Zia on the subject and refused to withdraw his name despite Zia's personal intervention. He went on to win the majority vote. This election result came as a rude shock to Zia and Junejo.

The election of Mian Nawaz Sharif as the Chief Minister of the Punjab was not problem-free. In an MLAs' conference, soon after the elections, General Zia asked the military governors for the names of the likely candidates for the office of the chief ministership of the provinces. The name proposed by Lieutenent-General Fazle Haq (NWFP) did not evoke a discussion. General Jahan Dad (Sindh) stated that no elected member was suitable to become the chief minister. He proposed the name of Syed Ghous Ali Shah for that office. Afridi (Balochistan) stated that Jam Sahib of Lasbela enjoyed consensus support but, being too weak and corrupt, he would need to be carefully watched. He indicated that he had already cautioned Jam Sahib about his misdeeds. Jilani (Punjab) said that Mian Nawaz Sharif would be the automatic choice for a majority of the Punjab members. 'Why him?' enquired Zia. 'He is the one who enjoys support,' replied Jilani. 'Why not Malik Allah Yar?' Zia insisted. 'I don't think anyone other than Nawaz would be able to get elected,' said Jilani firmly. Though not convinced, Zia kept quiet. Nawaz Sharif was elected to be the Chief Minister of Punjab. Five years later, he was elected by the people to be their Prime Minister.

General Zia wished to appoint Dr Basharat Illahi, his brother-in-law, as the Governor of Punjab. The Chief Minister Mian Nawaz Sharif agreed. When Zia mooted the idea to Jilani, he advised the President against appointing his brother-in-law to succeed him, as, in his view, it would be tantamount to nepotism and would give him a bad name. Jilani suggested that in due course of time Basharat might instead be considered for membership of the parliament through the normal process of elections. Nawaz Sharif had also approached Mr Junejo to talk Zia out of this proposal. Mr Junejo suggested to

General Zia that a change be made. They jointly selected Makhdoom Sajjad Hussain Qureshi, Deputy Chairman of the Senate, to be made the Governor of the Punjab. Jilani supported the choice. Three years later, Dr Basharat Illahi became a Senator.

Some of General Zia's cabinet ministers had also been promised a seat in the Senate. Mr Ghulam Ishaq Khan and Lieutenant-General Jamal Said Mian contested the Senate seats from the NWFP and the Tribal Areas quotas respectively. The Governor of the NWFP, Lieutenant-General Fazle Haq, prevailed upon some of the candidates to withdraw from the contest. As a consequence, all the remaining candidates from the NWFP and the Tribal Areas were elected unopposed. Thereafter, it was easy for General Zia to get Mr Ghulam Ishaq Khan elected as the Chairman of the Senate, a post he filled with credit and distinction.

The Punjab Governor, Lieutenant-General Ghulam Jilani Khan, left the canvassing for the Senate seats to be done by the contesting candidates themselves. Two former federal ministers, Vice-Admiral Fazil Janjua and Dr Basharat Jazbi failed to get elected. The other three who contested the Senate polls successfully were Dr Mahbubul Haq, Lieutenant-General Saeed Qadir, and Dr Muhammad Asad. Sahabzada Yaqub Khan won the Senate seat from the Islamabad federal area.

Elections over, General Zia wanted some of his former ministers—now Senators—to be included in Junejo's federal cabinet. Mr Junejo wanted a maximum number of new political personalities to help establish his own credibility. Sahabzada Yaqub Khan was selected. Junejo accepted Dr Mahbubul Haq, albeit reluctantly. Despite General Zia's insistence, Mr Junejo declined to accommodate Dr Asad. A dejected Asad, who seemed to feel that Pakistan was worth living in only as a minister, resigned from the Senate and returned to the USA from where he had suddenly arrived to become a minister. Ambassador Ejaz Azim had requested President Zia to grant an interview to Asad, who was visiting Pakistan at that timed. Young Asad impressed Zia so much that the following day he was made a minister of state. Ejaz telephoned the President to express his surprise.[2] Zia told him, 'Asad was more surprised when I made him the ministerial offer.'

One of the first acts of the Junejo administration was to replace the information secretary, Lieutenant-General Mujibur Rehman. The change was quite understandable but the mode adopted was devious. General Zia had agreed with Mr Junejo's request to appoint an Information Secretary of his own choice. A senior bureaucrat conspired with the government-controlled information media to give wide publicity to an 'important' decision to be announced on a certain day. Mujib's removal, a routine affair, made headlines, as if he had been sacked unceremoniously. Junejo pleaded innocence when Zia protested to him on the issue. Made OSD (officer on special duty), Mujib became *persona non grata* overnight, with his official transport and other facilities withdrawn.

Mr Junejo wanted to demonstrate that he was a firm and independent prime minister. On his orders, those serving military officers who had completed three years or more while working in the civil departments of the government on deputation were reverted back to the military post-haste. Their replacements were not taken from the defence services. A feeling grew within the military that the affected officers had been victimized because of Zia-Junejo differences.

Such incidents took their toll. Initially, coolness replaced cordiality. The President-Prime Minister relationship became formal and official. With the passage of time, more problems developed, creating a gulf of mistrust and suspicion between the two, a gulf which kept widening.

In October 1986, Brigadier Mahmud Ali Durrani, Military Secretary to the President, was posted back to the army. When he made his farewell call on the Prime Minister, Mr Junejo surprised him by saying, 'I am trying to run the country in accordance with the Constitution. If the President did not like this Constitution he could have promulgated one similar to that of Sri Lanka.'[3]

The workload in the President's Secretariat decreased substantially after the lifting of martial law. Consequently, most of the military staff reverted back to the army. Just before the impending changes, the ever-inquisitive Lieutenant-General Fazle Haq enquired from General Zia, in an MLAs' meeting, if Lieutenant-General Syed Refaqat had been selected to replace the COS, Major-General Malik Abdul Waheed. The President's affirmative reply brought a quick retort from Fazli. With a wicked smile on his face, he caused loud laughter when he said, 'Between Refaqat [COS] and Aslam Khattak [Minister for Interior], the pair will see you through.'

The senior staff officers serving the President and the Prime Minister played a passive—nay, negative—role. Instead of removing the minor irritants which they could, they played the devil's advocate. The

Minister of State for Foreign Affairs, Mr Zain Noorani, once told me that Refaqat and Isani were taking the President and the Prime Minister on a collision course. On one occasion, Mr Junejo told Brigadier Mahmud Ali Durrani (President's Military Secretary) that, 'the President should appoint a more mature person as his Chief of Staff.'[4] Durrani brought this remark to the notice of the President. Many federal secretaries complained that, at times, they received divergent orders directly from the President and the Prime Minister, creating problems for them.

Uneasy Sindh

Despite the collapse of the MRD agitation, Sindh remained disturbed and tense. One reason was the free availability of weapons. The Afghan *jihad* produced side-effects in Pakistan. The weapon business boomed all along the Pakistan-Afghanistan border belt. The Tribal Areas became a weapons bazaar, where pistols, rifles, automatic weapons, grenades, mines, and explosives were freely available. These weapons filtered into population centres, passing through the porous border and clandestine routes. Once in the hands of political activists and anti-social elements, they were used to disturb the peace. Sindh became a victim of the proliferation of arms.

There was another fallout: with her borders with the Soviet Union and Iran closed, Afghanistan's global heroin trade started filtering through Pakistan. Crude heroin factories mushroomed in the safe haven of the Tribal Areas, outside the jurisdiction of Pakistani courts. The evil spread despite the government's attempts to contain it. Lust for easy money encouraged smugglers and fortune seekers to indulge in the narcotics trade. The number of heroin addicts increased in the country, not only posing hazards to health, but also raising the level of violence and crime.

During his frequent tours of Sindh, General Zia felt that the local administration tended to underplay the gravity of the law and order situation. There was usually a divergence of views of the police force and the feedback from the military sources deployed in that province. There was a tendency on the part of the administration to ensure that Zia met mostly the pro-government people. Some of the political leaders supporting the agitation did not wish to meet the President. Some others were kept away for reasons of local politics.

Mr Junejo's government inherited a disturbed Sindh. Lawlessness and an ineffective police force necessitated the frequent deployment of troops to restore law and order in the disturbed areas. Many criminals enjoyed the protection of feudal landlords who enlisted their support in order to keep their own estates trouble-free. The local administration was privy to this practice, but was too weak to net the culprits, who wielded immense political power.

The Prime Minister held two meetings to review the Sindh situation which I, as the Vice Chief of Army Staff, was invited to attend. The Governor, Jahan Dad, the Chief Minister, Ghous Ali Shah, and the Chief Secretary, Masood Nabi Noor of Sindh, all expressed their helplessness. After painting a gloomy picture, they urged that the control of the troubled areas be transferred to the army. The provincial government had always employed the police force half-heartedly because it lacked confidence in its ability and impartiality. I advised the others that the government should employ the police force and other civil armed forces to their full capacity, before calling on the army to quell the disturbances. I explained that the frequent and prolonged deployment of troops on internal security tasks had kept the army away from its primary operational duties for many years and pleaded that the army might be used sparingly, as a last resort, to enable it to train uninterruptedly. That advice was not taken kindly and the views expressed were reported to President Zia who, on one occasion, admonished the Commander 5 Corps (Sindh area) for not helping the Sindh administration enough. Zia raised the issue in the next formation commanders' conference, saying that the army should take extra interest in eradicating lawlessness in the Sindh province. To the embarrassment of the general officer, he disclosed that he had already spoken to the concerned corps commander on the issue. I interjected to tell President Zia that the fault, if any, was mine, and not that of the corps commander. I had directed the general officer that, while troops should be made available to the local administration immediately on demand, he need not show unnecessary exuberance to carry out civil work. The army intelligence had identified the miscreants and the big landlords who gave them protection. This information was given to the Sindh Government which found itself in a dilemma. It wanted to end the strife but was hesitant to touch the offending bigwigs for reasons of political expediency.

The law and order situation in Sindh had political overtones. It needed a political cum administrative solution as well as the economic uplift of the interior of Sindh. Besides, prolonged employment of military force for the maintenance of law and order erodes the people's confidence in the ability of the civil administration to provide them security and protection. It also generates ideas in the minds of the military that it can succeed where the civil administration has failed. When such ideas germinate in the minds of the power-seeking brass, the democratic system becomes a victim.

There was also a psychological angle. In March 1985, new governors were appointed in all the provinces. In the Punjab, Balochistan and the North-West Frontier Province, the new governors hailed from their respective provinces. In Sindh, the previous Governor, Lieutenant-General Jahan Dad, a non-Sindhi was retained. Though the Governor was respected, the regionalist Sindhis protested that their province had received stepmotherly treatment. They demanded that a Sindhi be appointed governor in Sindh to bring it at par with the other provinces. To add to their annoyance, the Governor appointed a Chief Minister who was not a member of the Provincial Assembly. The selection, legally correct but politically questionable, was resented. Eventually, the Governor as well as the Chief Minister had to leave their posts.

My appointment as Vice Chief in March 1984 removed me from the President's inner circle. My professional responsibilities became my primary occupation and my meetings with the President became infrequent, though we did occasionally meet to discuss matters which the President wished analysed. At times, I also met the Prime Minister to discuss Service matters. Such contacts were interpreted by the Inter-Services Intelligence Directorate (ISID) to imply that I was becoming close to Junejo. On three occasions, Lieutenant-General Fazle Haq enquired about the frequency of my contacts with the President and impressed upon me the necessity of keeping a regular link, notwithstanding the President's inclination to maintain a distance. I told him that it would be unfair for anyone to impose himself on the President. Fazle Haq felt that, as the President's close advisers had started colouring facts and providing filtered information to him, it had become all the more necessary to give him another view. I told Fazle Haq that it was the President's prerogative to select his team.

Prime Minister Junejo had strong views against Lieutenant-General Akhtar Abdur Rahman, the Director General of Intelligence (ISID). On one occasion he enquired why the general officer had been kept in service 'till further orders', well beyond the age and service limits prescribed for his rank. He was advised to raise the issue with the President as Akhtar took orders either from the Prime Minister or from the President. A smile spread across Zia's face when I apprised him of this discussion.

On two occasions, Junejo talked to General Zia about replacing Akhtar. Zia agreed in principle but felt that the ongoing Afghanistan situation demanded continuity in that appointment. Junejo persisted in his demand. Towards the end of 1986, the Prime Minister asked me to suggest some names for a new DGI. I discussed the issue with General Zia and suggested the names of Major-Generals Farrukh Khan and Ghulam Muhammad for the post. 'How about Hamid Gul?' enquired General Zia. I gave professional reasons for retaining that general officer in a command assignment. Zia agreed. The Prime Minister was given the names of Farrukh Khan and Ghulam Muhammad and he was also apprised of the discussion on Hamid Gul. Junejo consulted Zia and a few days later the Prime Minister sent for Major-General Hamid Gul and selected him to replace Akhtar.

General Zia's team members changed from time to time. He had inherited military subordinates who, by and large, served him loyally. They were a well-knit team, ever ready to discuss unpalatable issues and offer advice without reservation or sugar-coating. They possessed the courage of conviction to differ with him and explain their viewpoints candidly and, when required, forcefully. General Iqbal could be firm to the limit. Warm-hearted and buoyant, he did not mince his words while expressing his opinions. General Fazle Haq had advice to offer on every subject. He was lucid and clear in his presentation. At times, his assertive style bordered on rudeness. Once, he candidly acknowledged that General Zia and Razia (Fazle Haq's wife) deserved medals for tolerating him. General Jilani, a fine administrator, was mellow but insistent. For the officious General Abbasi customs, rules and regulations were biblical documents—sacred and inviolable. He was incapable of willingly taking a wrong decision. Nor could he be forced into such an exercise. General Sawar had the knack of simplifying a knotty problem in his easy and pleasant style. General Jahanzeb Arbab, the extrovert, spoke with clarity, conviction, and vehemence. On the occasions when General Rahimuddin spoke, he made his point. General Akhtar's approach was usually flexible. He knew what to say, where and how to get a nod of approval from the top. General Chishti was brief but adamant and forceful. His views could be brutally frank. General Hassan could say difficult things easily. He was modest yet firm. The soft-spoken General Jamal Said Mian had the flexible approach of the tribal society to which he belonged. He liked authority and wished to soft-pedal on controversial issues. General Saeed Qadir, vocal and exuberant, was ever ready to accept any challenging task. General Mujibur Rahman, the soldier turned media expert, kept his cool under the barrage of criticism which, as Information Secretary, he occasionally faced from his colleagues. With a meaningful smile, Jahandad had the knack of interjecting native humour even into a serious discussion. K. K. Afridi expressed his views with charm and elasticity. Superbly serene, Waheed spoke rarely, but whenever he did, it was invariably with conviction and firmness. General Zia listened to criticism patiently. He had the capacity to digest harsh views. The prolongation of Zia's rule took its toll as his senior colleagues gradually faded away from the scene and new faces took their places. The seniority gap between the chief and his formation commanders kept widening. The new incumbents were no less sincere, loyal, or intelligent. However, not having been involved in running the administration of the country, they were not as well equipped to offer advice on political and administrative matters as their predecessors had been.

Not a man for details, Zia usually spoke in generalities. He needed others to do much of his spade-work. The MLAs' conferences had provided him a reliable forum for an in-depth study of the multifarious problems. The frequency of such conferences decreased after the formation of the federal and the provincial governments in March 1985. The provinces then had civilian governors. Since General Zia was no longer the head of government, he lost first-hand contact with the affairs of the state. His own mini-Security Council—the MLAs' conference—no longer existed to analyse problems and suggest viable options to him. And he made no attempt to maintain contacts with his old colleagues and subordinates, whose advice had helped him to weather many a storm in the past. They were forgotten as if they did not exist. Gradually, General Zia became a lonely person, considered by the politicians as an unwelcome intruder in their field. General Zia's inner circle kept shrinking and, towards the closing stages of his rule, it had been reduced to a tiny group. Some in that group were highly ambitious; others held positions which were beyond their ability to handle; for yet others, loyalty implied blind obedience to the dictates of their boss. General Zia had no dearth of the advice of such a coterie of sycophants.

On two occasions, once in 1987 and the other in 1988, I found General Zia highly critical of the Prime Minister. He accused Mr Junejo of being irritatingly slow in taking decisions, lacking the magnanimity expected of his high office, harbouring a strong grudge against the defence services, and spending the bulk of his time winning over the support of the members of parliament by granting them petty favours and inducements. Weeks before his death, he was in a pensive mood. He named two persons who, in his assessment, played a double game between him and Mr Junejo. Both had been his close civilian colleagues over a number of years. He said in anguish: 'What should I do, when such friends betray my trust?'

Lieutenant-General Fazle Haq met the President in late 1987 and found him criticizing Mr Junejo in strong words. Zia narrated to him instances which had eroded his confidence in the Prime Minister. The former Governor sensed that the President was considering 'various options' for dealing with the situation. After meeting General Zia, Fazle Haq predicted to me that, 'Mr Junejo's days are numbered.' Subsequent events proved him right.

The axe fell on 29 May 1988. In an ill-conceived and ill-advised decision, General Zia dissolved the National Assembly and dismissed the government of Prime Minister Muhammad Khan Junejo. The provincial assemblies and provincial governments met a similar fate.

The Kingmaker

In the post-1985 election period Prime Minister Junejo and the Interior Minister, Muhammad Aslam Khan Khattak, were invited to attend two MLAs' conferences. In those meetings, the President said that the possibility of the imposition of martial law could not be ruled out as the military was unlikely to become a silent spectator if the country faced an internal threat. If it was an attempt to browbeat the new government, it was crude and unnecessary.

In another MLAs' meeting with Prime Minister Junejo attending, the President asked the Governors if they wished to stay in their appointments after the lifting of martial law. All except Jilani wished to stay in their posts. Soon after, Fazle Haq also changed his mind: in view of the two-year ban after retirement for taking part in politics, he too decided to quit his post. Zia and Junejo urged Jilani to stay on. 'Not a minute more,' said Jilani in a firm tone. The other two Governors,

Jahandad Khan and K. K. Afridi, had agreed to continue in their appointments. Afridi had been critical of the Chief Minister of Balochistan. It was the turn of the Chief Minister to react when martial law was about to be lifted. He demanded a change in the governorship. A surprised Afridi was relieved of his appointment and promised a diplomatic assignment. The outgoing governor took some erratic decisions during his last week in office, earning the ire of the Prime Minister. His promised diplomatic job became a casualty.

The last two MLAs' conferences were farewell get-togethers. The military era had given birth to a democratic order. The President used his hospitality and charm to ease out the old team smoothly. The mood was relaxed, pleasant, and jovial. To the surprise of his listeners, General Zia referred to Lieutenant-General Akhtar Abdul Rahman Khan, the Director General of Inter Services Intelligence Directorate, as the kingmaker. While the others stared hard and winked at Akhtar, he blushed, smiling his captivating smile, perspiration beading his not so well-cropped head. In March 1987, Akhtar was promoted to the rank of General and replaced General Rahimuddin Khan as Chairman of the Joint Chiefs of Staff Committee. At the formal dining out of General Rahimuddin Khan, General Akhtar sat next to the President. In this farewell speech for the outgoing Chairman of the JCSC, the President evoked loud laughter when he said that General Akhtar, the kingmaker, had himself become the king. May God bless General Akhtar's soul: he died along with General Zia in the tragic aeroplane crash.

The Backlash

With the frequent interruption of civil rule, the political leadership had developed a sense of unease and mistrust about the defence services in general and the army in particular. Given an opportunity, it cast aspersions on individuals and institutions who thus get dragged into a controversy. The defence services are the symbols of national unity, a national asset. They are not partisan. They are neither the personal domain of the service chiefs nor of the Prime Minister and the President. National interest demands that the prestige and morale of the services be kept high. They deserve respect and protection to discharge their defence responsibilities with full devotion and undivided attention. A clear distinction ought to be made between individuals and institutions: institutions deserve to be preserved, developed, and strengthened. Individuals may be criticized.

The democracy restored in 1985 was not the textbook version, but it was a leap forward. The martial law administration had held fair and free elections which all elected governments had failed to do since 1947. Even some of the sitting ministers in every province had lost their seats.

Martial law left scars on the defence services. Their performance did not come under political scrutiny. Their acts were not discussed in the parliament. They escaped the process of political accountability and the whip of criticism which helps to keep an organization on the rails. Psychologically, they developed a feeling that any question asked of them about their performance amounted to an interference in their duties.

The political leadership that came to power took steps to assert its authority. In some cases, the technique adopted was abrasive and fell short of magnanimity. It is not the intention here to list all the irritants which created a sense of uneasiness in the armed forces. The vibrations were soon felt by the government. On one occasion, Prime Minister Junejo asked me if it was true that his government was considered anti-army. He was informed of the specific instances which had caused concern to the soldiers. The Prime Minister assured me that the government wished to strengthen the armed forces and that the impression to the contrary was wrong.

The politicians had cause for agitation. It was an untenable situation that the President of the country, in a democratic polity, (after December 1985) was also the Chief of Army Staff. This arrangement was unreasonable, unjustified, and indefensible. General Zia had told his military colleagues that he would retire from military service at the time of the lifting of martial law. This did not happen. Also, he breached a commitment made to the members of the National Assembly. He had assured them that, on the lifting of martial law, he would retire from the army, and it was on that firm understanding that they had supported the passage of the Eighth Amendment to the Constitution. The amendment was passed, but to their bewilderment, General Zia reneged from his commitment. He developed a self-serving argument that he was 'a bridge between the defence services and the elected government.' The nation, though, needed full-fledged democracy, not bridges.

In December 1986, General Zia told me that he was planning to retire from the army by March 1987. Two months later, he changed his mind again.

General Zia learnt the power game fast. Throughout his long rule, he maintained direct contact with the defence services and refused to leave the coveted post of the Chief of Army Staff. He trusted the general officers to the extent necessary. Through a system of promotion, transfers, and retirements, he kept a firm grip on the military establishment.

Time rolled on. In 1988 Zia declared that he would remain the Chief of Army Staff till 1990, the year when the next elections were due. His death cut that period short.

CHAPTER 10

Interceding Links

Islamic Measures

Religion was central to General Zia's philosophy and much was done and undone in its name. Islam is a progressive religion which prescribes broad principles to regulate not only human behaviour but also the business of state. It provides the foundations of a just order, and the guidelines for raising a state structure in harmony with the requirements of the time. While the principles, being of divine origin, remain unalterable, consultation and participation constitute the essential ingredients of an Islamic government, in which no individual can become the sole custodian of the interests of the people.

Any established order can be changed either through a revolutionary process or in an evolutionary manner. The revolutionary method, speedy but painful, applies coercive power. The Iranian revolution is an example. An evolutionary change is slow but psychologically more palatable. It becomes easier to modify practised norms if the proposed changes are less controversial, are reformative in nature, and deal with issues concerning the welfare of the society. Such an approach prepares the people for harder measures that may be adopted later.

The Zia administration adopted an evolutionary approach to the Islamization of laws. For reasons of expediency, changes were first made in the penal laws which were easy to codify according to the tenets of Islam. Their introduction aroused concern in the Western world, where Islam was depicted as a religion excelling in harsh penal laws. Within the country, the reaction was mixed. The Western-educated elite and a part of the intelligentsia opposed the measures. A majority of the lower and lower-middle classes favoured the establishment of an Islamic polity. With the advantage of hindsight, it can be said that it would have been better to initiate the process by introducing the welfare measures like *zakat* and *ushr* first.

In Pakistan, some institutions run religious training schools with missionary zeal. In these schools, young boys, mostly from poor families in the rural areas, are enrolled to attend a course of instruction, generally free of charge. The subjects taught in such schools basically include a study of the Holy Quran and Islamic theology, with a sprinkling of other disciplines. The students are awarded a diploma after passing in-house examinations. The curricula of these institutions, being narrow-based, do not prepare the students for lucrative job opportunities. The appointments commensurate with their qualifications are few and inadequately paid. Besides, the syllabi of all such schools are primarily based on a particular *fiqh* (school of law) of Islam, with a sprinkling of exposure given to the teachings of other *fiqhs*. The diploma holders usually develop an inflexible attitude in jurisprudence and become insensitive to dissent. Their exuberance, expressed in flowing oratory, has occasionally been used to play on the raw sentiments of their less educated, simple, religious-minded, and captive audiences in mosques and at religious functions. Islam stands for unity, tolerance, and accommodation. The fiery speakers, carried away by their emotions, at times cause division and polarization in the Muslim *ummah*.

General Zia's government made a meek attempt to reorganize these religious schools. It was proposed to standardize and broad-base the syllabi of such schools with the inclusion of some secular subjects in the curriculum. An attempt was also made to affiliate the schools with the Secondary Boards of Education and the universities in the country. The government agreed to offer financial assistance to the schools, while they remained under private management. The school administrators accepted the financial offer, agreed to the inclusion of some secular subjects in the syllabi, and to the affiliation with the universities and the Secondary Boards of Education on a voluntary basis. They declined to accept the standardization of the syllabi and the holding of examinations centrally. The schools thus got some concessions without undertaking meaningful obligations. Public and *zakat* funds given to such schools were used to further polarize society. In fairness, only those institutions should enjoy government patronage and monetary assistance which enhance national unity and shun the creating of divisiveness in society.

General Zia felt that basically the religious schools did good work and, with government patronage and support, their shortcomings could gradually be overcome. This was his approach towards religion as a whole. He was called a regressive person, trying to reverse the tide of time, a hypocrite who used religion to keep himself in power.

Did he use religion as a ploy to befool the people? Religious faith being a commitment between a man and his Creator, it is impossible to peep into anyone's heart to learn the truth.

A religious streak had been clearly perceptible in Zia ever since he had joined the army. As a young officer, while he loved music, songs, and movies, he prostrated himself five times a day to offer prayers, an act which earned him the nickname of *maulvi*. He smoked heavily but stayed away from alcoholic drinks. His name was never linked with any scandal. As a division commander, he introduced prohibition in his formation. This was a time when drinking was allowed in the army as well as in the country. He gave a religious slant to the army on becoming the Chief of Army Staff. A practising Muslim, he neither imposed his beliefs on others nor forced them to perform rituals. He meditated at holy shrines during his travels, mostly in the serenity of night. In the army, his deep inclination towards religion was common knowledge even before he emerged on the national scene.

General Zia's religious fervour permeated his thoughts and his actions. For him, politics and theology went together: in an Islamic country, the mosque was as inseparable from the state as the soul from the human body. Zia considered that he had a godsent opportunity to serve the cause of Islam. The ruler of a Muslim country, he felt, had a moral and divine obligation to establish an Islamic polity as enunciated in the Holy Quran. His Islamization policies stemmed from this genuine belief.

Martial law is repugnant to Islam. Its imposition by Zia put a moral pressure on him. A person preaching religion was a hypocrite if he not only clamped martial law but also extended its duration to prolong his authoritarian rule. So ran the criticism against Zia. In his commitment towards Islam, Zia was sincere, firm, and outspoken. While there is ample scope to disagree with some of his policies—and there were sharp differences on the issue between him and his colleagues—his motive is hard to question. The prolongation of his military rule was essentially caused by the Bhutto factor and the fear of revenge. He started hating the PPP and the return of the party to power was not acceptable to him.

Zia enjoyed the power he wielded. A position of eminence and authority became an inseparable part of his life. He seldom discussed his post-retirement plans with his friends. Perhaps he had none. The prospect of leading life as an ordinary citizen became distasteful to him.

Economy

During the early seventies, the Bhutto government nationalized the private banks and some private sector industrial enterprises under the label of 'Islamic socialism'. The mix of politics with economy was more of a populist facade than a genuine policy tilt towards the Left. The superficially conceived and inadequately implemented plan tightened the already firm bureaucratic grip over the inefficient and over-staffed public sector organizations. The handsomely paid non-professionals nominated to run the state-controlled autonomous and semi-autonomous organizations developed vested interests and made the public sector industry subservient to the lethargic government machine with disastrous economic consequences. The balance sheets of the once profit-bearing taken-over industries dipped into the red. Instead of retrenching surplus staff, the government decided to subsidize the inefficiently run units as a measure of political expediency. This amounted to spending public funds to promote inefficiency. Mr Bhutto also discarded the practice of preparing five-year development plans and instead worked on a yearly basis.

The Zia administration reintroduced the system of five-year development plans and disinvested the taken-over minor industrial units to their previous owners. However, it did not restructure the inherited economic order with a system in which the free market mechanism played a dominant role. The economic policies in the Zia administration lacked innovative and revolutionary vision and basically moved within safe grooves. Four factors influenced the adoption of the *status quo* approach in the field of national economy. These were: the government's preoccupation with the Bhutto case; Pakistan's involvement in the Afghanistan *jihad* and its fallout effect on her national security; the lack of economic expertise of General Zia and his close military colleagues; and the over-conservative and risk-free policies adopted by the minister for finance, Mr Ghulam Ishaq Khan, the high priest of economics in the Zia era, whose advice on economic matters had biblical sanctity for General Zia.

Zakat

Zakat is one of the five mandatory pillars of Islam, the other four being *Kalima*, prayers, fasting, and the pilgrimage to Mecca. *Zakat* is a yearly religious tax payable by all Muslims at a rate of 2.5 percent on designated assets. The money so collected is spent exclusively on the succour, relief, and rehabilitation of the poor, widows, and orphans, and on community welfare measures like hospitals, schools, orphanages, etc. The *zakat* fund in Pakistan has three sources of income: one, compulsory *zakat* deduction from all time deposits, securities, and other assets held in banks on the first of the month of Ramazan each year. The deduction is made only when the income on these assets becomes available; two, any voluntary contributions deposited in the *zakat* fund; and, three, grants and gifts.

The *zakat* Ordinance was promulgated in 1979, and the first compulsory deduction was made four years later. The institution of the *zakat* system, welcomed by the people to provide relief to the poor, was a step in the right direction.

The *zakat* Ordinance created a difficulty. The Shiite Muslims, a minority in Pakistan, pointed out that the *zakat* Ordinance impinged on their faith. Stating that their system of collecting and distributing *zakat* was different, they sought exemption from the provisions of the *zakat* Ordinance and held a protest rally in Islamabad to get their demand accepted. In mid-1981, the Shiites gathered in Islamabad to protest against the application of the *zakat* Ordinance to them. Calm returned to Islamabad when the Shiite leaders negotiated a settlement with the government by which this sect was exempted from the payment of *zakat* if they provided to the banks an affidavit of belonging to the Shiite faith.

The settlement peeved the hardliners in the majority Sunni sect. They apprehended that by succumbing to the Shiite demand the government had created a crack in the unity of Muslim ranks. The orthodox Sunni scholars also felt that the lust for money might tempt some worldly-wise Sunni Muslims to file false affidavits to avoid paying the *zakat* tax. This was not without justification. For the believers, *zakat* is a divine obligation. Many people prefer to distribute *zakat* directly to the poor and have little faith in the bureaucratically-run *zakat* system.

The Judicial System

The Anglo-Saxon judicial system was introduced by the British rulers in the subcontinent which had different customs, traditions, religions, and, above all, different values of right and wrong. The law is reasonable and fair but the legal process is complex, cumbersome, expensive, and time-consuming. In a country with low per capita income and poor litigants, the quest for quick justice is like asking for the moon. Court cases take years or decades to be decided, causing the people mental and financial hardship. The grant of adjournments is liberal and court proceedings can be dragged on through technicalities and procedural formalities. It is a rebuke to Pakistan's legal system that her courts are clogged with pending cases and the backlog keeps increasing. The public suffers helplessly. The executive branch cannot intervene. The judiciary maintains that the workload is more than can be handled by the number of judges, the investigative process is slow and corrupt, and the production of witnesses during the trial is delayed. The judiciary may be of the opinion that the law is adequate, but even a seemingly perfect law, if it does not provide speedy justice, is worth a second look.

It was to replace such a delay-prone and expensive system that the Zia administration tried to introduce the system of Islamic jurisprudence to provide relatively inexpensive and speedier justice to the litigants. The proposal aroused a mixed reaction. It was resisted by some people on ideological, administrative, and personal grounds. Ideologically, the western-minded intelligentsia and members of the legal profession, accustomed to the Anglo-Saxon law, opposed the change. On the administrative plane, it was argued that to replace a well-established system might create confusion. At the personal level, lawyers who had a vested interest in the system feared a slump in their earnings. They also did not relish the idea of any person being elevated to the bench who was trained in a system other than the Anglo-Saxon law. By the time the Zia administration was replaced by the elected government, the draft law for the establishment of Islamic courts was ready and was inherited by Prime Minister Junejo's government. The latter did not consider it prudent to implement it.

General Zia had strong views on the weaknesses of the 1973 Constitution and the inadequacy of the prevailing legal system. He wanted to bring about changes in both.

Not surprisingly, the proposed introduction of *Shariah* Laws caused unrest in the judiciary. Expressing the concern of his colleagues in the Supreme Court and the Chief Justices of all the high courts, the Chief Justice of the Supreme Court, Mr Justice M. Anwarul Haq, wrote a lengthy letter to General Zia, urging that the existing privilege of the courts to adjudicate and interpret the laws should not be impaired; the 1973 Constitution be used as an instrument for the Islamization of the existing laws; at least one right of appeal should be given in all cases; and persons not belonging to the judicial services and not qualified for appointment to the supreme court according to the provisions of the Constitution should not be inducted as members in these courts. Mr Justice Anwarul Haq concluded his letter by offering some political advice: 'the legal community should not be alienated in a matter in which their cooperation and wholehearted support was most needed.'

The process of political evolution emerges out of the specific requirements of a society. General Zia spoke frequently against the suitability of the Anglo-Saxon laws for Pakistan. His political and religious convictions did not diminish his personal respect for the honourable members of the judicial profession. Martial law did not interfere in the normal functioning of the Supreme Court of Pakistan, the high courts, and the civil courts. They enjoyed total freedom of action. However, he desired that these courts should not interfere in the functioning of the military courts created under the law, except in the cases of judicial review as ordered by the Supreme Court. While martial law and the judiciary are not the best of friends, they have coexisted in Pakistan over prolonged periods of time, with an undercurrent of unease.

In a society in which it is sometimes difficult to separate fact from fiction, where the investigating agencies enjoy immense unchecked power, where witnesses can be pressurized and won over, and where trials can be prolonged for an excessive period of time, decisions could be based on cooked-up evidence and fabricated 'facts'. General Zia wanted passionately to replace this system with the provisions of Islamic jurisprudence. He failed to appreciate that the prevalent social and administrative malpractices, which had corrupted the Anglo-Saxon legal system, could equally render the proposed Islamic order ineffective. He was not impressed by the logic that any system is as good as the people who run it.

General Zia firmly believed that Pakistan had her own culture and traditions rooted in her history and nourished by a religion which provides the broad parameters of an Islamic polity. He felt that Pakistan's Constitution and her judicial system should be based on such realities and that she ought to blend the religious and political aspirations of the people in systems which bore her own distinctive stamp.

In Zia's perception it was wrong to slavishly retain a colonial heritage in an Islamic polity. It was right for Pakistan to enforce the laws of the *Shariah*. He felt that procedural and other difficulties would gradually be corrected. But a start in that direction, he thought, was necessary and overdue. It was his obsession to move in that direction.

Constitutional Amendments

Pakistan's higher judiciary has given some highly controversial judgments on constitutional matters. These judgments have been severely criticized at home and abroad. The trend started early: in October 1954, Governor-General Ghulam Muhammad dismissed the Constituent Assembly. The Federal Court upheld the executive decision in a judgment that has been widely criticized. Four years later, the Constitution was abrogated and the country was placed under martial law. In the Dosso case (1958), the court upheld the legitimacy of martial law on the grounds that a 'successful revolution destroys the constitution.' The power of the gun prevailed over the rule of law.

The 'legitimacy' of General Yahya Khan's martial law was not questioned in the courts during his unfortunate rule. Thereafter, he was declared a 'usurper' by the Supreme Court in the Asma Gilani case in 1972. That bold decision was pronounced when Yahya, defeated in war, was physically out of power and politically dead. He was one man who was condemned without being heard. On the promulgation of martial law in July 1977, the judges of the Supreme Court and the provincial high courts took fresh oaths, notwithstanding the earlier ones taken by them under the 1973 Constitution. Their act came under criticism on legal and personal grounds. In the Nusrat Bhutto, case the Supreme Court justified the imposition of Zia's martial law in 1977 under the 'law of necessity', as the country faced the danger of civil war.

A decade later, in 1988, Prime Minister Junejo was dismissed and the National Assembly was dissolved by President Zia. The Supreme Court upheld the decision of the Punjab High Court in declaring that the President's action was invalid in law. The judgments were given after the death of General Zia.

In 1990, President Ghulam Ishaq Khan dismissed the Prime Minister and dissolved the National Assembly. That act was upheld by the Supreme Court. In 1993, President Ishaq made a mockery of the

Constitution and damaged his personal image when, after developing differences with Prime Minister Nawaz Sharif, he hobnobbed with the opposition and used the constitutional axe once again to dismiss the Prime Minister. The Supreme Court of Pakistan judged his act to be unconstitutional.

In the Nusrat Bhutto case judgment, the power of 'judicial review' was retained by the civil courts. Its implementation crippled the administration and rendered the military courts ineffective. In some cases, the high courts granted stay orders to persons facing trial in the military courts or convicted by them. The vacation of the stay orders took time. The resultant delay adversely affected the immediate deterrent value of the sentences awarded by the military courts. The provincial martial law administrations were thus peeved and frustrated. The aggrieved parties, seeking quick justice from the military courts, questioned whether the country was ruled by martial law. As the situation existed, while the judges exercised control, the onus of responsibility lay with the executive branch. Complaining that they were made to box with one hand tied behind their backs, the executive requested the ouster of the jurisdiction of the superior courts in respect of cases tried in the military courts. Some of the governors suggested abrogation of the Constitution for the duration of martial law.

The Minister for Law, Syed Sharifuddin Pirzada, suggested to the President that the issue should be discussed with the Chief Justice of Pakistan, Mr Justice S. Anwarul Haq. A meeting was held in the President's House on 15 October 1979. Besides the President, it was attended by Mr Justice Anwarul Haq, Chief Justice of Pakistan, Mr Justice Mushtaq Husain, Chief Justice of the Lahore High Court, the Chief Election Commissioner, Syed Sharifuddin Pirzada, Minister for Law, and the COS. The predicament faced by the executive branch came under discussion. Mr Justice Anwarul Haq abhorred the idea of abrogating the Constitution and forcefully stated that he would not be a party to any such suggestion. General Zia sought a solution which could meet the administrative needs while upholding the sanctity of the superior courts. Mr Justice Mushtaq Hussain asked for a copy of the Constitution which, luckily, was handy. The two judges retired to an adjoining room. They returned to say that one possibility could be to amend Article 212 of the Constitution. A brief discussion ensued between them and Mr Pirzada on the language of the proposed amendment. A consensus was reached and it was decided that

Mir Muhammad Ali, the draftsman, would get the amendment cleared by the Chief Justice of Pakistan and Mr Justice Mushtaq Hussain. He did so the following day and, in the process, incorporated a further modification suggested by the two judges. Article 212-A relating to the establishment of military courts or tribunals was thus inserted in the Constitution on 16 October 1979.

General Zia wished to make major changes in the 1973 Constitution. These were opposed by his military colleagues on the plea that it had taken the country twenty-six years to frame an agreed Constitution. It would be unwise, they argued, for a non-elected administration to change its basic structure. They counselled him to amend it sparingly.

The period between the referendum and the general elections was mostly devoted by General Zia to making constitutional amendments. Many constitutions were studied. The main architects of the amendments were Mr A. K. Brohi and Mr Sharifuddin Pirzada, the two top experts in constitutional law, and some other scholars. Pirzada felt that the number of amendments should be small. The proposed amendments were discussed twice in the MLAs' meeting in a cursory manner. On both occasions, the President verbally explained the changes, but members were not shown the written text. The Chief of Staff, who held copies of the proposed amendments, was directed not to show them to any one.[1] The President's military colleagues remained unaware of the full text of the proposed Constitutional amendments till these appeared in print in the Press. They were thus given a sense of participation in their adoption without being taken into full confidence. This was gamesmanship bordering on hypocrisy.

The President's military colleagues had advised him to promulgate the constitutional amendments before the general elections were held. By such a measure, the members of the newly elected assembly would have contested the elections under the amended Constitution thus giving it their tacit approval. Since the President had only partly taken his colleagues into confidence, he held the amendments close to his chest till after the elections were held. The amendments were promulgated on 17 March 1985, twenty days after the elections and just five days before the inaugural session of the National Assembly. The changes made were excessive and they created a strong political backlash.

According to the 1973 Constitution, only a member of the National Assembly could become the prime minister. On the President's advice, Mr Pirzada prepared an amendment to Article 91, whereby the prime minister could also be nominated from amongst the indirectly elected members of the Senate. The Chief of Staff argued against this amendment and forcefully pleaded that if the 237 directly elected members of the National Assembly could not produce a prime minister, one might as well say goodbye to parliamentary democracy. The President found it hard to ignore that advice. In the presence of the Minister for Law, he deleted that amendment.

There was a reason behind that proposal. General Zia for a while toyed with the idea of elevating Mr Ghulam Ishaq Khan, the Minister for Finance, to the office of the prime ministership. It had been planned to get Ishaq elected as a senator. A senator under the existing law could not be elected to become the prime minister. Hence the amendment.

Provisional Constitution Order 1981

The hurdles faced by the executive branch were partially removed by the amendment made in Article 212 of the Constitution. The bickering, however, continued. Martial law and statute law are poles apart. To administer the former with the ground rules of the latter was like attempting to reach the moon riding a horse-driven buggy. Both the judiciary and the executive were unhappy. The provincial governors complained that the dual control was exploited by law-breakers for delaying the ends of justice and diluting the deterrent effect of the law. They wanted the military courts to function without civil interference. On their part, the judiciary considered the military courts an intrusion into their domain. Syed Sharifuddin Pirzada and Mr A. K. Brohi proposed that the lacuna be legally removed. The MLAs conference endorsed their scheme. This paved the way for the promulgation of CMLA Order Number 1 of 1981, on 24 March 1981. It came to be know as the Provincial Constitution Order 1 of 1981.

The PCO required the invited judges to take fresh oath under it. A few declined. The oaths to the high court judges were administered in the respective provincial capitals. The oath-taking ceremony for the judges of the Supreme Court was fixed for the afternoon of 25 March 1981. About two hours before the appointed time, the Chief Justice of Pakistan sought an urgent meeting with the President.

Elevated to the supreme court bench on 16 October 1972, Mr Justice S. Anwarul Haq had become the Chief Justice of Pakistan on 23 September 1977. He was due to retire on 10 May 1982, on attaining the superannuation age of 65 years. General Zia met him in the presence of Syed Sharifuddin Pirzada and the author. Visibly agitated, Anwar criticized PCO 1 of 1981 and expressed his inability to take oath under it. General Zia asked him to reconsider his decision but he declined. 'I will be sorry to lose the benefit of your advice,' said Zia, but 'I reluctantly accept your wish.'

After Anwar's departure, Pirzada informed the President about the *inter se* seniority of the remaining supreme court judges, pointing out that the next seniormost judge was Mr Justice Muhammad Halim, one of the dissenting judges in the Bhutto case, who had another eight years to serve as a judge. 'Good luck to Halim,' said Zia, 'I hold nothing against him. The seniormost judge should become the Chief Justice.' Minutes later, Mr Justice Muhammad Halim was sworn in by Zia as the Chief Justice of Pakistan.

Transformation in Balochistan

In the years 1973-7 under the Bhutto government nearly three infantry divisions were deployed in Balochistan to restore normalcy to that troubled province. At that time, some foreign analysts predicted an early secession of Balochistan. Such conjectures underestimated the vitality of the people of Pakistan for forging unity in diversity. Eight years later, at the time of lifting of martial law in 1985, not a single soldier was deployed in the previously troubled areas of Balochistan. The peace and tranquillity that prevailed was the envy of the other provinces.

The Zia administration took a political decision to grant amnesty and launch an extensive economic uplift programme to improve the life of the ordinary people living in an oppressive feudal society. Some voices were raised within the administration, doubting the wisdom of a benign policy. By and large, the political wisdom of applying the economic balm brought normalcy to Balochistan.

The people in the hitherto troubled areas became partners in development activities. Those who had earlier taken up arms against the government began to receive contracts from it to implement a variety of development programmes. The prospect of financial gains and a brighter future brought about a healthy change in the psyche of the people. A handful of once mighty *sardars* found themselves on a downhill slope, fearful of losing their unquestioned age-old supremacy. This loss of power was painful. Some *sardars* preferred to leave their country rather than face a decline in their traditional influence. Sardar Khair Bakhsh Marri and Mr Ataullah Mengal left Pakistan to go into self-exile.

Centrifugal Pulls

The federal-provincial relations in Balochistan and the NWFP during the Bhutto administration created misgivings in the country about central interference in provincial matters. The apprehensions persisted even after the fall of the Bhutto government. Two close Bhutto associates and cabinet ministers added fuel to the fire. Mr Abdul Hafeez Pirzada and Mr Mumtaz Ali Bhutto, who had played key roles in the drafting of the 1973 Constitution, started demanding enhanced powers for the provinces. On the issue of provincial rights, the military governors of the provinces faced great psychological pressure. Despite the fact that the Constitution was held in abeyance, they jealously protected provincial rights lest they be accused of betraying the interests of their respective provinces.

The governors appointed by Zia had held their appointments over prolonged periods of time. Some flaunted authority, others became overly-possessive of their domain, yet others became hypersensitive to criticism. In their personal conduct, while some were humble and approachable, others became stiff and aloof. They considered their views on provincial matters superior and felt that others were less qualified to offer any advice on the subject. While it was their responsibility to safeguard the interests of their provinces, it was sometimes forgotten that they were mere appointees of the President.

Those governors who belonged to the provinces of which they were the chief executives came under local pressure to stand up for the rights of their provinces. Others belonging to different provinces did not wish to be blamed for not advocating the cause of their provinces, simply because they had the domicile of another province. Such conflicts and pressures had a negative impact. With the passage of time, the governors became increasingly critical of the federal government. By overplaying their political sensitivities, the smaller provinces demanded and generally secured extra financial allocations and other concessions from the federal government. The Punjab was invariably asked not to press for such demands and to display the proverbial magnanimity of the elder brother.

This does not imply that there was friction between the provinces and the federal government. By and large, they operated on the same frequency. Zia ran a mature and balanced team which agreed on almost all routine issues on the basis of unanimity or consensus. However, on ticklish and fundamental issues like the apportionment of the Indus water, the distribution of financial resources, and the construction of the Kalabagh Dam, there was a lack of consensus, which left the issues undecided. There was a lack of political will to grapple with those knotty problems, lest they be later accused of compromising provincial rights.

On major controversial issues, General Zia trod the political path with caution to avoid causing a rift in his team. The governors creating the hurdles took the line of least resistance by arguing that such sticky matters be left for a representative government. This was an attempt to sweep the problems under the carpet. The provinces became more vocal in their demands, fair or unfair, and blamed the federal government for their own weaknesses and failures.

Such centrifugal pulls had started surfacing during the declining years of the Bhutto administration. The trend continued during the Zia era, sowing the seeds of disunity.

The Politics of Violence

With the exit of Bhutto, sanity deserted his followers. Vendetta replaced politics. Zia, hated no less earlier, now became totally unacceptable. 'The dictator must go' was the bruised cry. Any means were considered fair to achieve that end. 'If he cannot be replaced democratically let other measures be taken to destabilize his government or eliminate him' was the feeling. From early 1979 onwards, the Inter-Services Intelligence and the Intelligence Bureau started reporting that a PPP-sponsored underground movement had been set up with the financial, moral, and technical support of some foreign powers. The strategy was carefully worked out. The Zia administration was painted black in the western media. Internal peace was disrupted through acts of sabotage and violence to create panic and anarchy. Some political opponents of the PPP were killed. Civil servants were threatened with reprisals for co-operating with a military government. Efforts were made to create dissension in the armed forces. Two military officers deserted the service and joined the PPP protest wagon in London. Attempts were made to kill General Zia. The leaders of the underground movement freely travelled between Afghanistan, Syria, Libya, Britain, the UAE, and India. In some of these countries they had reportedly established contact with the ruling elite.

The administration took preventive measures. While some plans were nipped in the bud, others had a degree of success. Some incidents are discussed to illustrate the pattern of anti-state activities:

1. The hijacking of a PIA aircraft
2. The Al-Zulfiqar Organization
3. The London Plan

The Hijacking of a PIA Aircraft

On 2 March 1981, a PIA Boeing 720 airliner, with 148 persons on aboard, on a flight from Karachi to Peshawar was hijacked by three armed persons who had the plane flown to Kabul, landing there at 4:57 p.m. This was the beginning of a gory drama which ended 324 hours later on 15 March 1981. During that agonizing period, one passenger was killed by the hijackers, while all others on board remained under extremes stress and anxiety, uncertain of their fate.

The three-man hijacking team was led by Salamullah alias Tippu, who identified himself by the false name of Alamgir. He announced that the hijackers were members of Al-Zulfiqar, a terrorist component of the People's Liberation Army led by Murtaza Bhutto, the son of Mr Zulfikar Ali Bhutto. He also claimed responsibility on behalf of his group for the bomb explosion in the Karachi stadium during the visit of His Holiness Pope John Paul to Pakistan on 16 February 1981. This was widely reported in the Press.

Initially, the hijackers demanded the release of five of their colleagues detained by the police in connection with the murder of a student at the University of Karachi. They also stated that Radio Pakistan should not broadcast views and news harmful to their image.

The Kabul authorities welcomed the hijackers and did not permit Pakistan's negotiating team at Kabul Airport to establish direct contact with them. A special PIA plane sent by Pakistan on a mercy mission to evacuate the passengers returned to Peshawar because the Afghan government refused permission for it to land at Kabul airport. In disregard of its international responsibility, the Kabul government adopted a partisan attitude, urging Pakistan to yield to the blackmail; it kept providing support and facilities to the hijackers. Some passengers later reported that the hijackers were initially equipped with one pistol and that they saw some bags being carried into the aircraft at Kabul. Afterwards, the hijackers appeared armed with machine-guns and hand grenades.

On 7 March 1981, Major-General (Retired) M. Rahim Khan, Secretary General in the Ministry of Defence, addressing a press conference, stated: 'The Kabul authorities had actively colluded and connived with the hijackers. According to authentic information available with the Pakistan Government, Murtaza Bhutto had arrived in Kabul one week before the hijacking incident. The government also had information that previously Murtaza had been in touch with an international terrorist called Carlos.'

While providing details of the events of 2 March 1981 at Kabul airport, Major-General Rahim Khan said: 'Murtaza Bhutto had embraced Afghan officials and thanked them for putting him in touch with the hijackers. Murtaza told the Afghan officials that he identified the hijacker as his man and that he was happy that he had performed the mission entrusted to him.'

The hijacker later said in a message broadcast over the radio that he was working under the direction of 'our leader Murtaza Bhutto.'

The safe haven of Kabul encouraged the hijackers to demand the release of 91 prisoners and detenus lodged in Pakistani jails. Pakistan refused to yield to pressure.

On 6 March 1981, the hijackers killed one passenger and heartlessly threw his body out of the aircraft at the Kabul airport. The victim was Tariq Rahim, Second Secretary at the Pakistan Embassy in Iran and a former aide-de-camp of Prime Minister Bhutto. Major Tariq Rahim had been on a visit to Pakistan because of the death of his father, Major-General Kazi A. Rahim Khan. He had graduated from Sandhurst Military College and had been commissioned in the Armoured Corps. He had been especially selected to serve on the personal staff of the Prime Minister. Such appointees are treated as part and parcel of the family. Little did Tariq know that he would meet such a tragic end at the hands of the supporters of Mr Bhutto whom he had served loyally as a member of the family.

The unprovoked killing of an unarmed passenger was widely condemned. Afghanistan was accused of encouraging terrorism. As diplomatic pressure mounted on Kabul, the hijackers got the aircraft refuelled and, on 8 March 1981, had it flown to Damascus, Syria.

The Syrian attitude was correct but they adopted the tactics of prolonged negotiations to wear out either the hijackers or Pakistan. The hijackers' demand for the release of prisoners was scaled down to 54. They kept threatening that more passengers would be killed if their demand was not met. The Syrian authorities were reluctant to use force to end the hijacking.

As time passed, public anxiety in Pakistan increased. Under pressure, the government indicated its willingness to release a few detenus. The hijackers held their ground and refused to compromise on their demands.

An emergency cabinet meeting, with all the provincial governors attending, was held to discuss the hijacking issue. The views expressed therein ranged from a flexible approach to a firm refusal to yield to terrorist pressure. Lieutenant-General Fazle Haq, the Governor of the NWFP, informed the cabinet of a 'prevailing view in Peshawar' that the government had adopted a hard line because most of the passengers on board the hijacked airliner hailed from the NWFP. The Governor clarified that, while he did not personally share that view, it was his duty to apprise the cabinet of the feelings voiced in his province. After hearing the Governor, the cabinet ministers refrained from expressing their viewpoint further. The issue was clinched: the cabinet yielded to the hijackers' demand.

The hijacking drama ended on 15 March 1981, when the three hijackers surrendered to the Syrian authorities. Their leader walked down the gangway shouting 'I fight for Bhuttoism.'

By that time, Pakistan had flown 54 prisoners to Syria; they were granted political asylum by that country. They were PPP activists undergoing different terms of imprisonment for the criminal offenses committed by them.

Al-Zulfiqar Organization (AZO)

An underground movement was started after Bhutto's execution. Some young and fiery die-hard members took to terrorism, with revenge as their slogan. Mr Bhutto's two sons, living in self-exile, formed the People's Liberation Army (PLA) with its headquarters in Kabul. Murtaza Bhutto became the overall organizer and Shahnawaz Bhutto took charge of its militant operations. On 5 January 1981, the birth anniversary of Bhutto, the PLA was renamed the Al-Zulfiqar Organization (AZO).

The AZO adopted the Soviet model in its organizational structure. Murtaza Bhutto became the Secretary General of the Politburo and Shahnawaz Bhutto the Chief of the People's Army. A security wing was created to protect the organization and to cover the terrorists. This turned out to be a difficult job. In 1982, the Central Committee was dissolved and the AZO was brought under the direct control of KGB and KHAD (WAD)—the Soviet and the Afghan intelligence agencies respectively. The honeymoon was short-lived. The Bhutto brothers started resenting professionals controlling and directing their hitherto freelance actions. By the end of 1982, the AZO Headquarters had been shifted to New Delhi and Tripoli, Libya. Afghanistan continued to serve as a base for launching sabotage activities in Pakistan and for providing training facilities and a safe haven to the terrorists.

Research and Analysis Wing (RAW), the Indian intelligence agency, gave a red carpet reception to the Bhutto brothers during their frequent visits to India. They served India's purpose of destabilizing Pakistan. During Indira Gandhi's rule, RAW's covert activities in Pakistan increased substantially. Pakistani agents were recruited, cultivated, trained in India, and launched through the porous border to commit acts of sabotage and murder against designated targets in Pakistan. RAW persisted with its covert operations even after the AZO was supposedly disbanded in 1989. In fact, its activities were only temporarily suspended.

The recruitment of agents was easy. Politically motivated sympathizers were lured with incentives of foreign travel, service abroad, and the prospect of easy money and positions of eminence in a future PPP government. Some others were recruited from the lower strata of society for money, wine, and sex.

Training camps emerged in India, Afghanistan, and Libya. Their number fluctauted and at one time twenty such camps were functioning in Afghanistan, thirty-five in India, and eight in Libya. The former Soviet Union and Syria also provided patronage and assistance. The trainees were imparted instruction in the handling of small arms, rocket launchers, time bombs, and explosives, for conducting sabotage activities. After indoctrination, they were grouped into hit teams of three to five men. The hit teams infiltrated into Pakistan through unfrequented routes, committed acts of terrorism, and exfiltrated into India and Afghanistan.

Ayaz Sammo, Ilyas Siddiqui, Javed Malik, and Rehmatullah Anjum assassinated Chaudhry Zahur Elahi, a staunch political opponent of Bhutto, at Lahore on 25 September 1981. They returned to India after committing the murder and subsequently escaped to Kabul. Another team set the General Post Office in Lahore on fire on 1 September 1982, attempted an explosion at the residence of Khawaja Muhammad Safdar, a prominent politician, and killed a guard at the residence of a judge at Lahore on 5 September 1982. On 13 September 1982, Mr Zahoorul Hassan Bhopali was killed at Karachi by an AZO terrorist hit team. One of the team members, Ilyas Siddiqui, was also gunned down by his colleagues because of his inability to escape after the gory act due to an injury sustained by him. On 2 March 1981, a PIA aircraft was hijacked to Kabul, as narrated earlier.

On 7 February 1982, a Pakistan Air Force plane with General Zia and his personal staff on board took off on an internal flight from Islamabad airport. Moments later, it was fired at by a Soviet-origin short-range surface-to-air missile (SAM 7) from the city end of the runway. The missile failed to hit the target. The investigation led to the recovery of a missile of a similar type from a house in Lahore.

Such were the acts of terrorism committed by the AZO. Space does not permit all the incidents to be narrated, but the pattern was identical. The AZO terrorists also organized acts of terror in some foreign countries to gain international sympathy.

A group of terrorists went from India to Libya for an 'important task'. Briefing done, they were to fly back to New Delhi, adopting a carefully selected circuitous route to perform 'a sensitive mission' against the Pakistan delegation attending the Non-Aligned Summit meeting in New Delhi in March 1983. In New Delhi, the group was to meet a 'contact' at a designated place. The flight plan for the return journey to India was Tripoli-Athens-Dubai-New Delhi. Another group given yet another task, that of hijacking a PIA aircraft, travelled on the Kabul-Dubai-New Delhi route. The plan misfired. They were arrested at Dubai airport and brought to Pakistan. Another hit team travelled in batches from New Delhi to Athens-Rome-Vienna in June 1984. At Vienna, they planned to raid the Canadian Embassy reception and arrest the ambassadors of Pakistan, the USA, and Britain. On a tip-off, the Austrian security agencies arrested the gang on 6 July 1984. An Austrian court sentenced them to rigorous imprisonment for terms ranging from seven to thirteen years.

In September 1981, ex-cadet Ejazul Haq secretly went to India. Cultivated by RAW, he was given an Indian passport at Bhopal under a false name—Abdul Rehman. The agent then requested a visit visa to re-enter Pakistan on his fake passport. While so doing, he was arrested in May 1982. The fake passport was later shown by me to the Indian Ambassador in Islamabad when he called on me along with the visiting Indian Foreign Secretary; I also offered to let them meet the person if they so desired. In her effort to combat terrorism, Pakistan not only wanted to identify those who fired the guns but also those who paid for the bullets.

In the AZO acts of sabotage, innocent lives were lost and public property was damaged. Many of their planned acts failed, resulting in the arrest of the terrorists. Their interrogation revealed the *modus operandi* of the AZO and the mode and manner of support provided to it by foreign intelligence agencies. While it created panic in Pakistan, the success rate of its operations was low. The PPP was accused of abetting and supporting a terrorist organization. The PPP denied the allegation as false and mischievous but was put on the defensive. While collaborating with its foreign masters, AZO became a victim of its own follies. Its two main supporters, India and Afghanistan, did not lend assistance to it either for the love of Bhutto or in pursuit of any democratic ideals. It served their national interests to weaken Pakistan by keeping it involved in internal strife. The external interference continued even after the AZO was disbanded. When the Benazir administration came to power in 1988, it complained of the Indian hand in the Sindh disturbances.

For thirteen years, the PPP questioned the existence of the AZO and denied its involvement in terrorist activities. It termed it a myth concocted by the Zia regime intelligence to defame the Bhutto family. Much to the embarrassment of his mother and sister, the suspense was finally broken by Mir Murtaza Bhutto himself. In an exclusive recorded interview given to a Pakistani journalist from Damascus, Syria, he claimed responsibility for raising the AZO in 1979 in Afghanistan and launching armed resistance inside Pakistan. 'We suspended our activities' in Pakistan, disclosed Murtaza, during the twenty month prime ministership of Benazir Bhutto. 'I wanted to return to Pakistan then,' said Murtaza, 'but my mother and sister stopped me.' After the dismissal of the Benazir government 'we restarted our activities [in Pakistan],' acknowledged Murtaza.[2]

While declining to disclose the sources of weapon supplies, Mir Murtaza confessed that the AZO had made two failed attempts on General Zia's life, including an abortive missile attack on the President's aircraft. Questioned about the murder of Chaudhry Zahur Elahi, Mr Zahoorul Hassan Bhopali, and Judge Nabi Sher Junejo, his reply was, 'I cannot speak about the individual operations ... those who abused their position were also taken care of.' About his involvement in the PIA hijacking case he said, 'The hijacking was not authorized by me. It was the result of a spontaneous decision made by our commanders in Karachi ... but once the hijacking took place, I could not disown my people and decided to make use of it.'

The AZO enjoyed the hospitality and support of Libya, Syria, Afghanistan, India, the Soviet Union, and 'some Palestinians'. In addition it received financial assistance from some other foreign countries. President Zia once complained to the visiting head of state of an Arab country that a part of the money given by him to the Bhutto family was spent on destabilizing Pakistan. The distinguished guest confessed that, although he was helping the Bhutto family, he had it conveyed to the recipients that the assistance provided should not be used to harm Pakistan.

The London Plan

The desire to bring about Zia's exit at any cost led some of his political opponents to extreme measures. A plan was hatched to subvert some disgruntled junior officers in the armed forces, provide them with weapons, ammunition, and explosives smuggled from India with the help of Research and Analysis Wing (India's main intelligence agency, RAW) and create anarchy in the country. The conspiracy plan was prepared in the safety of distant London, where it was easier to cook up unsavoury plans without arousing the suspicion of the Pakistan intelligence agencies.

RAW's involvement provided professional expertise to the conspirators. While the hush-hush planning started in the bars and restaurants of the capital of England, between the conspirators and a certain Joshi, representing RAW, the remaining elements of the plan were slowly and systematically pieced together. The venue of the meetings was regularly changed as the RAW representative was no novice to this game.

The process of recruitment back home proved difficult. Despite hectic attempts, no senior military officer fell prey to the design. The success in this field came from amongst some majors working in the Inter Services Selection Board detachment located at Gujranwala. They in turn cultivated some of their friends. A group of about two dozen officers were thus subverted. Some of them had limited prospects for further promotion for health and service reasons. The ideological indoctrination was initially carried out by, Raza Kazim, a pseudo-intellectual lawyer of Lahore with a Marxist background. He also made a modest financial contribution but later withdrew from the gang after learning that the plan involved shooting in anger.

There was an urgent need for co-ordination. One major went to London on a secret visit, met the master-mind, tied up operational details, collected some funds, and returned to Pakistan to report progress to some of his close confidants. He travelled abroad without taking permission from the military authorities as required under the rules.

In December 1983, the planner in London displayed great urgency in the early implementation of the effort. It may be recalled that the MRD had launched an agitation in the country on 14 August 1983. It had gained some momentum in Sindh only and by December that year that province was in turmoil. The execution of the London plan in that time-frame was linked with the developments in Sindh. There was a flurry of telephone calls from the London end to the co-conspirators in Pakistan, emphasizing that time was of the essence and that RAW was ready to play its part in the game.

A final meeting was held in London to tie up loose ends. D-Day was fixed when RAW was to hand over the lethal cargo, comprising weapons and ammunition, to the Pakistani agents across the Indo-Pakistan border at a carefully selected location, not far away from the city of Lahore. This transfer took place as planned without a hitch. So thought RAW and the conspirators. In reality, they had been outwitted. The rest was a matter of details which, for security reasons, are omitted.

The drama had a gory end. In the darkness of night on 3 January 1984, some conspirators were arrested at Lahore when they came to the appointed place to take delivery of the weapons. In the resultant skirmish, one person of the law-enforcing agency was killed and a conspirator wounded. Those taken into custody quickly blurted out the details and implicated others who were also bagged. The game was up. The man in London spent a sleepless night finding out what had gone wrong and where.

Seventeen persons faced trial in December 1984. Those convicted included Majors Aftab Ahmad Chaudhary, Muhammad Sadiq, Nisar Hussain Bukhari, Muhammad Akhtar Shirazi, Squadron Leaders Tahir Maqsood and F. M. Shehzad, and Captain Muhammad Sibtain. The remaining accused were acquitted by the trial court either by giving them the benefit of doubt or for lack of sufficient evidence against them. The London end was operated by a founder-member of the Pakistan People's Party.

The Knack Of Survival

General Zia's assumption of power started a debate about his leadership qualities. To occupy the national centre stage was a task unfamiliar to a professional soldier. Despite his brilliance, a firm political base, and shrewdness, Mr Bhutto brought about his own downfall. Could Zia succeed where Bhutto had failed? Most observers did not think so. General Zia surprised them by his tenacity, foresight, and damage control mechanisms which enabled him to rule the country for over eleven years. The August 1988 air crash was an unforeseen intervention, but there was no imminent danger of his political collapse. His administration was sustained by a number of favourable factors.

The prevailing political structure in the country was fragile and disorganized and could at best generate lukewarm political pressure. There was no serious challenge to military rule. The only organized major party—the PPP—was in disarray. While Nusrat Bhutto was politically inexperienced, Benazir Bhutto, young and emotional, did not relish the thought of working with her 'uncles'. The mother and daughter purged the party of some members and sidelined others. The weakened PPP indirectly strengthened the hands of the administration. The PPP's cavalier approach to major policy issues and its resort to violence in politics weakened its cause.

The PPP-sponsored acts of violence and the AZO anti-state activities generated public ire. These acts included the cold-blooded murder of the political leaders, Chaudhry Zahur Elahi and

Mr Bhopali, a spate of sabotage activities by the AZO, a bomb explosion during the visit of His Holiness the Pope at Karachi in February 1981, and the Indian support to the AZO. Such misadventures helped the government to seize the initiative and take countermeasures. The PPP's attempt to inject violence into politics proved counter productive.

Hunger is a devastating weapon. While political hunger can be contained for limited periods, the needs of the physical appetite must be met on a continuing basis to avoid empty stomachs bringing down seemingly well-established mighty rulers. Barring one year, the harvests of the major crops—wheat and rice—were good. The storage capacity for foodgrains was doubled and measures were taken to keep the price index of essential items of daily need within the purchasing power of the consumers.

The Soviet occupation of Afghanistan rang alarm bells in Western Europe and the USA. Pakistan's Afghan policy boosted the image of Zia's leadership beyond the borders of Pakistan. It directly helped in consolidating his rule.

It is a chilling thought that most Pakistani rulers have left the political scene in ignominy. Against this background, General Zia, a non-elected authoritarian ruler, baffled his critics by staying in power for over a decade. His success was the result of a combination of many factors—firmness, good luck, anticipating events, seizing fleeting opportunities, favourable international developments, realpolitik, and a wily approach. Above all, for most of the time, he had a well-knit team of experienced administrators and advisers who knew their jobs and served him loyally and dutifully. While some of them were abrasive and uppish, all were generally fair in their words, deeds, and decisions. Towards the end of his rule, his yes-men put a ring of isolation around him and fed him with information which he liked to hear. With their glib-tongued falsehoods, they kept convincing him that, he, a Caesar, had a Brutus chasing him. These small men in high positions inflicted on him, as Shakespeare's Mark Antony said, 'the most unkindest cut of all.'

Agha Shahi Quits

Knowledgeable and articulate, Mr Agha Shahi, a civil administrator turned diplomat, rose to the zenith of his professional life to the envy of many of his colleagues. Promoted to the rank of Foreign

Secretary in 1973, Agha Shahi held that appointment for four years. At 4:30 a.m. one morning in July 1977, he was woken up by the telephone ringing. Brigadier Khawar Latif Butt asked him to meet General Zia in the latter's office at 8.30 a. m. that day. This was Shahi's introduction to Zia's martial law. Days later, he was promoted as Secretary-General and, in January 1978, became Adviser on Foreign Affairs with the rank of a Cabinet Minister. Subsequently he became the Foreign Minister of Pakistan.

After the execution of Bhutto, some bureaucrats distanced themselves from the Zia administration. Some sought voluntary retirement and jobs elsewhere. A few others requested that they be given low-key appointments or foreign postings. Years later, some of those thus obliged sought favour of the Benazir administration by complaining that the previous government had victimized them by sidelining them outside the bureaucratic mainstream.

Some faint-hearted bureaucrats panicked when they received anonymous threats from the Al-Zulfiqar Organization, threatening them of dire consequences for serving an 'illegal' government. While a vast majority of the civil servants, including Ghulam Ishaq Khan and Agha Shahi, ignored such threats, some felt apprehensive and insecure.

Mr Agha Shahi served the government with devotion and loyalty and enjoyed the trust and support of General Zia. In August 1980, on reaching the normal age of retirement, he requested that he be retired. He was prevailed upon to keep serving. This reflected Zia's confidence in Shahi.

Mr Sultan Muhammad Khan's appointment as Pakistan's ambassador to the US did not please Mr Agha Shahi. His suggestion to post Sultan anywhere except in Washington, because Pakistan was pursuing a non-aligned foreign policy, was not accepted by Zia. During their service, the two contemporaries had developed some differences, but both had promised Zia that they would work together without any recrimination.

In March 1981, Mr Agha Shahi consulted Mr Ghulam Ishaq Khan about his intention to seek retirement because 'pressures and strains were damaging his health and he had neglected his personal affairs for too long.' At that time, a PIA aircraft had been hijacked. Mr Ghulam Ishaq Khan suggested to Mr Agha Shahi that, notwithstanding his personal desire, the time was not appropriate for him to leave. Shahi agreed.

INTERCEDING LINKS

Sensing that Mr Agha Shahi might repeat his request to quit, General Zia decided to select a sucessor. I asked Sahabzada Yaqub Khan if he would be willing to fill in the Shahi slot, if and when vacated. He responded positively. From then onwards, Yaqub Khan was included in the Pakistan delegations which held talks in the USA and India. He also represented the country at the Non-Aligned Summit meeting. In February 1982, when Mr Agha Shahi resigned, Sahabzada Yaqub Khan replaced him as the Foreign Minister.

Shahi, a career diplomat, had neither developed any policy differences with General Zia nor did he lose his confidence. He retired from service with the satisfaction of a fine diplomatic innings to his credit.

CHAPTER 11

Relations with Iran

An air journey to Iran in the pre-revolution era left an indelible mark on the memory of a first-time visitor. The lobbies and each of the passenger lounges of the Mehrabad Airport were decorated with larger than life portraits of His Imperial Majesty, King of Kings, Aryamehr Muhammad Reza Pehlavi, the Shahinshah of Iran, Her Imperial Majesty the Empress, and His Imperial Highness Reza Pehlavi, the teenaged Crown Prince. The imposing trio gave one the uneasy feeling that the royal family was watchfully looking down on all the passengers.

As the visitor entered the lobby of any hotel, he once again saw portraits of the three, prominently displayed on a spacious wall. During his stay in Iran, he would see them repeatedly in all public places, hotels, offices, shops, restaurants, cinema houses, and on carefully selected prominent roadsides. The personality cult was total; the Shah was omnipresent. To those who knew Iran well, he was no less omnipotent. The people of Iran showed admirable patience, bearing with the autocratic monarchical system for 2,500 years.

Muhammad Reza Pahlavi, the symbol of a proud nation with a rich heritage, was born in Tehran on 26 October 1919. He was designated crown prince and heir apparent at the age of seven, during the coronation ceremony of his father, Reza Shah. During the Second World War, Reza Shah co-operated with Germany. The German invasion of Russia in June 1941 witnessed an attack on Iran by British and Russian troops. The position of Reza Shah became untenable and he was forced to abdicate. On 16 September 1941, with British troops threatening the periphery of Tehran, he signed the last act of his rule: 'I, Shah of Iran, by the grace of God and the nation, have taken the grave decision to withdraw and to abdicate in favour of my beloved son, Muhammad Reza Pehlavi.'

Three years after the abdication, he died in Johannesburg, mostly unsung and largely unwept. Inheriting a weak and poor Iran from his father, the Shah's future appeared uncertain. His long rule was trouble-ridden. He gained valuable experience in handling a series of internal crises and emerged from them more powerful and confident. The young Shah of Iran lifted his nation from the debris of war to guide its destiny for the next thirty-seven years. Much of Iran's oil income in the early days of his reign went to the coffers of the British-controlled Anglo-Iranian Oil Company. After the nationalization of the oil industry, Iran became the mistress of her own resources. In December 1973, oil prices rose substantially. The new-found oil wealth made Iran fabulously rich almost overnight. In 1972, Iran had accumulated a debt of $3 billion. Two years later, her oil revenue jumped to an impressive figure of $19 billion. All the debts were paid, and Iran became a creditor nation. The Shah developed a vision of Iran emerging as the dominant power in the region. Iran prepared an ambitious plan for the purchase of arms costing $4 billion to 8 billion each year.

Power and wealth intoxicated the ambitious Shah. He saw Iran as the fifth industrial nation of the world. As Iran's military muscles grew in strength, so also did the Shah's ego expand. In a press conference held at Tehran on 23 December 1973, he had some unsolicited advice to offer: 'The West has to learn to live within its means. It must search for other sources of energy than oil. If the people in the West want to produce hippies and indulge in leftist talk they should do this at their own expense and not at the expense of other countries like Iran.' He went on to add: 'They [West] want to export their degenerated ideas, which they call democracy, but that is something we cannot accept.'

Encouraged by the United States of America, the Shah assumed the role of policeman of the region. He started looking beyond the borders of his country and casting covetous eyes around to establish Iran's sphere of dominance. The United States, in pursuit of her own global interests, helped to build up Egypt, Israel, and Iran as the pre-eminent regional powers.

Oil wealth and American patronage brought about a discernible change in the Shah's attitude. While dealing with the United States, he no longer considered himself a junior partner. He invested Iranian money in American and Western European business houses. He planned to dominate the Gulf region and let Iran emerge as a military and economic power to make her presence felt in the areas beyond her immediate periphery. In an interview given in 1976, the Shah explained the rationale of acquiring military power to Heikal in the following words: 'I will give you an explanation of our defence policy.

I live in an area which, as I recall, you yourself in one of your weekly articles called the centre of gravity of the world. I belong to this area; I have a stake in it which I intend to preserve. I have a function in it which I intend to exercise. I have a policy which I intend to pursue. There can be no stake, no function, no policy, which is not backed by military power.'[1]

The Shah went on to explain further: 'The Iranian air force ought to be strong enough to protect the whole area from the Gulf to the Sea of Japan. India is going to collapse. India and Pakistan will become natural markets for Iranian industrial projects, but I shall have to protect Pakistan against Indian aggression. I am against any division of Pakistan; India wants that, but I am against it.'[2]

Iran demonstrated its will and capacity when on 1 November 1971, her forces occupied the three tiny islands—Abu Musa and the two Tumbs—located in the Straits of Hormuz. These were owned by Sharjah and Res el-Kheimah but claimed as Iranian property by the Shah. Iranian troops were used to deal with the pro-communist revolution in Dhufar, Oman. The Shah aided and abetted the Iraqi Kurds to rise against their government. He cut off aid to them when Iraq signed the Algiers accord in 1975 on Iranian terms. The Shah's views on the Gulf region and the Indian Ocean were given by him to Heikal in these words: 'The Gulf is going to be the centre of gravity and the centre of conflict for world mastery over the next twenty years. The Indian Ocean is a vacuum where there will be a clash between the two superpowers, and we should play a part in this. I foresee a prolonged period of chaos in the Indian subcontinent.'[3]

By 1977, the Shah appeared all-powerful, ostensibly in full command of his country and enjoying international prestige and status in excess of the size of his nation. He had initiated the 'White Revolution' at home, promising to his people the benefits of agrarian reforms, better education, development efforts, the emancipation of women, and administrative changes. Some writers identified this progress and development with the person of the Shah. In their assessment, modern Iran was synonymous with its ruler. The Western media projected him as a firm and enlightened leader with the vision and capacity to build Iran as a bastion of peace and progress.

What the Shah failed to provide to his subjects was human dignity and freedom of association and expression. Absolute monarchy was the order of the day. Too much power was concentrated in too few hands. The new-found oil wealth had created islands of prosperity in an ocean of poverty. The people faced suppression and terror. The country was run through an authoritarian system, and authority was exercised through powerful law-enforcing agencies, and the invisible hand of SAVAK (the State Security and Information Organization). SAVAK was instituted in Iran to combat what the Shah called 'communist subversion after the disastrous Mosaddeq episode.'[4]

SAVAK, created in 1957, was notorious for its ruthless efficiency. Modelled on the lines of a combination of the American FBI-cum-CIA, it expanded fast and developed remarkable techniques in penetrating its target areas. It worked in close liaison with Israel's Mossad and the CIA.

The Shah's dislike for Mosaddeq was total. However, to the majority of the Iranians, Dr Muhammad Mosaddeq epitomized the vanguard of the movement for a political struggle against the tyrannical imperial rule. In his autobiography, the Shah commenting on the performance of SAVAK, said, 'it had become the favourite target of the international press.' He further disclosed that 'The number of SAVAK employees at the end of 1978 had not risen beyond four thousand.'[5]

The authority and coercive power enjoyed by those four thousand specially selected and trained personnel must have been considerable to earn the wrath of the people, which they did in good measure. To the vast majority of the Iranians, SAVAK symbolized an organization of state terror, resulting in the torture and murder of fellow citizens. It was an organization beyond the pale of state laws.

For two decades, SAVAK was effectively used to ferret out extremists who supposedly posed a threat to the monarchy. What the Shah willed, SAVAK implemented loyally. It used torture to extract confessions. In 1975, the Ministry of Interior publicly claimed that '174 young urban guerrillas had been shot following trial by secret courts' during an unspecified period.[6]

The actual number of those tortured and killed without trial would remain a matter of speculation. Stempel records: 'Political assassination became relatively common. Between 1971 and 1978, over 300 police, military, and government employees and approximately 10 foreigners were gunned down in the streets.'[7] Amnesty International's report of 1976 identified 7,500 political prisoners in Iran. Other estimates ran ten times higher. The government never admitted to more than 3,000 persons held in custody.

SAVAK had spread its tentacles far and wide in Iran, its informers, agents, and stringers combing the political trouble-spots and feeding it with a variety of information. The numbers performing covert intelligence work remains undisclosed. The Shah put their strength around 4,000; others estimated it at twice that figure.

The people of Iran feared SAVAK: they could be detained without trial for prolonged periods of time. Many died during the period of incarceration and torture. Others languished in jails, undergoing long terms of imprisonment. For yet others, the agony was cut short. They were shot with or without stage-managed trials.

In the closing years of the Shah's rule, Iran had become a virtual police state. The country was administered efficiently and the basic essentials of everyday life were available in abundance. The Press and the people could differ with the government on trivial issues. On matters of substance, criticism was unwelcome. The intelligence net was spread wide. It covered bureaucrats and ministries, universities and business houses, the gentlemen of the Press and the clergy, the armed forces and the police. The Shah and all that was decreed in his name on issues of policy and state security were sacrosanct and not open to discussion. Those who violated this unspoken dictum soon felt the grip of SAVAK.

However, SAVAK was not the only organization which did intelligence work in Iran; there were others in this field. The military intelligence (J2) network was effective and elaborate. It operated within its prescribed limits. In 1963, an Imperial Directorate was created, whose chief reported to the Shah and to no one else. Its declared task was to achieve inter-ministerial co-operation and that of other organizations including SAVAK. There was also a Special Bureau to undertake special projects, but its power base was small. There were special groups formed to combat terrorism. They organized counter-guerrilla attacks quietly and efficiently.

The Shah was mindful of the turbulence and glory of Iran's past. One of his desires was to go down in history as the architect and creator of a prominent symbol depicting Iran's cultural heritage. The place chosen for this demonstration was Persepolis. The occasion was the commemoration of two and a half thousand years of monarchy. In October 1970, sixty-eight kings, princes, and heads of state assembled among the ruins of the former Achaemenian capital, Persepolis, to witness the twentieth century's most grandiose extravaganza. The tented village was subsequently preserved as a tourist resort. The lavish three-day show, designed to affix the seal of legitimacy to the Pehlavi dynasty, reportedly cost the Iranian taxpayers no less than $120 million.

At the diplomatic and official levels, Iran and Pakistan enjoyed mutual understanding. Being neighbours, they had prudently established cordial relations. Regrettably, not much was done to develop close and fraternal links between the peoples of the two countries in vital fields covering the social, cultural, educational, and economic sectors.

Iran, Pakistan, and Turkey were members of the Regional Cooperation for Development (RCD). Created with considerable fanfare, its declared objectives mostly remained unachieved. The RCD-sponsored commercial projects were too few in number and too small in size to create a meaningful impact on the economy of the member states. On a comparative basis, while Turkey and Pakistan faced financial constraints, Iran was better placed. The oil price hike in the mid-seventies made Iran fabulously rich and no less arrogant. Notwithstanding the occasional rhetoric of its leaders, the RCD essentially remained a paper organization in which loud claims were seldom matched by deeds. The internal developments in the three countries kept their leaders mostly inward looking.

The RCD countries were also members of the Baghdad Pact—later renamed CENTO—a toothless organization. It was a military treaty without any troops committed to it. CENTO periodically conducted training exercises in which the diplomatic and ceremonial elements outweighed their military value. The CENTO membership at best gave only psychological protection to its member countries. For Turkey, her membership of NATO was of primary importance. Her orientation was essentially towards Europe. CENTO aroused limited interest in that country. Her participation in CENTO activities was a symbolic demonstration of her friendship with Iran and Pakistan. The major concern of Iran was her border dispute with Iraq and the problem of the Kurd minority in the two countries. Her relations with the Soviet Union were satisfactory. Pakistan's security concerns emanated from an overbearing India, which had signed a Treaty of Peace and Friendship with the Soviet Union.

There were two faces of Iran: if prosperity was visible in parts of some major cities, poverty was all-pervading in the countryside. Tehran was a city of contrasts—a posh northern half and ghettos in the south. The urban elite wore Western-style dresses and was distancing itself from Eastern culture. The rural majority retained their traditional clothes and style of life. The upper class liked hard drinks, many of them ate pork, and they were less concerned about observing fasts and offering prayers. The less affluent people were deeply religious and practised their faith. The defence services were respected and enjoyed a high social status. Foreign dignitaries were entertained in offices, clubs, and public places, but they were seldom invited to visit the homes of military officers: fraternization with foreigners was considered taboo.

The market mechanism prevailed in trade and industry. The currency was freely convertible and consumer goods and the necessities of life were available in abundance. The police force was efficient. The crime rate was low. Unchaperoned women could move about freely at all hours of the day and night. The police treated anti-social elements harshly. Tehran and other cities were expanding fast. The traffic in Tehran was chaotic with too many cars plying on roads not designed to carry them. One witnessed considerable commercial activity in the cities.

On the negative side, the Press, radio, and television networks were docile. Freedom of expression was limited. Most Iranians gladly discussed world issues with foreigners, but gave evasive replies when questioned on their domestic politics. Those speaking fluent English would suddenly develop a language barrier when asked a searching query regarding Iran. Many Iranians talked more freely when alone. In the company of their fellow-countrymen, they usually looked around before answering a knotty question. They were mortally scared of the Gestapo-like activities of both SAVAK and J2.

The Gulf region contains 62 per cent of the known oil reserves of the world. The oil crisis of the seventies greatly increased the wealth of the militarily weak, politically fragmented, and sparsely populated Gulf states. The concentration of immense wealth in a fragile and friction-ridden region brought with it the seeds of turmoil and conflict.

Iran considered the Gulf area vital to her interests and security. She desired to control the Straits of Hormuz. The Shah made no secret of his new-found vision of Iranian influence and her expanding zone of interest. On 14 May 1973, he told, Arnaud de Borchgrave of *Newsweek* that, 'Not only do we have the national and regional responsibilities but also a world role as guardian and protector of 60

per cent of the world's oil revenues.' In December 1974 he proposed
' a regional defence force between Iran, Egypt and the Arab States.'[8]

The oil crisis hit the economies of the West so hard that the United States threatened to use force to maintain the flow of oil. To protect her long-term interests in the region, she sold weapons to Iran, Saudi Arabia, and Kuwait.

The American interest in Iran dates back to 1883, when a US diplomatic mission was opened in that country. At that time, Russia and Britain were the dominant powers in the region. The Anglo-Russian Treaty of 1907 divided the region into two zones of influence. It was a compromise between the Russian wish to obtain access to the warm waters of the Arabian Sea and the British desire to protect her lifeline to India. The American influence took a decisive turn when US troops arrived in Iran in 1942 to maintain the flow of supplies from the Gulf to the Soviet Union. From 1943 onwards, the United States was firmly anchored in Iran. On 1 December 1943, the Allied leaders—Roosevelt, Churchill, and Stalin—in a conference held in Iran signed the Declaration of Tehran. It paved the way for the implementation of the Anglo-Soviet Treaty of Alliance that required the British and Soviet troops to withdraw from Iran within six months after hostilities ceased. The end of the Second World War changed the dynamics of power. British influence declined and the vacuum in Iran was filled by the United States.

The United States started providing economic and military assistance to Iran. In the process, it made political inroads in the domestic struggle for power. Within a few years, CIA became a factor in the politics of Iran.

Iran faced political turmoil in 1953. The Prime Minister Dr Muhammad Mosaddeq, wanted the Shah to reign, not rule, and did not hesitate to attack the kingship publicly. To an authoritarian monarch, the arrogance of his own appointed Prime Minister was unacceptable. On 16 August 1953, the Shah dismissed Dr Mosaddeq. The wounded Prime Minister took the last refuge of politicians to demonstrate his popularity. He resorted to street violence which forced the Shah to flee Iran and to take refuge in Rome. It was now the turn of the CIA to act. It acted with speed.

The loyal Iranian politicians, aided and abetted by the American intelligence agency, intervened. Pro-Shah demonstrations were held in Tehran. General Fazlollah Zahedi, appointed Prime Minister by the Shah, collected the loyal army units. On 22 August, the Shah returned to Tehran and occupied the Peacock Throne once again. Dr Mosaddeq was arrested, tried, sentenced to imprisonment, and kept in a house near Tehran, where he died in captivity in 1966.

The CIA helped the Shah to regain power. While it took discreet credit, it maintained that some key Iranian personalities were keen to establish a stable government—a task in which it provided a helping hand.

From 1953 onwards, the American influence and presence in Iran kept increasing. So did her commercial activity which accelerated substantially after 1973. The US military sales to Iran registered a sharp rise as demonstrated in the statistics given below:[9]

($ in millions)

Year	Orders	Deliveries
1969	235.8	94.8
1970	134.9	127.7
1971	363.9	8.6
1972	472.6	214.8
1973	2,171.3	248.4
1974	4,325.3	648.6
1975	2,447.1	1,006.1
1976	1,794.4	1,927.9
1977	5,713.8	2,433.0
1978	2,586.9	1,792.9

In the closing years of the Shah's rule the military arsenal was overflowing with state of the art weapons. He acquired the arrogance of power and a self-appointed role in regional and world affairs.

Despite differences in their political systems, Iran and Pakistan had a very friendly relationship. Their 565 mile-long common border was demarcated and was peaceful. Pakistan understood the genesis of the Iran-Iraq dispute, Iran's reservations about the Soviet Union based on past history, her interest in Afghanistan where the Soviet Union had made deep inroads, and her deep and abiding concern about the security of the Gulf region. On her part, Iran showed understanding of Pakistan's problems with India and Afghanistan and her friendly ties with communist China. Both the countries valued their relationship with the United States and Turkey, and shared their perceptions about the Soviet Union.

RELATIONS WITH IRAN

Pakistan's friendly bonds with some Arab countries occasionally caused ripples in Iran because of the age-old Arab-Iranian rivalry. For example, in February 1974, the Shah of Iran did not personally attend the Islamic Summit Conference held in Lahore because of the presence of Colonel Qaddafi of Libya. Despite such occasional pinpricks, the general pattern of the Iran-Pakistan relationship was one of mutually beneficial friendship and co-operation.

General Zia visited Iran in September 1977. The Shah and General Zia met alone in the Niavaran Palace, perched at a height in Shemran, in a corner of Tehran. The majestic building gave a panoramic view of the landscape of the sprawling capital below. The Shah appeared extremely confident and cheerful. While the other members of the Pakistan delegation waited in an adjoining room, General Zia informed his host of the circumstances under which a popular movement had led to the fall from power of Bhutto's government. The Shah was well informed about Pakistan's internal developments. He asked searching questions about the composition and efficacy of the Pakistan National Alliance and the political leanings of its component parties. His reservations about the PNA, couched in diplomatic verbiage, were unmistakably conveyed . He told General Zia that, in his own country, he had had a long and bitter experience of dealing with the ultra rightist elements. Based on that experience, he found it difficult, he said smilingly, to trust the gentlemen sporting beards and wearing turbans. Given a chance, they would play on the sensitivities of their captive audience in religious gatherings and create problems for the government. 'Trust them after taking due care,' advised the experienced Shah.

Speaking with visible emotion, the Shah claimed with pride that he had always handled the *mullahs* firmly in Iran to keep them in their proper place. A policy of appeasement towards them would be an invitation to disaster, said the Shah. General Zia told His Majesty that the rightist parties in Pakistan were patriotic and loyal and that he anticipated no major difficulty from them. The Shah expressed his misgivings and stated that he had shared his personal experience with his distinguished guest as he was a well-wisher and friend of Pakistan. He again advised General Zia not to put his faith blindly in those who excelled in the art of exploiting religion for political ends. They were a volatile community, repeated the Shah, and he advised Zia to handle them with care.

After the *tete-a-tete*, the two delegations had lunch at the Palace. At the table, the Shah spoke on a variety of subjects with confidence, knowledge, and poise. He displayed a penetrating grasp of world affairs and expressed his views on them in a lucid style. He spoke fluent English with a French accent. The rules of royal protocol were rigid. When the Shah spoke, others listened attentively.

As the luncheon participants came out of the dining-room, a senior Iranian military officer was waiting in the lobby. He gave a smart salute to his monarch and started talking to him. He kept his right hand at the salute position throughout the duration of his conversation with the Shah. It was a degrading sight. A military salute is a formal and dignified form of greeting. It enjoys respect and status. In Iran it perhaps symbolized personal loyalty—a tradition corrupted to the limit of absurdity—to satisfy the personal ego of an absolute ruler.

* * *

Mecca, Medina, and Jerusalem are the three holy cities for all Muslims. For the Shiites in Iran, the city of Qom, where the grave of Masoumeh (Fatima), the sister of Imam Reza is located, constitutes their religious capital. It has been so since the beginning of the sixteenth century when the first Safavid Shah, Ismail, made Shiism the official religion of Persia. Over a period, Qom, with its peculiar mystique, has developed as a centre of religious studies where the mosque schools train Shiite religious scholars. Fisher says about Qom: 'It is a repository of the Shiite tradition, a centre of conservatism rejected by many Iranians and lauded by others; and it served as a focus of opposition to the Shah on moral grounds.'[10]

So firmly was the Shah of Iran established on his throne in the fall of 1977 that even his worst critics could not imagine that he was in fact sitting on a smouldering volcano which would erupt within months to sweep him out of power, and that Qom would be the epicentre of a religio-political upheaval. In November that year, he and the Empress visited the United States of America where, at Williamsburg, they were greeted by some masked individuals who shouted insults at them.

In Iran, the first major riots took place on 7 January 1978 in the city of Qom, in which an undisclosed number of people died. In the words of the Shah, 'their death was wrongly attributed by the *mullahs* to the crimes perpetrated by the Savak.'

From that day onwards, the writ and control of the Shah was on the wane. His popularity graph dipped fast. He took a number of administrative measures, including a change of cabinets, to restore order and regain the initiative. He found the task difficult—nay, impossible. On 19 August 1978, a cinema in Abadan was set ablaze, resulting in the death of 477 persons who were either burnt alive or asphyxiated. The shadows started darkening over Iran. The country was in turmoil.

As the Shah's government lost its grip on the administration, it turned towards religion to earn the goodwill of the people in general and of the Shiite hierarchy in particular. Casinos and gambling clubs were closed and the Hijra calendar was introduced. Such cosmetic measures proved ineffective. The people no longer sought concessions from their ruler. Their target was the royal head.

While Iran burnt with hatred of the Shah, Pakistan's ambassador in Tehran, Ghiasuddin Ahmad conceived a bright plan. He repeatedly suggested that General Zia should urgently visit Tehran to demonstrate Pakistan's friendship towards the beleaguered Shah in his hour of trouble. In his assessment, the Shah was likely to weather the political storm, as his defence services were loyal to him. Pakistan's gesture at that critical time, in the view of Ambassador Ghiasuddin Ahmad, was unlikely to be forgotten by the Shah, a friend of Pakistan. The ambassador's optimism about the Shah's ability to control the situation was belied by media reports. The Foreign Office felt that, notwithstanding the negative Press opinion, the advice of the experienced ambassador, who was present on the spot, should be given greater reliance. A three day visit to Iran, from 9-11 September 1978, by President Zia was thus planned. This turned out to be a diplomatic blunder.

Just one day prior to the planned visit, a tragedy of serious magnitude shook Iran. 8 September was a Friday. On that day, the police clashed with demonstrators in Tehran and used excessive force, resulting in large-scale killings. On the 'Black Friday', as it came to be called, over 2,000 persons lost their lives. The government put the death toll at 85 persons. The tragedy reverbrated in the corridors of power in Iran. Violence erupted in different parts of the country. Prime Minister Hoveyda resigned and many cities were placed under martial law. Even at that belated stage, General Zia's projected tour should have been postponed. But it was not. The wisdom of hindsight was not available then.

On his arrival at Mehrabad Airport at 4:35 p.m. on 9 September 1978, General Zia was presented with a guard of honour. From the airport, the entourage was flown in helicopters to the guest house—Aghdesia Palace. General Zia's meeting with the Shah was arranged for 7 p.m. at the Saadabad Palace, which was to be followed by a dinner. Ambassador Ghiasuddin Ahmad briefed the Pakistani delegation at the Guest House. He expressed his thanks to General Zia for accepting his advice to visit Tehran at a time when other friends of the Shah were either lukewarm or ice-cold to him. 'In the long run,' said the ambassador, 'the visit would pay dividends.'

Explaining the latest developments, the ambassador indicated that the Iranian cabinet was divided on how to deal with the situation. While some advocated a tough stance, others felt that such a step would be counter-productive. Martial law had been imposed in some cities as a measure of compromise. The ambassador was convinced that the Shah's difficulties were temporary and the agitation against him would not succeed as the military, a key factor as assessed by him, continued to be loyal to the King.

Three Pakistani military officers serving in Tehran had a different view. Commodore Akbar H. Khan, Colonel Tariq Rafi and Lieutenant-Colonel Sajid, who did not attend the ambassador's briefing, were of the unanimous view that the political situation in Iran was critical and that the Shah's days were numbered; in their assessment, he had become a symbol of hatred and mistrust for the people. It was their considered opinion that events would take a decisive turn against the Shah within a matter of weeks. The countdown for the Shah had started, they concluded. They were surprised to hear from me that the ambassador's view on the subject were just the opposite. They frankly admitted that the ambassador had not found it convenient to consult them on the issue.

General Zia found the Shah off-colour that evening. He displayed visible signs of anguish and anxiety. His internal turmoil was writ large on his sunken and ashen face. His spirits were low. He took pains to explain that the agitation was foreign-inspired. The CIA had a hand in it to keep him in check. He had complained sternly about it, he said, to the American ambassador in Tehran. The Shah went on to add that the Soviet Union had also been active in Iran for decades and had made deep inroads. He complained that the *mullahs* were exploiting the sentiments of the people for their own vested interests. Throughout the meeting, the Shah was visibly morose and frequently took deep breaths. He confessed that his experiment of forming the

Rastakhiz (Renaissance) Party had failed and he had been proven wrong in his assessment that it represented all citizens. He lamented that Iran had too many political parties, some with two members only. The Shah bitterly criticized the Afghan rulers. He narrated an incident in which an Iranian Air Force transport aircraft, carrying twelve persons and some generator sets for the Iranian embassy in Kabul, was surrounded at the Kabul Airport with tanks. A rumour was set afloat in Kabul that Iran had sent the aircraft to hijack some imprisoned Afghan leaders.

At the dinner-table the Shah was unusually serious and quiet. He talked very little and ate even less. The comedown in his appearance and style was distinctly noticeable. The lofty eminence once associated with him was conspicuously absent.

General Zia's tour of Iran was ill-timed. Besides causing inconvenience to his hosts, who were deeply shaken by the internal turmoil, a rumour circulated in Tehran that Pakistan had offered military assistance to Iran. There was no truth in it. An American reporter, S. Talbot, had interviewed the Shah just before General Zia's arrival in Tehran. After recording the interview, he told a member of the Pakistan delegation that 'the Shah was shattered.' The impression of Pakistan's delegation was the same.

The next morning, Zia's entourage flew to Mashhad, where the mortal remains of Imam Reza, the eighth Shiite Imam, are buried. The surroundings of the imposing mausoleum were under extensive repairs and extension. The Governor-General of Khorasan extended all the diplomatic courtesies, but the city was tense and emotionally charged and its people were agitating against the government. The disturbances in Iran were widespread. The people had risen in revolt against the ruler. The edifice of monarchy had decayed. Its collapse was a matter of time.

By the end of 1978, the deterioration was rapid and vividly evident. In August of that year, the Shah had announced that fresh elections would be held in the spring of 1980. The declaration became a nonevent. Iran was passing through a militant phase in her national life. The Shah employed conventional methods in dealing with an unconventional situation. Prime ministers were changed in quick succession. Efforts were made to form a government of national unity. Each change weakened the Shah and united the opposition against him. By the close of 1978, it was clear that any measure short of the exit of the Shah would not satisfy his opponents. Mr William Sullivan, the United States ambassador to Iran, sent a telegram to Washington on 12 November 1978, expressing the opinion that the Shah's end was in sight and some alternative would have to be found. The following day, President Carter declared in a press conference that 'the US would hate to see Iran disrupted by violence', and on 30 November elaborated further, saying that the US would not become involved and 'did not approve of interference by another country.'[11]

On 5 January 1979, General Robert Huyser, an American holding the appointment of Deputy Director of NATO, secretly visited Iran but avoided calling on the Shah till his presence was reported to the ruler. The Shah was indignant. He was bewildered when the General eventually called on him along with the American Ambassador. Heikal records that General Huyser undiplomatically asked the Shah: 'When are you leaving, Sir? Have you fixed the date?' Such a blunt approach was uncharacteristic and undignified, even by American standards.

The Soviet press reported, 'General Huyser is in Tehran to foment a military coup.' Washington observed a meaningful silence about the General's presence in Iran. There was wide speculation about his mission. It was alleged that his task was to persuade the armed forces to shift their loyalty from the Shah to the new Prime Minister, Shahpur Bakhtiar. There was another view that he had urged the military leadership to remain loyal and united behind the constitutional government. There was also a third view: 'Huyser had been sent to Iran by President [Carter] to assess the future of U. S. military programmes in the country. Of special concern were sensitive American electronic equipment and aircraft.'[12]

Long after the event, General Rabi, Commander-in-Chief of the Iranian Air Force, while deposing at the trial which preceded his execution, said: 'General Huyser threw the King out of the country like a dead mouse.'[13]

In 1981, Pakistan's honorary consul general in Houston had hosted a dinner in honour of a visiting Pakistani delegation in Washington. During that dinner, Mr Agha Shahi enquired from the from the National Security Adviser in the Carter Administration, Dr Zbigniew Brzezinski, the purpose of General Huyser's 1979 visit to Tehran. He replied that Washington's failure to take a timely decision frustrated the objective of that visit. The prevailing confusion has been well described by Heikal in these words: 'American policy was in complete disarray. Everybody blamed everybody else—Brzezinski blaming Vance, Vance blaming the military, the military blaming the CIA, and the CIA complaining that it was not being given a free hand.'[14]

The hour of decision had finally struck. On 16 January 1979, the Shah and the Empress quietly flew out of Tehran to 'take several weeks of holiday.' The announcement of the royal departure was made by the American Secretary of State, Mr Cyrus Vance. The Shah was never to return to Iran again, alive or dead. The pathetic story of his exile, leading to his death, is an eye-opener. He died brooding over his betrayal by Iran's close ally—the United States of America. He was cold-shouldered by those who once took pride in claiming his friendship. As a king, he had been above the law. Stripped of his kingdom, he became an accused person, evading the hands of the law. Once a mighty king, he became an international orphan in exile. His friends closed their doors on him. He died of cancer, a broken man, befriended only by Anwar Sadaat of Egypt.

The story of the Shah's exile illustrates the frailty of the so-called human giants and the unreliability of friendship linked with power. After leaving Tehran, the Shah had planned to visit Jordan first. King Hussein politely declined the honour. Perforce, the Shah's party travelled to Egypt where it had lived at Aswan, the winter resort on the Nile. After a five-day stay, the group moved to Morocco, from where the Shah was scheduled to go to America. Here, the Shah learned that he would not be welcomed in the United States. Morocco also became a reluctant host. A dejected Shah and a morose Empress advanced their visit to the Bahamas where they intended to stay for a prolonged period of time. Their desire could not be fulfilled because the Bahamas declined to extend their visa facility. On 10 June 1979, the seriously ailing Shah reached Mexico.

It was the turn of President Carter to get cold feet. He had it conveyed to the Shah that, while the time was not opportune for the exiled couple to visit the United States, they could have access to the medical facilities available in that country, when needed. In late October, the Shah reached New York, and underwent surgery.

On 4 November 1979, the American embassy in Tehran was occupied by militant students who seized more than fifty Americans as hostages. The United States came under Iranian pressure to stop providing a medical haven to the deposed Shah. America yielded to the Iranian demand. The Shah had no choice but to leave that country. By the end of November, he had recovered sufficiently to be able to travel. He planned to return to Mexico, but, at the last moment, the Mexican Government refused to provide a fresh visa on the grounds that it would hurt Mexico's 'vital interests'. The noose was tightening around the Shah's neck. The world started shrinking for him. Austria, Switzerland, and South Africa also turned down his requests for a visa. Initially, Britain had promised to grant him asylum. Subsequently, she backed down and had it diplomatically conveyed to him that it would be awkward for her to let him stay in that country.

The United States finally arranged for the exiled couple to stay at Contadora Island in Panama, where they arrived on 15 December. Within a month, the Panamanian authorities had had second thoughts. As part of the psychological offensive, it was declared that the Shah was a virtual prisoner and the technical possibility of his extradition to Iran could not be ruled out. Privately, the Shah was asked to ignore that statement. He was also conveyed President Carter's advice not to go back to Egypt as it might endanger President Sadaat's position and the peace process that was underway in the Middle East. The Shah was exasperated. With his kingdom gone and his health in shambles because of a fast-spreading cancer, he also faced the possibility of extradition as the new government in Iran sought his return to face trial. Ultimately, he returned to Egypt where, on 28 March, his cancer-ridden spleen was removed. He died in Egypt, unwept and unsung except by his close family members and friends. The Shah had ruled Iran for thirty-seven years. During that period he had enjoyed absolute and unquestionable authority. The Iranian revolution toppled the 'Peacock Throne'. His life of blazing glory was in sharp contrast to his inglorious end. His mortal remains lie buried in a foreign land, away from the country which he and his ancestors had once ruled with all the panoply of power and wealth.

* * *

Ayatollah Ruhollah Khomeini, the father of the Islamic revolution in Iran, had been forced out of his motherland by the Shah of Iran. He spent eighteen years in exile in Iraq before moving to France on 6 October 1977. While in France, he had lived in a small villa at Neauphle-le-Chateau, about twenty-five miles from Paris. The Shah's dislike of the religious scholar is amply reflected in his own words: 'The June [1963] troubles were completely "black" and gave free rein to pure and simple vandalism. The instigator of the riots, pillaging and arson was a practically unknown person. He was an obscure agitator, the Ayatollah Khomeini, who was opposed to our agrarian reforms, to the emancipation of women and generally to the principles of the White Revolution. He had no support in the country and his audience was, therefore, considerably limited. He was neither condemned, nor even judged, he was simply requested to go and exercise his incendiary eloquence elsewhere.'[15]

Ayatollah Khomeini worked patiently to unite his people, to create an opportunity to topple the Shah, and to stage a triumphant return to his homeland. With the passage of time, the number and strength of his followers grew. So did the worry of the Shah. In 1977 the Shah prevailed upon the government of Iraq to extradite Ayatollah Khomeini. A weak Iraq yielded to the demand of her powerful neighbour, and the Ayatollah took up residence in France. The departure of the Shah from Iran was a signal to the religious leader to end his exile. He proved to the world that his one-time enemy, the Shah, had grossly underestimated his strength and misjudged the popularity and support that he enjoyed among the teeming millions of Iran.

At 11 p.m. on 30 January 1979, Islamabad received a message from Ayatollah Khomeini's Camp Office in France, enquiring if a Pakistan International Airlines aircraft could be made available to fly him to Tehran. A confirmation was sent and the PIA was directed to get an aircraft ready at short notice. The Camp Office at Neauphle-le-Chateau had simultaneously made a similar request to the French government also, which provided an Air Force Boeing for the journey. The following day it was reported that Tehran would not permit any aircraft carrying Ayatollah Khomeini to land on Iranian soil. A message was flashed from Islamabad to the Camp Office at Neauphle-le-Chateau, welcoming the Ayatollah's aircraft at any airport in Pakistan, in case a landing was denied to it in Iran. But such a situation did not arise. Ayatollah Khomeini, the leader and hero of the Iranian revolution, returned to Tehran on 1 February 1979 and received a tumultuous welcome, the like of which had not been witnessed in that country before. The Shah's rule had collapsed in Iran. The revolution was triumphant.

The success of every revolution lies in its ability to destroy the old order which it replaces. The planners of the Iranian revolution showed by their style and conduct that they were determined to ensure the success of their effort, irrespective of the consequences and the costs involved. Having set their aim, they moved vigorously to achieve their goals in a short span of time. International criticism and pressure failed to deflect them from their set course. For a while, confusion prevailed in Iran. Multiple power centres mushroomed, each claiming the support of Ayatollah Khomeini. Every revolution takes time to complete its task. It goes to the credit of the leaders of the Iranian revolution that the teething difficulties in Iran were soon overcome and the writ of the revolution was established. After having put her house in reasonable order, Iran was ready to receive visitors from outside.

A two-man delegation, comprising Mr Agha Shahi and myself, went to Iran on a goodwill mission in March 1979. As we entered the Royal Tehran Hilton, we were greeted by a group of youngsters, carrying automatic weapons who introduced themselves to us as *Pasdaran*. The hotel was under their charge. The only other occupants were four American citizens who were awaiting a flight to leave ran. Tehran. The hotel rooms bore bullet marks.

The Ministry of Foreign Affairs was under reorganization. The delegation was taken to two different rooms before entering a third to meet the Foreign Minister. He apologized for the inconvenience and explained that the government was in the process of settling down. Some persons attired in religious robes were present in the ministry.

Our delegation engagements in Iran included a visit to Bahishte Zehra, the cemetery outside Tehran, and a call on Ayatollah Khomeini at Qom. At Bahishte Zehra, there were hundreds of young Iranians chanting slogans against the exiled king and condemning the atrocities allegedly committed by SAVAK under his orders. They were thus paying homage to those who had fallen victim to the oppressive rule of the Shah in the cause of their country's freedom.

The trip to Qom was memorable. The roads were a sea of humanity and the car moved at snail's pace, pushed by emotionally-charged youngsters to the residence of their great spiritual leader. They were shouting, 'Death to the Shah! Death to America! Death to America's friends!' Pakistan came in the last category.

Ayatollah Khomeini lived in a small carpeted room, virtually unfurnished and undecorated. It had no chairs. He sat on a mattress on the floor. He worked, rested, and slept in the same place. We sat down on the floor and were introduced by an interpreter. Ayatollah Khomeini spoke of the urgent need for unity amongst the Muslim *ummah*, and stressed the importance of good neighbourly relations between Iran and Pakistan. He especially enquired about the welfare of the Shiite community in Pakistan. He spoke in a low, soft voice and, for his age, appeared to be in good health.

Back in the hotel, we were led to our rooms by two machine-gun-carrying youths. As the door was opened, one of them spoke in fluent English: 'You may sleep comfortably. We will guard you at night.' The visit confirmed that Pakistan would have to make efforts to establish cordial relations with the post-revolution administration in Tehran. Iran had reservations about Pakistan. The cobwebs of doubt in the bilateral relations needed to be removed in the mutual interest of both the countries.

In the early post-revolution period, Iran adopted a simplistic approach in her foreign policy. It was based on hostility against the Shah and suspicion towards the United States. The division was sharp and discernible: everything that the Shah did was wrong; his politics were faulty and based on evil. The revolution was the embodiment of all virtue; what it stood for was justified and unquestionable. The Shah's friends were assumed to be opposed to the revolution. Countries having friendly relations with the United States were suspect. Under such circumstances, the warmth traditionally associated with Pakistan-Iran relations in the past cooled noticeably. Some additional irritants surfaced. Iran convinced herself that her revolution was an exportable commodity and her neighbours should be its first recipients. She took undue interest in the activities of the Shiite sect in Pakistan and established contacts with its leadership. This was unacceptable to Pakistan. It was in the long-term mutual interest of both countries to shun interference in the internal affairs of each other and to re-establish a cordial, strong, enduring, and brotherly relationship for their common good. Post-revolution Iran misjudged Pakistan's position *vis-a-vis* the Shah. President Zia's visit to Iran in September 1978 had created doubts in the minds of the new Iranian leadership. It took them time to understand that the visit was not against their revolution. Sometimes a diplomatic misjudgement carries a heavy cost.

The Iraq-Iran war started in October 1980. As Chairman of the Organization of the Islamic Conference, General Zia undertook a tour of Iran and Iraq in October 1980 in an attempt to stop the fratricidal war. A small delegation accompanied him. Emotions were at a high pitch in both the countries. Iran laid down two conditions for a cease-fire—the branding of Iraq as the aggressor and the removal of President Saddam Hussein from power. These demands left little room for any diplomatic initiative to succeed.

General Zia's programme in Tehran did not include a call on Ayatollah Khomeini. This was an indication of Iranian coolness towards Pakistan. While driving to Tehran airport on his way to Baghdad, General Zia told President Bani Sadr that, without meeting the spiritual leader, he was returning thirsty from a friendly Iran.

Because of the ongoing hostilities it was not possible to fly direct to Baghdad. The aircraft took a circuitous route, travelling south-west from Tehran, crossing the Gulf, flying over Kuwait, and landing in Amman, Jordan, as Baghdad airport was closed. While approaching Amman, President Zia received an invitation from King Hussein to spend the night in Jordan and have dinner with him. His Royal Highness Prince Hassan received General Zia at Amman airport.

At the dinner-table, the discussion centred around the Iran-Iraq war. General Zia briefed King Hussein about his talks with the Iranian leaders. King Hussein treated General Zia, who, a decade earlier, had served in Jordan at a time when it had serious problems with Syria and the Palestine Liberation Organization, with special kindness and affection. Prince Hassan kept the dinner party lively with his occasional full-throated laughs.

The next morning, Zia's entourage, accompanied by Prince Hassan, made a short air journey to a military base on the Jordan-Iraq border. From there, a four-hour road journey took the party to Baghdad.

The Pakistani delegation met President Saddam Hussein and his team of ministers and high-ranking officials in an underground operations room. Prince Hassan was present. President Saddam Hussein rejected the conditions put forth by Tehran. He talked in a conciliatory tone, without compromising Iraq's position. He explained that the Algiers accord had been imposed on Iraq by the late Shah and was thus invalid. The Iraqi capital was hit by Iranian rockets during Zia's meeting with the Iraqi authorities. Emotions ran high in the streets of Baghdad. Baghdad radio was repeatedly broadcasting war songs, the favourite being an account of the battle of Qadisiyah, where an Arab army had met and defeated the main force of the Persian army in AD 637.

The gulf between Iran and Iraq was too wide to be bridged. Both expected Pakistan to support them. Pakistan enjoyed a friendly relationship with both of them. She adopted a neutral position in the

Iraq-Iran war and played a role through the OIC to find an amicable settlement. As time passed, Pakistan's position and sincerity were better understood by both these countries. Her relations with Iran took a positive turn when Iran realized that her policy of isolation was detrimental to her interests.

The Iran-Iraq war came to an end when a cease-fire was effected on 20 August 1988 through the good offices of the Secretary General of the United Nations Organization. This was in contrast to the unsuccessful attempts which the Organization of Islamic Conference had made for eight years to negotiate a settlement between the two warring Muslim countries. The internal divisions of the Muslim *ummah* were once again too obvious to miss.

CHAPTER 12

Turmoil in Afghanistan

As the Tsarist empire expanded southward in the late nineteenth century, the possibility of a Russian advance into India worried her British rulers. They realized that: 'The safety of India depends on the degree of control which the rulers in India can exert on the mountains of the Hindu Kush and the Oxus Valley beyond, for only thus can the "barbarians" be kept at arm's length.'[1]

The concept of converting Afghanistan into a buffer state between the Russian empire and Imperial India was thus born. The British adopted the forward defence policy on the north-west frontiers of India to achieve that aim. The European empires, Russia and Britain, stopped at the Oxus River in the north and at the Durand Line in the east of Afghanistan.

The Durand Line agreement, establishing the border between Afghanistan and British India, was signed by Amir Abdul Rahman Khan on 12 November 1893. In 1905, Abdul Rahman's son and successor, Habibullah, committed himself to abide by the agreement concluded by his late father.[2] The Treaty of Rawalpindi (1919) and the permanent Anglo-Afghan Treaty (1921) further reaffirmed the Durand Line.[3] On Nadir Shah's accession to the throne in 1930, the validity of the Treaty of 1921 was reaffirmed by an exchange of letters between the British Secretary of State for Foreign Affairs and the Afghan Minister in London.[4]

After the partition of the Indo-Pakistan subcontinent, Mr Noel Baker, the Secretary of State for Commonwealth Relations, told the House of Commons on 30 June 1950: 'It is His Majesty's Government's view that Pakistan is, in international law, the inheritor of the rights and duties of the old Government of India, and of His Majesty's Government in the United Kingdom, in these territories, and that the Durand Line is the international frontier.'

This was repeated in the British Parliament by the British Foreign Secretary, Lord Home, on 3 November 1955, and by the British Prime Ministers, Sir Anthony Eden, on 1 March 1956, and Mr Harold MacMillan, on 20 May 1960.[5]

The former deputy foreign minister of Afghanistan, Abdul Samad Ghaus, writes: 'In 1944 when the British departure from India appeared inevitable, the Afghan Government had informed the Government of British India that it hoped to be consulted should a change occur affecting the fate of the Pushtuns living East and South of the Durand Line. In their reply, the British observed that the Durand Line was an international boundary, and, therefore, Afghan interest stopped at that end.'[6]

Pakistan's application for membership of the United Nations came up for discussion in the United Nations General Assembly on 30 September 1947. Speaking on the occasion, the Afghan representative, Mr Abdul Hussein Khan Aziz, said: 'We cannot recognize the NWFP as part of Pakistan so long as the people of the NWFP have not been given an opportunity, free from any kind of influence, to determine for themselves whether they wish to be independent or to become a part of Pakistan.'[7]

Afghanistan was the only country to cast a negative vote. The Afghan proclamation was enigmatic: a country advocating democracy to a neighbour while denying it to its own people. From 1947 onwards, Afghanistan maintained that she had 'a political difference' with Pakistan concerning the future of the Pushtuns, without elucidating that 'concern'.

Pakistan shares a 1,500 mile-long border with her land-locked neighbour—Afghanistan. Bonds of history, religion, culture, traditions, and language exist between the two peoples. Afghanistan's external trade has historically been routed through the port of Karachi, Pakistan. It is a country traditionally ruled by bullets, not ballots, in which coups and palace intrigues have changed governments. Bacha-i-Saqao was executed on 3 November 1929. His successor Nadir Khan, later called Nadir Shah, was assassinated on 8 November 1933. Muhammad Zahir Shah, the next king, was ruling Afghanistan when Pakistan was born. On 17 July 1973, Sardar Muhammad Daoud, enjoying Soviet support, ousted King Zahir Shah, his cousin and brother-in-law, from power in a bloodless *coup d'etat*. Having lost his throne, King Zahir Shah went into exile. Sardar Muhammad Daoud suspended the Constitution and became the Head of State. The kingdom vanished. An Afghan republic emerged. For the people of Afghanistan, the change-over was merely symbolic. They continued to be denied the fruits of democracy.

For three decades, Pakistan-Afghanistan relations remained strained. Afghanistan exploited her friendship with India and the Soviet Union to garner their support against Pakistan. On 24 October 1974, the Soviet Premier, Aleksei Kosygin, advised Pakistan to normalize relations with 'our friendly neighbour—Afghanistan.'[8]

On 8 February 1975, the Chief Minister of the NWFP, Mr Hayat Muhammad Khan Sherpao, was killed in a bomb explosion in Peshawar. The Bhutto government accused the National Awami Party for the murder and arrested its top leadership, implicating the Afghan government. The government declared that, by interfering in Pakistan's internal affairs, a neighbouring foreign power was 'totally betraying the principles of peaceful coexistence of sovereign states.'[9]

The Minister for Interior, Khan Abdul Qayyum Khan, threatened to take 'counter-measures', if compelled. In a sharp reaction, Afghanistan termed the Pakistani action 'politically motivated' and suggested that the solution lay in respecting the 'aspirations of the Baluchi and the Pushtun people'.[10]

The Afghan dissident leaders Engineer Gulbadin Hikmatyar and Professor Burhanuddin Rabbani had escaped to Pakistan in 1974. Their operations inside Afghanistan, with encouragement provided by Pakistan, hurt the Afghan administration. Kabul realized that covert activity was a double-edged weapon and the two countries could mutually benefit if their inter-state relations were improved. A dialogue resulted.

At President Daoud's invitation, Prime Minister Bhutto visited Afghanistan from 7 June to 10 June 1976. Their tete-a-tete recognized the need for replacing tension with cordiality for the well-being of the two countries and for creating regional stability. President Daoud asked Mr Bhutto to create a healthy climate by ending internal security operations in Balochistan. He pleaded for a sympathetic consideration of the grievances of the Pushtun and the Balochi people. Mr Bhutto cited examples of the negative attitude of some Pushtun and Baloch leaders. He indicated to his host his resolve to settle the issue amicably. The secession of East Pakistan, said Mr Bhutto, had made the people weary and opposed to the demands of greater autonomy to the provinces. President Daoud raised the question of the arrest of the NAP leaders and the disturbances in Balochistan. Mr Bhutto cleverly shifted the blame to others. Abdul Samad Ghaus, the interpreter, records what Mr Bhutto said: 'We in Pakistan have to be careful about the mood of our generals. But I am sure that in due time I will be able to get around this difficulty.'[11]

At that time, Mr Bhutto was at the height of his power and authority. A strong-willed person, he took no nonsense from anyone. The army, under General Tikka Khan, obeyed him loyally and implemented government orders in letter and spirit.

President Daoud paid a five-day return visit to Pakistan in August 1976. His arrival and departure ceremonies at Islamabad were a lavish affair. So was his visit to the historic Shalimar Gardens in Lahore, where he addressed the citizens of the city. The public relations effort was superb. Mr Bhutto used all his charm to enchant his honoured guest. At the negotiation table, not much progress was made. The two sides generally maintained the positions held by them in their June 1976 meeting. The 'spirit of Kabul' prevailed, but no more warmth was added to it. With the NAP leaders still facing trial and Balochistan in turmoil, the prevailing realities had not undergone a change. The two sides agreed to continue their discussions. The stalemate persisted during the next one year.

After the fall of his government, Mr Bhutto was to claim that an agreement between Pakistan and Afghanistan was virtually reached during the Daoud visit.[12] Historical records do not support this conclusion. There was a meeting of minds but an agreement was not in sight. For eight long months after August 1976, no further progress was made on the issue. Bhutto's own political difficulties enmeshed him from March 1977 onwards.

Soon after General Zia came to power in July 1977, Pakistan took the initiative of establishing high level contact with Afghanistan. On 10 October 1977, General Zia arrived in Kabul on a two-day 'goodwill mission'. The simple airport ceremony included inspection of a smartly turned-out guard of honour. That evening, Zia met President Daoud at Gul Khana Palace for an extended *tete-a-tete*. He took the opportunity to apprise his host of the political developments in Pakistan. On bilateral relations, he expressed the hope that the two countries would rise above the bitterness of the past and start a new era of peace and friendship. General Zia said that pragmatism demanded the removal of the hurdles which had obstructed the path, clearing the way and marching on a course of friendship and co-operation in the future. Both the countries faced dangers, said the General. The factors uniting them outweighed their differences, they needed reconciliation, not confrontation. Pakistan was keen to develop a mutually beneficial brotherly relationship with Afghanistan.

President Daoud narrated the discussions he had held with Mr Bhutto. He reciprocated the sentiments expressed by General Zia and stated that his country wanted peace in the region. He hoped that a way would be found to settle the problem with Pakistan on a fair and honourable basis.

The meeting enabled the two leaders to establish a personal rapport. Both beamed with confidence and looked cheerful as they emerged from their room to join the other guests for dinner. The banquet was a formal diplomatic affair, commensurate with the rich traditions of Afghan hospitality.

In the second round of exclusive talks held the next morning, both the leaders decided to meet again in Pakistan soon. This was followed by a lunch. At the luncheon table, General Zia narrated the gist of his talks with President Daoud. The tour re-established contacts at the highest level. Pakistan-Afghanistan relations took a turn for the better.

On 1 January 1978, the Hyderabad Tribunal, trying the NAP leaders, was abolished. This decision brought peace to Balochistan, restored confidence in the NWFP, and paved the way for an amicable settlement with Afghanistan.

At the invitation of General Zia, President Daoud visited Pakistan from 5 to 8 March 1978. During their lengthy private talks, President Daoud reflected on the past suspicions which had influenced the policy options of the two countries. 'While Pakistan looked towards the West,' said President Daoud, 'Afghanistan moved in another direction.' It appeared that Afghanistan desired better ties with her Muslim neighbours, in her own national interest. Significantly, he disclosed that the emerging thaw between Pakistan and Afghanistan was not to the liking of 'some' countries. Daoud apprehended the risk of 'this region being destabilized,' adding, 'our bilateral friendship is thus of mutual advantage.'

President Daoud congratulated General Zia for taking a bold decision in releasing the Pashtun and Baloch leaders. He warmly appreciated Pakistan's gesture and hoped that the leaders, now free, would play their part in the political life of their country. A difficult job had been made easier, he said, and it would help in reaching a final settlement. He looked to the future with hope and talked about bilateral economic co-operation and cultural exchanges.

General Zia thanked President Daoud for sharing his wide comprehension and agreed with his views. He was keen on reaching a final settlement to the mutual benefit of both the countries. Their bilateral relationship, according to Zia, had a vast potential which should be gainfully developed.

The banquet for President Daoud was carefully planned. Several prominent Pakistani politicians were present on the occasion including the freshly released political leaders: Khan Abdul Wali Khan, Mr Ataullah Mengal, Mr Khair Bakhsh Marri, and Mr Ghaus Bakhsh Bizenjo. President Daoud was visibly pleased to meet them. He mixed with the guests freely and talked to them in a pleasant and warm manner. He displayed a subtle sense of humour. On one occasion, while commenting on the communist factions in Afghanistan, he said: 'They are like water melon—green from outside but red deep within.'

In his speech, President Daoud noted with satisfaction the opening of a new chapter of understanding and goodwill with Pakistan and stated that his talks 'had proved extremely useful and productive.'[13]

Before his departure for Kabul, he addressed a press conference in Rawalpindi in which he was pointedly asked: 'Did the "political difference" between the two countries figure in his talks with General Ziaul Haq?' President Daoud replied crisply: 'Everything was discussed and, with the passage of time, everything would fall in its proper place and time would take care of everything.'[14]

The Afghan delegation did not wish to issue a joint communique at the end of the visit; Pakistan accepted that suggestion. It was decided that the two leaders would meet again in Kabul after a few months.

Before his departure from Pakistan, President Daoud extended his hand for a warm handshake and told General Zia: 'This is the hand of a Pathan promising to establish friendly relation with Pakistan on a firm and durable basis. In the past thirty years, we had taken a stance on an issue. Give me a little time to mould public opinion in my country to effect a change. I intend to convene the Afghan *Loya Jirga* [Tribal Grand Assembly] to take a decision to normalize relations with Pakistan.'

Pathan traditions are deep-rooted and time-tested. Just as their enmity can be passed down from one generation to another, their friendship is equally proverbial—strong, durable, and trustworthy. General Zia was of the opinion that President Daoud would fulfil his commitment. Fate had something else in store for the region.

On 27 April 1978, General Zia was holding a martial law administrators' conference in General Headquarters, Rawalpindi, when the first news about trouble in Afghanistan was received. The fighting which had erupted in Kabul was reported to be an armed *coup* against the government and the situation was confused and unclear. General Zia was asked about Pakistan's response in case President Daoud made a request for assistance. 'I will not hesitate to provide help,' was his prompt reply. The rapid and gory events in Kabul precluded such a course.

* * *

'American foreign policy is controlled by jackasses,' said Mr Nelson Rockefeller on 28 April 1978, at the lunch-table, in the Khyber Rifles Officers' Mess near Landi Kotal, a small town near the Pakistan-Afghanistan border. A day earlier, President Muhammad Daoud had been assassinated in a *coup d'etat* in Kabul.

Mr and Mrs Rockefeller had arrived in Islamabad on 26 April 1978. After a day's visit to Peshawar, their destination was Kabul, where Mr Rockefeller was scheduled to dine with President Daoud on 28 April 1978. The massacre in Kabul forced them to reschedule their tour itinerary. The couple returned to Islamabad in the afternoon of 28 April for a brief halt before proceeding eastward to India and Nepal. They were received at the airport by a small group of officials and the US Ambassador, Mr Arthur W. Hummel Jr. Mr Rockefeller, looking visibly moved, said: 'It is a sad day. I was to have dinner with him [Daoud] tonight.'

After a two-hour stay at the State Guest House, the couple returned to the airport. While boarding his personal aircraft, Mr Rockefeller said: 'I see your [Pakistan's] difficulties. We are with you.'

The official American perception about the developments in Afghanistan was less clear. Washington considered it an internal fight.

History had come full circle. President Daoud had seized power on 17 July 1973, with the support of communist military officers. His assassins were none others than those same officers.

President Nur Muhammad Taraki, who replaced the assassinated Daoud, kept the details of his take-over close to his chest. Unlike democracy, a *coup* takes place in a cloak of secrecy. Despite the official blackout, the pieces of information woven together make an interesting story.

Mir Akbar Khyber, an important communist ideologue of the pro-Soviet Khalq Party in Afghanistan, was killed by an unknown assailant on 17 April 1978. It was claimed by the People's Democratic Party of Afghanistan (PDPA) that he had been murdered by government agents in an attempt to liquidate the left. His death created an uproar. Fiery speeches were made at his burial ceremony, blaming the government for the murder. Put on the defensive, the administration reacted belatedly. On 26 April 1978, Kabul announced the arrest of seven leaders of the Central Committee of the Khalq Party for 'anti-constitutional activities'. Those put behind bars included Mr Nur Muhammad Taraki and Mr Babrak Karmal. The *coup* leaders decided to implement their plan.

Just before midday on 27 April 1978, a column of tanks from the Pul-i-Charkhi barracks occupied the Ministry of Defence. The next target was the Presidential Palace, where a cabinet meeting was being held. The ministers dispersed quickly. After a brief clash with the security forces in the streets of Kabul, the insurgents gained control of the outer perimeter of the palace by 3 p.m. By that time they had achieved another important success. Bagram airfield was under their control. It was then a matter of time. The Afghan Air Force joined the operation and the presidential palace was attacked with rockets. At 7 p.m. the Kabul radio broadcasts in the Pushto and Dari languages said: 'For the first time in the history of Afghanistan, the last remnants of monarchy, tyranny, despotism, and power of the dynasty of Nadir Khan has ended and all powers of the state are in the hands of the people of Afghanistan.'[15]

It also announced the death of President Daoud and his brother Sardar Naim, killed while 'madly resisting' the demand for surrender.[16] The Constitution was abrogated, Mr Nur Muhammad Taraki emerged as the new dictator, and the country was renamed the 'Democratic Republic of Afghanistan'.

There is another version. According to this, President Daoud, Sardar Naim, their family members, and two ministers remained besieged in the presidential palace during the night between 27 and 28 April. The insurgents entered the palace in the early morning of 28 April, after overcoming the resistance offered by the palace guards. 'First some thirty members of Daoud's family were shot in front of his eyes, then several members of his government and finally Daoud himself.'[17]

In the months preceding the *coup*, President Daoud's government was faced with internal and external difficulties. Strains on the Afghan economy had increased public resentment, affecting Daoud's personal popularity. Despite his advanced age, Daoud undertook two strenuous external tours to muster support. Iran offered economic assistance. Some Arab countries promised help. Relations with Pakistan took a turn for the better. To diversify her dependence, Afghanistan had hired experts from the Western countries to work on bilateral economic projects. Such developments alarmed Moscow, whose government considered the foreign experts imperial agents. The Kremlin was unhappy about the resurgence of Islam in Iran and Pakistan. The prospects of Afghanistan following the same route sent shivers down the spine in Moscow. A rightist government in Afghanistan was unacceptable to the Soviet Union because the Soviet republics just north of the Oxus River had sizeable Muslim populations.

The Soviet Union felt that President Daoud had served his purpose and was now dispensable.

Daoud's assassination destabilized Afghanistan and the region, causing grave concern in Pakistan. It could also slow down, if not halt, the ongoing dialogue between the two countries. For a while, it was not clear whether the new leadership would adopt a positive approach towards Pakistan, or would accuse Daoud of adopting a soft policy with her eastern neighbour. Pakistan expected that, because of internal compulsions, it would adopt a confrontational policy. The fog cleared fast. As the *coup* established its writ in the country, Pakistan recognized the new regime. She was not the first but was among the few countries to do so early on.

An Afghan cell had been created in the Foreign Office in July/August 1973. It met regularly for the next three years, under the chairmanship of either Prime Minister Bhutto or Mr Aziz Ahmad, and gave out policy guidelines. The Inspector General Frontier Constabulary and the DGISI worked in concert to conduct intelligence missions inside Afghanistan. The Afghan leaders, Gulbadin Hikmatyar and Rabbani, came into contact with the Pakistani authorities during this period. The Pakistani intelligence agencies also kept communication channels open with the deposed king, Zahir Shah, who was living in exile in Italy. Gradually, the cell became dormant during the final stages of the Bhutto administration.

TURMOIL IN AFGHANISTAN

On 2 May 1978, the Afghan Cell was reactivated in the Foreign Office. Its task was to analyse the available information and suggest policy options. The defence plans were updated as a destabilized Afghanistan had adversely affected the security of Pakistan.

The *coup* leaders in Afghanistan claimed that their 'revolution was secure' and that only 100 persons had lost their lives. The figures given by other sources vary from 1,000 quoted by Louis Dupree[18] to 5,000 by the *Economist*,[19] and 10,000 by ORBIS.[20]

Mr Nur Muhammad Taraki was called the 'true son of the people'. The real power-broker was probably Hafizullah Amin, the Foreign Minister. A US-educated physics graduate and a former bureaucrat, Amin was a diehard communist, indoctrinating the armed forces with Marxist philosophy.

The regime's infighting surfaced within a short span of time. By July 1978, the Parcham party was purged and many of its top leaders, including Babrak Karmal, were eased out on diplomatic assignments in distant countries. In December 1978, a Treaty of Friendship was signed between the Soviet Union and Afghanistan.

In February 1979, the oppressive rule of the Shah of Iran came to a violent end. In the same month, the United States' Ambassador in Kabul, Mr A. Dubbs, was assassinated. The Carter administration continued business as usual, as if these were routine events. Inside Afghanistan, the influence of Mr Hafizullah Amin was on the rise. In July 1979, he became the Minister for Defence and Interior.

Turbulence in Afghanistan caused concern but Pakistan did not lose hope. During General Zia's visit to Iran in September 1978, he had a brief informal stopover in Afghanistan to meet President Nur Muhammad Taraki.

General Zia and his entourage, which included ministers Agha Shahi and Mustafa Gokal touched down at the Kabul International Airport at 9:50 a.m. on 9 September 1978. Mr Hafizullah Amin and Mr Muhammad Aslam Wattanjar received Zia. Kabul airport looked like an operational air force base, with military aircraft and helicopters on the runway, some with their crews standing beside their craft. The security arrangements were extra tight and the reception ceremony simple. The delegation travelled by cars to Paghman Tapa, about 25 kilometers away. Mr Hafizullah Amin accompanied General Zia in his car. Soldiers were conspicuous in the city. About thirty tanks guarded the Presidential Palace, renamed the People's House.

307

The people stared at the visitors with blank eyes and bewilderment writ large on their unsmiling faces. Kabul appeared a living graveyard.

On reaching Paghman Tapa, the delegation was introduced to 'Comrade' Nur Muhammad Taraki who told General Zia: 'The royal family had exploited the Afghan nation for 200 years. Now everything belongs to the people. The revolution has given land to eleven million people. They are now its owners. Our revolution enjoys the support of 98 per cent of the Afghan population. In our new system, individuals do not matter. They can be changed or replaced. It is the party which counts.'

The discussion ran like this:

Zia: As Muslims, we believe that all land belongs to Almighty Allah and man is His custodian on earth.

Taraki: All land belongs to the tiller.

Zia: Human beings must fear God.

Taraki: God is *aadil* [just]. We don't have to fear a just God.

Zia: People have certain obligations towards God and human beings.

Taraki: To serve the people is to serve God.

The two Muslims disagreed on the interpretation of Islamic philosophy. Mr Taraki expressed Afghanistan's opposition to military pacts and enquired abrasively and undiplomatically: 'Why don't you give up your membership of CENTO?'

Ignoring the question, General Zia indicated that his country had no differences with its neighbour and suggested that, in case Afghanistan felt otherwise, Pakistan would be prepared to discuss the subject. Mr Taraki expressed satisfaction on the smooth operation of the transit facilities provided to his country through Pakistan. Then, completely out of context, he counselled: 'If France has refused to provide a reprocessing plant to Pakistan, why don't you ask the USA to build one for you?' This was a dig—Afghan style—at Pakistan's relations with the USA.

Mr Agha Shahi interjected: 'All the developed countries do not wish to share nuclear technology with the developing world.' Taraki quipped: 'Not all of them.' General Zia felt that mutual co-operation would benefit both the countries. Agreeing, Mr Taraki said, 'We will solve our problems peacefully.'

Mr Taraki displayed a sharp mind and a sharper, though blunt sense of humour. General Zia informed him that his Iranian tour would include a visit to the holy city of Mashhad. 'So you will perform two pilgrimages in one trip,' was his immediate response. His dislike of the Shah of Iran was evident. When General Zia introduced Mr Ghulam Mustafa Gokal, Pakistan's Minister for Ports and Shipping, as 'Mr Onassis of Pakistan', Taraki shot back: 'He is free to find his Jackie.'

During lunch, Mr Taraki took pains to emphasize that Khalq was the only political party in Afghanistan. Mr Hafizullah Amin added: 'Parcham is not a political party. It is the name of a magazine.' Then suddenly, with a mischievous smile on his face, Mr Taraki looked at General Zia and said: 'Let us compare notes on how we implemented our respective revolutions.'

Volunteering to speak first, he said: 'We had been planning for thirteen years to bring about a revolution.' After a short pause he said: 'It was so decided amongst ourselves that control would be assumed by whosoever was free at the decisive moment.' Pointing towards Mr Hafizullah Amin, he said, 'He, being out of jail, issued the orders to implement the plan.'

There was a moment's silence. Mr Taraki looked towards General Zia and said, 'Now let us hear how you implemented your revolution.'

'Pakistan, in fact, had no revolution,' said Zia, adding, 'I simply spoke to Mr Bhutto on telephone to inform him that I had taken over the administration of the country. I also promised him his personal safety.'

The four-hour stay in Kabul was brief but interesting. It helped to establish a personal level Zia-Taraki contact. Some personal impressions: Mr Muhammad Aslam Wattanjar was a quiet and uninspiring young man, showing no spark; the quick-witted Mr Hafizullah Amin spoke with confidence; Mr Taraki's sudden rise to power had left him wanting in the poise and dignity expected of a head of state.

Pakistan's Red Shirt leader, Khan Abdul Ghaffar Khan, was residing in Jalalabad, Afghanistan, at the time of the *coup d'etat.* Pakistan's Consul in Jalalabad called on him on 15 August 1978. Khan Abdul Ghaffar Khan was unhappy with the Kabul regime because it would not agreed to toe his line on Pakhtunistan. The Khan told the Consul that the Afghan Government lacked roots and their claim of public support was superficial. He predicted the fall of the Taraki government as it was 'born in violence and had caused indiscriminate bloodshed.' He disclosed that he had told Mr Ajmal Khattak (a Pakistani follower of Ghaffar Khan living in self-exile in Afghanistan) to tell his *naiks* (protectors) that they were treading the path of destruction, devastation, and misery and were heading towards a dark future. The old man was proved right by later events.

During the sixth summit conference of the Non-Aligned Movement (NAM) held at Havana, Cuba, in September 1979, General Zia and Mr Taraki had an exclusive meeting. It was a diplomatic courtesy affair. On his journey home, Mr Taraki spent a few days in Moscow, where he was awarded high protocol. Back in Kabul, the infighting in the ruling clique took a violent turn, in which he was killed in the People's Palace in September 1979. The new strongman who assumed power was Mr Hafizullah Amin.

Mr Hafizullah Amin's rise to power disturbed Moscow which considered him power-hungry and of dubious ideological conviction. Declassified Politburo documents released after the collapse of the Soviet Union indicate that the KGB had prepared a plan to remove him from the scene and Moscow had approved its implementation.

Amin's government invited Pakistan's Adviser on Foreign Affairs to visit Afghanistan for bilateral discussions to remove any misunderstandings. Mr Agha Shahi's arrival in Kabul, planned for 22 December, had to be postponed at the last moment because the airport was reportedly snow-bound. The visit was rescheduled for 29 December.

On 26 December 1979, Soviet troops landed in Kabul. The following day, Amin was killed in the presidential palace by the Soviet forces which were 'protecting' the building. The official report stated that he was executed after being sentenced to death by a Revolutionary court for 'crimes committed against the Afghan people.' Mr Babrak Karmal, leader of the Parcham Party, reappeared from the political wilderness, virtually riding on the Soviet tanks, to be installed as the new President.

On 28 December, a poker-faced Mr Azimov, the Soviet Ambassador in Islamabad, informed General Zia that his country had sent a 'limited military contingent' to Afghanistan at her request to assist her in dealing with 'foreign interference'. Reading from his notes, the ambassador added that the contingent would be withdrawn as soon as its task was done. Asked who had requested for the Soviet forces, he promptly replied: 'Mr Babrak Karmal.'

The Ambassador blushed with embarrassment when the next question was put to him: 'How could Mr Babrak Karmal make a request when he had no position of authority in Kabul and was in fact serving abroad as an ambassador in an East European country?' He fumbled for words and admitted that he was not is possession of all the facts.

It was subsequently declared by the Soviet Union that the Soviet military contingent had been sent in response to requests made 'from time to time' by the Afghan leadership under the provisions of the Soviet-Afghan Treaty of Friendship of December 1978. It was a nice, vague statement to suit all occasions. Churchill had once complimented the Soviet diplomacy by saying that 'the Soviet foreign policy is a riddle wrapped in an enigma.' Lytton had put it more acidly: 'Be more scared of Russian diplomacy than its arms.'

The Soviet decision to invade Afghanistan was taken secretly, without following its own constitutional requirements. Reportedly, the hawks gave Brezhnev the choice of taking action in Afghanistan or quitting.[21] Earlier, by the fall of 1979, over 5,000 Soviet civilian and military advisers had been inducted in Afghanistan.[22] The hush-hush decision to employ the military was known to not more than two or three persons, apart from the President of the USSR.

The Afghans revolted violently against the occupation of their country by the Soviet Union and its surrogates. Its internal security situation, previously simmering, erupted into an open armed conflict —rightists versus leftists. During the next nine years, the Afghan freedom fighters kept the torch of freedom burning with their sweat and blood. In the process, they suffered. Their near and dear ones were killed; their houses and property were destroyed; they were evicted from their lands; their honour and life became unsafe. Confusion and chaos prevailed. The Soviet Union eventually paid a high price for its unprovoked aggression.

Tolstoy once said, 'the two most powerful warriors are patience and time.' The prolonged resistance of the Afghan freedom fighters against a superpower won them the admiration of the free world. The Soviet occupation was condemned, year after year, by the Arab League, the Organization of Islamic Conference, the Non-Aligned Movement, the South Asian Association for Regional Co-operation, the European Economic Community, by the world at large, and by the United Nations General Assembly.

Fifty-one countries, including Pakistan, called upon the United Nations Security Council to deplore the Soviet action and demanded the withdrawal of foreign troops from Afghanistan. The Soviet Union kept blocking the resolution by invoking its veto right. It was her 113th such attempt in the Security Council. The issue was then debated in the United Nations General Assembly which, on 14 January 1980, adopted a resolution with 104 votes in favour, 18 against, and 18 abstentions, demanding the withdrawal of the Soviet forces. That pattern of voting subsequently became an annual feature in that organization till the signing of the Geneva Accord in 1988.

The rape of a weak neighbour stunned the world and threatened regional and international peace. It set a dangerous precedent. If Afghanistan could be a victim, some other country might meet a similar fate in the future to satisfy the ego of some other bully.

Human beings love their ancestral environments. It is not easy for a person to leave his hearth and home to take refuge in a foreign land. As continuing upheavals made life inside Afghanistan unsafe, people started migrating to neighbouring Pakistan and Iran, in search of protection, food, and shelter. A trickle at the beginning, the tempo of the flow accelerated when the Afghan administration adopted a scorched earth policy against political dissidents. Men, women, and children trekked long distances over roads, tracks, and unfrequented routes on trucks, camels and donkeys, and on foot in search of security in Pakistan. By January 1980, over 400,000 persons had reached Pakistan. Their number crossed the one million mark in August of that year and had reached the staggering figure of three million by early 1988.[23]

The refugees were initially lodged in tented village-size camps. The tents did not provide relief to the undernourished refugees from the oppressive heat of Pakistan's summers and the biting cold of its winters. Necessity being the mother of invention, the tents were soon replaced by temporary mud huts. Most of the camp villages were located in the NWFP and Balochistan, along the border with Afghanistan. The Afghan refugees were housed in 344 camps located as under:

Province	Number of Camps	Refugees
NWFP	251	2,238,905
Balochistan	76	672,107
Punjab	16	180,032
Sindh	1	20,076
Total	344	3,111,120

The refugees created administrative, social, and ethnic problems, and placed a heavy economic burden on Pakistan's resources. Despite such difficulties, the people of Pakistan provided humanitarian assistance to them in the tradition of neighbourly brotherhood and in the spirit of Islam. The able-bodied Afghans, after leaving the women, children, old and sick male members of their families in Pakistan, returned to their ancestral areas to wage war against those who had usurped their freedom.

The Soviet military intervention was condemned worldwide, with America setting the tone. Carter called it 'the greatest threat to peace since World War Two.'[24] He asked Brezhnev to withdraw his forces or face serious consequences.[25] The State Department called it 'blatant military intervention in the internal affairs of an independent state.'[26] China strongly condemned the Soviet aggression and asked for the withdrawal of Soviet forces from Afghanistan.[27] The British government declared that the people of Afghanistan had the right to choose their own government without outside interference. France voiced concern.[28] The response from India was muted. The Indian delegation to the United Nations saw no reason to doubt the Soviet claim that its troops had moved into Afghanistan at the invitation of the Afghan government.[29]

A destabilized Afghanistan and the presence of Soviet military forces on her western border worried Pakistan. If the Soviets were allowed to consolidate their hold in Afghanistan, their next target could be Pakistan and Iran. The oil-rich Gulf region was just one country away from the Soviet Union. To subjugate Pakistan would fulfil the age-old Soviet desire to gain access to the warm waters of the Arabian sea. If such were the plans of the Soviet Union, would it vacate the aggression in Afghanistan? President Zia once said: 'It would be the miracle of the twentieth century if the Soviet forces were to withdraw from Afghanistan.'

The large-scale induction of the Soviet troops into Afghanistan brought about a fundamental change in the regional geopolitical environment. Pakistan's security came under enhanced threat. Her eastern border with India had seldom been tension-free. Turmoil in Afghanistan made her western border also insecure. Pakistan was thus faced with a two-directional threat to her national security.

All eyes were focused on Pakistan. Would she buckle under pressure and acquiesce in superpower aggression? The Western countries quickly changed their tune. The arch critics of the autocratic military ruler of Pakistan began to woo him. They suddenly discovered Zia's hitherto unknown 'sterling qualities' and the special importance of Pakistan in the changed circumstances. President Carter telephoned General Zia, reaffirming US support in case of Soviet aggression against Pakistan. There was a flurry of high level visitors to Pakistan, all promising support. These included the British Foreign Secretary, Lord Carrington, on 18 January 1980, the UN Secretary General, on 23 January 1980, and the Secretary General of the OIC, Habib Chatti, on 25 January 1980.

The choices available to Pakistan were hard. Firstly, she could accept the *fait accompli* as she lacked the capacity to challenge the Soviet Union. Secondly, she could provide open and full support to the Afghan freedom struggle, despite the risks involved. And, thirdly, she could give overt political, diplomatic, and humanitarian support to the refugees with covert assistance to the *Mujahideen*.

No choice was cost- or pain-free. The soft-liners argued that it was dangerous for Pakistan to risk her own security for the sake of another country, even a Muslim neighbour. Their reasons included the inherent weakness of Pakistan, the ambivalent attitude of India on the Soviet invasion, the possibility of India and Afghanistan acting in concert against Pakistan, the grave risk of incurring the active hostility of a neighbouring superpower; and the unreliability of a distant United States of America. These were sound arguments, difficult to ignore. It could also not be ignored that the danger posed to Pakistan's national security could not be averted by a policy of appeasement.

Pakistan refused to accept the inevitability of the situation. A passive approach, like a slow poison, could damage the country. The storm in Afghanistan could transcend territorial frontiers and engulf Pakistan. Besides, it was unethical to acquiesce in an unjust and unprincipled action.

Of her own free will, Pakistan adopted the third option to protect her national interest and to uphold a vital principle. She criticized the Soviet military intervention in Afghanistan because it was against internationally recognized norms and principles, enshrined in the Charter of the United Nations, which prohibited member states from interfering in the internal affairs of other countries. Pakistan's position was supported by the Organization of Islamic Conference, on whose initiative the 7th plenary meeting of the United Nations General Assembly adopted a resolution laying down, among others, four principles to settle the Afghanistan problem. These were:

1. The preservation of the sovereignty, territorial integrity, political independence, and the non-aligned character of Afghanistan.
2. The right of the Afghan people to determine their own form of government and choose freely their own economic, political, and social system.
3. The immediate withdrawal of all foreign troops from Afghanistan.
4. The creation of the necessary conditions to enable the Afghan refugees to return voluntarily to their homes in honour and safety.

For eight long years Pakistan remained under relentless Soviet pressure. On 12 February 1980, the Soviet Foreign Minister, Mr Andrei Gromyko, warned Pakistan that by converting itself into a 'springboard for further escalation of aggression against Afghanistan', Pakistan was taking a grave risk. The tone and tenor of the Soviet diplomatic barrages from 1980 through 1988 remained unchanged. The Soviet Union accused Pakistan of providing training and other facilities to the Afghan *Mujahideen* and warned her of 'unpredictable consequences'. Moscow flooded Islamabad with harshly worded messages indicating that Pakistan was 'hurting Soviet interests.' Pakistan was accused of being in a state of 'undeclared war' with Afghanistan. She was warned that if she persisted with her attitude, the onus of responsibility for the consequences that might ensue would rest on her.

On her part, Pakistan repeatedly denied having provided military facilities to the resistance movement. She claimed to follow a steadfast course, based on the universally recognized principles of non-interference and non-intervention in the internal affairs of another country. She provided humanitarian assistance to the refugees who had taken shelter in Pakistan. She argued that the basic cause of the conflict—the induction of Soviet forces in Afghanistan—should be removed and the people of that country should not be denied their inalienable right to be the masters of their own destiny.

The Soviet diplomatic *demarches* were supported by military threats and provocations. During the period 1980 to March 1989, Pakistan's air space was subjected to intrusion by the Afghan Air Force on 2,730 occasions, killing or wounding 1,355 civilians. In the same period, Pakistan's territory was violated by artillery fire 2,599 times in which over 1,000 persons were killed or wounded The year-wise records of the violations of Pakistan's air and land space are summarized in Annexure 1. The considerable damage caused to property remained unassessed. Pakistan faced these provocations calmly. Such arm-twisting tactics and threats of hot pursuit were a part of Soviet psychological pressure to coerce Pakistan into submission.

The Soviet and Afghan intelligence made deep inroads into Pakistan, particularly in areas close to the Durand Line. Their subversive activities were aimed at creating anarchy and destabilizing the government, while the border and air space violations caused panic. The government was blamed for not ensuring the safety of the people. Retaliation by Pakistan would have hurt the people of Afghanistan, who needed sympathy and assistance, not bullets fired at them in anger. The Soviet and Afghanistan attempts to exert military pressure on the border areas was an act of desperation, not strength. The 100,000 Soviet troops were absorbed in the Afghan war. This quantum of force was inadequate for invading Pakistan. Besides, the attack on Pakistan would have created political issues of larger dimensions. The Soviet Union was not unaware of US commitments to Pakistan in the face of communist or communist-sponsored aggression.

Besides the influx of Afghan refugees, there were other negative spill-over effects. Pakistan became a market for Afghan arms. The free weapon trade enabled local miscreants to equip themselves with sophisticated hardware. This gave birth to the phenomenon called the Kalashnikov culture in the country. During the ten-year period, 1,617 cases of sabotage were carried out in which 890 persons were killed and 3,201 wounded. The breakdown of sabotage incidents, year-wise, and the casualties caused by them is at Annexure 2.

Pakistan also faced the menace of narcotics. The opium and heroin produced in Afghanistan found an outlet to the Western countries through Pakistan. Opium cultivation in Pakistan showed an increase.

The influx of weapons and the narcotics trade were the inescapable consequences of the porous Pakistan-Afghanistan border. No government in Pakistan could have prevented this phenomenon. Movement of goods, services, and people traditionally takes place unhindered across the Durand Line into the contiguous tribal territory of Pakistan.

The invisible fallout was more serious. Pakistan's humanitarian assistance to Afghanistan was not without a price. Under cover of monitoring the flow of goods and services provided by them to the *Mujahideen*, the donor countries increased their diplomatic and other presence in Pakistan. This included a sprinkling of their intelligence personnel. In the final analysis, the flow of aid tapered off, the Afghan crisis underwent a change, but many of the foreign intelligence appendages became permanent parts of the regular embassy staff of the countries concerned.

It is for historians to debate whether the induction of Soviet military forces into Afghanistan could have been avoided. An article, 'Secrets from CIA Archives in Tehran', suggests that the Afghanistan invasion might have been averted.[30] The archives of the CIA and the State Department documents held in the US Embassy in Tehran had been seized by Iran in 1979. This was said to be the most extensive loss of secret data in the history of the diplomatic service. The article claimed that five months before the Soviet tanks entered Afghanistan, Moscow had used diplomatic contacts to convey its intentions to the United States to test her reaction. Implicit in those messages was the Soviet claim to a 'legitimate' sphere of influence in this region and her responsibility for preventing the breakdown of law and order in a neighbouring state. The article drew the conclusion that, had Washington contradicted the Soviet assertion and warned Moscow against a military adventure, the tragedy that befell Afghanistan might have been avoided. The Carter administration did not publicly reveal the Soviet military intention that summer. Washington's silence was presumably taken by Moscow as a tacit green signal for its military intervention in Afghanistan. The United States neither confirmed nor denied the substance of that article.

General Zia had kept President Carter informed about the serious developments in Afghanistan. Soon after the assassination of President Daoud, he wrote a long letter to Carter conveying his deep concern to America about the danger in Afghanistan and its implications for the region. The Carter administration dismissed Pakistan's apprehensions as overreaction. It preached human rights but failed to protect them. This was a time when Pakistan-US relations were at an all-time low. Pakistan had informed the United States that, notwithstanding difficulties in their bilateral relationship, there was a need to act in unison in Afghanistan. America agreed in principle but did little in reality.

President Ronald Reagan took office in January 1981. His election as US President brought about a perceptible change in US policy. The United States and Pakistan established a closer relationship. Washington started providing weapons to the Afghan freedom fighters. At first, their flow was a trickle and the weapons provided were often outdated. Nor were the semi-literate Afghan *Mujahideen* trained to handle sophisticated weapons. Gradually, the amount of aid and the type of weapons improved. Correspondingly, the scope and intensity of fighting in the freedom struggle increased, reaching a high mark in the years 1985-7. The American assistance to the Afghan *Mujahideen*, which kept increasing, was a critical factor in tilting the operational balance against the Soviet Union. In the final analysis, America provided over two billion dollars of covert assistance to the Afghan freedom struggle. The supply of US weapons was controlled by the CIA at the Washington end. It started as a covert affair. Leaks in the American Press gradually made it an open secret. At the Islamabad end, the weapons were distributed to the Afghan freedom fighters through the Inter-Services Intelligence Directorate (ISID). Initially, the role of the ISI Directorate was limited in scope, confined to intelligence work and some co-ordination. Gradually, it kept expanding and ultimately it was fully involved in *Mujahideen* activities. As a matter of policy, the ISI Directorate role was low profile during the life of General Zia. Zia kept a firm grip on all its operational matters. His policies were loyally implemented by DG ISI Lieutenant-General Akhtar Abdur Rahman.

The induction of modern weapon systems, like the anti-aircraft Stinger missiles, and the handling of explosives for the demolition of military and economic targets justified the need for training the *Mujahideen*. The training was imparted in *ad hoc* camps organized by the ISI Directorate, with instructors provided by the army. While the top military leaders and the cabinet members were generally aware that Pakistan was supporting the Afghan struggle, the details were kept secret.

Since US assistance to the *Mujahideen* started as a covert affair, the ISI Directorate was used as a channel. Besides ensuring the secrecy of the effort, it had the expertise to advise the *Mujahideen* on guerrilla tactics. The ISI Directorate received the weapons from the CIA, stored them, and distributed them to the *Mujahideen* groups on the basis of their performance in Afghanistan. The system worked well. In the process, CIA-ISI contacts developed. General Akhtar and the director of the CIA, William Casey, exchanged visits, approved the psychological warfare plans, and shared the intelligence data on Afghanistan between their two agencies. Inside Pakistan, Akhtar met the leaders, sometimes alone and on other occasions in the company of General Zia. On occasion, Foreign Minister Sahabzada Yaqub Khan was also present. Such meetings were seldom publicized. The lines were clearly drawn. General Zia set the policy guidelines; Akhtar did the ground work. The Army had no direct involvement in the struggle raging inside Afghanistan. Its operational task was to defend the country, along with its sister services.

As fighting intensified inside Afghanistan, the involvement of the ISI in that struggle increased. It started handling operational matters for which it lacked expertise and resources. Military operations and military intelligence are two different subjects, even though they go side by side. In all armies of the world, they are handled by separate departments, under specialized military experts. For reasons of secrecy these were combined in the ISI Directorate to support the *Mujahideen* struggle. This was a calculated risk, the merits and demerits of which should have been subjected to indepth professional analysis. It worked well under the guidance and personal control of Zia. Akhtar, a loyal and dutiful subordinate, had no illusions. He knew his own limits and marched in harmony with the tune expertly played by Zia. When criticized in the Afghan Cell and the military formation commanders conferences about the statistics of casualties and loss of equipment in the Afghan war, Akhtar usually disclosed the obvious, while concealing the vital details, knowing that General Zia, who invariably presided over these meetings, was well aware of the actual facts. Zia was usually briefed in advance of these meeting.

The system suddenly collapsed with the death of General Zia. The Benazir administration had a different policy on Afghanistan. She spoke of the futility of the *Mujahideen* operations and sought a quick end to the conflict, without evolving an alternative action plan. With wavering political support and a lack of professional guidance, the ISI Directorate was left alone to handle the workload. In early 1989, edged on by the CIA, the ISI Directorate committed the *Mujahideen* to a conventional military attack for the capture of Jalalabad. The mission failed. The half-trained guerrilla fighters were incapable of launching a set-piece attack against a well-defended city. The

Jalalabad fiasco exposed the ISI Directorate. When the town did not fall despite its firm assurance that it would, the ISI became a target of criticism.

A disillusioned Benazir made a partial policy change. In 1989, for the first time, the Chief of Army Staff, General Mirza Aslam Beg, who had succeeded to that position after the death of Zia in August 1988, was actively inducted into the Afghan war with a co-ordinating role given to him. In this capacity, he started meeting the *Mujahideen* leaders and advised the ISI Directorate on military and political matters. This created a dichotomy. Not surprisingly, the ISI Directorate and General Headquarters soon started pulling in different directions. For inexplicable reasons, high level meetings on Afghanistan, in which policy decisions were taken, were also attended by the US ambassador in Islamabad, Mr Robert Oakley, who earned the nickname of 'the Viceroy of Pakistan.'

Zia had suspected that, at some stage, America might undercut Pakistan. He had ordered the ISI Directorate to prevent Americans from meeting the *Mujahideen* leaders and commanders on their own on Pakistani soil. This policy was fully implemented during his lifetime. The situation underwent a change after his death. The Benazir administration was too weak to resist American pressure. The American officials started meeting the *Mujahideen* leaders directly, to the exclusion of the Pakistani officials. The Americans had their own policy objectives to achieve. Leaning towards the moderates, they told those Afghan leaders, who in turn informed Pakistani authorities, to distance themselves from Pakistan as she had a soft spot for the fundamentalist Afghan leaders.

There was another factor at work. The intimate involvement of *Mujahideen* leaders with the ISI Directorate worked to the disadvantage of the Foreign Office, engaged in the Geneva talks. While they knew that the *Mujahideen* conducted their operations with foreign weapons and Pakistani support, the Pakistani negotiators were generally unaware of the details. The ISI Directorate frequently briefed the Foreign Office about the *Mujahideen* operations, but without disclosing their own contribution and the nature of the material support received from abroad.

The United States was not alone in providing assistance to the Afghan *Mujahideen*. Some Arab countries, notably Saudi Arabia, made financial contributions, mostly in concert with America. Such developments further chilled Pakistan-Soviet relations. The assignment of Pakistan's ambassador in Moscow during the Afghan crisis was thorny. On a regular basis, he faced diplomatic threats and angry statements. The ambassador's messages to Islamabad were seldom cheerful in tone and tenor. Professor Yuri Gankovsky, Chairman of the Department of South-West Asia, Institute of Oriental Studies, Moscow (later President of the Soviet-Pakistan Friendship Society), once narrated to him a Russian proverb about two elephants: When the elephants fought, the grass got trampled. And the grass met the same fate when elephants made love. The message was clear: stay out of the superpower rivalry.

In Islamabad, the Soviet ambassador was no less aggressive. He invariably had something urgent and less than pleasant to convey to the government. He once suggested that Pakistan should seal her border with Afghanistan to prevent the entry of 'insurgents' into Afghanistan. He was told that the porous mountainous nature of the border precluded such a possibility. Pakistan would not object if Afghanistan, supported by the Soviet forces, closed the border from its own side. The ambassador said dejectedly: 'It is not possible.'

It was also proposed by the Soviet Union that the Afghan refugee camps be shifted away from the border belt and the Afghan leaders separated from their people. The purpose of such impractical suggestions was to create a rift between the refugees and the people and government of Pakistan. Pakistan was told that the Soviet support to Afghanistan was enduring and irreversible. It would be of advantage to Pakistan, so ran the argument, not to miss the historic opportunity for the sake of expediency. A positive approach would pave the way for a lasting settlement of the issue which had long defied solution between Pakistan and Afghanistan.

To face the Soviet wrath for a full decade was an unenviable situation. Sceptics felt that it was foolhardy Pakistan to get involved in an unequal contest. However, the inner strength of *jihad* defies quantification in mathematical terms. At times, the pressure became unbearable. Under such conditions, many senior bureaucrats and, politicians wavered, and intellectuals questioned the wisdom of Pakistan's Afghan policy. The moral and diplomatic pressure from the world community, exerted from a safe distance, had its limits. It did not prevent the killing of Pakistanis, which had psychological repercussions within the country, and led to questioning of the validity of Pakistan's policy and the imperatives of its security. However, Zia stood firm. Increase in pressure hardened his resolve to lead his nation from the front. He was convinced of the righteousness of the cause and he followed the course relentlessly. Zia's inner circle supported him on this issue.

At the policy-making level in Islamabad, the Afghan Cell meetings were held frequently, in which policy options were considered and decisions taken. The meetings were invariably presided over by the President and were attended by the relevant governors, federal ministers, and concerned officials. The topics discussed included the diplomatic options available in handling the Afghan situation, the humanitarian aid received from donor countries and international organizations and its utilization, logistic issues concerning the welfare of the refugees, and the law and order problem. Each meeting lasted many hours. Decisions on the diplomatic approach were implemented by the Ministry of Foreign Affairs. The Ministry of States and Frontier Regions and the provincial governments took care of the administrative efforts concerning the care of the refugees. The business of the supply of weapons to the *Mujahideen*, handled by the ISI Directorate, was not discussed in the meetings. This was handled separately for reasons discussed earlier. One subject which caused anxiety was the disunity in the ranks of the Afghan *Mujahideen*. Despite considerable efforts, not much headway was made in this regard. Afghan tribal society is very possessive of its rights. It does not shed power if it can help it.

The inevitable happened. The dynamics of the game of power eventually came into play. As war raged in Afghanistan, the participants of the Afghan Cell meetings became aware of who was fuelling it from Pakistan. Since this subject was not analysed, oblique references were made by the participants. In some meetings, the Foreign Minister, Sahabzada Yaqub Khan, complained that the Foreign Office faced the difficulty of defending Pakistan's Afghan policy which was made, to a large extent, by 'other departments'. It was not desirable, he pointed out, to place all the Afghan eggs in one basket. It was a faulty approach, according to him, that the provision of equipment, as well as planning, implementation, supervision, intelligence, operations, and the analysis of the operational tasks were all handled by the same agency.

The Junejo administration (March 1985) initially supported the Zia approach on the Afghan dispute. By late 1987, it started to drift from the previous course.

Pakistan had started supporting the freedom struggle at a time when world attention had yet to focus on events in Afghanistan. In the process, the *Mujahideen* developed implicit faith in Pakistan, and they felt assured that the Zia administration would neither waver in its determination to support their cause nor compromise their interests for reasons of expediency. To them, as to some others, 'Zia was almost a mystical leader in the region'.[31]

As the war gained in intensity inside Afghanistan, diplomatic efforts were initiated to find a political solution to the dispute. These included the 14 May 1980 proposal by Babrak Karmal for bilateral talks between Afghanistan and its 'neighbours';[32] the European Economic Community proposal put forward by Lord Carrington on 30 June 1980; and the three-member OIC Committee directed to hold negotiations with the representatives of the Kabul regime without recognizing it.[33] The United Nations General Assembly had asked its Secretary General, on 20 November 1980, to appoint a representative for seeking a political settlement of the Afghan issue. On 2 January 1981, Pakistan requested the UN Secretary General to nominate a special representative to handle the Afghanistan problem. Kabul agreed to talk to Iran and Pakistan under UN auspices.[34] On 11 February 1981, the UN Secretary General nominated Mr Javier Perez de Cuellar as his special representative.

Indirect talks started in Geneva on 25 June 1982. Between 1982 and 17 April 1988, ten rounds of talks were held between Pakistan and Afghanistan, resulting in the signing of the Geneva Accord. The Afghan *Mujahideen* did not participate in these discussions, though they were kept fully informed of their progress by Pakistan. So was Iran, which had stayed out of the Geneva talks. Iran had adopted a two-track approach on the Afghan struggle. Politically, it supported the *Mujahideen*. Those Afghan refugees who had taken shelter inside Iran were mostly moved away from the border belt and kept in camps under strict supervision and their movements were controlled. Iran started taking a greater interest in the Afghan freedom struggle at about the time when the Geneva Accord was signed. Obviously, her eyes were focused on the post-settlement era.

In December 1987, Mr Mikhail Gorbachev informed the US President, Ronald Reagan, of the Soviet intention to withdraw her forces from Afghanistan. Later, the Soviet Foreign Minister expressed Moscow's desire to complete the pulling out process within 1988. The stage was set for the accord.

At that crucial point of time, a divergence of opinion surfaced in Pakistan. General Zia, the architect of the Afghan policy, wanted the Geneva accord to *ipso facto* include an agreement on the formation of a broad-based transitional government in Kabul. He issued firmly-worded statements to this effect. The Soviet Union, for reasons of her own compulsion, had de-linked the withdrawal of forces from other factors. As a measure of pressure tactics, she fixed a deadline, 19 March 1988, for the signing of the Geneva Agreement. A stalemate ensued at Geneva.

Pakistan's Afghan policy was not free from criticism. Some political parties (other than the rightists) castigated the Zia administration for following a dangerous course. They blamed General Zia for fanning the Afghan dispute to prolong his autocratic rule. Prime Minister Junejo was called an ineffective head of government and a puppet nominee of the President. Policy decisions, they argued, were taken by the President. Zia-Junejo differences already existed. Their echoes were clearly heard in the corridors of power in Islamabad. The climax was reached in 1988. To weaken General Zia, Mr Junejo played a political card. The National Assembly debated the Afghan policy, and a majority of the members spoke in favour of reaching an early settlement at Geneva, as advocated by the Prime Minister. He then called an All Parties Conference on a country-wide level, outside the National Assembly, to elicit the views of the political leaders on the Afghan issue. A majority of the assembled leaders advocated an early settlement. These efforts eroded the position of General Zia and strengthened Mr Junejo's stance. As a consequence, Pakistan decided to sign the Geneva Accord without first reaching a settlement on the vital question of the formation of an interim government in Afghanistan.

The strategy was sound. A political problem needed a political solution. The Junejo government, however, adopted a simplistic approach in handling a complex subject. Their negotiating stance betrayed a lack of skill and finesse. International negotiations on complicated political issues are seldom easy to handle. They require professional competence, patience, a sense of humour, strong nerves, and an ability to persevere in a less than congenial atmosphere. A good negotiator, like a poker player, keeps his cards close to his chest and knows how and when to call a bluff. Pakistan adopted an open approach during the crucial final stage of the Geneva negotiations. By holding well-publicized debates on her foreign policy, Pakistan compromised her own manoeuvrability at the negotiating table. To the delight of the Soviets, these debates highlighted policy rifts in Pakistan. Moscow found Pakistan wavering and divided. The Soviet Union seized the opportunity, hardened its negotiating position, declined to compromise, and, as part of pressure tactics, kept accusing Pakistan of adopting a negative approach in concluding a peaceful settlement of the issue. Pakistan's chief negotiator at Geneva issued statements indicating that he was awaiting the nod from Islamabad. Put on the defensive, Pakistan lost the initiative.

In the final analysis, it was the two superpowers who reached an agreement on the details of the Geneva Accord, after a flurry of cipher messages exchanged between Washington, Moscow, and Geneva. The parties concerned directly then signed on the dotted line.

It is of some importance to consider how, when, and why the issue of the formation of an interim transitional government was de-linked from the question of the withdrawal of Soviet forces. Mr Zain Noorani, Pakistan's Minister of State for Foreign Affairs, said: 'In Washington, I was told that so far as the question of a transitional government was concerned, the Soviets had also been asking for it. In fact, it was only on the insistence of Pakistan that the US had persuaded the Soviet Union to de-link the withdrawal of troops from this question. Mr Shultz told me that Sahabzada Yaqub, who was then Foreign Minister, had persuaded him to get the Soviets to agree to this. It was, therefore, difficult for the US to go back to the Soviets and argue with them in reverse.'[35]

There is another version. At about the time when Mr Junejo was busy meeting the Opposition leaders, General Zia did his own homework on the Afghanistan issue. In March 1988, I received an invitation from the President. On reaching the Army House, I learnt that I was to meet the President, along with Mr Ghulam Ishaq Khan, Mr Agha Shahi, and Lieutenant-General A. I. Akram, the Director General of the Institute of Regional Studies, Islamabad. In that meeting, General Zia was asked to give reasons for the United States agreeing to the withdrawal of Soviet forces without simultaneously demanding the formation of a transitional government. General Zia stated that the Soviet Union had initially been keen to negotiate on both the issues together, but the two superpowers could not reach an agreement on the modalities. At that stage, Mr Shultz had suggested to Mr Shevardnadze that they should de-link the two issues and settle the question of withdrawal first. The Soviet Union agreed. Pakistan was informed about this development long after the two superpowers had already reached an agreement on this point. She was thus faced with a *fait accompli*. In reply to another question, Zia stated that the Soviet decision to pull out her troops from Afghanistan had in fact taken Pakistan's Foreign Office by surprise. It had not done adequate homework to meet such a contingency.

The Geneva Accord helped the United States to achieve her strategic goal of securing the withdrawal of Soviet forces from Afghanistan. Moscow had been humiliated. The remaining elements of the Afghan dispute were not of vital concern to her. She was in fact in search of an Afghan solution in which the *Mujahideen* did not emerge as a dominant power. Their 'fundamentalism', an asset to the United States while resisting the Soviet invasion, was now held against them. Pakistan's sustained and substantial support to the Afghan resistance struggle had helped to defeat the Soviet intervention.

Moscow had miscalculated her military venture. The Kremlin learnt the hard way that Afghanistan was not just Kabul. The writ of the Soviet-installed government was confined to the bigger cities. The freedom fighters dominated the vast countryside, ambushing Soviet and Afghan government troops and destroying bridges and equipment. With mounting losses and no sign of a military victory in sight, the Soviet Union realized that the problem needed a political solution.

The Soviet Union lost three top leaders in quick succession. General Secretary Leonid Brezhnev died in November 1982. President Zia attended his funeral in Moscow on 15 November 1982, where he met his successor, Yuri Andropov. In failing health, Mr Andropov looked tired, lacking enthusiasm and dynamism. General Zia found him polite and businesslike, relying heavily on his notes. He told President Zia: 'Please stop interference from Pakistan if you wish the Soviet troops to withdraw from Afghanistan.'

On Mr Andropov's death in February 1984, Mr Konstantin Chernenko became the General Secretary. He died in March 1985. This time too, President Zia took part in the funeral ceremony held in Moscow. While there, he met the new General Secretary, Mikhail Gorbachev. The meeting was less than cordial.

Gorbachev's assumption of power brought wide-ranging changes in the Soviet Union's policies. In February 1986, in his address to the 27th Congress of the Communist Party of the Soviet Union, he described Afghanistan as a 'bleeding wound', and added: 'We would like in the near future to withdraw the Soviet troops stationed in Afghanistan.'

In May 1986 Dr Najibullah replaced Mr Babrak Karmal. Two months later, Mr Gorbachev, in a speech made at Vladivostok, referred to the Soviet 'window to the East' and expressed the desire to improve relations with all Asian states. In November that year, Mikhail Gorbachev visited New Delhi where he talked about an 'independent non-aligned neutral Afghanistan' and adopted a conciliatory tone towards Pakistan.

After protracted negotiations spread over six years, the Geneva Accord was signed on 14 April 1988. The Soviet Union now called her military intervention in Afghanistan 'a great mistake' and an act which 'was uncalled for, unnecessary and without public support.' Foreign Minister Shevardnadze said: 'We used to call it an international duty but it would be more correct to call it an invasion.'[36]

The Soviet Union paid a heavy price for its Afghan adventure. The Soviet Prime Minister, Mr Nikolai Ryzhkov, declared in June 1989 that the war in Afghanistan had cost his country 70 billion US dollars—an average of nearly 8 billion US dollars per year. On 25 May 1988, General Alexei Lizichev, head of the Chief Political Directorate of the Army and the Navy disclosed in a news conference held in Moscow that 13,310 Soviet soldiers had died in the war in Afghanistan up to the beginning of May of that year. He gave the number of Soviet wounded as 35,478, with 311 men listed as missing in action. Even if these statistics are accepted as correct, the cost of the misadventure was heavy. The equipment losses suffered by the Soviet Union included 800 tanks, 1,113 armoured personnel carriers, 7,766 vehicles, 882 guns and mortars, and 1,486 aircraft and helicopters.

The Afghan government admitted having lost 195,000 troops and supporters killed and another 80,000 wounded. The decade-long struggle had left its scars on all facets of Afghan life. Over 2,000 kilometers of paved roads and 3,000 kilometers of secondary roads were damaged. This constituted seventy per cent and twenty-five per cent of the two types of road respectively. 350 bridges of various types and spans located in different parts of the country were rendered inoperative. Twenty per cent of the total transport fleet, constituting 5,000 trucks, was destroyed. Five million heads of cattle, twenty per cent of the total livestock population, were killed. Another 1.35 million heads of cattle were moved out of Afghanistan. The insurgency curtailed traditional exports: fruits, vegetables, nuts, carpets, skins, cotton, and natural gas. Major crop production in the agricultural sector dropped between thirty and seventy-five per cent, affecting wheat, rice, cotton, and sugar beet.

The Geneva Accord was a compromise on the conflicting interests of different groups. It had weaknesses: the Soviet withdrawal did not end hostilities in Afghanistan and the freedom struggle continued; over three million refugees remained in Pakistan. The projections of Pakistan's intelligence services and the CIA about the inability of Dr Najibullah's government to survive after the Soviet forces had left Afghanistan proved wrong. The Afghans failed to reach a consensus on the formation of a broad-based caretaker government.

At the policy level, the changes of governments that took place in Pakistan had their own impact. The Junejo administration had weakened Pakistan's position on the Afghanistan issue. With Junejo's exit in May 1988 and Zia's death in August that year, the Afghan policy fell into disarray. Benazir Bhutto's administration demonstrated a lack of direction in its Afghan policy initiatives.

A number of factors helped to bring about the Geneva Accord. These included the unwavering support given by Pakistan to the Afghan struggle; the generous help provided by the USA, the Arab countries, and the world at large; the Soviet Union's decision to disengage; and, above all, the relentless struggle waged by the people of Afghanistan to regain their freedom. Their heroic deeds have won them the applause of the free world. The end result of the Geneva Accord might have been different if the *Mujahideen* had been direct party to it. The story of the Afghan struggle is incomplete without rich tribute being paid to the 1.2 million Afghan men, women, and children who died in the combat, upholding the torch of their country's freedom. Their courage was a beacon of light. Their passion for liberty was irresistible. They displayed an indomitable will. These were the traits which helped the Afghan nation to achieve what President Zia had once called the 'miracle of the twentieth century'.

ANNEXURE 1

GROUND/AIR VIOLATIONS STATISTICS

Year	Violations			Casualties		
	Air	Ground	Total	Air	Ground	Total
1980	192	–	192	Statistics		
1981	120	27	147	not available		
1982	67	26	93			
1983	102	125	227	11	8	19
1984	165	129	294	277	165	442
1985	348	405	753	107	50	157
1986	774	663	1,437	152	308	460
1987	657	778	1,435	723	310	1,033
1988	292	435	727	85	165	250
1989	13	11	24	–	1	1
TOTAL	2,730	2,599	5,329	1,355	1,007	2,362

ANNEXURE 2

SABOTAGE INCIDENTS AND CASUALTIES

Year	Number of Incidents	Killed	Injured
1980	14	32	27
1981	29	6	13
1982	66	20	60
1983	104	13	91
1984	77	71	180
1985	127	74	180
1986	381	214	694
1987	414	269	1,437
1988	395	185	511
1989 (up to March)	10	6	8
TOTAL	1,617	890	3,201

CHAPTER 13

An Unequal Friendship

Pakistan's relations with the USA have had a chequered history. From the time of Partition, Pakistan felt threatened by the hegemonic attitude of her much larger neighbour. India's continual threats and the crises she imposed on Pakistan forced the latter to look for ways to ensure her territorial integrity. Prime Minister Liaquat Ali Khan's visit to the US in May 1950 and the Korean crisis of 1951 brought Pakistan close to the USA. A flurry of high-level meetings between the two countries in 1953 set the stage for mutual co-operation. On 19 May 1954, the Mutual Defence Assistance Agreement was signed. The same year, Pakistan joined the South-East Asia Treaty Organization (SEATO) and, a year later, the Baghdad Pact, later renamed the Central Treaty Organization (CENTO). She became 'America's most allied ally in Asia.' In 1959, the Pakistan-US Bilateral Agreement of Co-operation was signed, and the US agreed to provide military aid to Pakistan.

The US military equipment helped to replace some obsolescent hardware, but the price paid by Pakistan was high. She became addicted to US assistance and her indigenous defence production effort was neglected. The diplomatic cost was higher still. Pakistan earned the ire of the nearby superpower, the Soviet Union.

The Sino-Indian border clash in 1962, and the speed and manner in which the US rushed military aid to India, aroused doubts in Pakistan about her own status as an ally and placed a 'tremendous strain on Pakistan's friendship with America'.[1] In her search for peace and security, she developed friendly ties with China, a step that was highly distasteful to the US.

In the Indo-Pakistan war of 1965, the United States suspended military aid to both India and Pakistan. The arms embargo hit Pakistan hard because, unlike India, she was almost totally dependent on the US for the supply of weapons. The US policy amounted to encouraging India to aggress against Pakistan.

During the Nixon administration, there was an upturn in USA-Pakistan bilateral relations. Pakistan earned the appreciation and the gratitude of the US policy-makers when she played a role as a bridge between that country and China. The US attitude during the East Pakistan crisis of 1971 was generally sympathetic. It helped to end the war on the West Pakistan border. In the Bhutto era, the relationship remained cool.

There emerged a new area of friction. In 1976-7, Pakistan's efforts to acquire nuclear technology were opposed by the United States. In April 1977, the United States suspended project aid to Pakistan on the grounds that the latter had concluded an agreement with France to buy a reprocessing plant. Pakistan was advised to cancel that agreement. When she did not buckle under to US pressure, in September 1977, the Carter administration cut off military and economic assistance to Pakistan. This was subsequently restored in October 1978 after France, yielding to the US demand, suspended the reprocessing plant contract. Pakistan-USA relations reached a new low in 1977-8, when President Jimmy Carter visited Tehran and New Delhi but meaningfully avoided including Islamabad in his tour itinerary.

In July 1977, the Zia administration had to contend with a sagging economy, a depleted treasury, chilly Pakistan-American relations, and a World Bank and International Monetary Fund reluctant to help Pakistan. The United States exploited Pakistan's weakness and exerted diplomatic and economic pressure on her to give up the Chashma reprocessing plant and to sign the Non-Proliferation Treaty.

In September 1978, while attending the 33rd session of the United Nations' General Assembly, Mr Agha Shahi, Pakistan's Adviser on Foreign Affairs, and I met the American Secretary of State, Mr Cyrus Vance, in New York. Mr Agha Shahi made a request for US assistance in Pakistan's efforts to seek loans from the World Bank and the IMF. Mr Vance gave an evasive diplomatic response.

The details of the Shahi-Vance meeting were communicated to Islamabad. Mr Agha Shahi received instructions to seek an appointment either with President Carter or Mr Vance for a message to be conveyed to them before returning to Pakistan. The State Department indicated that Mr Vance had an extremely busy schedule during the coming few days. Mr Agha Shahi returned to Pakistan with this diplomatic rebuff.

The assassination of President Daoud of Afghanistan in 1978 initially failed to shake off the lethargy of the Carter administration. The indifference shown by it to Pakistan's assessment as conveyed to Washington was hard to comprehend. America considered the events in Kabul an internal strife in a distant West Asian country. The Vietnam syndrome had made her a prisoner of her own power.

The Afghan government celebrated the first anniversary of the Saur Revolution on 27 April 1979. During the year, a civil war had broken out in Afghanistan. Afghan refugees had started crossing into Pakistan from 1978. This influx increased in 1979, and especially after the Soviet invasion in December of that year. Waking up from its slumber, the US government reacted in April 1979. Pakistan was informed that America recognized the Durand Line as the Pakistan-Afghanistan international boundary and was prepared to send a team to Islamabad to discuss the security problems of the region. The United States also expressed its willingness to conditionally lift its embargo on economic aid to Pakistan, her nuclear programme notwithstanding.

The Soviet action had caught the US napping. America found herself ill-prepared to reverse the tide. Her concern was shown in President Carter's State of the Union address on 23 January 1980 in which he said that: 'Any attempt by an outside force to gain control of the Persian Gulf region will be regarded as an assault on the vital interests of the United States of America.' This pronouncement set the pace for the establishment of a US Rapid Deployment Force. It also showed that American vital interest was in the Gulf region—not in Afghanistan.

In the changed geo-strategic political environment, the Carter administration realized the importance of Pakistan. A United States delegation, comprising Dr Zbigniew Brzezinski, the National Security Adviser, and Mr Warren Christopher, Deputy Secretary of State, visited Pakistan in February 1980. During the negotiations, Dr Brzezinski emphasized that an enduring friendship with Pakistan was in the vital interest of the USA. The problem of Afghanistan, he said, was strategic and global in nature. The Soviets should not be allowed to consolidate in Afghanistan and the cost of their presence should be as high as possible. He expressed American unhappiness over the ambivalent stand taken by India on Afghanistan but advised his hosts not to prejudge India. He urged that, 'we should prevent India from becoming a full-fledged ally of the Soviet Union.'

Mr Warren Christopher felt that the US Congress would be prepared to reaffirm the 1959 defence agreement with Pakistan, giving it 'contemporary vitality'. Pakistan inquired if the United States would be prepared to upgrade the 1959 agreement to the level of a binding treaty. 'This would not be possible,' was the reply. The 1959 agreement, as it stood, had not been honoured by America in the past. Moreover implementation was subject to Congressional approval. Such an approval depended on the unpredictable environment and the mood of the American Congress at the time.

The United States offered a $400 million economic and military aid package to Pakistan, spread over a period of eighteen months. It was described by Dr Brzezinski as 'seed money'. Pakistan was informed that the US law would be amended to provide her economic and military assistance by suspending the Glenn and the Symington Amendments which prohibited such assistance to a country that had acquired uranium enrichment or reprocessing technology. Pakistan declined the offer. General Zia telephoned President Carter to inform him of the failure of the talks.

The aid offer would not have enhanced Pakistan's defence capability. The United States was overly-sensitive to the Indian objections. Mr Robert Goheer, the then US ambassador to India, issued a statement which was published in the August 1980 issue of the US Embassy publication, *SPAN*. In this statement, the ambassador said, 'What we did not offer Pakistan, namely large arms supply and a permanent new treaty, is an important measure of the significance which we now attach to our relations with India.'

If the Carter administration had its difficulties, so had Pakistan. The doves in the Foreign Office in Islamabad forcefully argued that Pakistan was in a difficult position, facing the Soviet wrath on her Western border and Indian hostility in the East. Under the circumstances, they felt that it would be imprudent to reject the American offer and risk annoying that superpower. An angry America, in their assessment, could create immense economic problems for Pakistan by prevailing upon the aid-giving countries and agencies to suspend their support to her.

Mr Ghulam Ishaq Khan and I opposed the acceptance of the aid offer. By accepting the aid, Pakistan would have earned the ire of the Soviet Union, without enhancing her defence capability. Mr Agha Shahi agreed with the assessment. If America wished to check Soviet expansionism in the region, she could not afford to lose Pakistan, as the only other access to Afghanistan—via Iran—was closed to her. Pakistan rejected the aid offer.

The public rejection of the aid offer caused bruised feelings in Washington; the US was surprised at Pakistan's negative response, despite her pressing needs. A foreign correspondent asked General Zia the reasons for the rejection. Without concealing his inner feelings, General Zia replied that: 'When the Soviet weapons are breathing fire on Pakistan's border, what can she buy with that measly amount to enhance her national security?' He himself posed a counter-question: 'Peanuts?'

In that off-the-cuff remark, he meant no personal disrespect to President Carter who had been a peanut farmer. That comment was overplayed by the media and 'peanuts' soon entered the glossary of political journalism. A poem by Felicia Lamport appeared in the US Press. It reads:

> Says Pakistan's Zia
> The very idea
> Is far too absurd to discuss.
> You people must be nuts
> To offer such peanuts
> As 400 million to us.
> Though peanuts may do
> For your Washington crew,
> Your stinginess ought to abash you.
> If you want us to spar
> With the U.S.S.R.
> You'd better come up with a cashew.

I recall a visit to the United States in mid-1979, when I went to a department store in New York city to buy a gardening implement. I requested an employee to guide me to the relevant section of the store. While walking together, we started talking. The employee enquired which country I was from. When I told him that I was from Pakistan, he inquired if I knew Zia. Feigning ignorance, I asked him which Zia he meant. 'Zia, the President,' the American elaborated.

I said I did not know him personally. The American said with utter frankness that he thought the guy was crazy to dismiss Carter's offer of $400 million in aid as 'peanuts'.

The man in the shop was not the only foreigner who had difficulty in understanding Pakistan's position.

During the Islamabad meeting in February 1980, Dr Brzezinski had indicated that: 'The rejection of the aid package would produce a negative impact on US public opinion which was not easy to mobilize.'

He then enquired about Pakistan's response if Washington chose to unilaterally announce the offer of the aid package. General Zia told him that, in such an eventuality, Pakistan would release to the Press full details of the mutual discussions held with him.

Despite the rejection of the aid package, the United States expressed a desire to help Pakistan but on her own terms, assuming that economic constraints would compel her to soften her attitude.

Deputy Secretary Warren Christopher visited Islamabad to convey the US desire to strengthen bilateral relations if Pakistan could hold back her ongoing nuclear programme. Such a gesture, Christopher argued, would enable the Carter administration to escape the provisions of the US laws that prohibited the grant of aid to Pakistan. He made a pointed remark that, while expanding ties with Pakistan, America could not ignore her relations with other countries, meaning India. The tone and tenor of the dignitary's remarks and the substance of the talks indicated that the US looked at Pakistan through the prism of India. America retaliated promptly when Pakistan declined to oblige. Project aid to Pakistan was stopped. Employing the age-old carrot and stick technique, fiscal pressure was applied on Islamabad to extract political concessions. Under US influence, the IMF, the World Bank, and the Consortium countries acted in concert to exert an economic squeeze. Pakistan's requests for loans and debt rescheduling were parried and she was advised by the officials of the IMF and the World Bank to improve relations with America.

There were other irritants. These included the execution of Mr Bhutto and America's fears of a rise in religious fervour in Pakistan. The unfortunate burning of the United States embassy in Islamabad on 21 November 1979 also proved a damper. The Holy Kaaba in Mecca had been desecrated and taken over by a group of misguided people. The extreme emotional stress fuelled the sentiments of the people of Pakistan. A report that the incident had a secret American hand behind it unleashed these emotions. In a frenzy, some students in Islamabad set the US Embassy on fire. Much damage had already been done to the building—and to bilateral relations—by the time it transpired that the rumour of US involvement was a piece of mischief.

A few days earlier, an event in Tehran—the hostage crisis—had severely jolted the already rocking Iran-US relations. If Reza Shah was considered a 'demon' in revolutionary Iran, his ally, America, was called the 'Great Satan' by the post-Shah rulers. After considerable hesitation, America permitted Reza Shah to get medical treatment in that country on 'humanitarian grounds'. The Shah reached New York on 27 October 1979. For the people of Iran, this was like showing a red rag to the bull. 'Our protecting the Shah is like our protecting Adolf Eichmann' wrote a former US Ambassador Andrew Young, to the United Nations.[2] In retaliation, on 4 November 1979, about 500 Iranian students seized the American Embassy in Tehran and the US citizens trapped inside the building became hostages. The seizure was hailed by the people of Iran and approved by the Iranian government. The hostage crisis ended 444 days later, on 4 January 1981, when America had to return Iranian assets worth $7.9555 billion (which had earlier been seized by her) to secure the release of 52 Americans hostages held in Tehran. This event was considered a matter of national humiliation in the US. Washington felt that Pakistan's policy on the 'Iranian outrageous' action was less than even-handed. Consequently, their inter-state relations became cooler still.

Despite these differences, the two countries did share common apprehensions regarding Afghanistan, and exchanged intelligence reports. On the eve of the Islamic Foreign Ministers Conference in May 1980, President Carter conveyed to President Zia his hope that Pakistan would exercise the same firm leadership in the May session of the Islamic Conference as she had displayed at the extraordinary session in January 1980. President Carter's letter was accompanied by an offer for resumption of the dialogue between the defence establishments of the two countries, on a private and unpublicized basis, without entailing obligations on either side. Pakistan did not show any enthusiasm for engaging in a serious dialogue with the United States under such pressure.

In October 1980, President Zia, as Chairman of the Organization of the Islamic Conference, addressed the United Nations General Assembly. The Soviet military intervention in Afghanistan was the focal point of that address.

While President Zia was in New York, former President Richard Nixon called on him. During an hour-long conversation, Nixon displayed a penetrating grasp of the international geo-political situation. He appreciated Pakistan's stance on the Afghanistan crisis. He recalled with gratitude the assistance given by Pakistan in arranging Dr Henry Kissinger's secret visit to China on 9-11 July 1971. Pakistan's nuclear programme, said Mr Nixon, was not favoured by the US. He told General Zia: 'I do not know the details of your nuclear effort.

If you have weapon capability, personally I won't mind if you get over with it.'

President Zia informed his guest that, despite his sustained efforts, Pakistan's relations with India were less than cordial. 'Mrs Indira Gandhi has assured me,' said Zia, that 'India wished to normalize ties with Pakistan and had no aggressive designs against it.'

Nixon retorted: 'I hope you did not believe her.' He went on to elaborate that, immediately prior to the 1971 Indo-Pakistan war, Mrs Indira Gandhi had given similar assurances to the United States and other countries.

President Zia had a meeting with President Carter at the White House on 3 October 1980. The two Presidents met privately in President Carter's office for over half an hour. Dr Brzezinski and I were also present. President Carter was pleasant and gentle, and the discussion on some sensitive issues, including Afghanistan, was held in a cordial atmosphere. General Zia surprised President Carter by not discussing Pakistan's security and economic needs. President Carter himself broached the issue and offered to provide F-16 fighter aircraft to Pakistan. General Zia thanked his host and said: 'I do not wish to burden you with Pakistan's problems at a time when you are pre-occupied in an election campaign. Let us defer this issue till after the US elections.' I paid a visit to CIA Headquarters and held a discussion on matters of mutual interest, concerning Afghanistan.

The US election result of 1980 was an expression of disapproval of some of the fundamental premises of the post-Vietnam foreign policy. The wide margin of President Ronald Reagan's victory reflected the electorate's dissatisfaction with the weak state of the economy and the decline in America's international position. The landslide victory was a mandate for restoring America's strength and her primacy in international affairs.

It is for the people of the United States to judge what position they would like to give to President Carter in the roll of honour of the American Presidents. The people of Pakistan would remember him for testing their willpower and endurance in times of extreme stress and crises faced by them. On most occasions, he was less than sympathetic towards Pakistan. The Carter administration misjudged the resilience of Pakistan. It had concluded that the Soviet pressure on Pakistan and her security compulsions in the face of her economic difficulties would compel her to backtrack and agree to a bilateral relationship with the United States, more or less on US terms.

Pakistan-American relations remained at a low ebb throughout the Carter presidency. Pakistan's difficulties might have been accentuated if President Carter had won the election in 1980. With the change of administration in Washington and the assumption of office by President Reagan, American thinking on the international position and the situation in Asia underwent a change. The Soviet military intrusion into Afghanistan became a primary concern in the United States.

In April 1981, the Deputy Assistant Secretary of State for Near East and South Asian Affairs, Mrs James Coon, testifying before a subcommittee of the Foreign Affairs Committee of the House of Representatives stated that: 'Pakistan had become a front line state. ... a stronger, more self-confident Pakistan, capable of resisting direct or indirect Soviet pressure through Afghanistan is ... essential for the protection of free world interests in the region.'

Five months later, the US Under Secretary of State for Security Assistance, in his testimony before the same Committee, stated on 18 September 1981 that: 'A strong, stable and independent Pakistan is an essential anchor to the entire South-West Asian region.' Secretary of State General Haig also spoke along similar lines in November 1981.

The United States suggested a redefinition of a mutually acceptable basis for a bilateral relationship with Pakistan. The US offer created hopes and suspicions in Pakistan. Within the government, two schools of thought emerged. One was in favour of accepting the offer, while the other was sceptical of American intentions. Those who were against accepting the offer argued along these lines: the Reagan administration might wish to keep the Soviet Union engaged in Afghanistan for global or bilateral strategic reasons, in which case Pakistan might unwittingly become a party to the superpower rivalry. American friendship had lacked consistency in the past, and, at critical junctures in Pakistan's national life (in the 1962 Sino-Indian conflict and in the 1965 Indo-Pakistan war), the United States not only interpreted her 1959 agreement obligations unilaterally but also adopted measures which, in the perception of Pakistan, were one-sided and unfair to her. Iran and Vietnam were quoted as examples of the unreliability of American support. The American connection might erode Pakistan's status in the Non-Aligned Movement. The United States might demand that, as a *quid pro quo*, Pakistan should compromise on her nuclear programme; Pakistan becoming a conduit for the supply of weapons to the Afghan *Mujahideen,* granting bases to US forces, or becoming a party to a USA-Middle East 'strategic consensus' against the Soviet Union, were quoted as possible hurdles. The American connection, in the eyes of the critics, could be an added threat to Pakistan's security. It would provide an excuse to the Soviet Union, and her proxy and her friend—Afghanistan and India—to unite in harming Pakistan singly or collectively.

Those in favour of accepting the Unites States offer agreed with most of the apprehensions expressed above. However, they felt that the remedy lay in communicating Pakistan's apprehensions to the United States in clear and unambiguous terms. Their arguments ran thus: the Reagan administration should be given a fair opportunity to prove its *bona fides.* A judgement on its sincerity and motives should be reserved for the present. Both the superpowers had their strategic objectives in the region; so long as they did not clash with the vital interests of Pakistan, she need not feel unduly concerned about them. Pakistan should guard her interests and ensure that her support was not taken for granted and that she was not used by others.

On the issue of Pakistan-US bilateral agreements, it was argued that some of the expectations of both sides were high and perhaps not justified. The United States had helped Pakistan in the diplomatic, economic, and defence fields in the past. Bilateral assistance apart, the United States' influence on the donor countries and international financial institutions, on whom Pakistan was dependent, was an important factor. Pakistan need not worry unduly about Indo-USA friendship, if it did not hurt Pakistan's vital interests.

As a fresh to entrant in the Non-Aligned Movement (NAM), Pakistan was over-sensitive about her neutral status, with the proverbial zeal of a new convert. The Foreign Office over-played the importance of this factor. To the surprise of the Americans, Mr Agha Shahi insisted and Mr Ghulam Ishaq Khan agreed that the military component of the package must be fully paid for by Pakistan, in order to demonstrate her neutrality. General Zia went along with the views of his two ministers.

There was unanimity on some issues. One, Pakistan should not compromise on her nuclear programme. Two, she should avoid becoming a conduit of arms supplies to the *Mujahideen.* Three, she should not provide military bases to any foreign country.

The intervention of the Soviet forces in Afghanistan had posed a serious threat to the security of Pakistan. Her resources were stretched to the limit on two fronts—India and Afghanistan. Pakistan did not have the capacity to face the Soviet Union alone. It was, therefore, desirable to accept the offer of the United States. The Indian hegemonic aspirations in South Asia were also a factor in Pakistan's deciding to give a positive response to the aid offer made by the Reagan administration.

Mr Agha Shahi led a delegation, of which I was a member, to Washington in early 1981. The State Department under the Secretary of State, General Alexander Haig, was sympathetic towards Pakistan. He criticized the Carter administration for its lack of effective response in the face of Soviet expansionist designs in Africa, Asia, and elsewhere. Without indulging in polemics, he came to the core of the problem, condemned the Soviet intervention in Afghanistan, and expressed the US desire to strengthen bilateral relations with Pakistan: 'for the mutual benefit of both the countries.'

General Haig, a confident extrovert, knew his facts, spoke with clarity, and quickly grasped the other's point of view. He was apprised of Pakistan's apprehensions about the inconsistency of US support in the past. It was conveyed to him that a mutual relationship, lacking in durability and dependability, was unlikely to serve the long-term cause of peace and friendship. It was also explained that Pakistan would neither compromise on her nuclear programme nor accept any external advice on internal matters. General Haig stated that it was for Pakistan to solve her internal affairs. He assured us that Pakistan's nuclear programme would not become the linchpin of the new relationship.

After a working lunch with General Haig, the delegation met Vice-President George Bush who praised Pakistan for facing an ugly situation on her border with courage and determination, and promised US support in meeting the 'common danger.'

The high point of the day was the meeting with President Ronald Reagan. He entered the cabinet room of the White House with a broad smile and warmly greeted the delegation. Looking very fit and agile for his age, President Reagan had an aura of charm and dignity. He spoke in a congenial, captivating style, optimism oozing from his words. He bitterly condemned the Soviet intervention in Afghanistan, praised Pakistan for adopting a bold Afghanistan policy, and expressed American support for her security and stability.

While sitting in the White House cabinet room facing President Reagan, one's mind went back to the fall of 1978, when the then Secretary of State, Mr Cyrus Vance, did not find it convenient to meet Mr Agha Shahi for the second time. Just three years after that episode, the Pakistan delegation had met the Secretary of State, the Vice-President, and the President of the United States in just one day. The Soviet military adventure in Afghanistan had turned Pakistan into a front-line state. The United States needed Pakistan's support to halt and repulse the polar bear.

A technical delegation from Pakistan visited the United States in July 1981 to evaluate the purchase of American military equipment. It had indepth but inconclusive discussions with the US authorities. The delivery schedule of the F-16 aircraft created a hurdle. Pakistan wanted to get the first batch within one year. Quoting production difficulties, the US authorities stated that the time-frame for delivery could not be less than twenty-seven months. I remarked that it was incomprehensible that the US could not provide at least some aircraft in less than the stated period. Their early delivery would demonstrate US concern for the security imperatives of Pakistan. I went on to say that if that was the final position, the delegation would return to Pakistan to report the failure of the talks to the government. The leader of the US delegation suggested that discussion be held on those items of hardware on which there was mutual agreement. I replied that negotiations on such items could follow the settlement of the F-16 delivery schedule. The Pakistan delegation returned without clinching the issue.

President Zia wrote to President Reagan, highlighting the threat posed to Pakistan's security by the Soviet military presence in Afghanistan, and the need for a quick response from the US to demonstrate her concern. He suggested that at least some F-16s could be provided within a year, to improve Pakistan's defence capability. President Reagan responded positively.

A balance in the imperatives of the national interests of the two countries was reached after prolonged consultations. An agreement was concluded in September 1981, by which the United States was to provide a package of $3.2 billion, spread over the years 1982-7, in economic assistance and military sales, divided on a fifty-fifty basis. But for the misplaced diplomatic anxiety of the Foreign Office, the terms of the agreement could have been much softer. It was a peculiar case of a buyer wanting to pay more.

The agreement came under discussion in the US Congress. In November 1981, Mr James Buckley, the US Under Secretary of State, introduced the Pakistan package. In his testimony before the Senate Foreign Relations Committee, he said that: 'With the Soviet invasion of Afghanistan, Pakistan has found itself thrust into the unwelcome status of a front-line state. . . . Pakistan had the option of succumbing to pressure, of accepting the status quo or resisting them. Pakistan elected to condemn the occupation of Afghanistan. . . . a strong, stable and independent Pakistan is an essential anchor to the entire South-West Asian region.'

Congress approved the agreement, subject to the condition that the assistance to Pakistan would be suspended '. . . if it transfers a nuclear explosive device to any non-nuclear state or receives a nuclear device from any country or detonates such a device.' Congress was assured by the US administration that the aid would not upset the military balance between India and Pakistan.

Pakistan made it patently clear to the US authorities that she would not grant bases on her soil. The United States understood Pakistan's position and did not raise this subject.

The economic and military sales package was approved after a rough passage through Congress. The Congressional hearings appeared to suggest that, in the US perception, Pakistan had a role in the USA-tailored strategic scheme for the region. Despite pressure from Congress, the Reagan administration stood firm on its commitments to Pakistan and consistently underscored the importance of a viable and strong Pakistan to protect the strategic interests of the United States in the region, to contribute to regional security, and to resist intimidation by the Soviet Union.

While on a visit to Pakistan, Mr Arnaud de Borchgrave of the American weekly *Newsweek* said that 'the American television specializes in destroying leaders.' The US Congress is no less brutal to American allies. They are stripped naked during Congressional hearings in the name of freedom of expression. The pressure generated on Capitol Hill provides a welcome opportunity to the US administration to obtain concessions from their allies before bills concerning them are approved by Congress.

Pakistan is a developing country. The United States is a superpower. A measure of inequality and unfulfilled expectations is a built-in element of the unequal relationship between them. At times, the undercurrents of this reality have created avoidable acrimony and bitterness in the relationship. There is also the Indian factor. In the game of realpolitik, India has an edge over Pakistan. Her size, population, industrial base, a large market, and democratic institutions make her an important factor in South Asia. It does not reflect well on Pakistan's diplomatic effort that a threat to her from a large, antagonistic, and hegemonic India does not usually fall on receptive ears in the United States and is generally viewed with a lack of understanding and sympathy. For Pakistan, the Indian threat is serious and perennial in nature. On the other hand, the hostile situation on Pakistan's western border was perceived much more clearly and readily by the Americans, in the context of Soviet global and regional policies, particularly in the Gulf region.

After the passage of the aid bill by the US Congress, the tactics of the Reagan administration changed. It started showing increased concern about Pakistan's nuclear programme. It invariably referred to the Sword of Damocles hanging over Pakistan's head, by pointing out that the aid ran the risk of being cut off if Pakistan became a nuclear weapon state. Pakistan was subjected to pressure to sign the Nuclear Non-Proliferation Treaty (NPT). She was also urged not to enrich uranium beyond the level used for commercial purposes. Pakistan maintained that a fair and practical approach to achieve non-proliferation in South Asia was to negotiate a regional agreement on the issue, to which all countries of the region should be party. Towards the closing stages of the Zia administration, America accepted this logic.

The United States showed interest in some other fields. They were:

1. Joint surveillance operations.
2. Fuel storage facilities in Pakistan.
3. Port operation and cargo maintenance.
4. Joint naval exercises.

Pakistan conveyed her reservations through diplomatic and other channels.

The narcotics problem caused anxiety to the United States and Pakistan. The production of opium in Pakistan and the trafficking in heroin and other narcotic substances through Pakistan to America and other Western countries assumed serious proportions. Pakistan fully shared American anxiety in the matter. The two countries worked together closely on an anti-narcotics drive. As a consequence, poppy production decreased from 800 metric tons in 1979 to 40 metric tons in 1984-5. In the post-1985 period, its production again showed an upward trend.

The aid package for the years 1982-7 was implemented to the mutual satisfaction of both countries. In September 1984, President Reagan wrote to President Zia conveying US willingness to extend assistance to Pakistan beyond 1987. A fresh package for the next six years, 1988-93, was finalized in March 1986. It covered an outlay of $4.02 billion. By this time, the American attitude towards Pakistan had undergone a change. She made an abortive attempt to link the economic component of the assistance to other economic policy objectives desired by her. Reason prevailed when Pakistan did not agree to the US demand.

The military portion of the aid package was provided on easier terms but with a stiff proviso. Under a law passed in 1985 exclusively for Pakistan, called the Pressler Amendment, the US President was required to issue a certification to Congress every year that Pakistan did not possess a nuclear device and that the continued aid would induce it not to have one. By making a law applicable to a single country, the United States adopted a double standard in her policy. Strict conditions were attached to aid to Pakistan, while the nuclear programmes of countries like Israel, India, and South Africa were glossed over.

In December 1982, President Zia undertook a state visit to the United States. Beside Washington DC, the major cities visited by him were New York, Houston, and San Francisco. The two Presidents met privately on 7 December 1982, before holding formal talks the same day. Their talks centred on the situation in the Middle East and South-West Asia, with particular reference to the Afghanistan crisis and the Iraq-Iran conflict. On bilateral relations, the United States reaffirmed her commitment to Pakistan's security. She expressed her concern about nuclear proliferation and drug trafficking. Pakistan reiterated her position and indicated that she was no less concerned about these matters.

I had gone to the United States ahead of General Zia's visit. Besides meeting the Chief of Staff, I met some officials in the State Department.

President Zia addressed a largely attended press club meeting in San Francisco. Conspicuous among the audience was a group of about half a dozen Sikhs from India, wearing multi-coloured turbans. After the function, they requested a brief meeting with General Zia. The request was granted. Six Sikhs came to the President's hotel suite that evening to 'greet him on his visit to San Francisco.' They had been living in the United States for a number of years. As the conversation shifted to the Indo-Pakistan subcontinent, the Sikhs expressed concern about the welfare of their community in India. They lamented, with obvious emotion, that 'we are treated as second-rate citizens in our own country.' President Zia advised them to live as good and loyal Indians. One of them replied: 'We value your advice, Mr President, but deep in our hearts we have a feeling of unease. We blame ourselves for not getting the fruits of freedom. At the time of partition, Hindus got India, Muslims established Pakistan, *aur Sikh Sikh he rahe.*' (. . . and Sikhs were left high and dry.)

Vice President George Bush visited Pakistan in April 1984. In a meeting held at the hill resort of Murree, he mentioned to General Zia that Pakistan's nuclear programme could become a hurdle in their mutual relationship. Zia reassured Bush that the programme was peaceful.

On 23 October 1985, General Zia addressed the United Nations General Assembly. The same day, he also had a meeting with President Reagan in New York. The two leaders reviewed the situation in Afghanistan and agreed that the freedom fighters were hurting the Soviet interests in that country. They agreed to continue exerting diplomatic and military pressure on the Soviet Union to withdraw her military forces from Afghanistan.

Pakistan's nuclear programme also came under discussion. President Zia was told of US apprehensions in this regard. On his part, President Zia stressed the importance of adopting a regional approach in seeking a fair and equitable settlement of the issue.

Some analysts have stated that Pakistan had kept the military pot boiling in Afghanistan in order to get aid from the United States. This argument is fallacious and untenable. The foreign policy of the United States—a superpower—was designed to promote her own global and national interests, and not tailored at the behest of any other country. The critics ignored the fact that Pakistan had started providing assistance to the Afghan refugees in 1978. American aid to Pakistan was approved in 1981 and started reaching that country the following year.

Nor had the Soviet Union consulted Pakistan before dispatching her military forces to occupy Afghanistan. The invasion was in pursuit of her perceived national interests. It is naive to argue that Pakistan could manipulate the policies of the USA or the USSR on vital issues of war and peace.

Strategic and environmental changes, contemporary events, shifts in policies, the dictates of national security, and many other factors influence the foreign policy options of nations. Pakistan-USA relations have faced this phenomenon in the past and will do so in the future as well.

During his visit to Pakistan in August 1988, Secretary of State, Mr George Shultz, said that: 'The United States' relations with Pakistan are based on long-standing shared purposes and common goals and America's support rests on a broad bipartisan base.' That statement was made on the death of President Zia and was meant to reassure Pakistan. The 'shared purpose', the 'common goals', and the 'bipartisan base' can undergo a change. East Pakistan is an example: it was amputated despite the US commitment to preserving the integrity of Pakistan. Defence Secretary Frank Carlucci said that 'the security relations between Pakistan and USA will continue after the Afghanistan problem is solved.'

After his election as the forty-first President of the United States, Mr George Bush said on 10 November 1988: 'I would like to reaffirm my commitment to a stable Pakistan. The United States and Pakistan have a historic relationship which I will preserve and further strengthen.'

Notwithstanding such assurances, nations formulate their policies on pragmatic considerations assessed in cold logic. The US decision in 1981 to provide aid to Pakistan was primarily influenced by the Soviet intervention in Afghanistan, which threatened her vital political, economic, and strategic interests in the Gulf region. Other factors were minor and contributory. The US Afghan policy enjoyed bipartisan support in the Congress. So strong was the US concern that, as a measure of tactical necessity, she temporarily relegated her concern about Pakistan's nuclear programme to the back burner.

A decade later the situation changed appreciably. The withdrawal of the Soviet forces from Afghanistan had served the strategic interest of the United States. Her primary objective achieved, the remaining elements of the Afghan dispute were of secondary importance to her.

Political changes took place elsewhere. In 1990, the socialist order in Europe collapsed. The totalitarian system in Poland, Hungary, East Germany, Bulgaria, Romania, and Czechoslovakia fell to pieces. The

Iron Curtain disappeared. So did the Berlin Wall. The Warsaw Pact became meaningless. The North Atlantic Treaty Organization (NATO) was reshaped. East Germany and West Germany were united. The emergent unified Germany started radiating signals of hope and fear to Europe.

More significantly, the twin menace of prolonged political repression and economic stagnation caused the disintegration of the Soviet Union from within into fifteen independent states. This tilted the equilibrium of world power in favour of the United States, which became the sole superpower.

The collapse of the Soviet Union produced its impact on South Asia. India, linked with the erstwhile Soviet Union by a treaty and the recipient of large economic and military aid from her, suddenly lost a benefactor. Facing the inevitable, she turned towards the United States which was more than ready to reciprocate. An Indo-US linkage emerged. It involved bilateral co-operation in the diplomatic, political, economic, and military fields.

Another fallout of the Soviet political implosion was the emergence of the Central Asian Republics as independent countries. This aroused fears in some western countries about the creation of an Islamic bloc in the region. Such anxiety did not take into consideration the reality that the Muslims were internally too weak and divided to pose a threat to any power bloc except themselves. An emerging Indo-US axis aims at checkmating the rise of a united Islamic bloc in the Central Asian region and at destabilizing China.

In the emerging geopolitical scenario, Pakistan-US relations, following the pattern of their chequered history, again nosedived. Pakistan's ongoing nuclear programme is not acceptable to the policy-makers in Washington.

Pakistan expects that the world attitude on all nuclear and allied matters should be even-handed and non-discriminatory. The performance of all countries on this issue ought to be judged on a fair and uniform basis. Any deviation from a universally accepted principled course would, in the long run, damage the image and claim to impartiality of the United States.

CHAPTER 14

The Nuclear Ballyhoo

In late 1976, the foundations of a laboratory complex were laid in Kahuta, an obscure village on the outskirts of Islamabad. The brick and mortar work over, technicians and technologists replaced the masons and plumbers. The place hummed with hush-hush activity. Under tight security, most of the initial project work was completed in three years without arousing suspicion.

The Engineering Research Laboratories (ERL—later renamed Dr A. Q. Khan Research Laboratories) established on 31 July 1976, shifted into the new buildings. Its previous location, comprising old, dingy, leaking huts, resembling junk shops, had served the purpose. The tiny centrifuge pilot project at Sihala was conceived and fabricated there.

Pakistan's open society excels in making a hash of its secrets. Headlines about Kahuta aroused the curiosity, surprise, and ire of the Western world. Some nations saw it through eyes of the cameras fitted in their satellites, while others collected bits and pieces of information through intelligence sources and fabricated juicy and often exaggerated tales. The 'secret' became an open secret. Kahuta rapidly rose from anonymity to extreme prominence.

The ERL enrichment plant elated Pakistan and stunned the world. A country unable to produce needles and ball-bearings had fabricated, through an indigenous effort, centrifuges which required special metallurgy, extremely tight tolerance limits, and microscopic accuracy. The complicated header pipe system was laid, the cascades were erected, a monitoring system was established, and, under the watchful guidance of a bunch of talented Pakistani scientists, the ultra-centrifuges started spinning at the phenomenal speed of 70,000 to 80,000 revolutions per minute. The orchestrated din raised by the Western countries notwithstanding, Pakistan pursued her goal. The labour bore fruit. General Ziaul Haq announced in December 1981 that, 'We have the capability to enrich uranium.'[1]

This laudable achievement was due to the dedication of technologists and technicians who had toiled hard to break the technological barriers erected in their path by the industrially advanced countries. Pakistan had joined the select group of a few countries which possessed the technology to enrich uranium. The pioneer and godfather of the Kahuta enrichment plant was a modest, soft-spoken, physical metallurgist, Dr Abdul Qadeer Khan. Years later, he was decorated with the high award of *Hilal-i-Imtiaz* 'for his singular and monumental contribution in the field of nuclear science.'

Born in Bhopal, India, in 1936, the young Khan migrated to Pakistan in 1952, graduated from the University of Karachi, studied at the famous Technische Universitat at Charlotenberg, West Berlin, and obtained a master's degree in metallurgical engineering from the prestigious Technical University of Delft, Holland, in 1967. In 1972, he completed his doctorate in Physical Metallurgy at the Catholic University of Leuven, Belgium. The young Dr A. Q. Khan was employed for four years in the Physical Dynamics Research Laboratory (FDO) in Holland which worked with URENCO, a joint venture of the governments of West Germany, Britain, and the Netherlands. In October 1975, he came to Pakistan and decided to avail of an offer made to him by Mr Bhutto to serve in the country. He resigned from the FDO and established the ERL in 1976.

A scientist-cum-technologist of high calibre, Dr A. Q. Khan's professional knowledge was combined with a practical approach. Gifted with enthusiasm and passion, he faced technological barriers and bureaucratic hurdles in his way with contempt and vigour. Not a favourite of the penny-pinching administrators, he enjoyed a great measure of fiscal autonomy and independence of action which enabled him to show results. His insatiable professional ego was surpassed only by his desire for creating a firm technological base in Pakistan.

The Kahuta plant was conceived, designed, and established by Pakistani personnel and is operated by them. The Western countries made it a target of criticism for self-serving reasons. That a Third World Muslim state has achieved a breakthrough in nuclear technology is not liked by those who arrogate to themselves the role of sole custodians of this technology. Their desire to monopolize nuclear technology—hard to justify on the planes of logic, law, morality, or fair play—is realpolitik in its naked form.

THE NUCLEAR BALLYHOO

Nuclear technology serves four distinct functions. These are:
- Nuclear reactors for power generation.
- The atom for peaceful projects.
- The technology factor.
- Nuclear weapons.

Nuclear Power Generation

Pakistan's growing industrial and agricultural development is largely dependent on her ability to meet her expanding power needs. Her known reserves of oil, gas, and coal are limited. So is the hydroelectric potential. Solar energy is not yet economically viable. A widening gap exists between the energy needs of the country and their availability. This can be filled by nuclear power.

Pakistan's solitary 137 MW natural uranium fuelled heavy water moderated reactor, the Karachi Nuclear Power Plant (KANUPP), inaugurated in November 1972, was built with Canadian assistance. The Indian nuclear explosion of 18 May 1974 caused a setback to Pakistan's nuclear programme. Some contracts signed by Pakistan with the supplier states were either cancelled or not honoured. These included the provision of a heavy water plant by Germany, a fuel fabrication plant by Canada, and a reprocessing plant by France. In addition, Canada stopped providing fuel materials, heavy water, and spare parts for KANUPP. Pakistan was thus punished for the act committed by India. Taking the plea that the Indian explosion had necessitated stricter control, the Canadian government, in violation of the KANUPP agreement, linked the fulfilment of her contractual obligations with Pakistan's signing the Non-Proliferation Treaty (NPT). The Canadian demand was rejected as it was untenable in law.

Pakistan signed a Memorandum of Understanding (MOU) with China in 1989 for the building of a 300 megawatt nuclear power plant in the country. A contract to this effect was signed in 1992. By another deal signed in 1989, France promised to establish a 900 megawatt nuclear power plant in Pakistan. Both the plants would take seven to eight years to complete, after the signing of the contracts. These would be under the International Atomic Energy Agency safeguards.

While the Chinese contract is likely to be implemented, the French had a motive in luring Pakistan with the offer of the plant lollipop. It was a clever manoeuvre to pave the way for getting herself released from the reprocessing plant contractual obligation. Naively, Pakistan took the bait and quietly signed a settlement on the reprocessing plant issue with France on unfavourable terms. The details of the agreement were not made public. The stage was thus set for France to wriggle out of her nuclear power plant offer. It would be easy for her to coin an excuse to do so.

In 1955, nuclear power plants produced a mere 5 megawatts of electricity throughout the world. In 1992, 425 such plants were operating in 30 countries, contributing 17 per cent of the total global electricity generation.[2] Four-fifths of them were in rich countries. As announced by the IAEA, by 1993 the number of nuclear plants in the world had increased to 430, and 55 additional reactors were under construction in 18 countries.[3] Pakistan generates a bare 0.2 per cent of its electricity from nuclear power. In contrast, seventy-three per cent of the electricity consumed in France in 1992 came from the nuclear plants. The percentages for some other countries were: Belgium, 59.9; Hungary 46.4; Germany, 30.1; UK, 32.2; USA, 22.3, and India, 3.3.[4] This demonstrates the energy predicament of Pakistan. Her hydro potential, besides being limited, is influenced by technical, social, and economic considerations, precluding large scale exploitation. Fossil fuel generation is expensive. An increase in nuclear power generation is the most viable option.

The Atom For Peaceful Projects

Like many other countries, Pakistan uses nuclear technology in the fields of agriculture, medicine, and industry. Some Western countries had initiated the 'atom for peace' programmes in different part of the world.

The Technology Factor

Nuclear technology supplements conventional technology in promoting the industrial growth of a country. Mechanical, electrical, and chemical engineering services and processes can be revamped and modernized. A specialized base is created in the fields of electronics, computer technology, and automation. The research and development effort trains its demographic resource. A nuclear programme provides immense technical rub-off in a variety of fields. One leader maintained that, 'No country without an atom bomb could properly consider itself independent.'[5]

The flow of knowledge defies man-made checks and barriers. In the annals of history, every technology, once conceived, has spread. Nuclear technology is no exception. It cannot be kept chained in the backyards of a few selected countries for self-serving and spurious reasons. Monopolists may delay the spread of nuclear technology through coercive tactics but sooner or later it will reach the have-not states. It is no wonder that, despite restrictions and embargoes, a dozen or more countries in 1994 are known to be either in possession of nuclear weapon technology or close to getting it.

Nuclear Weapon Capability

By coincidence or design, the permanent members of the United Nation's Security Council became the first five countries in the world to possess the nuclear bomb—the United States in 1945, the USSR in 1949, Great Britain in 1952, France in 1960, and China in 1964. A thesis was then developed that the further horizontal proliferation of nuclear weapon capability should be prevented. But the Big Five retained for themselves the unchecked option of proliferating nuclear weapons vertically. The self-righteous approach implied that world peace would be safeguarded if nuclear weapons remained only in the 'balanced and mature' custody of the five nuclear weapon states. The arrogance implicit in condemning an overwhelming majority of the countries of the world as a bunch of irresponsible and trigger-happy states is an insult to humanity. Their attempt to perpetuate their political, nuclear, economic, and technological domination of the world is hard to defend.

The nuclear attacks on Hiroshima and Nagasaki were the most horrible acts committed in the twentieth century. Facing lifelong agony, the survivors in these nuclear-afflicted cities envied the dead. Historians will debate, *ad nauseam,* the justification of the atomic strikes, 'Little Boy' on Hiroshima, and 'Fat Man' on Nagasaki in 1945, when Japan was virtually on the verge of defeat. Was it militarily justified, politically desireable, and morally valid to kill 240,000 people in Hiroshima and 87,000 in Nagasaki, besides maiming countless others, to expedite the Japanese surrender? Japan faced the trauma because it did not possess comparable coercive power to deter the attacker from doing what it did with impunity. The victor feared no risk of retaliation from the vanquished.

There was belated moral retribution. Colonel Paul W. Tibbets, flying the Enola Gay that unleashed 'Little Boy'—the first nuclear bomb used in combat history—felt, 'a sense of shame for the whole human race.'[6] 'My God! what we have done'[7], exclaimed Captain Robert A. Lewis, the co-pilot of the Enola Gay. A feeling of guilt also engulfed Professor Robert J. Oppenheimer, who was asked if he had moral scruples about the loss of lives. He replied, 'Terrible ones.'[8] He became what the Bhagavadgita acidly describes: 'I am become death, the all-devouring.'[9]

Remorse was felt by others as well. One policy-maker writes, 'I have questioned them [atomic attacks on Japan] myself and so have a good many Americans . . . I think Nagasaki was unnecessary and Hiroshima debatable.'[10]

The men in power felt differently. President Harry S. Truman called the nuclear strike on Hiroshima 'the greatest thing in history.'[11] Speaking just before the fiftieth anniversary of the Japanese attack on Pearl Harbour, President George Bush, in response to a demand made in Japan that America should apologize for launching the atomic strikes in 1945, emphatically said, 'We mourned the deaths of civilians, but the use of the bombs which led to Japan's surrender, had saved millions of American lives.'[12] That statement, coming from a person placed so high in public life, was so low in content. It reeked of racial discriminination and double standards for mankind. Besides, the argument that 'millions' of US lives were endangered in 1945 was a distortion of history.

Over the millennium, the power game has been played with relentless consistency. While the tactics have changed with time, the strategy has endured. In realpolitik, the strong wish to become stronger to dominate the weak. Domination is achieved through the possession of power—economic, diplomatic, technological and military. Nuclear weapons provide the ultimate power. Those who have it, wish to retain it, and prefer to deny it to others. Those who do not possess it, strive to acquire it. Only those nations are temporarily not in the race who know that the goal is presently beyond their reach. Such is the reality of the game of power.

The Proliferation Race

The United States emerged out of the Second World War as the only nuclear weapon power. That *fait accompli* was tolerated by other nations as a matter of political expediency. Their national interest spurred them to end the one-nation domination.

The Soviet nuclear explosion in 1949 protected her from the danger of nuclear blackmail. The two power blocs looked for security. The United States adopted a policy of containment to check Soviet expansionism through pacts—NATO, CENTO, and SEATO. The Soviet Union established the Warsaw Pact and kept the West occupied by initiating communist bush-fires around the globe.

The national interests of France and Britain prevented them from subordinating their national security needs to the perennial goodwill of an external friendly power. Both became nuclear weapon states.

Till 1960, the nuclear club was the exclusive preserve of the white race. Then, China exploded a nuclear device in 1964 'to break the nuclear monopoly'.[13] She declared 'solemnly on many occasions that at no time and under no circumstances will China be the first to use nuclear weapons [against any country]'.[14] A policy statement issued in 1971 made this commitment explicit. It said, 'China develops nuclear weapons because she is compelled to do so under imperialist nuclear threats ... China is not yet a nuclear power, nor will she ever be a "nuclear superpower"—practising the policies of nuclear monopoly, nuclear threat and nuclear blackmail.'[15] Chairman Mao had earlier described the philosophy of politics by saying that 'political power grows out of the barrel of a gun.'[16] Marshal Chen Yi, feeling rather ineffective without the weight of a nuclear force, had once lamented that, as Foreign Minister, he felt he could not straighten his back. He had stated that, even if they had to pawn their pants, China should develop a nuclear arsenal so it could deal on equal terms with other nuclear powers.

The vertical proliferation of nuclear weapons started swelling the arsenal of the Big Five. By the year 1990, over 90 per cent of the world's nuclear armaments were held by the Soviet Union and the United States. After 1945, 'The superpowers have contemplated the use or threat of use of nuclear weapons on numerous occasions and often these were directed at non-nuclear states.'[17] The hinted or implied threats, usually couched in diplomatic language, were made sometimes implicitly and on other occasions explicitly but invariably in a manner that the recipient state understood their import without any ambiguity. For example, following the shooting down of the American U-2 spy plane over Russia in 1960, the Soviet Union had publicly announced that Peshawar (from where the plane had taken off) had been put on the Soviet maps.

South Africa and Israel clandestinely became nuclear-weapon states. The acquisition of weapon-grade nuclear capability by them and their nuclear tests were not only denied but also covered up by their strategic allies. 'The Israeli secret was shared, sanctioned, and, at times, wilfully ignored by the top political and military officials of the United States since the Eisenhower years,' writes Hersh, who goes on to say that the American officials (who spoke to him), 'realized the hypocrisy of the American policy pretending that Israel's nuclear arsenal does not exist.'[18]

In June 1974, President Nixon offered to sell nuclear power reactors to Israel and Egypt without requiring either of them to ratify the Non-Proliferation Treaty—a condition imposed on other countries, including Pakistan. This was done despite the fact that the 'US had believed since 1968 that Israel possessed nuclear weapons capability.'[19] After Nixon's resignation in 1974, the Ford administration pursued this sale plan even when the CIA had submitted a summary to the US government which conceded that 'We believe that Israel has already produced nuclear weapons.'[20] Such double standards eroded US credibility.

Mr Ephrain Katzir, the then President of Israel, said in December 1974, that 'it has always been our intention to develop a nuclear potential. We now have that potential ... Israel could convert (this) capability into fact ... in a few days.'[21] The CIA reported in September 1974, that 'we believe that Israel already has produced nuclear weapons.' The disclosures made later in 1986 by Mr Mordechai Vanunu, a former technician in Israel's Dimona nuclear facility, substantiate these reports. Mr Vanunu, in his story published in *The Sunday Times*, revealed the presence of a plutonium reprocessing facility built with French assistance.[22] This was later confirmed by Professor Francis Perrin, France's High Commissioner for Atomic Energy from 1951 to 1970.[23] Vanunu also revealed the presence of facilities that were manufacturing critical components that could be used in nuclear devices.

Leonard Spector has quoted statistics to prove that since 1981 South Africa has been in a position to produce highly enriched uranium suitable for manufacturing nuclear weapons.[24] Several so-called 'threshold countries' including Argentina, Japan, Brazil, Spain, India, Pakistan, Israel, North Korea and South Korea, are known to be actively pursuing nuclear programmes. Till 1991, Iraq was considered a threshold country. Her defeat in the 42-day punitive military operation by the US-led allied forces in February-March 1991 resulted in the scrapping of her nuclear- and chemical-weapon installations. It was then discovered that the western assessment of Iraq's nuclear potential was exaggerated—perhaps deliberately. Iraq's nuclear potential was destroyed in 1992 under UN orders.

The Global Nuclear Scenario

The 1991 collapse of the Soviet Union ended the era of the bipolar world. The United States emerged as the pre-eminent power. The Soviet disintegration raised questions about the control of the strategic and tactical nuclear-weapons located or deployed in four of her erstwhile republics, now independent countries. The possibility of the loss, leakage, or pilferage of tactical nuclear weapons, or their falling into unauthorized hands, could not be ruled out. It also resulted in the leakage of technology, when many Soviet nuclear scientists and technicians were hired by West European countries, India, Israel, and China for assistance in their respective nuclear programmes. The risk was partly contained by the decision that about 35,000 nuclear warheads scattered across the territory of the disintegrated Soviet Union—in the emerging states of Russia, Ukraine, Kazakhstan and Belarus—would be withdrawn to storage sites in Russia. The modalities for this arrangement have largely been negotiated.

The end of the Cold War created a window of opportunity for peace in which the US and the former Soviet Union concluded bilateral agreements—START in July 1991 and START II in January 1993—limiting their strategic arsenals from 10,000 to 3,500 warheads each by the year 2003. The perceptible reduction, a step in the right direction to ease nuclear tension, became inevitable because of the changed global political climate. A closer scrutiny reveals that the weapons to be scrapped are surplus, of older vintage, and no longer cost-effective to maintain. Beyond the year 2003, the USA and Russia (replacing the Soviet Union) will continue to possess an overkill capability. Nuclear experts consider about 1,000 nuclear warheads adequate to sustain the maximum nuclear deterrence theory. Some analysts scale down this number to between 300 and 100 warheads.

Britain, China, and France are not committed to reducing their nuclear stockpile. Besides, all the nuclear weapon powers, except China, are unwilling to pledge the no-first-use of nuclear weapons.

The US decision to reduce her tactical nuclear weapons is a positive development. So is the agreement between Argentina and Brazil to move away from their bilateral nuclear race. The nuclear issue in North Korea is being addressed. With Iraq's nuclear capability destroyed, Israel remains the sole (clandestine) nuclear weapon power in the Middle East. She enjoys the acquiescence of her strategic supporters for retaining her status—at least in the foreseeable future. South Africa has already acceded to the Non-Proliferation Treaty.

The global nuclear scene, despite the projected arms reduction by America and Russia, remains murky and vexing. The nuclear countries strive to retain their supremacy on a permanent basis. They preach world peace but prepare for war.

India's Nuclear Capability

The foundation of India's political amibition is based on Pandit Jawaharlal Nehru's vision of his country as one of the world's four great powers—a 'pivot'—with a right to intervene in her neighbourhood.[25] 'In a large country like India', said Nehru, 'it is always possible to find facts and trends to justify a particular thesis, and then this becomes the accepted basis for a new argument.'[26] Under Nehru's guidance, India's nuclear programme was conceived as weapon-oriented *ab initio*. Nehru clearly defined the Indian nuclear policy when he said, 'Indeed, I think we must develop it for peaceful purposes. Of course, if we are compelled as a nation to use it for other purposes, possibly no pious statements of any of us will stop the nation from using it that way.'[27] In 1957, Dr Homi J. Bhabha said that, given the green signal, India would take 'three years for the atom bomb and five years for the hydrogen bomb'.[28] In 1958 Nehru declared, 'India has the know-how to make nuclear weapons in 3-4 years but will never do so.'[29] Nehru had no pretensions of retaining the Gandhian philosophy of non-violence as an element of Indian policy. In 1962, he said, 'Do we all believe fully in non-violence, taking it to its utmost conclusion? I suppose not.'[30] Nehru's successors in office consistently pursued the nuclear path in all fields. Mrs Indira Gandhi stated in 1965, 'We are building atomic know-how and competence.'[31] In September 1971, during the Fourth Geneva Conference on the Peaceful Uses of Atomic Energy, Dr Vikram Sarabhai, the Chairman of the Indian Atomic Energy Commission, publicly announced India's interest in carrying out an underground nuclear explosion. Prime Minister Indira Gandhi told the Rajya Sabha in November 1973 that the 'Indian Atomic Energy Commission is constantly reviewing the process in the technology of underground nuclear explosions from both theoretical and experimental angles.'[32] Mr C. Subramanyam, the Defence Minister in the Charan Singh cabinet, was more explict, ' I am not naive enough to declare on behalf of all future generations and governments that India will not make nuclear-weapons.'[33]

The policy statements were matched by a rapid expansion in India's nuclear facilities in multidirectional fields. It is a tribute to India's ingenious diplomacy that she portrayed her 1974 nuclear implosion as 'peaceful'. Four years later, Prime Minister Morarji Desai announced that India would not conduct further nuclear tests 'even for peaceful purposes.'[34] Facing severe criticism for making this commitment, he explained that he had renounced explosions but not ruled out blasts. In 1985, Prime Minister Rajiv Gandhi stated that his country could produce nuclear weapons in a matter of 'months if not weeks.'[35]

Mr K. Subrahmanyam, the former director of India's Institute of Defence Studies and Analyses when asked 'if India needed a nuclear bomb' replied, 'We need to exercise the nuclear option absolutely. If we don't, India will not be a united country in fifteen years.'[36] General K. Sunderji, former Chief of Staff of the Indian Army (retired April 1988) said, 'Our [Indian] defensive strategy is dissuasive. The important thing is it must be credible. The enemy must realize you have the will to use that capability. It might have to be demonstrated at certain points.'[37]

'We don't want to be blackmailed and treated as Oriental blackies,' declared Kawal Ratna Malkani, Vice President of the Bharatiya Janata Party in January 1993, adding with pride, 'Nuclear weapons will give us prestige, power and standing. An Indian will talk straight and walk straight when we have the bomb.'[38] The Indians are welcome to walking straight and her neighbours will be relieved to hear them talking straight.

India's unwavering intention of becoming a nuclear-weapon state was unambiguously stated on 11 June 1994 by Prime Minister Narasimha Rao in these words: 'We do not want to give up the choice of producing a bomb. We are keeping the nuclear option open.'[39]

In 1994 India had a stockpile of 500 kilograms of weapon-grade plutonium in separated form, in addition to 1,000 kilograms of reactor-grade plutonium. A foreign expert calculates India's 'weapon-grade plutonium stocks (by 1995) to above 425 kilograms, enough for fifty to sixty bombs.'[40]

India's vast nuclear programme pre-dated the Chinese nuclear explosion in 1964. It was thus not a reaction to a perceived threat from China as usually claimed by the Indian policy-makers. With a vision of her own greatness, India is striving to become a regional pre-eminent and global power. Her nuclear weapon choice is designed to enhance her international image and provide the means to project her power and influence within the region and beyond. In her perception, nuclear weapons and the threat of their use will enable her to impose her own brand of neocolonialism in Aisa.

India's Missile Programme

The space race between the two superpowers was triggered with the launching of Sputnik by the Soviet Union in 1957. The importance of space research for scientific and defence purposes became apparent to the defence planners. The Indian National Council for Space Research was soon established. In 1972, the Indian Space Commission was created to plan, manage and execute activities in space science and technology in the field of application.

India soon developed a comprehensive programme for the development of missiles, propellants, space vehicles, and control systems. This programme serves to project her power beyond her borders. Agni, an intermediate range ballistic missile (IRBM) with a declared range of 2,500 kilometers, is the most advanced Indian missile. 'We now have a carrier on which both conventional and non-conventional weapons can be delivered over a long range,' said A. P. J. Abdul Kalam, the godfather of Agni, adding, 'whether we should go nuclear or not, I would not like to comment.'[41]

The Agni missile, and its future upgradation to ICBM level, poses a threat to all the countries neighbouring India, as well as to the littoral states of the Indian Ocean. It can reach out to the southern parts of China, the whole Gulf region and the US military base in Diego Garcia. Besides, the ASEAN countries, Australia, Japan, USA, and the European countries could perceive a potential threat to their trade routes in the Indian Ocean.

Prithvi, a surface-to-surface missile, with a declared range of 250 kilometres, is planned to be deployed against Pakistan 'by the end of 1994.'[42] This date was later modified to June 1995. In the anti-tank class, India has the Nag missile. The Indian surface to air missiles include Akash and Trishul which is also 'a supersonic sea-skimmer.'[43]

The external assistance has been persistent and sizeable. The 'US aid to India's missile programme was extensive.'[44] Some other countries outstripped the American generosity. France launched India's sounding rockets and licensed her to build the Viking high-thrust liquid rocket motor. The technology for the missile guidance system was provided by Germany. Besides, she sold crucial know-how about composite materials and test facilities. The USSR sold SA-2 Guideline surface-to-air missiles and advanced rocket engines.

The introduction of nuclear weapon capability and ballistic missiles by India in South Asia has radically changed the regional power equilibrium and added a new dimension—more dangerous than before—to the threat posed to India's neighbours, particularly Pakistan. India has all along enjoyed superiority over them in conventional weaponry. The induction of missiles in her military inventory has made the region more turbulent.

India deserves credit for her systematic approach in achieving her perceived goals. After her nuclear capability was demonstrated in 1974, she entered the space age in 1980 by launching Augmented Satellite Launch Vehicle 3. Agni, test-fired in 1989, gave her the capability to carry nuclear and conventional warheads over long distances.

Pakistan's Security Concern

India rushed her troops to Kashmir (1947), marched into Junagadh and Manavadar (1947), invaded Hyderabad (1948), absorbed Goa (1961), and Sikkim (1975). She provoked the Sino-Indian border clash in 1962. By fuelling the insurgency in Sri Lanka, she manoeuvred to induct 30,000 Indian troops into that country under the guise of a peace-keeping mission. In 1988, she air-lifted troops to the Maldives to thwart a *coup* suspected to be Indian-inspired. She has forced three wars on Pakistan.

Pakistan does not aspire to an arms race in South Asia. The Indian chauvinism has created perennial regional hostility and forced Pakistan to look for security elsewhere. She relied heavily on external sources of military hardware and security guarantees and, in the process, ignored to develop indigenous defence production efforts. The external crutches proved unreliable during the periods of crises. India's nuclear implosion in 1974 foreclosed Pakistan's nuclear option. Faced with a hard choice—either opt for a balance of terror or face a perpetual terror of imbalance—she adopted the honourable course.

The history of nuclear weapons, short as it is, and the logic of nuclear deterrence, lead to some inevitable conclusions. Nuclear weapons can preserve peace and prevent war when both the adversaries possess them. Their immense destructive power and the unacceptability of the catastrophe unleashed by them prohibit their use in war as an instrument of policy. By this logic, their inherent destructive ability makes them a potential weapon for peace.

Alternatively, when only one of the adversaries possesses a nuclear arsenal, the other becomes vulnerable to threats and blackmail. Pakistan faces such a risk as India has demonstrated both her nuclear weapon capability and their means of delivery.

Threats to Pakistan

During the mid 1980s, Pakistan received a number of reports from its missions abroad and through intelligence channels, indicating an Indo-Israeli collusion against the Kahuta uranium enrichment plant. The *Hindustan Times* reported the loss of a file, 'Attack on Kahuta', from the office of Prime Minister Indira Gandhi. The projected overt threats involved a commando-type surgical operation and air action. Pakistan shared her information and concern with some friendly countries, including America, which apprised Israel. The persistence of the reports prompted General Zia to say that, 'India might launch an air strike against Pakistan's nuclear facilities in a manner similar to the Israeli attack against Iraq.'[45] Indira Gandhi denied the charge. On 22 September 1984, a reliable source from a foreign country reported the imminence of an air strike. Pakistan informed India that an attack on her nuclear installations would be treated as an act of war. The *New York Times* reported that, 'Indira Gandhi received a recommendation for attacking Pakistan nuclear facilities, but turned it down.'[46] An indication of what was being planned was perhaps picked up independently by the US as well. On 10 October 1984, Ambassador Deane Hinton said in Lahore that the US would be 'responsive' if India attacked Pakistan, of which he saw a clear danger.[47] It is significant that the threat signals decreased significantly after November 1984, except one serious reporting in mid-1985. It may be recalled that Prime Minister Indira Gandhi was assassinated in India on 31 October 1984, as a consequence of the Indian Army's misadventure against the Sikh holy shrine, the Golden Temple, in Amritsar.

Little did Pakistan know then that one important source of the leakage of information was America itself. On 21 November 1985, Jonathan Pollard, an American Jew working in the US Navy, was arrested while attempting to seek refuge in the Israeli Embassy in Washington DC.[48] He was later found guilty and sentenced to life imprisonment for spying for Israel. Pollard worked in the US Navy for five years as a civilian on a highly sensitive assignment, became a Mossad agent, and received a regular pay of $1,500 per month from Israel, besides availing all paid foreign visits and accepting expensive gifts for his wife. He handled top secret CIA satellite photos of Pakistan's nuclear installations and details of the defence purchases made by Saudi Arabia, Jordan, and Egypt from the US. He disclosed that Tel Aviv's secret service not only concentrated on Israel's neighbours but also focussed on Pakistan, Libya, Iraq, and Algeria. He delivered to the Mossad a complete CIA file on Pakistan's atomic programmes. In 1994, President Clinton denied clemency to Pollard because of 'the enormity' of his crime.

Pakistan's Nuclear Programme

Much of what has been said and written about Pakistan's nuclear programme makes a cocktail of facts, fiction, and falsehood, expertly orchestrated by the vested interests to create the effect of a melodrama. Mr Bhutto's statement of 1965 saying that, 'if India builds the [nuclear] bomb, we will eat grass, but we will get one of our own', has often been quoted in and out of context to justify the conclusions drawn.

That statement was an echo of the fears and sentiments of the people of Pakistan whose democratic psyche impels them to agree to disagree on many contentious issues, sometimes silently and sometimes violently. The nuclear programme, aimed at promoting national security, enjoys national consensus and bipartisan support. It is perceived to be a sensible and irreversible course. Those countries which oppose this programme either have a motive of preserving their own cartels or wish to realize their hegemonic aspirations.

KANUPP establishes Pakistan's nuclear non-proliferation policy. She could have legally claimed that Canada's violation of her international commitment to meet the running needs of KANUPP had automatically released this project from IAEA inspections and safeguards. However, Pakistan has voluntarily kept this power plant under the IAEA inspections as a measure of her sincerity.

Pakistan's nuclear programme, small in size and limited in scope, started at a leisurely pace. An Atomic Energy Committee formed in 1955 was given such a low priority that it functioned under a medium-ranking bureaucrat, in an obscure ministry in the federal government. The all-pervading bureaucratic control contrasted with such job insecurity that the services of the atomic energy personnel could be terminated on fifteen days notice. The half-hearted approach produced casual results.

In 1958, the Atomic Energy Committee was upgraded to the Pakistan Atomic Energy Commission (PAEC), with Dr Nazir Ahmad as its first Chairman. Dr I. H. Usmani became the Chairman PAEC in 1960 and held that position till 1972. During this period, the basic infrastructure was created in the fields of agriculture, medicine, power generation, and the training of technical manpower was started.

Mr Munir Ahmad Khan became the Chairman of PAEC in 1972. He held this appointment till 1991. In this period, Pakistan struggled hard to face the conflicting challenges of external pressures on her nuclear effort and the internal needs and aspirations of the country.

The Indian nuclear implosion polluted the international nuclear scene. The countries providing nuclear help to India felt cheated, took countermeasures, and introduced technological barriers for all the developing countries. Out went the Atom for Peace programmes and their like. In came the embargoes and restrictions imposed by those who enjoyed a monopoly on nuclear technologies, fuels, materials and know-how. They formed a cartel, the London Suppliers Club, to check the transfer of nuclear technology and sale of such items of dual-purpose machinery and equipment. This negative approach frustrated even the industrial growth of the developing countries. Pakistan's modest indigenous effort toward developing a nuclear capability, the only one in the Muslim world, was singled out for added criticism and condemnation. She was advised, cajoled, cautioned, warned, intimidated, and threatened in attempts to force her to abandon her research and development effort. The United States of America took the lead in frustrating even those agreements that Pakistan had concluded with other countries.

Working in such an adverse environment, Pakistan's nuclear development effort achieved success in some areas. KANUPP kept running despite the stoppage of spare parts, fuel materials, and technical services by Canada. By trial and error, Pakistan became self-sufficient in the front end of the nuclear fuel cycle. This involved the exploration of uranium, its mining and refining, and making reactor fuel for the power reactor. The much-publicized success in the enrichment of uranium was the most noteworthy achievement.

There were frustrations and failures. The secrecy of the programme was compromised. Foreign intelligence agencies made inroads into Pakistan's systems and organizations. Pakistan learned the hard way that, while discussing issues of vital security concern, discretion and prudence were better virtues than exuberance and projection.

Some goals remained elusive. Pakistan's projected target of fabricating eight reactors in the country by 1990 to produce 1,000 MW of nuclear energy failed even to make a start. On the one hand the planned goals were too ambitious to achieve. On the other, the acquisition of this technology by Pakistan would not have served the political, economic, and other interests of the supplier states. During this period, Pakistan did not produce any power reactor indigenously. On the retirement of Mr Munir Ahmad Khan, Dr Ashfaq Ahmad became the Chairman PAEC.

The French Deal

On 18 October 1974, PAEC signed an agreement with a French firm, Saint-Gobain Techniques Nouvelle (SGN), for the construction of a reprocessing plant at Chashma. In February 1976, the International

Atomic Energy Agency, France and Pakistan signed a tripartite agreement by which Pakistan agreed to submit the Chashma plant to international controls and inspection by the IAEA officials. The US delegate at the IAEA Board of Governors voted in favour of the tripartite agreement. On 18 March 1976, Pakistan and France signed an agreement for the construction of the Chashma reprocessing plant.

In June 1976, the US Congress adopted an amendment to the Foreign Aid Appropriations Bill, called the Symington Amendment, which prohibited economic and military assistance to any country which tried to acquire enrichment or reprocessing technology. Armed with this law, the Secretary of State, Dr Henry Kissinger, visited Pakistan in August 1976, to persuade Islamabad to give up the French reprocessing plant. As a *quid pro quo*, America offered to sell us jet fighters. When Prime Minister Bhutto declined to yield, Kissinger threatened that, if voted to power, the Democrats would 'make a horrible example of you.' Simultaneously, the United States pressurized France to cancel her deal with Pakistan.

In December 1976, the French Council for Nuclear Policy decided to discontinue export of reprocessing technology *prospectively* (emphasis added) and stated that the contract already signed with Pakistan would be implemented. This commitment proved short-lived. Buckling under to US pressure France began to stall on the contract, and in June 1977 proposed patently unacceptable additional conditions in an attempt to provoke Pakistan to revoke the agreement. Simultaneously, Pakistan faced intense US pressure to rescind the French agreement. In September 1977, the United States cut off military and economic assistance to Pakistan when she refused to cancel the deal with France.

In January 1978, the British Prime Minister, Mr James Callaghan, during his visit to Pakistan told General Zia that, while he appreciated Pakistan's desire to acquire a reprocessing plant from France, Britain was against the spread of nuclear technology for military purposes in the overall global context. He expressed doubt if France would provide the plant to Pakistan. It showed that the Western countries had worked in unison to enable France to wriggle out of her contract obligation with Pakistan.

America made France swallow her national pride. In June 1978, the French Council on Foreign Nuclear Policy revoked the Pakistan contract. The credibility of French assurances repeatedly given to Pakistan that she was too independent a nation to yield to external pressure on policy issues suddenly evaporated into thin air. The unpleasant task of communicating the French decision to Pakistan fell to the Secretary of the Council for Foreign Nuclear Policy, Mr Andre Jacomet.

Mr Jacomet, in his earlier visits to Pakistan, had vainly attempted to lure her into accepting a non-existent co-processing technology, reportedly still at the drawing-board stage. If and when developed, this technology was meant to enrich plutonium well below the weapon-grade level. Pakistan rejected this proposal with the contempt it deserved and declined to accept any deviation from the contract commitment.

Before arriving in Pakistan in July 1978, Mr Jacomet visited Tehran to elicit Iranian support to the French proposal. The government of Iran declined to intervene. France also drew a negative response on this issue from Saudi Arabia.

A visibly tense Jacomet met General Zia. Moral guilt was writ large on his tense face. He delivered a personal letter from President Giscard D'Estaing and talked vaguely of the French desire to co-operate with Pakistan on her needs for nuclear energy and nuclear know-how. Mr Jacomet made a vain effort to explain that France had independently taken a decision against the export of reprocessing technology. This was not the first time in history that a French emissary had lied so blatantly.

General Zia maintained a dignified calm. In a measured tone, he said, 'France is an honourable nation. I did not think that she would break a contract. But she was doing so.' 'The letter was very polite,' said Zia in a press conference held later in Rawalpindi, 'but in military terms, it was a lemon.'[49]

The French decision to 'suspend' the contract caused no surprise in Pakistan. While Pakistan lost a plant, France lost her credibility and dignity. Could she be trusted any longer to honour her openly negotiated international agreements? This question was hard for the Third World countries to ignore.

Mr Jacomet carried back to Paris a written reply from General Zia for President D'Estaing. In that letter, General Zia declined to accept the French reasoning and felt that the matter remained open for further discussion. He also reserved Pakistan's right to protect her legal interests.

With the Pakistan-French contract out of the way, the United States promptly restored economic and military aid for Pakistan in October 1978. The American-French link became visible.

US Pressure

The timings of the US-led diplomatic tirade by the West against Pakistan were carefully synchronized to take advantage of her difficulties, domestic and economic. In 1977, the Bhutto administration faced public wrath against the rigged elections held in March that year. The country was internally polarized. The prolonged massive agitation had severely affected the national economy and the treasury reserves had dipped low—very low indeed. America exploited Pakistan's political and economic vulnerability to torpedo her nuclear programme. The economic lever was used when diplomatic *demarches* failed to move first Bhutto and then General Zia from the nuclear route. Under US influence, the World Bank, the International Monetary Fund and Western donor countries applied the economic squeeze. Foreign loans became hard to obtain and Pakistan's requests for debt rescheduling were kept pending. Even approved projects and those which had already cleared the economic viability criteria were put on hold. Some World Bank and IMF officials told their Pakistani counterparts that the economic taps would start gushing out aid provided Pakistan played the nuclear ball game as desired. Standing firm on principles, the Zia administration declined to compromise and withstood pressures. The rougher the going became, the stronger grew Pakistan's resolve not to trade her security concern for aid. Pakistan-US relations remained tense and at a low ebb during the period 1977-9.

The Soviet military intervention in Afghanistan suddenly eased external pressure. Pakistan's nuclear programme remained irksome for the US administration but it no longer was an obstacle in developing a closer relationship with her. The other Western countries and agencies followed the US lead. It became expedient for the West to coexist with the ground reality in Pakistan. A decade later, soon after the Soviet forces had withdrawn from Afghanistan, the US hostility to Pakistan's nuclear programme resurfaced with renewed vigour. The US strategic objective in Afghanistan achieved, Pakistan was targeted once again.

THE NUCLEAR BALLYHOO

A United States-led disinformation campaign was launched against Pakistan's nuclear programme by the Western countries. Phoney films were made. Sponsored books were written. Articles based on information leaked out by intelligence agencies carried sensational tales about Pakistan's 'clandestine' nuclear activity. They claimed that the country was only a 'screw-turn' away from making a bomb. It was alleged that Libya and some other Arab countries had financed Pakistan's nuclear programme and Niger had diverted the yellow cake to her. Fictitious stories were circulated that Pakistan had secretly detonated a device in China. Such attempts were designed to damage Pakistan's relations with friendly countries. Interestingly, during this period, Pakistan received periodic offers for the sale of enriched uranium through vaguely quoted sources in Sudan, Switzerland, Greece, Kuwait, Abu Dhabi, Nepal etc. The US secretly planted a highly sensitive and advanced electronic monitoring device near Kahuta to collect classified information. The security agencies soon detected it. It is now kept as a museum piece. This indicated the extent to which the intelligence organizations of certain Western countries tried to spy on, bait, implicate, and discredit Pakistan.

Pakistani traders importing items of common use for the civil sector industry were accused of indulging in business malpractice and ulterior motives were attributed to their routine business transactions. The fact that the government of Pakistan did not exercise control over the business dealings of her private citizens was conveniently ignored.

It was alleged that Pakistani businessmen tried to import from the United States small quantities of zirconium, kryptron switches, and maraging steel without obtaining export permits. In all the three incidents, the accused were trapped by CIA agents who first lured them into buying the material. The alleged defaulters faced trial in the USA under US law in US courts, which resulted in their acquittal on the main charges. Strangely, the public leakage of such attempts always coincided with the discussion on Pakistan's aid programme in the US Congress.

Maligning Pakistan became the favourite activity of the Western countries. A Dutch court carried out a farcical trial. Dr A. Q. Khan was prosecuted, without his knowledge or presence, for trying to obtain a technical piece of information based on available published literature which the Public Prosecutor felt was classified. A lower court in Holland convicted Dr A. Q. Khan without even hearing him.

An appeal was filed in the High Court of Amsterdam in 1983, which set aside the patently absurd judgment of the lower court. On 16 June 1986, the Dutch government finally dropped all the charges. While this act made no news in the Western press, the unjust trial was given wide publicity by the Western news media.

With the shutters down on external technological assistance, Pakistan pursued a policy of increased self-reliance. This was a frustrating and yet a rewarding experience. Frustration came with the hurdles faced so frequently. To overcome those difficulties gave immeasurable satisfaction. With patience, innovation, and greater perseverance, Pakistan achieved self-reliance in the manufacture of a large number of jigs, tools, machines, and instruments of critical importance. When a comprehensive account of Pakistan's nuclear programme is written, a word of gratitude should be expressed for those countries which closed the tap of nuclear technology on Pakistan. It created a realization in the policy-makers and the scientists at home that all substitutes to self-sufficiency were transitory and unreliable. Dependence on external crutches breeds internal lethargy and provides a mirage of security. When attention was focused on achieving indigenous capability, gradually light started appearing at the end of the research tunnel.

The success achieved by Pakistan was given a mischievous twist by the vested interests. Their imagination ran wild. The rumour mills churned out juicy, tales, implicating Pakistan in dicey deals. The BBC went to the extent of showing a PIA plane in flight, supposedly carrying dollar bills from Libya to Pakistan. Libya's mercurial leader, Qaddafi, had earned the ire of many countries by his freelance policies. It was alleged that Libya had financed Pakistan's nuclear programme. As a *quid pro quo*, so it was surmised, a Pakistani-made nuclear bomb might be given to Qaddafi, which could endanger the security of Israel. The acquisition of nuclear technology by Pakistan could thus pose a danger to peace.

The fictitious and mischievous accusations coined by the rumour-mongers were expertly projected by the Western-controlled media. No external power has invested even a penny in Pakistan's nuclear research and development programme. Pakistan is not naive enough to compromise her freedom. Nor is she a crazed nation, unmindful of nuclear hazards. Her track record is that of a responsible country playing a moderating role in world conflicts. This is borne out by the balanced approach she has consistently adopted in the United Nations General Assembly. Her relations with Libya have had a chequered history. These have mostly been anything but enviable most of the time.

The Libyan Reality

Prime Minister Bhutto, claiming to be a progressive socialist, had strengthened diplomatic ties with countries like North Korea, Syria, Libya, and with the Palestine Liberation Organization. Qaddafi's visit to Pakistan during the Islamic summit conference held in Lahore in 1974 was a high-water mark in the Pakistan-Libya relationship. Mr Bhutto developed an enduring personal equation with Colonel Qaddafi. The Libyan unhappiness about the fall of the Bhutto administration in July 1977 made her relations with Pakistan cool.

During General Zia's informal visit to Libya in 1978, his call on Qaddafi was delayed by 45 minutes. That discourtesy did not go unnoticed. Pakistan-Libya relations dived low.

The following year, it was Qaddafi's turn to feel hurt when Bhutto was executed, despite the Libyan request for clemency. Qaddafi maintained personal contacts with and supported the Bhutto family. Pakistan's intelligence agencies reported Libya providing financial assistance to some Pakistani dissidents involved in anti-state and terrorist activities within the country. This created further strains between the two countries.

Both the countries made diplomatic efforts to repair the damage. During his visit to Pakistan, the Libyan leader Major Abdussalam Jalloud suggested that the past be forgotten and an improvement be made in the bilateral relationship. In an after banquet *tete-a-tete* with General Zia, Major Jalloud suggested the raising of an Islamic army —with Libyan money and Pakistani manpower—to be stationed in his country. Such an army, claimed Jalloud, would protect the interests of the Islamic world. Some other like-minded nations could subsequently join this force. General Zia responded favourably. The same night, he discussed the proposal with Mr Ghulam Ishaq Khan, Mr Agha Shahi, and me; we all opposed the venture. It was not appropriate for Pakistan, we argued, to get involved in Libya's dispute with her neighbours. Nor should Pakistan take sides in an inter-Arab conflict, except in the case of a gross violation by some country, we contended. General Zia agreed with this advice. Minutes later, he met Jalloud again to express Pakistan's reservations. Jalloud was disappointed. Pakistan-Libya relations deteriorated once again.

In 1981, Libya expressed a desire to hire Pakistanis, preferably ex-soldiers, for guard duties. The selected persons were taken to Libya. Their passports were withdrawn and they were interned in special camps for military training. Those refusing training were subjected to harsh treatment. Training completed, some were secretly sent to Lebanon to participate in *jihad* against Israel'. The unwilling guardsmen turned make-shift 'soldiers' wrote home their tales of woe, which were splashed in the Press. A government delegation led by Mr Ghulam Dastgir Khan, Minister of Labour and Manpower, visited Libya in November 1981 and managed to end the misery of the Pakistani labour. They were brought back home at Libya's expense. This episode chilled the inter-state relations still further.

Pakistan's Foreign Minister, Mr Agha Shahi, was invited to visit Libya in mid-January 1982, to improve bilateral relations. In an obvious reference, Dr Ali Abdussalam Treiki told Mr Agha Shahi that Pakistan-Libya relations took priority over the life of an individual. Foreign Minister Abdul Atti Ibrahim al Obeidi told Shahi that the time was ripe to develop better bilateral ties. Colonel Qaddafi, however, showed his bitterness. He expressed his desire to overcome the 'tragedy' of Mr Bhutto's execution and went on to make the accusation that General Zia's government was suppressing the popular forces in the country. When corrected, Qaddafi quickly volunteered to mediate in Pakistan's internal dispute. The autocratic leader did not care to remember the manner of his own rise to power and the absence of democratic institutions in the country he ruled with an iron hand. As had happened with the Shah of Iran, the new-found oil wealth had clouded Qaddafi's vision. Speaking with an air of importance, he stated that Pakistan should not accept US influence and that Libya would oppose American hegemony over her. That uncalled for advice depicted the abrasiveness of a person who was not a fresh entrant in international diplomacy. Knowing that President Zia was to visit some countries in Europe at the end of January 1982, Qaddafi suggested to Agha Shahi that the Pakistani President might stop over in Tripoli, as it was important for the two leaders to meet. Shahi pointed out General Zia's tight itinerary but Qaddafi repeated his request.

General Zia's tour of European countries brought him to Bucharest on 21 January 1982. Pakistan's ambassador in Libya, Mr Shahid M. Amin, was called there for a firsthand briefing to review the Libyan request for General Zia's possible stopover at Tripoli, during his homeward flight at the end of his scheduled visits. The ambassador recommended an affirmative response. Qaddafi's discussion with Shahi had created misgivings and Pakistan's reply had taken note of it. The ambassador returned to his post with the message that President Zia was prepared for a two-hour stopover at Tripoli on 27 January 1982, if an assurance was given that he would be given the protocol of a head of a state and Pakistan's internal affairs would not be discussed. Libya hedged. Pakistan stood firm in her demand. Eventually, General Zia's visit did not materialize. Thereafter, throughout the rule of General Zia Pakistan-Libya relations did not develop closeness.

Between the years 1979-88, Libya did not condemn the Soviet military occupation of Afghanistan. At the UN General Assembly, she invariably voted against the Pakistan-sponsored resolution censuring the Soviet Union and urging her to withdraw her forces. Every year the resolution was approved by over 100 countries, with Libya and few others always opposing it.

Assessed in this background, the allegation that Libya had made a financial contribution towards Pakistan's nuclear effort does not make sense.

The Nuclear Approach

Pakistan has consistently expressed her willingness to place her entire nuclear programme under international safeguards, provided these are applied universally and on a non-discriminatory basis to all countries. Any derogation of that principle would imply that some countries were more sovereign than others. It is the unassailable right of all states to have access to nuclear technology. No country can abdicate her rights for the spurious and self-serving reasons advanced by others.

A visiting dignitary from the US administration (name deliberately omitted) met General Zia in Islamabad in 1980. While expressing US apprehensions about nuclear proliferation, he suggested that Pakistan should sign the Nuclear Non-Proliferation Treaty. General Zia told his guest that Pakistan would do so the day after India acceded to the NPT.

'But India is unlikely to join the NPT because of the China factor,' lamented the guest, and went on to advise, 'By joining the NPT Pakistan could put India under considerable moral pressure.'

Zia listed the nuclear installations in India which were outside the international safeguards and asked his guest, 'Why don't you put moral pressure on India to accept the international safeguards?' 'India won't accept that,' replied the visitor.

'Is Pakistan being unfair in expecting,' asked General Zia, 'that America should follow an even-handed approach in this matter? US concern on nuclear proliferation should not be selectively applied. And why does she discriminate between these two countries?'

The official's patience ran out. 'India has the facilities and we can't do anything about it,' said the guest. 'But, Mr President, you don't have that capability yet and America is not going to let you possess it.' The rabbit was out of the hat.

Pakistan's Nuclear Effort

PAEC produced yellow cake from indigenous uranium ore. In 1978 it made the first fuel bundle used in the nuclear reactor at Karachi. Nuclear medical centres are providing facilities for the treatment of cancer and for diagnostic services. New varieties of cotton, wheat, rice, and mungbean have been developed through nuclear techniques. But for the restrictive foreign policies, the negative attitude of the supplier states, and her own lethargy, Pakistan could have moved faster towards establishing nuclear power generating plants in the country to meet her growing energy needs. Her industrial development will remain elusive if her electricity production does not meet the expanding public and industrial demands. Pakistan is developing know-how and infrastructure, albeit at a slow pace, in the designing, engineering, and fabrication of nuclear power generating plants.

What Pakistan has achieved was made possible by the expertise of a group of pioneers who accepted the challenge with dedication. Starting from a small group, their number has expanded. Service to the country and professional satisfaction are their best rewards.

Pakistan has acquired the capability to enrich uranium to meet her modest needs. Uranium, a heavy and radioactive metallic element, was discovered in 1789 by a German scientist, Martin Klaproth. Streaks of different types of uranium ore deposits are found in some crusts of the earth. Uranium has different isotopes. The two common isotopes are uranium 235 (^{235}U) and uranium 238 (^{238}U).

Since the atoms of ^{238}U do not readily fission, this isotope cannot be directly used to produce nuclear energy. On the other hand, ^{235}U being fissionable, creates energy.

THE NUCLEAR BALLYHOO

For commercial and other purposes, ^{235}U has to be upgraded through a complicated physical process called 'enrichment'. When enriched to a level of 3.5 per cent, it is used as a fuel in the nuclear power plants or research reactors. These are called light water reactors. Hundreds of such reactors are operating in the world, producing nuclear power.

^{235}U, when enriched beyond 90 per cent, can be used as a core of an atomic bomb after converting the enriched UF_6 gas into uranium metal. It is also called the uranium bomb, like the one dropped on Hiroshima.

An atomic bomb can also be made from plutonium. The Indian nuclear explosion in 1974 was a plutonium bomb. So was the one dropped on Nagasaki.

Uranium enrichment is a complex process. The uranium ore found in nature is first converted into uranium oxide concentrate called yellow cake. The yellow cake is then further purified in a conversion plant and turned into uranium hexafluoride (UF_6). The UF_6 gas is fed into the ultracentrifuges in an enrichment plant. Through a process of high-speed spinning spread over a period of time, the heavy uranium 238 is separated from the lighter and fissionable uranium 235. The UF_6 is thus enriched to the required level and is further processed to be used as a fuel in nuclear reactors.

In the acquisition of uranium enrichment technology for Pakistan, Dr A. Q. Khan played a leading part. Being a pioneer in this field, he has earned for himself a place of perennial respect. He was ably assisted by a team of dedicated colleagues working under him— unknown and unsung in public—but by whose capability and contribution Dr A. Q. Khan himself swears. Many scientists serving in the PAEC have also performed acts of great distinction. Their behind-the-scenes contribution is notable and laudable.

At the policy level, Pakistan's nuclear programme had the patronage of two leaders —Mr Z. A. Bhutto and General Ziaul Haq. The conceptual input was initiated by Mr Bhutto. He left the scene early. At that time, the infrastructure was under construction and, barring some minor successes, the scientists were struggling to overcome the teething technological difficulties.

The Zia government inherited the programme, pursued it with great vigour against strong external opposition, removed its difficulties, withstood external threats, and put it on the rails. Given full patronage and sustained support, the scientists responded well.

Slowly, the rough edges were smoothened, the technical hurdles were crossed, and the pace of work gained momentum. Luck favoured General Zia who emerged as the real architect of the nuclear effort. The duration of his rule was long and the opportunities which came up were seized and well utilized. The geostrategic changes in the region enabled Zia and a handful of his close colleagues to develop Pakistan's nuclear programme from close to the start line, where they inherited it, to within striking distance of the goal post. This gladdened Pakistanis and saddened the nuclear monopolists and the potential aggressor.

The technological breakthrough was achieved despite the barriers created by the foreign powers, the diplomatic and economic pressures exerted on the country, and the venomous Western media blitzkrieg against Pakistan's nuclear effort. Mr Ghulam Ishaq Khan (later President) and the author monitored the nuclear programme on behalf of the President and provided general guidance cum financial support. The scientists worked with minimal research facilities and on modest emoluments.

In September 1987, Prime Minister Junejo in his address to the United Nations General Assembly stated that he had proposed a bilateral ban on nuclear testing to Prime Minister Gandhi of India. India rejected the initiative. General Zia said in an interview in July 1988 that the region had achieved 'a stable nuclear deterrent relationship based upon ambiguity as to whether India and Pakistan had nuclear weapons, and if they did, how many they possessed'.[50] Spector interprets this as 'the tacit acknowledgement that Pakistan may possess a *de facto* nuclear weapons capability'.[51]

The sudden death of General Ziaul Haq in a mysterious aircraft crash in August 1988 produced a negative impact on Pakistan's nuclear programme. The inexperienced and vacillating Prime Minister Benazir Bhutto proved too weak to withstand external pressure on the nuclear issue. Following a carrot and stick approach, President Reagan certified to the US Congress on 18 November 1988 that Pakistan did not possess a nuclear device. Simultaneously, Washington made it known to Islamabad that the bilateral aid relationship was on the rocks. The feeble policy-makers in Pakistan failed to comprehend that the US tactics were based on a grand design in which the special relationship with Pakistan had undergone a change after the Soviet retreat from Afghanistan. The aid was to be phased out anyway but in the interregnum Islamabad was to be kept guessing, in order to extract concessions.

In January 1989, President Ghulam Ishaq Khan, Prime Minister Benazir Bhutto, COAS General Mirza Aslam Beg, the Foreign Minister, and some others, decided in a joint meeting to freeze the enrichment of uranium at a low level. The decision was enforced and America was so informed, but the people of Pakistan were not considered worthy of this trust. This was incremental capitulation. Mr Nawaz Sharif, who succeeded Benazir as Prime Minister, kept the lid of secrecy on this issue.

Pakistan had walked into the trap laid for her. The US alleged that Pakistan had crossed a red line which disqualified her from receiving further US aid in accordance with US laws. President Bush did not issue the certification to the Congress in respect of Pakistan in 1989. In the American assessment, Pakistan did not possess a nuclear weapon but had crossed some unannounced prohibitive barrier. The Prime Minister, pleading innocence, maintained that if any barrier was crossed, it was without her knowledge.

Prime Minister Nawaz Sharif's government reiterated in 1992 'Pakistan's pledge neither to explode a nuclear device nor to transfer nuclear technology to other countries although she had the capability.' In the words of the Foreign Secretary, the candid announcement was meant to 'avoid a credibility gap.'[52]

On 20 November 1993, Prime Minister Benazir Bhutto stated that, 'The nuclear programme had been capped and frozen since July 1990,'[53] and held the Nawaz Sharif government responsible for it. General Aslam Mirza Beg announced that, 'To set the record straight, a meeting was held in the Presidency in January 1989 to deliberate the nuclear issue. President Ghulam Ishaq Khan, Prime Minister Benazir Bhutto, the COAS [himself] and three other very responsible persons attended. It was unanimously decided to put a restraint on uranium enrichment.'[54] When asked to comment on this issue President Ghulam Ishaq Khan declined to 'offer a comment' as he wished to stay 'clear of the controversy.'[55]

In August 1994, Nawaz Sharif, the leader of the Opposition, stated that Pakistan had a nuclear weapon, a claim prompty and forcefully denied by the Benazir government.

The Nuclear Debate

The official timidity in the face of an increasing threat posed by India increased the element of risk to Pakistan's national security.

There is a differing view. Some analysts maintain that, for economic and moral reasons, Pakistan should unilaterally opt out of a regional nuclear race. This argument belies the lessons of history. Economic and moral compulsions have seldom prevented aggression. Realpolitik is not governed by the lofty ideals of the puritans. Weakness and appeasement invite trouble. Nations that compromise their security under what they believe to be high moral principles invariably put their security in jeopardy. Running after mirages invites destruction. The Munich accord is too recent to be forgotten.

Can Pakistan seek an external security guarantee to meet her defence needs? The possibility of some country agreeing to provide a security umbrella to Pakistan is wishful thinking and unworthy of serious consideration. The collapse of the Soviet Union, a superpower, shows that no country can guarantee even her own integrity, much less that of another state. National security is too delicate a subject to be left to the changing whims and policies of outside powers. Pakistan knows too well that, despite the US commitment to preserve her unity and sovereignty, she was dismembered in 1971.

A seemingly fair approach is to apply a nuclear freeze on the nuclear capability of India and Pakistan at mutually agreed levels. Such expediency is unlikely to establish durable peace in the subcontinent. To freeze a gross nuclear inequality will perpetuate insecurity for the weaker country. Weapons do not cause wars. Conflicts do. The underlying causes of the regional conflicts should be politically removed to avoid the temptation of settling them through violent means. Pakistan cannot afford to ignore the superiority enjoyed by her neighbour in conventional weaponry.

Pakistani Proposals

Pakistan, a consistent supporter of a nuclear non-proliferation regime in South Asia, has good reason to feel insecure. The loss of East Pakistan and the manner in which it was brought about weighs heavily in her policy considerations. She has demonstrated her goodwill by advocating a bilateral discussion on the nuclear issue and has suggested to India the following specific proposals for the promotion of peace and confidence between them:

— Simultaneous accession by India and Pakistan to the Nuclear Non-Proliferation Treaty.

— Simultaneous acceptance by both the countries of full scope IAEA safeguards.

— Mutual inspection of each other's nuclear facilities.

— A joint declaration renouncing the acquisition or development of nuclear weapons.

— Establishment of a Nuclear-Weapon Free Zone in South Asia, an objective repeatedly endorsed by the UN General Assembly through various resolutions.

— Convening a conference on nuclear non-proliferation in South Asia under UN auspices with the participation of all countries in the region.

— A bilateral treaty to ban all nuclear tests.

— A five-nation conference — USA, Russia, China, India, and Pakistan—to examine the nuclear non-proliferation issue in the subcontinent.

India has rejected all these proposals. She has also declined to make alternative suggestions on the plea that nuclear disarmament is only valid in a global context. India avoids serious negotiations to gain time to complete her ongoing nuclear effort to produce a *fait accompli* and improve her bargaining position.

The nuclear programmes of India and Pakistan are based on the principle of ambiguity but for different reasons. India demands a share in the power equilibrium, Pakistan seeks security. Both the countries, assessed as nuclear-capable, are advised by the Western powers not to convert their nuclear capability into weapon systems. The Western society, in which a free lunch is taboo, arrogates to itself the right to offer free advice to sovereign states on the nuclear issues.

The nuclear game, worldwide, is a mix of openness, secrecy, and disinformation. Whereas the political, strategic, and psychological aspects are freely debated in most democracies, the economic cost is seldom accurately disclosed and the technological achievements made remain off limits for discussion.

An arms race between India and Pakistan—conventional or nuclear—may hurt both the countries. With greater resources, India can numerically outmatch Pakistan and stockpile nuclear weapons to achieve an overkill capability. This may provide some satisfaction, but its practical value is questionable. A minimum credible nuclear deterrent capability with India and Pakistan can promote regional security and help in reducing the level of their conventional forces.

India and Pakistan may have three nuclear options. The first, maintain the status quo and let nuclear ambiguity persist till it runs out its natural course. In the resultant no-peace no-war scenario, inter-state relations will remain brittle and the region may be perched on a volcano.

Secondly, India and Pakistan may agree not to make nuclear weapons, subject their nuclear facilities to international or bilateral inspection, and declare South Asia a nuclear-weapon free zone. This could involve capping and reversing of their respective nuclear-programmes under verifiable safeguards. It could also cover nuclear weapons, materials, and facilities, and all means of delivery. The nuclear weapons and their means of delivery already in their possession may have to be destroyed through mutually acceptable and verifiable arrangements.

The third choice could be to achieve a modicum of qualitative and quantitative parity, near parity, or even inequality, in the nuclear weapon field. An open-door policy could replace their existing closed approach. Such a status can be maintained till such time as a global strategy is evolved, whereby all the nuclear weapon states abjure nuclear weapons.

Since 1972, Pakistan has been advocating the creation of a Nuclear Weapon-Free Zone in the Indian Ocean in the U.N. General. In her perception, the emergence of a single nuclear weapon state in South Asia has enhanced the regional instability in general and her own in particular.

Some Western analysts speculate that nuclear weapons, if used in South Asia, would result in a catastrophe. Their apprehension is justified. Precisely for this reason, these weapons may never be employed as an instrument of policy by any country in any role against any people. In their turbulent history, India and Pakistan have committed grave errors of judgement in the past and their bilateral relations have seldom been a model of good neighbourly behaviour. Many a time their internal policies have caused eyebrows to be raised even within their own countries. But which country on earth has not committed intolerable excesses in the past, based on colour, creed, race, religion, and a variety of other reasons? Those who preach human rights, ethics, and morality to others are themselves guilty of tolerating ethnic cleansing being done as a matter of state policy in the heart of civilized Europe. India and Pakistan may not be the most perfect states in the world but neither is a crazy country either. It is strange that nuclear weapons are considered safe and acceptable in some hands but dangerous and unacceptable in others. If the strategy of nuclear deterrence can work in Europe, why can it not be effective elsewhere? Despite her overbearing attitude towards her neighbours, it is highly doubtful if India will use a nuclear weapon against Pakistan if she suspects retaliation in kind. The reverse is equally true.

Non-Proliferation Treaty

Less than six months after the end of the Second World War, a resolution was passed calling for 'the elimination from national armaments of atomic weapons and of all other weapons adoptable to mass destruction.'[56] Notwithstanding this call, nuclear weapons were produced. On 1 July 1968, 62 countries signed the Nuclear Non-Proliferation Treaty (NPT) with the goals of preventing the further spread of nuclear weapons and encouraging negotiations to end the nuclear arms race, with a view to general and complete disarmament. Not much progress has been made on Article VI of the NPT under which 'the signatories pledge to work toward universal nuclear disarmament.' Under Article X of the NPT, an extension conference will be held (in 1995) to determine whether the treaty should be renewed periodically or indefinitely.

The NPT, preventing the horizontal spread of nuclear weapons but permitting their vertical proliferation by a few states, has earned the odium of being discriminatory. A selective approach cannot promote international peace on a durable basis. If the non-nuclear weapon states are prohibited from possessing nuclear weapons to promote global peace, it should be equally binding on all the nuclear weapon states to eliminate all their nuclear weapons within an agreed time-frame.

By 1994, 163 countries had signed the NPT. France and China, after remaining out of the NPT fold for two decades, acceded to it in 1991. So have Argentina, Brazil, and South Africa. India and Pakistan have not signed the NPT, but for different reasons. India calls it discriminatory. Pakistan is prepared to sign the treaty, provided India does so.

The genuine security concerns of all countries can be met fairly and equitably. The countries with hegemonic motives ought to be censured and opposed. Others which fear a legitimate threat to their national security need to be reassured. Pakistan falls in this category.

Commenting on the Intermediate-range Nuclear Force (INF) Treaty signed between the USA and the USSR on 1 June 1988, Dr Zbigniew Brzezinski, the former National Security Adviser during the Carter presidency, said, 'I think arms control is basically a fraud. A lot of stupid people in the world think that cutting nuclear weapons by fifty per cent increases stability by fifty per cent. In some ways, the strategic relationship is likely to be more vulnerable.'[57]

In the annals of history, weapons of destruction have never remained the exclusive preserve of a selected few states. Advancement in technology improves the weapons systems. Those becoming redundant are replaced by a newer generation. A coercive approach to prevent the spread of nuclear weapons will encourage its clandestine growth. Such a development will inevitably be harmful for humanity.

Ideals and Reality

Total elimination of nuclear weapons to be achieved worldwide, within a reasonably short, agreed time-frame, should be the ultimate goal of mankind. Despite a commitment to this effect made under Article VI of the NPT, no worthwhile progress on this issue has been made in the last two decades. The nuclear weapon states seem to be in no mood to lose their monopoly. The realization that a global nuclear non-proliferation regime would best serve the cause of all humanity should emerge from within each country. The nuclear have-not states will be attracted to this goal if the Big Five set an example and fix a deadline for achieving total elimination of all nuclear weapons and their means of delivery. Their motives will be suspect if they hedge on this issue.

Nuclear weapons, after causing horrendous destruction in Japan, have helped to maintain peace. The assurance of mutual destruction helped to promote the mutual assurance of existence. The model of Europe can be duplicated elsewhere, including South Asia.

Nuclear proliferation is a reality in the subcontinent. The Indian nuclear capability and her imperial attitude pose security concerns to her neighbours in South Asia. Since nuclear weapons can only be deterred by nuclear weapons there is hardly a choice other than the nuclear option to checkmate the possibility of nuclear blackmail by a neighbour. A single nuclear weapon state, in a brittle and tension-ridden region, is a danger to peace, stability, and security. Whether or not such weapons will be unleashed in the future is debatable. One hopes that they will never by used. So long as they exist, the mere fact of their possession by one of the adversaries constitutes an unacceptable risk.

India and Pakistan face increasing economic, diplomatic, and psychological pressure from aid-giving states and institutions to halt, cap, and reverse their ongoing nuclear programmes. On this issue, both have shown restraint. While India has conducted only one nuclear weapon test, Pakistan has not even demonstrated her capability, besides freezing her uranium enrichment process. South Asia needs an even-handed nuclear approach to achieve the goal of nuclear non-proliferation. The rules of the nuclear game should be applied to both countries on an equal basis.

Disarmament and arms control in themselves do not ensure peace or guarantee security, but they reduce the risk of war. In South Asia the disarmament issue—nuclear and conventional—is directly linked with the larger question of national security. Tension in South Asia can be reduced by removing the causes of conflict. The dispute over Kashmir lies at the heart of the Indo-Pakistan differences. A settlement of this dispute will expedite the process of regional peace. The route to nuclear peace in the subcontinent passes through the state of Jammu and Kashmir. Herein lies the key to success and peace.

Strangely, the most ardent supporter of nuclear non-proliferation has the largest inventory of nuclear weapons and the biggest stockpile of fissile materials. The Western nuclear approach is based on the principle of domination. Human hearts are won by love, not weapons or threats. Durable peace can be better achieved through a policy of equal rights and equal security between countries. A tranquil South Asia will create beneficial commercial opportunities for the countries within this region and for the world at large.

Denunciation of nuclear weapons and their destruction are better options than the strategy of deterrence. However, if one country in a troubled region adopts a policy of deterrence, the other is hardly left with a viable alternative. In this scenario, neither India nor Pakistan can unilaterally renounce the nuclear option for reasons of security, public opinion and national prestige. Either both the countries jointly renounce the nuclear weapons or both should acquire them.

Given India's opposition, a nuclear weapon-free Indian Ocean, a desirable goal, is not presently visible on the regional horizon. Should India and Pakistan decide to retain their nuclear capabilities or translate them into weapon systems, then, based on ground realities, this region can be declared a nuclear weapon safe zone with an agreed mechanism created for nuclear safety and arms control measures. Sooner or later, they will surely come to realize that the subcontinent would be better off without nuclear weapons. In the interregnum, Pakistan retains the nuclear option, not as a weapon for war but as an instrument of peace.

CHAPTER 15

A Stormy Summer

1988 was a year of tragedy. Three events in quick succession shook Pakistan and altered the course of her history. In April 1988, a large arms and ammunition depot in Islamabad, which had been meeting the needs of the Afghan freedom struggle, was destroyed, just four days before the Geneva Accord was signed.

A month later, a political storm shook the country. The quasi-democratic Junejo government was unceremoniously shown the door by the very person who had inducted it into power with considerable fanfare three years earlier. By that constitutional coup, General Zia rocked the unsteady boat of democracy.

Soon thereafter, in August 1988, General Zia died in a plane crash and the country was plunged into uncertainty.

In the interregnum between the dismissal of the Junejo government and the elections due in November 1988, General Zia had formed a caretaker government without a prime minister. By that act, he concentrated in his person all the constitutional powers of the president and the prime minister. The parliamentary form of government was thus *ipso facto* converted into a presidential form through an executive fiat. The equilibrium of power between the head of state and the head of government ceased to exist. The balance swung exclusively in the direction of the president.

The first two incidents mentioned above were interrelated. The fallout from the second had already clouded the political horizon of Pakistan when Zia was abruptly removed from the national scene. The three events had a snowball effect.

Ojhri Camp

The rose gardens in Islamabad were in full bloom. Spring had added colour and fragrance to the otherwise dull routine of the expanding capital city—rich in bureaucrats and richer still in officialdom. The mellow sun and soothing morning breeze enhanced the architectural beauty of the well-planned city. The early morning chirping of the birds could no longer be heard as the rising sun lit the low-lying Margalla Hills with its golden rays. The din of transport taking people to work and children to school had just ended.

On 10 April 1988, the serenity of Islamabad was rudely shaken. At 9:35 a. m., a low intensity explosion on the outskirts of the city started a fire. Moments later, there was a louder bang. As frightened people came out of their homes, inquisitive about the strange phenomenon, all hell was suddenly let loose. A series of explosions in quick succession shook the twin cities of Islamabad and Rawalpindi. Panic replaced tranquillity. People ran helter-skelter in search of safety. At 9:45 a. m., an explosion of severe intensity jolted the two cities. It was recorded at 3.8 on the Richter scale. A rain of missiles then started pouring over the area. Unchecked and uncontrolled, they flew in all directions at random, hitting whatever came in their way. Islamabad became an undeclared and undefended battlefield. The deafening projectile fireworks lasted for a long time, leaving behind one hundred dead and 1,100 wounded. It was a catastrophe unprecedented in the history of Pakistan.

In view of the national calamity, President Zia, who was at that time attending the Organization of Islamic Conference mini-summit at Kuwait, cut short his visit and rushed back home. A three-day state mourning was declared in the country. The rockets had disrupted the telephone system and the water supply facility in Islamabad. So great was the havoc caused that two hundred bomb disposal teams combed the city for days to recover used shells and to defuse live bombs. The Minister of State for Defence, Rana Naeem Mahmood, was 'not only grieved but also ashamed on the tragic accident'.[1] But he stayed on in his post.

The explosion site was Ojhri Camp—a World War Two vintage cluster of brick barracks with tin roofs—located halfway between the twin cities of Islamabad and Rawalpindi. Built to low specifications for use during the war, the barracks should have ceased to exist many years earlier. Pakistan's financial constraints, which precluded replacing old structures with new ones, and the ingenuity of her people in saving old buildings from collapse, had kept Ojhri Camp going. At different times the Camp had housed different military units.

After the 1979 induction of the Soviet military forces into Afghanistan, weapons and ammunition from donor countries started filtering through Pakistan to the Afghan resistance movement.

The Inter-Services Intelligence (ISI) Directorate, dealing with the covert military support, selected Ojhri Camp to serve as an arms depot. It was essentially a transit facility, receiving the lethal cargo by train from the port city of Karachi, storing it for short periods, and then sending it in batches to its destinations by truck. The supply started as a trickle, for which the Camp had adequate storing facility. With the passage of time as the intensity of operations inside Afghanistan increased, so did the requirement of arms and ammunition for the *jihad*. The existing accommodation became inadequate. Some additional sheds were built to increase the storage capacity. Even then, the available space was inadequate for keeping the ammunition and explosives properly segregated as required under the prescribed safety regulation. Some *ad hoc* measures were taken and the results they produced were, understandably, far from satisfatory.

On 10 April 1988, boxes filled with ammunition and explosives were being manually shifted from the ill-fated sheds to the waiting transport for dispatch to other destinations. The loading work was performed by a group of hired civil labour under lax supervision. The boxes had previously been untidily stacked in the sheds to a height of approximately 9 to 10 feet. To save time and effort, they were being pushed down by the untrained and unsuspecting labour, and loaded on to the vehicles. The first hour and a half were uneventful. At about 9:30 a.m., a box containing 122 mm Rocket-A fell from the top of the stack while the men were trying to slide it down. It hit the ground with a thud and exploded on impact, starting a fire which caused panic amongst the workmen. Some persons ran in search of safety. Others were wounded, shocked, and unable to function. As the fire spread, there was yet another explosion which started another fire elsewhere in the shed. Soon a chain effect was created in which the ammunition started burning and the sheds were set ablaze. The intensity of heat generated and the process of sympathetic detonation activated the remaining rockets which started flying in all directions, causing havoc and panic.

The 122 mm Rocket-A was fitted with an inbuilt percussion fuse which, the experts claimed, could be activated by strong impact. In simpler language, this fuse had a point-detonating mechanism with no extra inbuilt safety device. A violent vibration could technically activate the firing pin which in turn would ignite the primer charge, causing the firing of the rocket. The rockets had been manufactured in a Third World country, perhaps not to high specifications.

The accident completely destroyed over 7,000 tons of arms and explosives. A large number of vehicles parked in the area were also burnt.

The tragedy stunned the people of Pakistan. The heavy loss of lives and property raised vital questions of national security and public safety. That an ammunition depot existed in the midst of a populated area without public knowledge aroused alarm. Caught on the wrong foot, the government came under biting criticism and took shelter behind an unconvincing argument that such accidents were not uncommon in other parts of the world. It forgot that two wrongs do not make a right.

Before the fire was brought under control, it had gutted the sheds completely. The loss in the terms of money remained undisclosed. On 12 April 1988, a Commission of Enquiry was formed to investigate the causes leading to the incident of fire in the ammunition depot; to point out security lapses and fix responsibility; to make recommendations for the prevention of such incidents in the future; and to make any other recommendations considered necessary by it. The two-man Commission was presided over by Lieutenant-General Imranullah Khan. It was directed to submit its report to the federal government within a period of ten days.

The Commission co-opted some military experts as technical members to facilitate its task. It submitted its report to the government on 22 April 1988; the report was neither made public nor presented to the National Assembly. A five-member ministerial committee was formed to examine it and to make recommendations on its implementation. The composition of the Committee was Mr Muhammad Aslam Khattak (Minister/Chairman), with Ministers Qazi Abdul Majid Abid, Mir Ibrahim Baloch, Malik Nasim Ahmad Aheer, and the Minister of State, Rana Naeem Mahmood, as members. The Committee reportedly developed differences during its deliberations and split into two groups. Aslam Khattak and Nasim Aheer came to be called the pro-Zia group. The other three ministers got the Junejo label. The committee authorized its Chairman to write its report. While doing so, Aslam Khattak took a broad political view of the incident and underplayed the blame attributed to the Director General of Intelligence. This prompted Rana Naeem to write a short paper on the issue, disagreeing with the Chairman on some points. Ibrahim Baloch and Qazi Abid supported Rana and appended their signatures to his paper.

Some members of the ministerial committee wanted strict action against all those responsible for dereliction of duty, including the policy-makers. These included General Akhtar Abdur Rahman, who headed the ISI Directorate till March 1987, and his successor Major-General Hamid Gul. The others took a lenient and broader view of the tragic episode. The Committee's recommendations were submitted to the Prime Minister but were kept classified.

General Zia's Chief of Staff, Lieutenant-General Syed Refaqat, disclosed that General Akhtar was opposed to the holding of a high-level enquiry. Instead, he felt that a departmental probe would be sufficient. The President was not happy either and he wished to stall the Imran Report. Refaqat prepared a long list of observations on the enquiry but time had run out as the Imran Report had already become the property of the government. 'Akhtar thoroughly hated Junejo,' said Refaqat.[2] If that were so, it is logical to assume that Akhtar might have influenced Zia's views on Junejo. Hamid Gul claims that on the day of the incident he had accepted responsibility for it and had offered himself for punishment. According to Hamid Gul, on the basis of the Imran Report, Junejo primarily held Akhtar responsible for establishing the depot in a heavily populated area and for keeping it there for so long.

The contents of the Imran Commission Report leaked out in bits and pieces. It transpired that, apart from its unsuitable location, the Ojhri Camp depot had been inexpertly managed. Some instances of security lapses, administrative failures, and lack of fire-fighting systems were brought to light. Earlier, fire had broken out once but was luckily brought under control and, unluckily, not reported in the Press. The lid of secrecy was kept tightly on. The Camp remained a hush-hush affair.

The successful Afghan freedom struggle was a thorn in the flesh of some countries. The ammunition blow up could have been an act of sabotage planned by an external source and implemented by some hired internal agents. Such a possibility could not be ruled out. It appears that the government, the intelligence agencies, and the investigators focused their attention on this aspect. The depot was located in a secluded area, protected from public access. Entry into it was not easy. Besides, despite considerable efforts, no trace was found of any time-fuse device or an explosive planted at the site of the accident. The sabotage theory might have appealed to those who wanted an excuse to cover up their own inefficiency. In the absence of any evidence to justify raising an accusing finger, it was clearly unsustainable. The sabotage theory was not proven.

An electric short circuit or the blowing up of defective ammunition could be the other two causes. These possibilities were firmly rejected for lack of evidence. A knowledgeable source disclosed on the basis of anonymity that the eyewitnesses' accounts confirmed that the fire was in fact caused by the mishandling of ammunition. The evidence to this effect was overwhelming and conclusive.

General Zia underplayed the severity of the accident. Mr Junejo disclosed that the then Director General Intelligence, Major-General Hamid Gul, had accepted total responsibility for the mishap and had volunteered to be retired or removed from his appointment.[3] Junejo went on to indicate the mitigating circumstances favouring Hamid Gul. As this general officer had inherited the depot location and had held the appointment for only one year, the major share of blame could not be apportioned to him. It was necessary to determine, said Junejo, why the depot was located in the midst of the twin cities in the first instance and then kept there for so long. The person to answer these questions and to get the major share of blame was General Akhtar Abdur Rahman. General Zia wanted to protect Akhtar and Hamid Gul. The stage was set for a showdown between the President and the Prime Minister.

Junejo Dismissed

Two high-level foreign tours had been planned in the month of May 1988. Prime Minister Junejo returned to Islamabad on 29 May after paying an official visit to the Philippines. The following day, President Zia was to undertake a tour of China. On the surface, the political sea was calm. The ministerial committee examining the Imran Commission Report on the Ojhri Camp fire had submitted its recommendations to the Prime Minister. A decision on it was to be taken after Mr Junejo's return from his Far Eastern tour.

If any turbulence was brewing below the apparently tranquil surface, Mr Junejo had blissfully underestimated its severity. Had he suspected that he would face the political guillotine on his return, he would scarcely have left the shores of Pakistan for a tour of the Philippines.

A beaming Junejo emerged from the green and white PIA aircraft as it landed at Islamabad Airport in the hot afternoon of 29 May 1988.

A day earlier, he had claimed in Manila that 'There is total constitutional rule in Pakistan with the Parliament enjoying full authority.'[4] In a 'business as usual' style, he gave the details of his successful tour to a group of waiting Press correspondents in the VIP lounge. The Press briefing over, Junejo departed, unaware that, in a building close by, the stage had been set to pull the rug from under his feet.

Towards the closing stages of the Prime Minister's Press briefing, some correspondents impatiently glanced at their wrist watches. The time was fast approaching for another engagement—a Press conference to be addressed by General Zia.

Arranged at short notice, President Zia's Press conference was a hush-hush affair. The President's Chief of Staff, Refaqat, gave a mere three hours to the Press Officer, Brigadier Siddiq Salik, to make the necessary arrangement as 'General Zia wished to explain details of his projected visit to China.'[5] This was a departure from the norm. Never before had Zia addressed the Press prior to undertaking a foreign tour. He invariably did so on his return from such trips. The subterfuge surprised Salik, but he nevertheless complied with the orders given to him.

General Zia was in a sombre mood. Reading from handwritten notes, he stunned the Press correspondents by announcing the dismissal of the Junejo government as well as the dissolution of the National Assembly under Article 58(2)(b) of the Constitution, which empowered the President to dissolve the Lower House of the Parliament.[6] The dismissed Junejo had held the post of the Prime Minister for a period of three years, two months, and seven days. General Zia argued that the 'National Assembly had failed to come up to its assigned role, to make a move towards the Islamization objectives and could not provide protection to the life and property of the people of Pakistan.'[7]

Elaborating the rationale of his decision in a televised address at 8:15 p.m. on 30 May 1988, General Zia stated that, 'the Prime Minister was compelled to succumb to unwholesome political pressure, which led to rampant corruption, nepotism, and maladministration, finally leading to a complete breakdown of morality and law and order in the country.'[8]

If the diagnoses made by Zia were hard to accept, the Draconian measures taken by him were harder still. Mr Junejo might not have been the ideal prime minister but he had inherited a difficult situation on assuming power. To run a democratic system while working under the shadow of an autocratic president was not an easy task. To dump responsibility for all the ills of the country in the lap of the prime minister was against the norms of justice and fair play. The President's act appeared vindictive. Mr Junejo termed it 'completely arbitrary' and claimed with considerable justification that he 'had introduced an element of decency and dignity into the politics of the country.'[9]

The four provincial governments were also dismissed and the provincial assemblies were dissolved under the orders issued by the respective Zia-appointed Governors. Two days later, caretaker governments were formed at the federal and the provincial levels.[10] Writing under the heading 'At the crossroads of destiny', a newspaper lamented that 'The country has been thrown into a welter of conjectures on how the crisis should or would be resolved.'[11] Zia and Junejo were not political rivals but any differences between them were part of the political process. Junejo consulted Zia frequently and gave him respect. Their mutual uneasiness emerged out of the power-sharing process. General Zia frequently wrote directives to the ministries. His senior staff officers pestered them for a quick response. Under the Rules of Business, the ministries were required to route their replies to the President through the Prime Minister's Secretariat. The delay annoyed Zia. His crafty staff blamed the Prime Minister for the delay. The gap between the President and the Prime Minister, created by suspicions, thus kept widening. Mr Junejo requested General Zia to address all the directives to him directly and he promised their speedy implementation.[12] This was in conflict with the Zia style—a direct personal approach. Such incidents created a bitterness which was exploited by the close advisers of Zia. They advocated pre-emptive action against the Prime Minister before Mr Junejo could cause grievous political damage to the President.

On 29 May, a visibly morose Salik entered General Zia's lounge. He had been summoned to draft the television speech which the President was to deliver on 30 May 1988. Sensing the disturbed state of mind of his speech writer, General Zia said: 'Salik, I have dismissed Junejo, not you. Why do you have a long face? Take some fresh air and cheer up before you start drafting my address.'[13] Salik complied with the orders. The President's address was stale, hackneyed, and unconvincing. Salik confessed afterwards that his heart was not in the text.[14] He asked me if he should seek premature retirement from the military service. I advised him against a rash act.

On 31 May 1988, General Akhtar Abdur Rahman was asked if Mr Junejo's dismissal had been inevitable. General Akhtar Abdur Rahman bitterly accused the Prime Minister of undermining the position of his own benefactor, Zia.[15] In an emotion-filled voice, he went on to disclose that the Intelligence Bureau had been tapping the telephones of the President and of his close political and military associates. This was startling news. The reply confirmed that Akhtar was privy to General Zia's action.

The Vice Chief of Army Staff, General Mirza Aslam Beg denied prior knowledge of the President's action.[16] On 29 May 1988, Beg, along with other services chiefs, had received the Prime Minister at Islamabad Airport on his return from the Philippines. After the airport ceremony, he returned home. There was a call from the President, asking Beg to meet him at his residence. This was just half an hour before the President's press conference. On arrival, Beg was taken to the sun-room, as some visitors were already sitting in the lounge. General Zia told Beg that he would be announcing the dismissal of the Junejo government at the press conference. Beg was directed to take any precautionary security measures that he considered necessary. Beg was prevented from asking questions as General Zia claimed to be in a hurry, saying, 'Well, it had to be this way.' General Beg claimed that he was totally taken by surprise and felt that the stage had been set by Generals Akhtar and Refaqat.

A few days after the event, said Beg, General Zia, talking to a group of senior military officers, gave reasons in justification of his action against the Junejo government. One, Junejo had blundered by rushing to sign the Geneva Accord. Pakistan could have extracted concessions from the Soviet Union, which was under pressure, before signing the Accord. The knotty issue of establishing a broad-based government in Kabul in the immediate post-withdrawal period should have been settled in advance. Second, Junejo had deliberately politicized the Geneva negotiations in Pakistan to weaken Zia's position. He gave it a sentimental colour for the sake of political expediency. Thirdly, Junejo would delay decisions, create minor hurdles in the way of Zia, and disregard his advice.

General Zia was displeased with the Prime Minister for not defending him during the National Assembly debate on the Eighth Amendment. During that discussion, many members of the Assembly had passed unsavoury remarks about Zia. Hamid Gul maintains that there might have been another factor. The approval of the budget by the National Assembly (due in June) would have indirectly given a vote of confidence to Junejo. Zia pre-empted the budget session.[17]

Immediately after announcing Mr Junejo's dismissal, General Zia directed the Signal Officer-in-Chief of the Pakistan Army, Major-General Hamid Hasan Butt, to take into custody the telephone monitoring equipment installed in the Intelligence Bureau (IB), lock the premises, and prevent the IB personnel from tampering with the Bureau's records. The orders conveyed personally on telephone by General Zia that evening were implemented. The records seized were not analysed by the army, as no instructions to this effect were issued to Butt. A military guard was posted at the locked room. On the orders of General Zia, the premises and the records were handed back to the new Director of the Intelligence Bureau, who was appointed soon thereafter.

While confirming the above narration, Butt disclosed that minutes after receiving the President's call, Major-General Hamid Gul (DGI) telephoned him to enquire if he had received the instructions from General Zia.[18] During the telephone conversation, as if thinking aloud, Hamid Gul apprehended that the IB would blame ISI Directorate for initiating the seizure of their records. Butt told him, 'Well those are the orders given to me.' 'I suppose,' replied Hamid Gul, 'you should carry them out.'

It is interesting to note the Zia technique. He did not pass the orders to Butt through his immediate superior, General Beg, even though the latter had met Zia only a couple of hours earlier. When questioned on this subject by the author, Beg disclaimed having firsthand information about this incident, saying that the President had issued some instructions to General Butt directly. Butt stated that, before implementing the President's orders, he had informed General Beg about them. Beg directed him to implement the instructions. General Zia occasionally reached out to subordinates personally. This was his style of subtly emphasizing on all his own pre-eminence in the hierarchy.

Another piece of information fits into this jigsaw puzzle. While discussing the Junejo dismissal with Lieutenant-General Imranullah Khan, General Zia had once told him that he was constrained to take pre-emptive action based on intelligence reports in his possession. Before his projected visit to China due to start on 30 May 1988, a session of the National Assembly had been called by the President. Zia disclosed to Imran that Mr Junejo had secretly connived to get a resolution passed by the Assembly calling upon the President to seek retirement from the Army and appoint a whole-time Chief of Army Staff.[19] The aim was to put General Zia under moral pressure and to remove him from his power base. The plan backfired as Zia struck first.

Mr Junejo braved the dismissal of his government with dignity. The brutal act must have hurt him grievously, but he bore it with poise. He criticized Zia's action as unjust and unfair and a blow to democracy. While so doing, he displayed anguish but not anger. In his public pronouncements, he eschewed acrimony against the person of General Zia. His upright response in the face of provocation won him respect and enhanced his public image.

General Akhtar was gifted with great perseverance. His unflinching personal loyalty to General Zia made him suspicious of others. Zia had superseded Akhtar in 1976 (as major-general) but with the passage of time had developed a strong liking for him. General Akhtar was always uncomfortable with Mr Junejo and criticized him in strong words in the military conferences. The feeling was mutual. On his part, Mr Junejo wanted Akhtar removed from the ISI Directorate—the sooner the better.

Mr Junejo tells a different story. He denied the existence of any proposal to pass a resolution in the National Assembly to cause embarrassment to General Zia.[20] He maintained that, despite the petty irritations and mischief caused by the President's staff, his relations with General Zia were normal. He would never stoop so low, he said, as to commit such an act. This was a figment of the imagination of General Akhtar who was extremely apprehensive regarding the Ojhri Camp fire incident and felt that the disciplinary axe would fall on him. Since Akhtar had selected that location in the midst of a populated area and did not shift the depot despite the passage of many years, he saw the noose tightening around his neck. Before he could be blamed and punished, he concocted stories, filled General Zia's ears with falsehoods, and pushed him into an unconstitutional act.

Asked if he had permitted surveillance of the telephones of General Zia and others, Mr Junejo denied the allegation. He stated that it was in his knowledge that, at one time, the ISI Directorate had bugged the President's telephone and recorded the conversation of General Zia's daughter. The tape was then played back to the President, blaming the Prime Minister for the mischief. Mr Junejo went on to disclose that on one occasion Akhtar's agents had photographed cars entering General Zia's residence. The photographs were then shown to the President with the remark that the watchful ISI security staff had 'managed to obtain them' to expose those who were 'spying on General Zia's visitors.'

Mr Junejo blamed General Akhtar and the President's Chief of Staff, Lieutenant-General Syed Refaqat for the dismissal of his government. He called Refaqat an 'intriguer' who had poisoned Zia's mind against him.

The Zia-Junejo relationship was seldom congenial or comfortable. In the assessment of Refaqat, 'Junejo wanted to reduce Zia to the status of President Fazal Elahi Chaudhry, not realizing that while Fazal Elahi was the creation of Bhutto, Junejo himself was the nominee of Zia.'[21] He further disclosed that it greatly irritated Zia when, on 16 May, the Prime Minister sent him a message through the Defence Secretary, Ijlal Zaidi, enquiring about his plan for his own retirement from the army.

Refaqat claims that Zia told him about his decision to dismiss the government a day before he acted.[22] Advocate Aziz A. Munshi drafted the dismissal order. While Refaqat did not express his views to the President on the justification of the harsh step, he apprised him of the constitutional provision which required an election to be held within ninety days of the dissolution of the National Assembly. Disagreeing with that interpretation, Zia told his COS that, 'A way can be found to overcome the hurdle. Pirzada [Sharifuddin] *ke pas kuch masala hai* [Pirzada has a trump card with him].'[23] Zia vaguely talked of a referendum. Refaqat recalled the Prime Minister's Secretary, Isani, telling him more than once, 'If there is any work, just order us and we will carry it out.'[24] Refaqat confessed that he understood the real import of that remark better after the event. By then, much damage had been done.

Hamid Gul had met the President hours before the latter held the fateful press conference on 29 May. He maintains that he was given no inkling of the President's decision.[25] After the event, when Hamid Gul broached the subject of holding an election, Zia told him, '*Dekhen gay*'[26] (we will see) and asked him to think of 'an appropriate question for a referendum.' Hamid Gul found the Zia-Junejo relations badly strained and felt that Refaqat was more to blame than Isani for creating tension between the President and the Prime Minister. He indicated that he met Zia for the second time around midnight on 29 May. While taking his leave he said, 'Thank you sir.' 'For what?'

enquired Zia. 'For not telling me about your decision in advance,' replied Hamid Gul, adding, 'You spared me the agony of being torn between duty and loyalty.'[27]

The President's action of dismissing the government and dissolving the assemblies was not challenged in a court of law during his lifetime. Soon after his death in August 1988, the issue was agitated in the court. The Lahore High Court in a judgment delivered on 27 September 1988 held that: 'The grounds given for the dissolution of National Assembly and the Provincial Assembly of Punjab are so vague, general or non-existent that the orders are not sustainable in law.'[28] The court ruled that, while the dissolved assembly could not be restored, polls should be held in November 1988, as announced by the Zia administration earlier. The Supreme Court of Pakistan upheld the decision of the Lahore High Court.

The Fatal Crash

It was 17 August 1988. A massive ball of fire suddenly went up in the air as the aircraft crashed. The mushroom cloud of flame and smoke was visible for miles in the bright, cloudless summer afternoon. The intensity of heat was unbearable. The velocity of the impact smashed the aircraft to smithereens, scattering bits and pieces of it over a wide area near the tiny village Basti Lal Kamal near the town of Bahwalpur. Parts of the aircraft, littered over the semi-desert area, burned. There were no survivors. The heavy death toll, thirty-one persons, included five general officers, two American citizens, and the President of Pakistan, General M. Ziaul Haq.

Three days later, the mortal remains of the late President were buried with full military honours, in the spacious compound near the elegant Faisal Mosque, at the foot of Margalla Hills in the heart of the capital city, Islamabad. Touching scenes were witnessed at the funeral. Over a million dazed mourners attending the last rites sobbed and wept as Zia's coffin was slowly carried towards its final resting place. Those present on the solemn occasion and sharing the grief included thousands of Afghan refugees, paying their homage to the person who had done so much for them for so long in vehemently supporting the cause of freedom in the nine-year long Afghan struggle against Soviet military aggression. Stunned, millions of Pakistanis watched the funeral proceedings live on their television screens.

Zia's body was carried in a helicopter from his modest home, the Army House in Rawalpindi, where he had spent the last twelve years of his life, to *Aiwan-e-Sadr* (President House) in Islamabad at midday on 20 August. On a hot and sultry day, with the sun blazing, the coffin was taken in an ambulance to a transfer point a few hundred yards away from the burial site. Here, wrapped in the green and white national flag, it was placed on a spick-and-span gun carriage. Soldiers, sailors, and airmen in their ceremonial uniforms and with clinking medals glittering on their chests, lined the route. A group of senior military officers, including the three services chiefs, smartly slow marched behind the gun carriage pushed by men in uniform. This was Zia's journey, in the military tradition, to his final resting place. For the last one hundred yards, the coffin was removed from the gun carriage. Carried on the shoulders of mourners, it was finally placed on a platform. The funeral prayers were performed in accordance with Muslim rites. A twenty-one gun salute was given. As the echoes were heard in the Margalla hills, the coffin was slowly lowered into the grave dug by the soldiers he had had the honour to command in life. The burial was witnessed by Mr Ghulam Ishaq Khan, the President of Pakistan, who had filled the vacancy left by Zia's death. He was flanked by delegates from thirty-five foreign countries, the friends and colleagues, and the admirers and the critics of late General Zia. All stood motionless and in silence with their heads bowed as the grave was filled with earth. Junejo, the man he had dismissed, was also present to lend his shoulder to the coffin and put a handful of earth into his grave as a mark of respect to the one who was no more. When a man is dead and gone, all is forgiven and forgotten. A smartly turned out tri-service contingent of tall, young, and handsome military men fired three salvoes in quick succession. From the background came the sound of the last post played by a dozen trumpeteers dressed in their blue ceremonial patrols. The grave was then submerged in a massive heap of floral wreaths laid by the assembled dignitaries.

Thus ended the rule of Zia who had 'presided over the destiny of Pakistan for over 11 years across violent upheavals in the region and political triumphs and trauma at home.'[29] Out of his forty-four years of military service, he was the Chief of Army Staff for an unprecedented period of twelve years. The Federal Cabinet honoured Zia, who died aged sixty-four, by locating his grave at such a prominent site 'as a recognition of his meritorious service for promoting the cause of Islam and implementing Islamic laws in Pakistan.'[30]

The questions raised in the wake of the fatal crash that killed Zia and others remain unanswered. What was the cause of the crash? Was it planned mischief? If so, who were those privy to the act? These vital questions were inexplicably consigned to history without a serious investigation. The Benazir administration showed indifference in probing the cause of the tragedy. The personal animus was so strong that Zia's death was considered good riddance. Emotionalism and political expediency made the government abdicate its responsibility. An enquiry was started later. The half-hearted effort was not taken to a logical conclusion. The time wasted might have resulted in the destruction of valuable evidence. The truth remains buried in a haze of mystery. No less intriguing in this regard was the attitude of the USA.

On the last day of his life, 17 August, Zia travelled to the Tamewali field firing range in an American-built four-engine Hercules C-130 military transport aircraft. His flight took him to the desert city of Bahawalpur from where he travelled to Tamewali in a helicopter. He spent a couple of hours witnessing field tests of the US-made M1 Abrams tank, which the Army was evaluating for induction in service. The trials were conducted under arrangements made by Major-General Mahmud Ali Durrani commanding 1 Armoured Division located in Multan. On arrival at the Bahawalpur Airport, General Zia was received by General Mirza Aslam Beg, the Vice Chief of Army Staff, who had arrived earlier that day from Islamabad in his small jet prop aircraft. Those accompanying Zia included the US Ambassador, Arnold Raphel, 45, the Chief of the US military mission in Pakistan, Brigadier-General Herbert Wassom, 49, and a group of Pakistan Army brass including General Akhtar Abdur Rahman. The trials over, President Zia returned to Bahawalpur in the same helicopter. General Zia then spent a couple of hours in the newly formed local corps headquarters where he was apprised of the progress of its raising. This presentation was not attended by General Akhtar. It was then time for *Zohr* prayers. Lunch was served soon thereafter. General Zia and his party then returned to the airport for the flight back to Islamabad. The aircraft to be used was the same that had brought the President to Bahawalpur in the morning. There was no change in its crew.

Before boarding the plane, Zia shook hands with the military officers on the departure line. While meeting Beg, he offered him a lift. Beg thanked the President. Zia had a look at the jet prop and said,

'You have your own plane also here.' From Bahawalpur Lieutenant-General Mian Muhammad Afzaal, the Chief of General Staff, boarded the C-130 aircraft. Like many other military officers, Afzaal had arrived a day earlier and was scheduled to travel back to Islamabad by a commercial flight on which his seat was already booked. That change of flight cost him his life. Also travelling in the aircraft was Major-General Muhammad Hussain Awan, a division commander.

At 4:30 p.m. on 17 August 1988, the VVIP flight, Pak One, with thirty-one persons on board, took off from Bahawalpur Airport. The take-off was perfectly smooth and trouble-free. For two minutes and thirty seconds, the aircraft kept gaining height and the pilot remained in contact with Bahawalpur control tower. Then came the disaster. Bahawalpur control tower suddenly lost radio contact with Pak One. This was a surprising development because the aircraft was flown by highly experienced cockpit crew. The sturdy turbo-prop, reputed for its reliability and safety record, remained airborne for another two minutes. Those agonizing one hundred and twenty seconds took Zia and others travelling with him to their rendezvous with death. Eyewitnesses on the ground saw the erratic behaviour of the aircraft, bouncing up and down before it hit the ground violently, nose down. So tremendous was the velocity that the engines ploughed several feet into the ground. The disintegrated aircraft, carrying 20,000 pounds of fuel in its wings, burnt fiercely for over four hours and burning pieces of wreckage were widely spread. Also burnt to death were the 31 persons on board. Barring a few badly charred and mutilated corpses, the rest were cut to small pieces of bones and flesh, beyond recognition. The human remains retrieved after an extensive search operations posed considerable problems of identification.

Unaware of the tragedy, General Beg took off from Bahawalpur minutes after Pak One was airborne. The destination of his jet prop was the military base Dhamial, near Islamabad. Beg recalls seeing a cloud of smoke rising in the sky soon after he left Bahawalpur. He did not suspect any mishap till the pilot informed him that the Bahawalpur control tower had lost contact with Zia's aircraft. This caused anxiety.

A helicopter that had taken off from Bahawalpur on its journey to Multan spotted wreckage at the scene of the accident. It hovered over the area at low altitude; from the widespread nature of the debris and the intensity of the fire, the pilot concluded that the loss was total,

A STORMY SUMMER

perhaps with no survivors. The pilot conveyed his impressions to Bahawalpur control tower as well as to the captain of the jet prop. He then landed close to the wrecked plane.

On hearing about the crash, General Beg diverted his aircraft to return to Bahawalpur. On board with him were Major-General Jehangir Karamat, Director General Military Operations, Brigadier Ejaz Amjad, and his aide. The jet prop was soon over the site of the accident. It lost height and circled around to enable Beg to see the wreckage, which was emitting smoke and fire. He learnt that the Corps Commander had rushed to the scene of the crash to take charge of the rescue work. A quick discussion took place in the jet prop. Jehangir Karamat and Amjad were of the view that, there being no survivors, it was more important for Beg to return to the capital than spend the remaining daylight hours in Bahawalpur. The Bahawalpur garrison had enough resources for launching a quick rescue and recovery operation. Beg's presence, in their view, was needed more in Islamabad where a power vacuum had suddenly been created because of Zia's death. Beg agreed with that assessment. The aircraft once again changed course and, without landing at Bahawalpur, flew back to Islamabad.

The news of Zia's death was withheld by the government for over three hours. This was a period of intense behind-the-scenes activity in Islamabad. For those hours, the country was without a president and the Pakistan Army without its chief. Both the appointments had been held by Zia. The Constitution provided that, in the event of the president's death or absence, the Chairman of the Senate would become the acting president. Mr Ghulam Ishaq Khan, the then Chairman of the Senate, was thus the automatic choice. The question of succession had been foreseen in the Constitution and its provisions were clear and unambiguous. There was no justification for deviating from the Constitution.

It was argued after the event that Zia's death was an opportunity for General Beg to assume control of the country, a course which he did not adopt for the sake of democracy. That the Army could have adopted an unconstitutional path was a possibility. It had done so in the past. The events that followed proved that military intervention would have been unwarranted, unjustified, and a gross violation of the Constitution.

Pakistan faced a peculiar situation then. After sacking the Junejo government, General Zia had formed a cabinet without a prime minister. This was in violation of the Constitution. His sudden death rendered the post of the president also vacant. If this vacuum created a desire in the military, to intervene in the constitutional process, the exuberance was totally misplaced.

After landing at Dhamial, General Beg drove straight to General Headquarters. He called Lieutenant-General Imranullah Khan, Commander 10 Corps (at Rawalpindi), Lieutenant-General Imtiaz Warraich, Joint Staff Headquarters, and Major-General Hamid Gul, Director General Intelligence, for consultations. In Beg's office, they, along with Major-General Jehangir Karamat, analysed the sudden development. Two options were considered. One, the army takes over control of the country and imposes martial law. Two, following the constitutional provisions, Mr Ghulam Ishaq Khan becomes the new president. They 'decided' in favour of the latter course.

The army view firmed up, it was time to consult the other two services chiefs. The Chief of Air Staff, Air Marshal Hakimullah Khan, and the Deputy Chief of Naval Staff, Rear Admiral Saeed Muhammad Khan were invited to meet General Beg. The Chief of Naval Staff, Admiral Iftikhar Ahmad Sirohey, was away from the country. The services chiefs agreed with the GHQ view that the Constitution should prevail. Mr Ghulam Ishaq Khan, the Chairman of the Senate, was then requested to visit General Headquarters where he was apprised of the views of the services chiefs. The time was now close to 7:30 p.m.

Mr Ghulam Ishaq Khan went to the Presidency and called an emergency meeting of the cabinet that night to which the chiefs of the three military services were invited. The news of the crash was then announced.

Late that night, Mr Ghulam Ishaq Khan addressed the nation on the television and radio networks. He announced a ten-day national mourning and declared a state of emergency in the country. He assured the nation that the election date, 16 November 1988, previously announced by General Zia, would remain unchanged. General Mirza Aslam Beg was appointed Chief of Army Staff. The appointment of the Chairman Joint Chiefs of Staff Committee was left vacant. This vacancy was caused by the death of General Akhtar Abdur Rahman, who had died in the aircraft crash.

It was improper for the military brass to call Mr Ghulam Ishaq Khan to the General Headquarters. Instead, they should have called on him to express their grief and loyalty. Ishaq had the constitutional right to become the President and the military had shown him no favour. He was too nice a person to fuss about the protocol and that too in an hour of national tragedy. It would have been prudent for the top military hierarchy to show him due courtesy.

General Zia's death raised some controversies. It was speculated that he had taken the decision to attend the tank demonstration reluctantly and was perhaps lured into accepting it by some insistent subordinates. The available evidence does not support this thesis.

The Armoured Corps Directorate (ACD) at General Headquarters was the sponsor of the tank evaluation process. It had detailed 1 Armoured Division to conduct the field trials and submit a suitability report. The evaluation programme was to conclude with the firing of the tank gun. ACD had informed Headquarters 1 Armoured Division weeks in advance that the final trials were likely to be attended by the President. 1 Armoured Division selected 17 August for holding the firing trials. While communicating the date to the ACD, it sought confirmation about the attendance of the President. It seems that the date selected, 17 August, did not suit Major-General Roshan Ejaz, Director-General Armoured Corps, as it coincided with the Hijra month of Moharrum. Roshan, a staunch practising Shiite Muslim, regularly attended religious congregations every night during the first ten days of Moharrum. 17 August 1988 corresponded to 3 Moharrum 1409 (AH). Perhaps he played a delaying game in the hope that the tank trials would be rescheduled after the tenth of Moharrum. Instead of sharing his predicament with General Durrani, General Officer Commanding 1 Armoured Division, and requesting him to alter the dates, he showed a lack of courage, telling him that the case had been submitted to the President's Secretariat to seek the President's convenience and that a response was awaited from them. This made Durrani helpless. As the trial date neared, Durrani received the same reply from Roshan. In desperation, Durrani contacted Brigadier Najib, Military Secretary to the President, to enquire as to when the President's availability to attend the tank trials would be known. Najib expressed surprise at the question, indicating that he had not received any summary from the ACD, seeking the President's approval. Durrani enquired if 17 August suited the President. He got an affirmative response and requested Najib to provisionally reserve that day for the demonstration, after obtaining the President's approval.

Durrani called the Chief of General Staff, Lieutenant-General Mian Muhammad Afzaal and gave him the gist of his conversations with Roshan and Najib. Things moved fast then. Post-haste, the ACD sent a summary to the President's Secretariat which confirmed that the President would attend the tank trials. The Staff Duties Directorate, GHQ, issued a programme on 11 August 1988, about General Zia's visit on 17 August. On 15 August, the Corps Commander at Bahawalpur was directed to give a presentation to General Zia on 17 August about his Corps problems. These developments indicate that General Zia's programme was prepared in advance and was finalized at least six days before 17 August 1988.

The presence of two Americans, Ambassador Raphel and Brigadier-General Wassom, at the demonstration site at Tamewali is well-documented at General Headquarters. On 9 August 1988, Lieutenant-Colonel Margave of the US Embassay in Islamabad conveyed to the ACD the US Ambassador's desire to attend the M1A1 demonstration scheduled for 17 August 1988. The following day, the ACD forwarded the request to the Chief of General Staff, Lieutenant-General Mian Muhammad Afzaal, along with a proposed list of VIP invitees. The CGS endorsed on the file, 'I recommend that both the US Ambassador and ODRP [Wassom] be allowed to witness the demo.' The VCOAS, General Beg, approved the proposal on 11 August with the remark 'yes'. Director-General ACD then endorsed the file thus, '... Following actions have been taken:

a. MS(P) is extending the invitation to the US Ambassador.

b. Brig Wassom is being, invited by W&E Dte (Weapons and Equipment Directorate).'

Ambassador Raphel had a meeting with General Zia on 16 August 1988 during which he accepted the President's invitation to travel in Pak One. The US Embassy aircraft was taken to Bahawalpur on 17 August but the Ambassador did not travel in it.

Conclusive evidence is not available to prove how General Akhtar, not concerned with the trials, came to travel with General Zia to see the tank demonstration. The record reveals that his name was included in the GHQ VIP invitees list, amended by the CGS, along with the addition of the names of Raphel and Wassom. GHQ was thus aware of his attendance.

A STORMY SUMMER

About four days before the trials, Akhtar called Durrani and jokingly complained that he had not been invited to attend a military function which the President was to grace. Durrani retorted that he held too humble a position to dare invite the Chairman, JCSC, the tri-services boss. Akhtar left Durrani with the impression that he would be seeking the President's approval to witness the trials. Durrani did not consider it relevant to inform anyone in the GHQ about his conversation with Akhtar.

On 16 August 1988, General Akhtar, while walking in the Rawalpindi Golf Course, met General Beg who was playing golf.[31] Beg recalls the conversation thus:

Akhtar: You have invited the American Ambassador to see the tank trials tomorrow but I have been left out.

Beg: I have not invited the Ambassador. If the President has done so, I am not aware of it.

Akhtar: I believe a lot of people will be attending.

Beg: Tomorrow's trial is exclusively for the President. I intend a repeat performance after a couple of days to which you and the Corps Commanders would also be invited.

Akhtar: Thank you.

General Beg's statement is at variance with the GHQ record. General Beg maintains that when he received President Zia at the Bahawalpur Airport, he was surprised to see General Akhtar emerging from the aircraft. Did the President's personal staff fail to inform GHQ about Akhtar travelling with the President? In the light of GHQ records on the subject, Beg's amazement is strange. Or was it a case of failure of staff co-ordination? As a matter of routine, the staff used to inform all concerned to ensure that general officers travelling with the President were given proper protocol.

The two instances illustrate General Akhtar's perseverance. He was eager to attend the trials even though the army authorities had not invited him. He did not wish to miss an occasion to meet the army brass and show his presence along with the President and the US Ambassador.

Not many of the bodies, or what was left of them were in any shape for autopsies to be performed. The prevailing urgency, it appears, was

405

to prepare the coffins and dispatch them speedily to the heirs. A less than professional effort was made to prepare a comprehensive chemical analysis report based on autopsies performed on all available pieces of flesh and bones. Based on two autopsies, the Chemical Analyst reported 'liver and lungs have the appearance of charcoal. No toxins, alcohol and carboxy-haemoglobin detected'. The histopathologist observed 'extensive burn injury of the liver and extensive burn injury of lungs.' The Pakistan Air Force Board of Enquiry in paragraph 33 of its report said: 'Autopsies on the bodies of the persons on the flight deck and the crew could have provided some definite answer towards their end. But, unfortunately, no proper autopsies on the flight deck crew were carried out.' Those in power maintained that the doctors were never forbidden to perform autopsies. That may be true. The fact that the doctors' effort did not satisfy the Board of Enquiry indicates that, at best, the task was done in a slipshod manner. From GHQ, General Beg urged the corps commander at Bahawalpur to dispatch the remains urgently, even without the autopsies. The directive was given by him on the internal GHQ telephone to the CGS, Lieutenant-General Shamim Alam Khan, who conveyed the instructions to the corps commander in the presence of Major-General Malik Abdul Waheed.

The remains of the two Americans were sent to their heirs through the US Embassy in Islamabad. Of those remains, some bones were later returned to Pakistan by the US government with the observation that they did not belong to the bodies of the two United States citizens.[32] This further illustrates the difficulty faced by the rescue operation in identifying the bodies.

The Pakistan Air Force held a Board of Enquiry to investigate the cause of the crash. At Pakistan's request, a US team of six air force accident investigators assisted the Board. After an eight-week investigation, it prepared a comprehensive report which mainly covered two aspects—security lapses and the cause of the accident. The part dealing with the security lapses was not made public by the government. For determining the cause of the crash, the Board hypothesized all possibilities. It analysed each possible cause comprehensively and gave cogent technical reasons for accepting or rejecting it. Through such a process of elimination, it discarded other possibilities and came to the conclusion that 'the most probable cause' of the crash was a 'criminal act of sabotage perpetrated in the aircraft leading to the crash of the aircraft'. The Board's charter of responsibility was limited. Functioning within its scope, it did a good professional job. The Board's specialized composition restricted its deliberations to the specific question it was required to probe and answer. As a follow-up of the Board's findings, a broad-based enquiry was warranted to identify the perpetrators of the crime. Such an enquiry should have had the services of experts with knowledge in the criminal, sabotage, legal, and counter-terrorism fields. The Benazir administration made a half-hearted attempt to probe the accident. The Zia factor weighed so heavily that it clouded its state responsibility to dig out the truth about the crash in which thirty-one human lives were lost. The government's apathy was indicated by the Minister of State for Defence, Mr Ghulam Sarwar Cheema, who said that 'the investigation into the Zia plane crash is dead and buried and those interested in finding details about it should telephone the heavens.' Such a callous approach to a human tragedy was beyond reasonable behaviour by a person in authority.

The Board had come to the conclusion that a low intensity detonation inside the cockpit could have caused the bursting of some innocuous container, apparently filled with air fresheners or soft drinks but in fact containing some poisonous gas to incapacitate the passengers. The agent used was so effective that the highly experienced cockpit crew members of Pak One were instantly paralysed and did not get a chance to give even the 'Mayday' signal. The forensic report supported the Board's findings. Some parts of the aircraft's wreckage were found to be contaminated with strong traces of antimony, potassium, sulphur, phosphorus, and, significantly, pentaerythritol tetranitrate (PETN)—an explosive used in sabotage operations.

Some American writers were quick to speculate on the involvement of the KGB and the Afghan WAD. Zia had earned the Soviet wrath over Afghanistan and paid a personal price, ran their argument. They took support from the Board of Enquiry which had observed that, 'the use of ultra-sophisticated techniques would necessitate the involvement of a specialist organization well-versed in carrying out such tasks and possessing all the means and abilities for its execution.' That the KGB was not the only agency which qualified to be suspected on the basis of the Board observation was a fact conveniently ignored. India and Afghanistan could be suspected. However, the available evidence did not lead one in their exclusive direction. Zia's death might have given them a sense of relief, but it would be unfair to raise an accusing finger without supporting evidence.

Could it have been an internal factor? Zia had been on the hit list of the Al-Zulfiqar Organization for long. While some internal agents were a party to the crime, the high level of sophistication precluded the possibility of the plan being entirely indigenous in nature. The *modus operandi* was different and more sophisticated, compared to the pattern of sabotage activities detected in the country at that time.

Another piece of information is relevant. A few minutes after 2 p.m. on 17 August 1988, an anonymous caller enquired from the editor of a daily newspaper if General Zia had been involved in an air crash.[33] This was full two hours before the ill-fated aircraft was even airborne. The call supports the sabotage theory.

If Zia was a red rag to the Soviet bull, he was not a favourite of America either. His policies on Islam and the nuclear programme caused concern in Washington. So pronounced was the American dislike that a plan had been made to ease Zia out of power. He was to be replaced by another general officer. The CIA plan misfired when the person chosen to replace Zia declined to oblige. The plan also failed to muster political support, for which an abortive attempt was secretly made. The Soviet military intervention in Afghanistan suddenly changed the situation. Zia's firm stand against the Soviet misadventure made him acceptable to the United States. It was a coincidence that Pakistan's Afghan policy and that of the Reagan administration enabled the two countries to develop a mutually supportive relationship. With the contemplated withdrawal of the Soviet military forces from Afghanistan, Zia was dispensable, as his utility had diminished in the US scheme of manoeuvre. Zia's religious fervour and pan-Islamic approach were strong irritants to Washington. His vision of a rightist Muslim government in Afghanistan, as in Pakistan, ran counter to the strategic interests of the USA and the USSR in this region. If Zia had stood firm against the Soviet Union, he was unlikely to yield to the United States either. His exit, in the assessment of the CIA, might have been desirable.

The US attitude in the wake of the crash was peculiar. Since a US team of experts was fully associated with the Board of Enquiry, America was aware of its findings. For inexplicable reasons, the Enquiry report was leaked to the American Press before it was officially released by the government of Pakistan. A pre-emptive story, quoting unnamed administration sources, suggested that the crash might have been caused by a malfunction in the aircraft, a possibility which had been fully examined and firmly rejected by the Board of Enquiry.[34]

Was it an attempt to create doubt? This theme was subsequently picked up by a section of the American Press. A State Department official said that 'the feeling here is that in the absence of any evidence that it was a criminal act or sabotage, it should be treated specifically as a plane crash with lots of unanswered questions.'[35]

Newsweek stated that, 'Last week Air Force Colonel Daniel E. Sowada, the Chief of the US team in Pakistan, reportedly told members of Congress that the Americans had found no evidence of mechanical failure. That testimony led several congressmen to question why the State Department failed to dispatch FBI agents to investigate the crash, which also led to the death of US Ambassador, Arnold L. Raphel. One possibility, suggested Rep. Dan Burton, was that the State Department was concerned that a full investigation might reveal that the Afghans—or their Soviet allies—had ordered that Zia be killed. "You have to surmise," said Burton, "that they'd rather not rock the boat."'[36]

American society claims to excel in human dignity and to abhor terrorism. Its concern for bringing back home the mortal remains of dead US citizens—be they soldiers killed in wars or people gunned down by terrorists—indicates its concern for human lives. US compassion did not measure up to its own proclaimed high standards when it came to the two Americans killed along with Zia. Under US law, the FBI enjoyed statutory authority to investigate accidents involving American nationals. US press reports indicated that the Secretary of State, George Shultz, advised the FBI to stay away from the investigation. Unless explained otherwise, the possibility of a cover-up attempt cannot be ruled out. If the CIA's conduct was aboveboard, the US government should have welcomed a comprehensive probe and taken an active part in establishing facts. The silence in Washington on this issue creates doubts. If international terrorism is neither investigated nor suppressed, it amounts to encouraging it.

On 17 August 1988, thirty-one human lives were lost. The delay in investigations might have destroyed valuable evidence. That loss is regrettable. Notwithstanding the delay, a concerted effort ought to be made to identify the perpetrators of the crime.

EPILOGUE

To tear down a system expertly is as easy a task as it is difficult to rebuild a system. Pakistan has alternated between military coups and corrupt, incompetent civilian rule. Her political system is firmly controlled by feudal lords and others who run political parties as their personal fiefs. The legislatures are dominated by such individuals and their descendants, whose major qualification is the accident of their birth. Politics in Pakistan is based on genes and means. Dynastic connections override efficiency.

It will be long debated why Bhutto rigged the 1977 elections when, by all indications, his party, the PPP, would have won handsomely in a fair contest. The rigging converted Bhutto's massive electoral success into his biggest political liability. Once self-assured to the point of cockiness, Bhutto was forced into a corner, bearing the unwashable stigma of moral guilt. Despite his considerable personal charm and skilful manipulation techniques, he failed to weather the political storm. His collapse was total. Once a political titan, he became a dwarf, desperately seeking to rehabilitate his lost image.

An immensely charismatic leader, Mr Bhutto was able, suave, articulate, and shrewd. A person of undoubted ability, he towered over his contemporary political rivals in the country. Handsome and consumed by passion both political and physical, he had an eye for the good things in life. An impressive orator, he spoke the language of the masses and knew the art of arousing public emotions and expectations. He awakened political awareness in the people and made them conscious of their rights. He seldom reminded them about their obligations towards the state.

De Gaulle writes, 'Every man of action has a strong dose of egotism, pride, hardness, and cunning. But all those things will be forgiven him—indeed, they will be regarded as high qualities—if he can make of them the means to achieve great ends.'[1] Judged by this yardstick, both Bhutto and Zia fell short of public expectations. Bhutto, the man of paradoxes, made a hash of the internal politics of Pakistan and jolted democracy through his dictatorial rule, quelling all opposition, introducing a personality cult, and considering all acts justified and democratic which brought power unto him. He brought

EPILOGUE

about his own downfall by failing to reach a political settlement during months of infructuous negotiations held with the PNA negotiators. He should have known that, while the stakes were high for him, his opponents stood to lose nothing if the talks failed. He destroyed institutions and democracy decayed under his harsh personalized rule.

The Zia era, a dilemma to many, poses numerous questions. This book records events from the point of view of an observer inside the political arena. No single work of this nature can ever claim perfection. Close proximity to the period under review, the debatable nature of events, and controversial personalities compound the issue still further. Many episodes described herein were seen by other participants, onlookers, and analysts from different angles. Their narration and opinions would help the historian in reaching an impartial assessment of this period.

The controversial issues of the Zia era were the justification for his rule, the execution of Mr Bhutto, the dismissal of Prime Minister Junejo's government, and the prolonged duration of Zia's tenure. The imposition of martial law was not a new phenomenon in Pakistan. In 1977, the possibility was evident to the quarrelling politicians, some of whom worked for it for their own ends. The military got sucked into the political swamp in a role foreign to its charter of responsibilities. The Supreme Court of Pakistan, by upholding the military intervention, put the seal of legitimacy on Zia's action. Seen in the broad political context, martial law was a negation of democracy, harmful for the country, and damaging for the military itself.

Mr Bhutto's execution might have been the most difficult and the most painful decision taken by General Zia. On the face of it, Zia remained steadfast in his conviction that the law must be administered uniformly, without considerations of fear or favour and irrespective of the position held in society by a convict. He declined to take a political view of a criminal case. It might be convincingly argued that democracy is not advanced by eliminating a person who might have been overweening and vindictive in the past. But, despite the fact that his military administration gave birth to a democratic order, Zia had no pretensions of being a democrat in the recognized Western sense of the word. Even if the Bhutto animus weighed in his fateful decision of rejecting the mercy petitions, Zia was not unaware of Pakistan's practical politics. He and Bhutto had parted ways. Zia was to live thereafter sitting on a time bomb, whether Bhutto was alive or dead.

The dismissal of the Junejo government signalled the political isolation of Zia from the mainstream of national politics. This decision—naive, absurd, and indefensible—reflected the political incompetence of the President's kitchen cabinet and of his other confidants who recommended the Draconian act. Zia had the habit of side-stepping those who differed with him too openly, too harshly, or too often. In the closing period of his administration, the number of his trusted associates was greatly reduced and those remaining would see darkness in the moonless night only when Zia so desired.

General Zia defied the assessment of his critics by remaining in the saddle for an unprecedentedly long period; he had no immediate plans for retirement when his life was suddenly cut short in mysterious circumstances. His views on the Islamic philosophy of life and his passion for introducing an Islamic order in Pakistan brought him into sharp conflict with his Western critics, who considered him a threat to their culture and way of life. The Western-controlled world media painted him in murky colours, partly for being a military autocrat, but largely because of his belief in the pan-Islamic concept. He was called a 'well-intentioned but increasingly maladroit military ruler'[2] and it was said that 'Zia's name has a death-rattle sound these days. There's a feeling he can't last much longer.'[3] Such predictions were proved wrong for obvious reasons. Firstly, the subcontinent was used to harsh politics. Secondly, Zia led a disciplined army and a mature team of senior officers to advise him. Thirdly, the political opposition in the country was too weak and fragmented to pose a serious threat to his administration. Fourthly, when Zia announced in July 1977 that enough was enough and he was stepping in to control national affairs, his act was generally accepted as inevitable by the people and the politicians in the country. The world considered it the internal affair of Pakistan. The Afghanistan crisis, emerging later, further diluted Western criticism against him. He seized this opportunity to tighten his grip on the internal developments in the country in a carefully planned manner.

Neither a charismatic personality nor a superb public speaker, Zia quickly learnt the art of statecraft and impressed the people by his simple habits, pleasant manners, humility, patience, and hard work. Contingency planning on political developments enabled his government to anticipate events, foresee crises, outplay their opponents, keeping them guessing about the next political moves, and making them react to political developments. The errors made by his political opponents were successfully exploited by Zia's government on more than one occasion.

Firm but not overbearing, Zia was seldom palpably excited. He retained his hold through active participation in formulating the foreign policy options, by maintaining unity in the armed forces, by retaining the post of Chief of Army Staff, and through firm administrative control on domestic affairs. His trust was qualified and he knew the source of his power. Significantly, he did not appoint even the best of his close associates to the coveted post of Chief of Army Staff.

Zia's Afghanistan policy, bold and firm, aimed at providing total support to the Afghan freedom struggle against the Soviet invasion of their country. This involved taking risks which his opponents felt endangered the security of the country. The withdrawal of the Soviet forces from Afghanistan reflected the success of Pakistan's Afghan policy. The infighting in Afghanistan after 1988 is, in part, the result of Pakistan's wavering support to that country during the crucial post-Zia period.

India was a disappointment for Zia. He had no doubts that Indian intentions about Pakistan were suspect. His peace offensive with this country was a shrewd move. His military instinct guided him against being caught in a two-front conflict. He kept his cool despite a barrage of provocative statements issued by the prime ministers of India. Those who accused him of being soft on India at best only saw the obvious.

Zia's Islamization programme, partly implemented, is hard to reverse in the post-Zia period. Barring the English-speaking intelligentsia and the elite, a great majority of the middle and the lower classes in the country support the process of Islamization of society. On the issue of religion, Zia was an idealist, an enlightened, practising Muslim, but not a bigot.

The Zia years did not see major economic changes in the country. The trial of Bhutto, the turmoil in Afghanistan, Indian bellicosity, and the *status quo* approach of the government's economic planners prevented the taking of long-term economic measures. His decade-long rule was in fact a period of economic consolidation.

Withstanding extreme external pressure, the Zia government actively pursued Pakistan's nuclear programme and considered it vital for national security. Zia was totally committed on this issue and the national nuclear effort made purposeful and significant headway during the period 1977-88.

Despite the fact that Zia achieved success in his foreign policy and created economic stability at home, military rule was a setback to the democratic order, and a negation of fundamental rights. It retarded the growth of incipient democracy, weak and ineffective as it was, but which deserved to be nourished and promoted. In the final analysis, the gains were tactical in nature and the losses of strategic dimension.

Zia, a human being, of flesh and bone, with a body and a soul, had sterling qualities as well as failings. He was neither a genius nor a con man. In many ways, he was a contrast to Bhutto, the person he ousted from power and hanged. His strong points were modesty, patience, piety, amiability, altruism, and graciousness.

Zia's death has left behind a big question mark. Who killed him? It was an act of terrorism. The sabotage theory points in two directions—the execution of Bhutto and Pakistan's nuclear programme. Bhutto, the designer of Pakistan's nuclear effort, had earlier alleged in 1977 that a foreign hand worked against him. In 1993, President Ghulam Ishaq Khan's premature exit from his high office because of an internal power struggle became a source of satisfaction to those foreign powers which considered him a hawk on the nuclear programme. As an old saying goes, uneasy lies the head that wears the crown.

NOTES

CHAPTER 1: THE GATHERING STORM

1. Quaid-i-Azam Mohammad Ali Jinnah, *Speeches and Statements 1947-48* (Services Book Club, 1989), 127.
2. *Confidential Appreciation of the Political Situation in India No. 9 of 1945*, 18 September 1945 (India Office Library and Records), L/1/1/777, file no. 462/22.
3. V. P. Menon, *The Transfer of Power in India*, 389.
4. *Dawn*, Karachi , 27 August 1947.
5. Lord Birdwood, *A Continent Decides* (London, 1953).
6. Justice Masud Ahmad, *Pakistan—A Study of its Constitutional History (1957-1975)* (Research Society of Pakistan, Lahore, 1978), 235-67.
7. Sir Ivor Jennings, *Constitutional Problems in Pakistan* (Cambridge University Press, 1957), 259–349.
8. Altaf Gauhar, *Ayub Khan*, (Sang-e-Meel Publications, Lahore, Pakistan, 1993), 96.
9. *Dawn*, Karachi, 29 October 1958.
10. Salman Taseer, *Bhutto—A Political Biography* (Ithaca Press, London,1979), 71.
11. Altaf Gauhar, *Ayub Khan: Pakistan's First Military Ruler*, 478.
12. Chaudhari Muhammad Ali, *The Emergence of Pakistan* (Wajidali (Pvt) Ltd., Lahore, Pakistan, 1988), 356.

CHAPTER 2: EAST PAKISTAN AMPUTATED

1. Full text of the Six Point Programme at Annexure 1.
2. G.W. Choudhury, *International Affairs* (London, April 1972).
3. Lieutenant-General S. G. M. M. Peerzada, interview with the author.
4. *Dawn*, Karachi, 28 March 1971.
5. Ahmad Raza Kasuri, *Idhar Hum Udhar Tum* (Britannica Publishing House, Lahore), 222; and *Daily Azad*, Lahore, 15 March 1971.
6. Lieutenant-General Sahabzada Yaqub Khan, conversation with the author.
7. Major-General Rao Farman Ali Khan, conversation with the author.
8. Peerzada, interview.
9. Lt-Gen Gul Hassan Khan, *Memoirs of Lt-Gen Gul Hassan Khan* (Oxford University Press, Karachi, 1993), 267.

10. *Daily Telegraph*, London, 9 March 1971.
11. *The Bangladesh Observer*, Dhaka, 19 January 1974. Mujib's address at the Awami League Council session in Dhaka.
12. Safdar Mahmood, *Pakistan Divided* (Ferozsons Ltd., Lahore-Rawalpindi-Karachi, 1984), 73.
13. Peerzada, interview.
14. *Far Eastern Economic Review*, 24 April 1971.
15. *Washington Post*, 12 May 1971.
16. *Dawn*, Karachi, 1 March 1971.
17. *Dawn*, Karachi, 15 March 1971.
18. Weekly *Current*, Karachi, 11-18 December 1977.
19. An article by Sultan M. Khan in *The Muslim*, 19 July 1983.
20. Peerzada, interview.
21. *The Pakistan Times*, Rawalpindi, 27 March 1971.
22. *The Pakistan Times*, Rawalpindi, 27 March 1971.
23. General Muhammad Musa, *Jawan To General* (East and West Publishing Company, Karachi, 1984), 187.
24. *The Irish Times*, 29 March 1972.
25. S. Brotra in *Washington Post*, 13 September 1971.
26. An interview given to the French television by Mrs Indira Gandhi on 8 November 1971.
27. *White Paper on the Crisis in East Pakistan* (Government of Pakistan, 5 August 1971), 48.
28. Major-General Sukhwant Singh, *The Liberation of Bangladesh*, (Vikas Publishing House (Pvt) Ltd, New Delhi, 1980), vol. 1, 93.
29. *The Hindu*, Madras, 5 April 1971.
30. *White Paper*, 53.
31. Interview in *The Nationalist* (Tanzania), 30 October 1971.
32. Sukhwant Singh, *Liberation*, 19.
33. Ibid.
34. *Yorkshire Post*, April 1971.
35. Sydney H. Schanberg, *New York Times*, 7 November 1971.
36. Lieutenant-General Ghulam Jilani Khan, conversation with the author.
37. Mr Agha Shahi, former Foreign Minister of Pakistan, conversation with the author.
38. Professor G.W. Choudhury, *The Last Days of United Pakistan* (C. Hurst and Company, London, 1974), 194.
39. *The Washington Post*, 14 December 1971.
40. Richard Nixon, *Leaders* (Warner Books Inc., New York, 1982), 272.
41. Signal No. G-0001 of 092300 December 1971. Full text is given as Annexure 2.
42. Full text at Annexure 3.
43. Major-General Rao Farman Ali, conversation with the author.

44. Shahi, conversation.
45. Ibid.
46. *The Ottawa Citizen*, 22 December 1971.
47. G.W. Choudhury, *The Pakistan Times*, 22 September 1988.
48. Choudhury, *Last Days*, 195.
49. *U.S. Foreign Policy for the 1970s*, President Nixon's Third Annual Foreign Policy Report to Congress, 9 February 1972, 145.
50. Full text at Annexure 5.
51. *Times of India* and *Hindustan Times*, Delhi, 20 April 1978.
52. In a democratic set-up in the country, the dominant intelligence agency is the Intelligence Bureau. The Directorate General Inter-Services Intelligence is more concerned with external threat than with internal matters. However, in a military regime the Directorate General Inter-Services may assume a more dominant role if so desired by the CMLA.
53. Promotion to and above the rank of lieutenant-colonel is suject to clearance by the government.
54. Jilani, conversation.
55. *The Muslim*, Islamabad, 21 December 1990.
56. *Pakistan Observer*, Islamabad, 12 February 1992.
57. Ibid.
58. *Dawn*, 9 December 1971.
59. *Weekly Outlook*, Karachi, vol. 3, No. 8, 25 May 1974
60. Narrated to the author by Mr Agha Shahi.
61. *Dawn*, 16 December 1971.
62. *Dawn*, 6 November 1971.
63. *Dawn*, 13 November 1971.
64. Mr Niaz A. Naik later Foreign Secretary, interview with the author.
65. *Keesings Contemporary Archives*, 25071
66. Writ Petition No. 509/78 filed by Fakhira Begum, wife of General Yahya Khan, under Article 199 of the Constitution versus the Federation of Pakistan in the NWFP High Court, Peshawar, on 16 June 1975.
67. *Nawa-i-Waqt*, Rawalpindi, 22 August 1988.
68. *Foreign Report*, Published by *The Economist,* London, 12 October 1977.

CHAPTER 3: PRELUDE TO INTERVENTION

1. *White Paper on the Conduct of the General Elections in March 1977* (Government of Pakistan, Rawalpindi, July 1978), 289-91.
2. 'The Day of Decision', *Dawn*, 8 March 1977.
3. *Observer*, London, 27 February 1977.
4. *The Pakistan Times*, 3 March 1977.

5. *Dawn*, 9 April 1977.
6. Jilani, conversation.
7. General Muhammad Iqbal Khan, interview with the author.
8. General Muhammad Shariff, conversation with the author.
9. Jilani, conversation.
10. Shariff, conversation.
11. *The Pakistan Times*, Rawalpindi, 1 June 1977.
12. *The Pakistan Times*, Rawalpindi, 11 May 1977.
13. Jilani, conversation.
14. Shahi, conversation.
15. *The Pakistan Times*, Rawalpindi, 10 June 1977.
16. Maulana Kausar Niazi, *Aur Line Cut Gai*, written in Urdu, meaning 'And Then The Line Was Cut Off' (1978).
17. Admiral Shariff, interview with the author.
18. Sharif, interview.
19. *The Pakistan Times*, Rawalpindi, 4 July 1977.
20. *Dawn*, Karachi, 5 July 1977.
21. *The Pakistan Times*, Rawalpindi, 4 July 1977.
22. Ibid.
23. *Dawn*, Karachi, 5 July 1977.
24. *The Pakistan Times*, Rawalpindi, 5 July 1977.
25. Professor Ghafoor Ahmad, *Phir Martial Law Aa Gaya* (Jang Publications Press, Lahore, 1988), 241.
26. Jilani, conversation.
27. *Newsweek*, 19 July 1977.

CHAPTER 4: THE MILITARY OPTION

1. Lieutenant-General Saghir Hussain Syed, conversation with the author.
2. *The Baltimore Sun*, 16 January 1972.
3. *Dawn*, 7 July 1977.
4. *The Pakistan Times*, Rawalpindi, 7 July 1977.
5. *Nawa-i-Waqt*, Lahore, 7 July 1977.
6. *Musawat*, 7 July 1977.
7. *Viewpoint*, 8 July 1977.
8. *Nawa-i-Waqt*, Lahore 7 July 1977.
9. *Nawa-i-Waqt*, Lahore 10 July 1977.
10. *Nawa-i-Waqt*, Lahore 16 July 1977.
11. *The Daily Telegraph*, 6 July 1977.
12. *Times*, 6 July 1977.
13. *The Daily Mirror*, 6 July 1977.
14. Lewis M. Simons in the *Boston Globe*, 6 July 1977.
15. *The Los Angeles Times*, 7 July 1977.
16. *The New Statesman*, London, 8 July 1977.

17. *The Statesman*, Delhi, 16 July 1977.
18. *Hindu*, Madras, 6 September 1977.
19. Reported in *Radiance*, Delhi, 7 August 1977.

CHPATER 5: VOYAGE OF DISCOVERY

1. Major-General Mahmud Ali Durrani, interview with the author on 10 December 1991.
2. *Dawn*, 27 March 1973.
3. *White Paper On The Performance Of The Bhutto Regime*, vol III, (Governmentof Pakistan, January 1979), A-92
4. Ibid., 39 - 40
5. Professor Ghafoor Ahmad, *Aur Election Nah Ho Sakay* (Jang Publishers Lahore, 1990), 89.
6. Lieutenant-General F. A. Chishti, *Betrayals Of Another Kind* (PCL Publishing House, Rawalpindi, first published by Asia Publishing House, London), 140.
7. *The Guardian*, 22 September 1977.

CHAPTER 6: THE POLITICAL JUGGERNAUT

1. *Kayhan International*, Tehran, 18 September 1977.
2. Simon Henderson, *The Financial Times*, 3 October 1977.
3. Ghafoor Ahmad, *Aur Election Nah Ho Sakay*, 348.
4. *The Economist*, London, 23 September 1978.
5. Dewan Berindranath in Patriot, New Delhi, 21 September 1978.
6. The text of Prime Minister Zulfikar Ali Bhutto's letter, dated 29 August 1978, is at Aannexure 1.
7. The text of President Fazal Elahi Chaudhry's letter, dated 7 September 1978, is at Annexure 2.
8. *The Transfer of Power 1942-7* (Her Majesty's Stationery Office, London), vol. 10, 512, 944
9. Jilani, conversation.

CHAPTER 7: VERDICT OF GUILTY

1. Victoria Schofield, *Bhutto: Trial And Execution* (Cassell Limited, London, 1979), 36.
2. Taseer, *Biography*, 187.

Chapter 8: THE TRAGIC END
1. Gavin Young, *The Observer*, 1 October 1978.
2. Chishti, *Betrayals*, 82 and 83.
3. Sir Morrice James, *Pakistan Chronicle* (Oxford University Press, Karachi, 1993), 75

Chapter 9: FROM THE PINNACLE
1. *The Pakistan Times*, Rawalpindi, 18 June 1989.
2. Lieutenant-General Ejaz Azim, conversation with the author.
3. Major-General Mahmud Ali Durrani, conversation with the author.
4. Ibid.

Chapter 10: INTERCEDING LINKS
1. Major-General Malik Abdul Waheed, conversation with the author.
2. Kamran Khan's article 'Murtaza Bhutto acknowledges existence of AZO', *The News*, Lahore, 16 September 1992.

Chapter 11: RELATIONS WITH IRAN
1. Muhammad Heikal, *The Return of The Ayatollah* (Andre Deutsch Limited, London, 1981), 106.
2. Ibid., 106.
3. Ibid., 100.
4. Muhammad Reza Pehlavi, *The Shah's Story* (Michael Joseph Ltd., 44 Bedford Square, London, 1980), 174.
5. Ibid., 174
6. Heikal, *The Return*, 120.
7. John D. Stempel, *Inside The Iranian Revolution* (Indiana University Press, USA), 25.
8. *The Pakistan Times*, Rawalpindi, 28 December 1974.
9. Stempel, *Iranian Revolution*, 73.
10. Michael M. J. Fisher, *Iran: From Religious Dispute To Revolution*, (Harvard University Press, Massachusetts, USA, 1980), viii.
11. Stempel, *Iranian Revolution*, 142.
12. Stempel, *Iranian Revolution*, 172.
13. Pehlavi, *The Shah's Story*, 188.
14. Heikal, *The Return*, 167
15. Pehlavi, *The Shah's Story*, 77.

NOTES

CHAPTER 12: TURMOIL IN AFGHANISTAN

1. W. K. Fraser-Tytler, *Afghanistan: A Study of Political Development In Central And Southern Asia*, 3rd edition (Oxford University Press, London, 1967), 282.
2. Olaf Caroe, *The Pathans* (MacMillan and Co Ltd., London, 1958), 464.
3. Ibid., 464.
4. Ibid., 464.
5. S. M. Burke, *Pakistan's Foreign Policy* (Oxford University Press, London, 1973), 85.
6. Abdul Samad Ghaus, *The Fall of Afghanistan* (Pergamon-Brasseys, Washington), 66.
7. *United Nations General Assembly Official Records*, 92nd Plenary Meeting, 30 September 1947.
8. *Keesings Contemporary Archives*, 17-23 March 1975, 27018.
9. Ibid.
10. *Asian Recorder*, 23-29 April 1975, 12557.
11. Ghaus, *The Fall*, 130.
12. Z. A. Bhutto, *My Dearest Daughter, Benazir Bhutto* (1989), 31.
13. *Asian Recorder*, 26 March -1 April 1978, 14237.
14. Ibid.
15. *The Pakistan Times*, Rawalpindi, 30 April 1978.
16. *Keesings Archives*, 23 June 1978, vol XXIV, 29037.
17. J. C. Griffith, *Afghanistan—Key to a Continent* (Andre Deutsch Ltd. London, 1981), 10.
18. M. Urban, *War in Afghanistan* (St. Martin's Press, USA, 1988), 8.
19. *The Economist*, 6 May 1978, 67.
20. *Orbis*, Spring 1979, 100.
21. *Observer*, London, 13 January 1980.
22. Urban, *War in Afghanistan*, 31, 32.
23. Brigadier S. Azhar, *Humanitarian Assistance Programme for Afghan Refugees in Pakistan* (Chief Commissionerate for Afghan Refugees, Government of Pakistan, Islamabad, July 1981), 13.
24. *American Foreign Policy Basic Documents (1977- 1980)*, No. 418, 248.
25. *International Herald Tribune*, 31 December 1979.
26. *American Foreign Policy Basic Documents* (1977-1980), No. 406, 809.
27. *Observer*, 31 December 1979.
28. *International Herald Tribune*, 31 December 1979.
29. K.P. Misra, *Afghanistan in Crisis* (Vikas Publishing House, New Delhi, 1981), 78.
30. *Globe*, London, May 1988.

31. M.C. Jaspersen, *Dawn*, Karachi, 1 October 1991.
32. *The Pakistan Times*, 17 May 1980.
33. Ibid., 23 May 1980.
34. Ibid., 6 January 1981.
35. *Herald*, Karachi, March 1989.
36. *Izvestia,* 19 February 1989.

CHAPTER 13: AN UNEQUAL FRIENDSHIP

1. Ayub Khan, *Speeches*, vol. IV, 36.
2. *Newsweek*, 26 November 1979, 9.

CHAPTER 14: THE NUCLEAR BALLYLOO

1. *Jang*, 18 December 1981.
2. *The Economist*, 21 November 1992.
3. *The News*, Islamabad, 12 May 1994.
4. *IAEA Year Book 1993* (International Atomic Energy Agency, Vienna), 7.
5. Charles de Gaulle quoted in *The New York Times*, 12 May 1968.
6. Paul W. Tibbets, 'Mission Hiroshima', reproduced in *The World at Arms* (The Reader's Digest Illustrated History of World War II, London, New York, 1989), 802.
7. *The World At Arms,* 438.
8. Ibid., 441.
9. *Bhagvadgita*, translated by Dr S. Radhakrishnan, chapter X, verse 34.
10. McGeorge Bundy, National Security Adviser during the Kennedy and Johnson administrations, *Newsweek*, 9 December 1991.
11. *The World at Arms,* 438
12. *The Muslim*, Islamabad, 4 December 1991.
13. William H. Overholt, editor, *Asia's Nuclear Future* (Westview Press, USA, 1977), 45.
14. Ibid., 45.
15. Ibid., 46.
16. Stuart R. Schram, *The Political Thought of Mao Tse-tung* (Pall Mall Press, London, 1963), 209.
17. Desmond Ball, *U.S. Strategic Forces, How They Should Be Used* (1982), 83.
18. Seymour M. Hersh, *The Samson Option* (Faber and Faber Limited, London, 1991), Author's note.
19. Leonard S. Spector, *Nuclear Proliferation Today* (Vintage Books, Random House, New York, 1984), 128.

20. Ibid., 128.
21. *Israeli Nuclear Armament,* quoted by Spector, *Nuclear Proliferation*, 129.
22. *The Sunday Times,* 5 October 1986.
23. *The Sunday Times,* 12 October 1986.
24. Leonard S. Spector, *Going Nuclear* (Ballinger Publishing Co., Massachusetts), 230.
25. Jawaharlal Nehru, *Selected Works* (Jawaharlal Nehru Memorial Fund, Teen Murty House, New Delhi, 1984), 439.
26. Jawaharlal Nehru, *The Discovery of India* (Asia Publishing House, Bombay, 1965), 241.
27. Debate in the Indian Parliament on the Indian Atomic Energy Bill, April 1948.
28. M.O. Mathai, *My Days with Nehru* (Vikas Publishing House, Delhi, India, 1979), 99.
29. Jawaharlal Nehru, *Collected Speeches* (Delhi, 1958), vol II, 505.
30. Quoted by Farhatullah Babar, *Regional Studies* (Quarterly Journal of the Institute of Regional Studies), vol. IV, No. 4, 1986, 17.
31. Bimal Prashad, *India's Foreign Policy* (Vikas, New Delhi, 1979), 401-10.
32. G. G. Mirchandani and P. K. S. Namboodari, *Nuclear India* (Vision Books, Delhi, 1981), 114.
33. K. Subramanyam, *Nuclear Myths and Realities — India's Dilemma* (ABC Publishing House, New Delhi, 1981), 15.
34. Desai, during his address in the United Nations General Assembly's special session on disarmament in 1978.
35. Leonard S. Spector, *The New Nuclear Nations* (A Carnegie Endowment Book, 1985), 83.
36. *Asia Week*, 30 August 1987.
37. *India Today*, New Delhi, 15 May 1988.
38. William E. Burrows and Robert Windren, *Critical Mass* (Simon and Schuster Ltd., London, 1994), 114
39. *Dawn*, 12 June 1994.
40. David Albright, *Arms Control Today*, June 1993.
41. Interview to *India Today*, reproduced in *Nawa-i-Waqt*, Lahore-Rawalpindi, 15 April 1994.
42. Ibid.
43. Ibid.
44. Burrows and Windren, *Critical Mass,* 97.
45. *India Today,* 29 July 1984.
46. *The Statesman,* 29 September 1984; and *Far Eastern Economic Review,* 4 October 1984.
47. *Far Eastern Economic Review*, 8 November 1984.

48. *Dawn*, 26 March 1994.
49. Jonathan Kendell, *International Herald Tribune*, London, 23 August 1978.
50. Stephen P. Cohen, quoted by Leonard S. Spector, *Nuclear Ambitions*, (Westview Press, Boulder, Colorado, USA, 1990), 100.
51. Spector, *Nuclear Ambitions*, 100.
52. Foreign Secretary Shehryar M. Khan's statement issued in Washington, *The News*, Islamabad, 8 February 1992.
53. *The Nation*, Lahore, 21 November 1993.
54. *The Pakistan Times*, Rawalpindi, 11 December 1993.
55. *Nawa-i-Waqt*, Lahore, 22 November 1993.
56. UN General Assembly Resolution 1 (1), 24 January 1946.
57. The treaty provides for the elimination of the INF missiles held by the two countries with a range of 500 to 5,000 kilometers within a period of three years.

Chapter 15: A Stormy Summer

1. *The Pakistan Times*, Rawalpindi, 13 April 1988.
2. Lieutenant-General Syed Refaqat, conversation with the author.
3. Mr Muhammad Khan Junejo, conversation with the author, 20 December 1991.
4. *The Pakistan Times*, Rawalpindi, 29 May 1988.
5. Brigadier Siddiq Salik, conversation with the author.
6. *Dawn*, Karachi, 30 May 1988.
7. Ibid.
8. *Dawn*, Karachi, 31 May 1988.
9. Ibid.
10. Ibid.
11. Ibid.
12. Junejo, conversation.
13. Salik, conversation.
14. Ibid.
15. General Akhtar Abdur Rahman, conversation with the author.
16. General Mirza Aslam Beg, conversation with the author.
17. Lieutenant-General Hamid Gul, conversation with the author.
18. Major-General Hamid Hasan Butt conversation with the author, 26 December 1991.
19. Lieutenent-General Imranullah Khan, conversation with author, 5 December 1991.
20. Junejo, conversation.
21. Refaqat, conversation.
22. Ibid.

23. Ibid.
24. Ibid.
25. Hamid Gul, conversation.
26. Ibid.
27. Ibid.
28. *Dawn,* 28 September 1988.
29. *Dawn,* 19 August 1988.
30. *The Pakistan Times,* 19 August 1991.
31. Beg, conversation.
32. Beg, conversation.
33. Maqbul Shariff, Editor, *The Pakistan Times,* in his reminiscences, in the weekly *Hurmat,* Islamabad, 14-20 August 1992.
34. *New York Times,* 24 October 1988.
35. *Newsweek,* 31 October 1988.
36. Ibid.

EPILOGUE

1. General Charles de Gaulle, quoted by Richard Nixon in *Leaders* (Warner Books, New York, 1992), 325.
2. *The Economist,* 10 June 1978.
3. *The Guardian,* 5 July 1978.

INDEX

Abbasi, Jan Muhammad, 63
Abbasi, Brigadier Z. I., 222
Abbasi, Lieutenant-General S. M., 202, 216, 217
Abid, Qazi Abdul Majid, 388
Afridi, Lieutenant-General K. K., 245, 247
Afzaal, Lieutenant-General Mian Muhammad, 400,404
Aheer, Malik Nasim Ahmad, 388
Ahmad, Aziz, 14, 41, 70, 71, 77, 78, 137, 306
Ahmad, Brigadier Niaz, 73
Ahmad, Dr Ashfaq, 365
Ahmad, Dr Nazir, 127
Ahmad, Dr Nazir, (scientist), 364
Ahmad, Ghiasuddin, 287
Ahmad, Justice Waheedudin, 184
Ahmad, Khalid, 63
Ahmad, Lieutenant-Colonel Mukhtar, 44
Ahmad, Major-General Nishat, 221
Ahmad, Professor Ghafoor: arrested 95, 97; cabinet minister, 158; miscellaneous, 123, 131; on elections, 148; on government-PNA dialogue, 83, 84, 156; PNA negotiator, 76, 79, 83
Ahmad, Tajuddin, 26
Ahmad, Waqar, 95, 98
Ahsan, Admiral S. M., Governor East Pakistan, 22, 23
Afghan refugees in Pakistan, 312, 313, 315
Akram, Justice Muhammad, 184, 186
Akram, Lieutenant-General Agha Ali Ibrahim, 43, 325
Al-Zulfiqar Organization, 264, 266-70, 408
Ali, Agha Muhammad, 21
Ali, Agha Zulfiqar, 73
Ali, Chaudhari Muhammad, 14

Ali, Jam Sadiq, 125, 126
Ali, Justice Qadeer, 141
Ali, Justice Yaqub, 100, 137
Ali, Mahmud, 154, 156, 158
Ali, Major-General Imtiaz, 44, 45, 98, 99, 111, 138, 213, 214
Ali, Mir Muhammad, 258-9
Ali, Sahibzada Farooq, 201
Ali, Salamat, 84
Alvie, M.A., 49
Amin, Hafizullah, 307,309,310
Amin, Nurul, Chief Minister, 7,39
Amin, Shahid M., 372
Amjad, Brigadier Ejaz, 401
Andropov, Yuri, 326
Ansari, Maulana Zafar Ahmad, 231
Anwar, M., 181
Arafat, Chairman Yasser, 41
Arbab, Lieutenant-General Jahanzeb, 126
Arbey, Darvesh M., 76
Asad, Dr Muhammad, 231,239
Attlee, Clement, 104
Awami League, 19,20,26; electoral success, 19, 20, 26; Four Point demand, 20,25; leaders escape to India, 27; outlawed, 27
Awan, D. M., 182
Awan, Lieutenant-General Azmat Bukhsh, 43
Awan, Major-General Muhammad Hussain, 400
Azim, Lieutenant-General Ejaz, 239
Azimov, S., 310
Aziz, Abdul Hussein Khan, 299
Aziz, Sartaj, 14
Badiner, Etienne, 183-4
Bajwa, Rafiq, 138
Baker, Noel, 298
Bakhsh, Pir Illahi, 7
Bakhtiar, Shahpur, 290

INDEX

Bakhtiar, Yahya: Bhutto's defence counsel, 182, 201, 203; election cases, 63, 64; political plans, 63, 64, 67, 71
Balochistan, emergency lifted, 173
Bashiruddin, Justice, 131
Batalvi, Ejaz Hussain, 181
Beg, General Mirza Aslam: Afghanistan war, 320; on General Akhtar's death, 405; on the nuclear issue, 307; on Junejo's dismissal, 393; on Zia's death, 309-402
Begum, Sherin Amir (Bhutto's first wife), 206
Behr, Edward, 88
Bhabha, Homi J., 358
Bhagavadgita, 354
Bhashani, Maulana, 39
Bhopali, Zahoorul Hassan, 268, 270
Bhutto, Benazir: death cell meetings with Z.A. Bhutto, 204, 205, 207; letter to Mir Murtaza Bhutto, 191-4; meeting with Major-General Saghir Hussain Syed, 205; on the nuclear issue, 377; on Zia's death probe, 407; policy on Afghan freedom movement, 320, 328; provocative statements, 132; request to attend soyem, 210
Bhutto, Mir Murtaza: acknowledges establishing AZO, 269; as roving emissary, 191; on terrorist activities, 267, 270; welcomes PIA hijackers, 265
Bhutto, Mumtaz Ali: detained, 95, 97; on 1973 Constitution, 262; on election strategy, 62
Bhutto, Muzaffar Khan, 209
Bhutto, Nawab Nabi Bakhsh, 206
Bhutto, Nusrat: as PPP Chairperson, 190; challenges imposition of martial law, 149; death cell meeting, 204, 205, 207; letter to General Ziaul Haq, 205; pleads stay of execution, 205; provocative statements, 132
Bhutto, Sardar Pir Bakhsh, 206
Bhutto, Shahnawaz, 267
Bhutto, Zulfikar Ali: achievements, 10, 12, 37, 38; admonishes President Fazal Elahi Chaudhry, 164,174; arrest, 95, 179, 182; arrest challenged, 182; as President, 37, 38; Aslam Khattak and Mian Jamal Shah on, 146; ban on National Awami Party, 166; clemency appeals, 195; convicted in Lahore High Court, 179; death cell meeting with wife and daughter, 204-5; defence counsels, 182; defiant politician, 21, 23, 26, 27; dismisses Balochistan government, 171; dissenting judgment, 187-8; elected unopposed, 63; election rigging 62, 65, 67; equation with Ziaul Haq, 44, 45; Fazal Elahi Chaudhry on, 101; Haji Maula Baksh Soomro on, 146; Hamoodur Rahman commission, 46, 47; hanged to death, 189, 206, 411; hanging countdown, 207-10; house search, 213; informed by Ziaul Haq of military taking over, 99; judgment of Courts, 176, 184, 187-8; Khan Abdul Wali Khan on, 140-1, 166; Lieutenant-General Gul Hassan Khan on, 139-409; Maulana Kausar Niazi on , 142-3; meeting with Indira Gandhi, 41; meeting with Sheikh Mujibur Rahman,39; meetings in death cell 204-5, 207; meets Corps Commanders, 70, 80; military option advice to General Ziaul Haq, 69; Muhammad Ayub Khuhro on, 142; Murree meeting with Zia, 113; on East Pakistan military action, 27; on General Ayub Khan, 10; on nuclear deterrence, 363, 366; on providing military base facility to USSR, 52; on sacking General Ziaul Haq, 88; on Sheikh Mujibur Rahman, 21; outrage in the National Assembly, 177-8; personality, 10, 104, 114, 189, 371, 410; political rise and fall, 104,105; political survival measures, 73-7; political traits, 107-8,189,206; relations with Afghanistan, 300-1; relations with Libya, 371; relations with USA, 77; relations with Yahya Khan, 20,23,51; review petition dismissed, 202; sons form Al-Zulfiqar Organization, 266-7; submissions in the Supreme Court, 185-6; tactics to win military support, 73-5;

427

talks with Pakistan National Alliance, 75, 79, 81, 83; trial, 182-9; trial implications, 180-1; trial, defence strategy, 182, 188, 190; White Papers on, 169-70; Zia on, 136; Zia relationship, 13, 133
Birdwood, Lord, 7
Bizenjo, Ghaus Bakhsh, 123, 140, 303
Bogra, Muhammad Ali, Prime Minister, 8
Bokhari, Syed Mukarram Sultan, 63
Borchgrave, Arnaud de, 282,343
Brezenski, Zbigniew: on aid relationship, 333, 335; on Arif, General K.M., 152; on the nuclear issue, 382; on USA policy on Iran, 290
Brezhnev, Leonid I., 313,326
Brohi, A. K.: advice on Constitution, 259, 260; advice on Islamization, 231; as cabinet minister, 154, 155, 157; election rules, 114; on advice to General Zia, 135-6; on Sharifuddin Pirzada, 160; Sheikh Mujibur Rahman's defence counsel, 38
Brown, Frederick, 77
Buch, Yusuf, 78-9, 89-92
Buckley, James, 342
Burki, H. K., 66, 79
Bush, George, 48, 341, 346, 347, 354, 377
Butt, Brigadier Khawar Latif, 93
Butt, Major-General Hamid Hasan, 394
Byroade, Henry, 78, 89-92
Callaghan, James, 366
Carlucci, Frank, 347
Caroe, Olaf, 165-6
Carrington, Lord, 314, 323
Carter, President Jimmy: attitude towards Pakistan, 314, 332, 333, 334; meeting with General Zia, 338; on US interest in the Persian Gulf, 290-1, 292, 314, 333; Pakistan rejects aid offer, 335
Casey, William, 319
Changez, Justice A. R., 131
Chatti, Habib, 314
Chauhan, Justice Karam Elahi, 184,186
Cheema, Ghulam Sarwar, 407
Cheema, Justice Muhammad Afzal, 231
Chernenko, Konstantin, 326

Chishti, Lieutenant-General F. A.: cabinet minister, 154, 155; Chairman Election Cell, 131, 161, 162; Commander Rawalpindi Corps, 46, 86; coup plan implementation, 93; on secret understanding, 211-12; retirement, 163,216; Zia confident, 68, 129
Chaudhury, President Fazal Elahi: as President, 93,98,103,163,164; advice to General Ziaul Haq, 101; clemency appeal for Z. A. Bhutto, 196-7; correspondence with Z. A. Bhutto, 164, 175; on Justice Yaqub Ali, 101; on Z. A. Bhutto, 101; resignation, 163, 164
Choudhury, Air Marshal Zafar, 43
Choudhury, G. W., 20,34,40
Christopher, Warren, 333, 336
Clark, Ramsey, 183
Constantine, Sir George, 9
Coon, James, 339
Cuellar, Javier Perez de, 323
Dad, Major-General Khuda, 38
Dalai, Camp, 123-5
Daoud, Sardar Mohammad, assassinated, 160, 304-6; gains power, 299; meeting with General Zia, 301-3; meeting with Z.A. Bhutto, 300-1; pledge to normalize relations with Pakistan, 303; visit to Pakistan 1976, 303
Daultana, Mumtaz Muhammad Khan, 7
Death of Hurs, 125-6
Desai, Morarji, 195,359
Dubbs, A., 307
Dupree, Louis, 307
Durrani, Major-General Mahmud Ali: on General Zia's visit for tank trials, 399, 403, 404, 405; on General Ziaul Haq, 121-2
Eden, Sir Anthony, 298
Ejaz, Major-General Roshan, 403
Elahi, Chaudhry Zahur, 123, 127, 131, 138-9, 143, 148, 156, 158, 198, 200, 268
Faisal, King Ibne Abdul Aziz Ibne Saud, 41
Gandhi, Indira: approves attack plan, 30-1; on the nuclear issue, 359, 362; on Pakistan's defeat, 359, 362; Simla Agreement, 41
Gandhi, Rajiv, 224, 359
Gankovsky, Yuri, 321

INDEX

Ghaus, Abdul Samad, 299
Gilani, Hamid Raza, 95, 96, 131
Gauhar, Altaf, 14
Goheer, Robert, 334
Gokal, Ghulam Mustafa, 154, 155, 157, 309
Gorbachev, Mikhail, 323, 326, 327
Gromyko, Andrei, 315
Gul, Major-General Hamid: as DGI, 244, 389; Junejo, Muhammad Khan, on, 390; on Junejo government dismissal, 396-7; qualities, 122
Habibullah, King, 298
Haig, General Alexander, 339, 341
Haleem, Justice Muhammad, 184,261
Hameed, General Abdul, 21, 22, 24, 29, 34, 35, 36, 38
Hameedullah, Dr, 231
Hamoodur Rahman Commission, 46, 47, 214
Haq, Air Marshal Inamul, 70,154
Haq, Chief Justice Anwarul, 46, 184, 186, 187, 203, 261
Haq, Dr Mahbubul, 14
Haq, Lieutenant-General Fazle, 151, 153, 229, 240, 243, 244,
Haroon, Mahmoud A., 155, 157, 198
Hasan, Mubashir, 42
Hashmi, Javed,156,158
Hassan, Admiral Muzaffar, 38
Hassan, Lieutenant-General Gul, 16, 29, 34, 38, 42-3, 49, 72, 117, 139-40
Hassan, Prince, 296
Hayat, Major-General Mahmud Aslam, 202
Heikal, Muhammad, 278, 290
Henry, Paul Mark, 35, 36, 57
Hersh, Seymour M., 356
Hidayatullah, Ghulam Hussain,7
Hijacking of PIA aircraft, 264-6
Hinton, Deane, 363
Hikmatyar, Gulbadin, 300, 306
Hummel, Arthur W., 111, 304
Hussain, Dr Ghulam, 87
Hussain, Justice Aslam Riaz, 76, 102
Hussain, Fazal, 181
Hussain, Justice Aftab, 176
Hussain, Justice Mushtaq, 114, 137, 176, 182, 183, 258, 259
Hussein, King, 118, 291, 296
Hussain, Major-General S. Wajahat, 45

Hussein, President Saddam, 296
Huyser, General Robert, 290
Hyderabad Conspiray Case, 165-8
Illahi, Dr Basharat, 238
Imam, Fakhar, 238
Imtiaz, Shahrbano, 201
India's nuclear programme, 358-61, 380, 383
Iqbal, Justice Sardar Muhammad, 137
Irshad, Chaudhry Muhammad, 123-4
Jacomet, Andre, 367
Jalloud, Abdussalam, 371-2
Jammu and Kashmir: Simla Agreement text, 58-60
Jan, Justice Sajjad Ahmad, on rigging, 74, 76
Janjua, Brigadier Amir Gulistan, 33
Janjua, Vice-Admiral Fazil, 236
Janjua, Lieutenant-Colonel, Rashid, 26
Jatoi, Ghulam Mustafa, 131, 215, 216, 219
Jaudel, Etienne, 183
Jazbi, Basharat, 236
Jinnah, Miss Fatima, 10
Jinnah, Quaid-i-Azam Mohammad Ali: death, 6; President, Muslim League, 5
Jogezai, Ali Muhammad, 149
Jogezai, Gul Muhammad Khan, 155
Junejo, Ali Bakhsh, 125
Junejo, Advocate Hayat M., 182
Junejo, Home Secretary Muhammad Khan, 63
Junejo, Muhammad Khan: General Akhtar Abdur Rahman, on, 393; as Prime Minister, 235- 41,392; attending General Zia's funeral, 398; background, 236; differences with General Zia, 237, 241, 393; dismissal as Prime Minister, 257, 390-1; Lieutenant-General Fazle Haq on, 246; minister in the Zia cabinet, 160, 162; Ojhri Camp inquiry, 390, 395; on General Akhtar Abdur Rahman, 390, 390-6; on Geneva Accord, 393; on Refaqat, Lieutenant-General, 241, 396; policy on Afghanistan, 322, 324, 325, 328; Refaqat, on 396; return from the Phillipines, 390-1; tasting power, 237, 240; Ziaul Haq, on dismissal of, 391-2

Kahuta, 349, 350
Kaikaus, Justice B. Z., 131
Kalam, A. P. J. Abdul, 360
Kallue, Major-General S. R., 179
Karamat, Major-General Jehangir, 401, 402
Karmal, Babrak, 305, 310-11, 323, 327
Kasuri, Ahmad Raza, 129, 176-8, 181, 184, 187
Katzir, Ephrain, 356
Khalil, Arbab Sikandar Khan, 123,149
Khaliquzzaman, Chaudhry, 6
Khan, Air Chief Marshal Zulfiqar Ali, 73, 76, 110
Khan, Air Marshal Asghar 65, 72, 83, 95, 97, 98, 107, 112, 131, 138, 146, 156
Khan, Air Marshal Hakimullah, 402
Khan, Air Marshal Rahim, 42-3, 49, 72, 140
Khan, Amir Abdul Rahman, 298
Khan, Brigadier Ishtiaq Ali, 73
Khan, Commodore Akbar H., 288
Khan, Dr A. Qadeer, 350, 369, 375
Khan, Fida Muhammad, 155, 157
Khan, Field Marshal Muhammad Ayub: as COAS, 16,17; as defence minister, 9; coronary thrombosis, 11; imposes martial law, 1, 16,142; Muhammad Ayub Khuhro on, 10; on General Yahya Khan, 28; ousts Iskandar Mirza, 9-10
Khan, General Muhammad Iqbal: as DCOAS, 224; opinion expression, 70; promotion and retirement, 216, 217; protocol issue, 153, 224
Khan, General Muhammad Yahya: delegates responsibility to Governor Malik, 35; detention, 50-1; imposes martial law,1, 11, 16; lust for power, 17,50; national elections of 1970, 19; on handling East Pakistan crisis, 11-12, 26-7, 35, 49; personality, 29; policy on East Pakistan, 20-8, 33-4; promotion to general, 28; relations with Z. A. Bhutto, 20, 21, 39, 50
Khan, General Rahimuddin: appointed Chairman JCSC, 217; governor and Corps Commander, 224; member of Zia team, 82, 228; nomination of Prime Minister, 234; protocol sensitivity, 153; trial of Sheikh Mujibur Rahman, 38
Khan General Sawar: appointed VCOAS, 216, 224; extension and retirement, 217, member Zia team, 82; protocol issue, 153; Public Affairs Committee, 198
Khan, General Tikka, 17, 25, 27, 43, 44, 70, 71, 73, 75, 95, 97
Khan, Ghulam Dastgir, 372
Khan, Islam Bahadur, 62
Khan, Justice Abdul Hakim, 102
Khan, Justice Gulbaz, 176
Khan, Justice Qaiser, 184
Khan, Major-General Kazi A. Rahim, 265
Khan, Khan Abdul Ghaffar, 144, 165, 309
Khan, Khan Abdul Qayyum 7, 39, 145, 149, 300
Khan, Khan Abdul Wali, 123, 138, 140, 143-4, 149, 165-7
Khan, Khan Liaquat Ali, 6, 331
Khan, Lieutenant-Colonel Mukhtar Ahmad, 128
Khan, Lieutenant-General Ghulam Jilani: as Governor, 216, 229; Brigadier Mahmud Ali Durrani on, 122; Intelligence anticipation of coup, 85-6; ISI assessment of 1977 elections fairness, 86; on appointment of General Zia as COAS, 44; on external aid for PNA, 78; on mini martial law,71; Senate elections, 239; serving beyond martial law period, 246
Khan, Lieutenant-General Habibullah, 154, 155
Khan, Lieutenant-General Imranullah, 394, 402
Khan, Lieutenant-General Aftab Ahmad, 43
Khan, Lieutenant-General Ghulam Hassan, 111, 155
Khan, Lieutenant-General Jahan Dad, 202, 243
Khan, Lieutenant-General Shamim Alam, 406

INDEX

Khan, Major-General Rao Farman Ali, 22, 28, 35, 36, 211-12
Khan, Mir Afzal, 131
Khan, Lieutenant-General Muhammad Akbar, 43
Khan, Munir Ahmad, 364
Khan, Nasim Wali, 85, 107, 131
Khan, Nawab, Muhammad Ahmad, 129, 176, 179, 203
Khan, Nawabzada Nasrullah, 79, 82, 83, 84, 95, 97, 11, 145, 147, 157
Khan, President Ghulam Ishaq: Agha Shahi consults, 274; as cabinet minister, 14, 154, 155, 157; as President of Pakistan,401-3; as Senator, 239; at General Ziaul Haq's funeral, 398; Brigadier Mahmud Ali Durrani on, 122; Brohi, A. K. on, 136; dismissal of Mian Nawaz Sharif's government, 257-8; economic expert, 253; Jam Sadiq Ali made Chief Minister,126; kitchen cabinet member, 151; military council, 110; nomination of Prime Minister, 234; nuclear programme connection, 376, 377; on Geneva Accord, 325; on Libyan proposal for Islamic army, 371; on US aid offer, 334, 340; promotion, 100; Public Affairs Committee, 198
Khan, Rear Admiral Saeed Muhammad, 402
Khan, Roedad, 14
Khan, Saeed Ahmad, 43,125,128,122
Khan, Sahabzada Yaqub: as foreign minister, 275; as Senator, 239; Governor, East Pakistan, 22-3; military assessment of East Pakistan situtation, 22-3; nomination of Prime Minister, 234; resignation, 24
Khan, Sardar Abdul Qayyum, 75, 135
Khan Sardar Shaukat Hayat, 123
Khan, Shahryar M., 377
Khan, Sir Muhammad Zafarullah, 14
Khan, Sultan Muhammad, 274
Khan of Hoti, Muhammad Ali, 154, 156, 157
Khanna, Brigadier D. K., 222
Khar, Ghulam Mustafa, Benazir Bhutto on, 193-4; escorts General Gul Hassan, 42;
General Gul Hassan on, 140; Hamoodur Rahman Commission Report, 214; Liaquat Bagh Case, 123; link with Ghulam Mustafa Jatoi, 216; meeting with General Ziaul Haq, 113-14; seeking election postponement, 131; self-exile, 162-3
Khattak, Ajmal, 123,310
Khattak, Muhammad Aslam, 122, 146, 240, 388
Khattak, Yusuf, 138,148
Khomeini, Ayatollah Ruhollah, 292-4
Khuhro, Muhammad Ayub, 7, 142
Khyber, Mir Akbar, 305
Kiyani, Major-General Hamid Asghar, 38
Kissinger, Henry, 48, 366
Kosygin, Aleksei, 300
Latif, Brigadier Khawar, 93, 94
Lewis, Captain Robert, 354
Liaquat Bagh case, 122-3
Lizichev, Alexei, 327
Lodhi, Lieutenant-General A. S. F., 200
London Plan, 270-2
MacMillan, Harold, 298
Mahbubul Haq, Dr, 14
Mahmood, Mufti, 26, 65, 66, 82, 85, 95, 97, 107, 112, 138, 145, 156
Mahmood, Rana Naeem, 386, 388
Majid, Lieutenant-General Malik Abdul, 43
Malik, Brigadier Muzaffar Khan, 44-5
Malik, Dr A. M., 27, 35, 36, 47, 55, 57
Malik, Major-General Abdullah, 70, 202
Malik, Major-General Ihsanul Haq, 211,212
Malkani, Kawal Ratna, 359
Mamdot, Khan of, 7
Manekshaw, General Sam, 31
Marri, Justice Khair Bakhsh, 102
Marri, Sardar Khair Bakhsh, 166, 171, 262, 303
Mazari, Sardar Sherbaz, 66, 95, 97
Memon, Ghulam Nabi, 64
Mengal, Attaullah, 166, 262, 303
Mian, Lieutenant-General Jamal Said, 155, 211-12, 239
Mir, Khurshid Hassan, 145
Mirza, Iskandar, 8, 9, 10, 14, 142

Mitha, Abubakar Osman, 38
Mosaddeq, Dr Muhammad, 283
Movement for the Restoration of Democracy, 218-20
Muhammad, Brigadier Said, 73
Muhammad, Chaudhry Yar, 204
Muhammad, Ghulam (Governor-General), 8, 14, 257
Muhammad, Mian Tufail, 107, 131, 145
Mukti Bahini, 30, 32
Munawwar, Raja, 231
Munir, M. (Chief Justice), 9
Musa, General Muhammad, 16,28
Mushtaq, Khondkar, 26
Naik, Niaz A., 49
Naim, Sardar, 305
Najib, Brigadier, 403,404
Najibullah, Dr, 327
Narcotics issue, 344
Nazimuddin, Khawaja, 7
Nehru, Jawaharlal, 358-9
Niazi, Lieutenant General A. A. K., 27, 34, 35, 36
Niazi, Maulana Kausar, 44, 81, 83, 95, 98, 131, 142-3
Nixon, Richard, 40, 331, 337-8, 356
Non-Proliferation Treaty, 381-2
Noon, Noor Hayat, 131
Noon, Viqarunnisa, 156
Noor, Masood Nabi, 242
Noorani, Maulana Shah Ahmad, 95, 98, 131
Noorani, Zain, 241,325
Nuclear pressure, 346
Nuclear proliferation, 355-7, 378, 380
Nuclear power, 351-2
Nuclear weapon capability, 353-4
Oakley, Robert, 320
Obeidi, Abdul Atti Ibrahim al, 372
Ojhri Camp fire, 386-90
Oppenheimer, Robert J., 354
Pakistan options on Afghanistan, 314
Pal, Justice Zakiuddin, 176
Patel, Justice Dorab, 184
Peerzada, Lieutenant-General S.G.M.M., 20, 21, 22, 24, 29, 38, 39
Pehlavi, Aryamehr Muhammad Reza, 276-81, 288-92, 336
Perrin, Francis, 356
Pirzada, Abdul Hafeez, 50, 71, 76, 79, 81, 91, 95, 96, 143, 207, 262

Pirzada, Sharifuddin, 114, 154, 156, 158, 160, 163, 203, 228, 258,259, 260, 261, 396
PNA (Pakistan National Alliance), 1, 2, 64-9
Pollard, Jonathan, 363
PPP (Pakistan Peoples Party), 1, 11, 19, 20, 64-9, 219
Prashad, Thakar, 31
Pressler Amendment, 345
Press statement of services chiefs, 74
Qaddafi, President Moammar, 41, 52, 371-3
Qadir, Lieutenant-General Saeed, 82, 239
Qureshi, Irshad, 211
Qureshi, Justice M. H. S., 176
Qureshi, Makhdoom Sajjad Hussain, 239
Qureshi, Sadiq Hussain, 45
Rao, Narasimha, 360
Rabbani, Burhanuddin, 300,306
Rafi, Colonel Tariq, 288
Rafiq, Khawaja Muhammad, 127
Rahim, Major Tariq, 265
Rahman, General Akhtar Abdul: as a subordinate,319; as DGISI, 88,389; Muhammad Khan Junejo on, 396; Ojhri Camp accident, 389; on Muhammad Khan Junejo, 393; on President Zia's fatal flight, 399; Pakistan-USA aid to Afghanistan, 319; Refaqat, Lieutenant-General Syed on, 389; style, 405; the kingmaker, 247; volunteer for VCOAS post, 218
Rahman, Justice Hamoodur, 46, 47, 136
Rahman, Lieutenant-General Mujibur, 113, 198, 239-40
Rahman, Sheikh Mujibur, 8, 12, 19-21, 23-7, 30, 31, 36, 38-40, 42, 133, 138
Rahman, Tufail Ali Abdur, 46
Ramay, Hanif, 139
Raphel, Arnold, 399, 404, 405, 409
Rasgotra, M., 222
Rashid, Rao Abdul, 86, 95, 96, 220
Rashid, Sheikh, 95, 143
Raza, General N. A. M., 48
Raza, Rafi, 61,71
Reagan, President Ronald, 318, 338, 341, 342

INDEX

Refaqat, Lieutenant-General Syed, 122, 229, 240, 389, 391, 396
Referendum, 75
Riaz, Major-General Muhammad, 88, 93, 109
Rockefeller, Nelson, 304
Roosevelt, President Franklin, 104, 283
Ryzhkov, Nikolai, 327
Sadaat, President Anwar, 291
Sadique Justice Muhammad, 131
Sadr, President Bani, 296
Safdar, Khawaja Muhammad, 156, 158, 238, 268
Sajid, Lieutenant-Colonel, 285
Salik, Brigadier Siddiq, 100, 102, 392
Samdani, Justice K. M. A., 182
Sarabhai, Vikram, 356
Savak, 282
Schanberg, Sydney H., 32
Schofield, Victoria, 177-8
SEATO, 331
Shah, Brigadier Muhammad Aslam, 95
Shah, Justice Ghulam Safdar, 184, 187-8, 203-4
Shah, Justice Nasim Hassan, 114, 184, 186
Shah, King Muhammad Zahir, 299
Shah, King Reza, 276
Shah, Mian Jamal, 146
Shah, Syed Ghous Ali, 238, 242
Shah, Syed Mardan Ali (Pir Pagaro), 75, 95, 97, 102, 107, 131, 148
Shah, King Nadir, 299
Shahi, Agha, 14, 33, 35-6, 41, 47, 48, 50, 79, 154, 156, 158, 274-5, 294, 307, 308, 310, 325, 332, 334, 340, 341, 371
Sharif, Admiral Muhammad, 71, 83, 110
Sharif, Nawaz Mian, 14, 238, 377
Shariff, General Muhammad, 43, 44, 45, 69, 71, 72, 83, 110, 216
Sheikh, Justice Abdul Kadir, 102
Sheikh, M. Akram, 43, 95
Sherpao, Hayat Muhammad Khan, 300
Shevardnadze, Edward, 32, 327
Siachen Glacier, 223
Shukla, K. K., 3
Shultz, George, 325, 347

Siddiqui, Colonel T. H., 100
Simla Agreement (text), 58-60
Simmons, Lewis M., 108
Sirohey, Admiral Iftikhar Ahmad, 402
Six Point Programme, 19, 53-4
Snowcroft, Brent, 48
Soomro, Haji Maula Bukhsh, 146,154
Soomro, Illahi Bukhsh, 233-4
Soviet troops enter Afghanistan, 310
Sowada, Daniel E., 409
Spector, Leonard S., 356
Subramanyam, C., 359
Subramanyam, K., 30
Suhrawardy, Hussain Shaheed, 8
Sullivan, Ambassador William, 289
Sunderji, General K., 221, 359
Syed, Lieutenant-General Saghir Hussain, 45, 98, 205
Symington Amendment, 334
Tajuddin Ahmed, 26
Talbot, S., 289
Talpur, Ali Ahmad, 158
Taraki, Nur Muhammad, 304, 305, 308-10
Tari, Mian Iftikhar, 123-4
Taseer, Salman, 11
Tashkent Declaration, 11
Tibbets, Colonel Paul W., 354
Tippu, Salamullah, 264
Tito, Joseph, 52
Treiki, Dr Ali Abdussalam, 372
Truman, President Harry S., 354
Turabi, Allama Aqil, 149
Umer, Major-General Ghulam, 29
US aid package, 342, 345
Usmani, Dr I. H., 364
US pressures, 344, 347
Vaidya, General A. S., 222
Vajpayee, Atal Behari, 41
Vance, Cyrus, 77, 291, 332
Vanunu, Mordechai, 356
Waheed, Major-General Malik Abdul, 218, 234, 406
Waraich, Lieutenant-General Imtiaz Ullah, 95, 402
Wassom, Brigadier-General Herbert, 399, 404
Wattanjar, Muhammad Aslam, 307

433

Wattoo, Mian Muhammad Yasin, 201
White Papers, 61,168-70
Yar, Malik Allah, 238
Yi, Marshal Chen, 355
Young, Gavin, 66
Younus, Brigadier Muhammad, 213
Zafar, S. M., 51
Zahedi, General Fazlollah, 283
Zaidi, Ijlal Haider, 14, 100, 396
Zakat Ordinance, 254
Zehri, Nabi Bakhsh, 146
Zia, Shafiqa, 117
Ziaul Haq, General: Abbasi, Lieutenant-General S.M. on, 217; aborted visit to Libya, 372-3; address 5 July 1977, 102-3; address at UNO, 346; animus against Z.A. Bhutto, 133, 215; appoints provincial governors, 100, 262; as a person, 2,116- 22, 215, 245, 249, 251-2; attitude after referendum 1984, 230; base facility to USSR, 53; Bhutto advice for military intervation, 80- 1, briefing; PNA leaders,82; Cabinet advice on Bhutto case, 194,200; Cabinet formation: January 1978, 153-4; June 1978, 155-8; August 1978, 157-8; Cabinet resigns April 1979, 161; clemency appeal President Fazal Elahi Chaudhry, 195-7; clemency appeals from foreign countries, 195; CMLA Secretariat establishment, 109; command of a division, 118; Constitutional Amendments, 257-60; Corps Commanders meetings, 80, 82; *coup d'etat*,; death, 385; decision on Bhutto's fate, 411; dinner for Henry Byroade, 78, 89-92; disbandment Hyderabad Tribunal, 167; early military life, 116, 18; Election Cell, 161-3; first press conference,112; funeral, 398; Ghulam Jilani Khan Lieutenant-General, on, 44-5; G.W. Choudhry on Bhutto to, 39-40; Islamic jurisprudence, 255; judicial system, 256-7; Junejo on, 392, 395; Martial Law Administrators conferences, 198, 200, 211, 215, 225, 227, 228, 233, 245, 259; martial law

working system, 110, 11, 153; meeting with: Andropov, Yuri, 326; Azimov, S., 310-11; Brzezinski, Dr Zbigniew, 333-4; Bush, George (Vice President), 246; Carter, Jimmy (President), 338; Gorbachev, Mikhail, 326; Jacomet, Andre, 367; Khar, Ghulam Mustafa, 113-4; Nixon, Richard, 337; political leaders (domestic), 135-47; Shahinshah of Iran, 285-6,288-9; Taraki, Nur Muhammad, 308-9; mercy appeal Nusrat Bhutto, 205; military apprehensions on PNA agitation, 80-1; M. Yusuf Buch's letter to, 78, 89-92; national election plan, 231; nomination of Prime Minister by, 235; on 1973 Constitution, 255; on Anglo-Saxon laws, 255, 256; on *coup* in Afghanistan 1978, 317; on elections, 133, 227, 230, 232-3; on Islam, 120,225; on Indian intention, 362,413; on Jatoi, Ghulam Mustafa, 216; on Khar, Ghulam Mustafa, 216; on Junejo, Muhammad Khan, 246; on Junejo's dismissal, 393, 394, 412; on Masood Mahmud, 181; on non-party elections, 231-2; on nuclear issue, 349, 367, 373-4; on Ojhri camp case, 390; on political parties, 231; on referendum 1984, 227-9; on Wali Khan, 167; on Western democracy, 225; plan to relinquish COAS post, 248-9; policy on Afghanistan, 313, 314, 320-2, 328; political internees' release, 114; postponement of 1977 elections, 133; Press reaction, 107-8; rapport with Bhutto, Z.A., 45; rejected President Carter's aid offer, 334-5; rejected mercy petition, 202; relations with General Muhammad Shariff, 134; relations with military Council, 110; relations with Arif, General K. M., 159-60; relations with Chishti, Lieutenant-General F. A., 161; responsibility of *coup d' etat*, 88; self appoints President of Pakistan, 164; services chiefs views on Bhutto conviction, 200; suspicions about

USA, 320; team members, 244-5; the *coup d'etat* night 5 July 1977: conversation with services chiefs, 98; knits martial law team, 110-11; meeting with President Fazal Elahi Chaudhry, 101; midnight conference, 94; conversation with Bhutto, Z. A., 99; visit to post-revolution Iran, 295-6; working habits, 118-20